FORTUNE'S MANY HOUSES

A Victorian Visionary, a Noble Scottish Family, and a Lost Inheritance

SIMON WELFARE

ATRIA BOOKS

NEW YORK   LONDON   TORONTO   SYDNEY   NEW DELHI

ATRIA
BOOKS

An Imprint of Simon & Schuster, Inc.
1230 Avenue of the Americas
New York, NY 10020

First Atria Books hardcover edition February 2021

ATRIA BOOKS and colophon are trademarks of Simon & Schuster, Inc.

For information about special discounts for bulk purchases, please contact Simon & Schuster
Special Sales at 1-866-506-1949 or business@simonandschuster.com.

The Simon & Schuster Speakers Bureau can bring authors to your live event. For
more information or to book an event, contact the Simon & Schuster Speakers
Bureau at 1-866-248-3049 or visit our website at www.simonspeakers.com.

Interior design by Kyoko Watanabe

Manufactured in the United States of America

1 3 5 7 9 10 8 6 4 2

Library of Congress Cataloging-in-Publication Data

Names: Welfare, Simon, author.
Title: Fortune's many houses : a Victorian visionary, a noble Scottish family, and a lost
inheritance / Simon Welfare.
Description: New York : Atria Books, [2021] | Includes bibliographical references and index.
Identifiers: LCCN 2020042155 (print) | LCCN 2020042156 (ebook) |
ISBN 9781982128623 (hardcover) | ISBN 9781982128647 (ebook)
Subjects: LCSH: Aberdeen and Temair, Ishbel Gordon, Marchioness of, 1857–1939. |
Aberdeen and Temair, Ishbel Gordon, Marchioness of, 1857–1939—Homes and haunts. |
Aberdeen and Temair, John Campbell Hamilton-Gordon, Marquess of, 1847–1934. | Aberdeen
and Temair, John Campbell Hamilton-Gordon, Marquess of, 1847–1934—Homes and haunts. |
Social reformers—Great Britain—Biography. | Politicians—Great Britain—Biography. |
Governors general—Canada—Biography. | Viceroys—Ireland—Biography. | Politicians'
spouses—Great Britain—Biography. | Governors generals' spouses—Canada—Biography. |
Viceroys' spouses—Ireland—Biography.
Classification: LCC DA565.A145 W45 2021 (print) | LCC DA565.A145 (ebook) |
DDC 941.1081092 [B]—dc23
LC record available at https://lccn.loc.gov/2020042155
LC ebook record available at https://lccn.loc.gov/2020042156

ISBN 978-1-9821-2862-3
ISBN 978-1-9821-2864-7 (ebook)

For Joanna
and in memory of
Alexander

I believe that a biography is more effectual than any other kind of literature in turning the mind into a new channel, and causing it to take an interest in the concerns of others rather than its own.

GEORGE HAMILTON-GORDON, 5TH EARL OF ABERDEEN

———

Despite her preoccupation with many charities and her way of turning night into day, there was, there is, something extraordinarily comfortable about Lady Aberdeen. She, too, is of the women who make home wherever they are.

KATHARINE TYNAN, IRISH WRITER

———

Not long ago, I had occasion to undertake various repairs and alterations in a house. Having once entered upon the work, I followed it up with some energy, and each renovation seemed to bring to light the need of some further remedial work. But I soon found that these operations were subject to unfavourable criticism. Some said, "This is a work of destruction"; others, "He has shifted that roofing and he'll not be able to get it up again"; others, "These workmen are a great nuisance, raising such a noise and dust—there's no peace"; and some would perhaps say or hint that "It did well enough for your predecessors; why not leave things alone?" To all this I paid very little attention; and what was the end of it? Why, everybody eventually admitted that a great and much needed improvement had been effected.

JOHN CAMPBELL GORDON, 7TH EARL OF ABERDEEN
SPEECH TO THE ABERDEEN JUNIOR LIBERAL ASSOCIATION
JANUARY 11, 1883

CONTENTS

A House on a Hill, a House in a Valley

Now, so long after, we disagree about what brought us one winter's day to a ruin on a hillside in North Eastern Scotland.

Mary is certain that we were simply hunting for a new home, but I am not so sure.

I think that we were tugged there by a long thread of family history. The odd thing is that we succumbed willingly, even with enthusiasm, although we knew that, less than a century before, building another house amidst these beguiling hills had brought financial disaster to the great Scottish family to which Mary, my wife, belongs.

What we found that first afternoon was a U-shaped barn—the Scots call it a steading—built of reddish granite, roofed with slates. The western end appeared to be in good repair. The farm machinery parked there was dry, though thick with bird droppings. The shafts of old carts had been stored across the beams: a few straddled them still. We climbed a ladder propped against the edge of a hayloft. Upstairs, in a dark chamber, in front of a small window, we found a wooden barrel. Whatever it had contained had leaked onto the flaking floorboards, forming a thick, sticky, orange puddle.

Back on the ground, we walked through the central cattle shed in the gathering gloom. The floor was still covered with straw and muck; the doors of the stalls flapped open or lay on the ground where they must have fallen when their hinges finally came away from the rotting pine posts, and part of the roof had collapsed. Slates, beams, and rubble barred the way to a smaller steading at the far end of the U. Its roof had sagged into a bow so deep and perfect that it looked as though it had been designed to cradle the wintry sky.

The remains of a cattle court lay in front. An abandoned car and a long iron tank lying on its side completed the picture of neglect and desolation.

Behind the steading, we could make out the crumbling concrete walls of a silage pit. Beyond it, a single willow tree perched on a knoll, a miniature version of the long, looming hill behind.

Just nearby, on the western side of the U, stood a small farmhouse, once home to the cowman, but now, we realized, in the early stages of gentrification.

But it was the view that made us both catch our breath: a vista of snow-dusted hills at the edge of a wide valley. High on the upper slopes, we could just make out flocks of sheep stoically cropping the grass beneath the crags. Below us, in the village, although it was barely three o'clock, lights were already shining at the onset of what the locals call "early dark."

The barn was too large for us: we had decided that as soon as we set foot in it. We were middle-aged; our children had left home; we knew that the house we had built on the other side of the county twenty years before, with its five acres of garden and as many bedrooms, was already too much to cope with. And yet . . .

We knew, too, that building here would be expensive, perhaps ruinously so. That was what an earlier generation had learned so painfully, after starting with high hopes, heady with the view and the prospect of life among these hills. And yet . . .

We remembered the wise words of the property experts about not letting hearts overrule heads, but instantly dismissed them. What hypocrites they were, we scoffed, for estate agents are nothing if not peddlers of dreams.

Enchanted, enslaved, overwhelmed with a sense of at last coming home, we signed a contract, hired an architect, argued with planners, drew up budgets, consulted lawyers, sold our house, pored over plans, and set the builders to work, much as Mary's great-grandparents, Johnny and Ishbel Aberdeen, must have done in the first years of the twentieth century.

Their place, the House of Cromar, which they commissioned in 1903, lay below us on the edge of the village of Tarland, in a wide "howe," or saucer-shaped valley, thirty miles to the southwest of Aberdeen; but unlike us, they had not come across the site by chance.

John Campbell Gordon, 7th Earl of Aberdeen, had inherited the land in 1872, along with other vast estates in the northeast of Scotland. At twenty-four, he found himself the owner of seventy-five thousand acres. Though there were some lairds to the north and west who could boast of even bigger spreads, the land they surveyed from their spartan castles was mostly moorland and mountain: fine for a day with a rod or a gun, but yielding little to placate the testy manager at the Edinburgh bank.

Johnny Aberdeen's fortunes far surpassed theirs: he owned, it was said, the largest parcel of prime arable land in Europe, bar those that belonged to emperors or kings. On it stood farms and villages by the score, and twenty miles north of Aberdeen, Haddo House, an elegant Palladian mansion designed by Scotland's most fashionable eighteenth-century architect, William Adam. Money flowed in from tenancies and fishing rights that stretched far along the banks of the River Dee downstream from Queen Victoria's own beat at Balmoral. Yet, in the last years of his life, Johnny's luck ran out—and so, crucially, did his money.

————

As the bills for our own house mounted in 2001, I often thought of this gilded couple struggling to make ends meet down in the village. Their financial fall from grace puzzled me. I did the sums. Today, those seventy-five thousand acres would be worth, at a conservative estimate, £300,000,000. No wonder that when Johnny died in 1934, his London lawyers felt they should spare the family the embarrassment of publishing his will. If they had done so, they would have had to reveal that, after all his debts and legacies had been paid off, Johnny Aberdeen had died with only £204 to his illustrious name. Even in twenty-first-century money, this amounts to a mere £10,000. Although he had made sure that the family fortune was not entirely depleted by making over Haddo and fourteen thousand acres surrounding it to his eldest son after the First World War, the cash in his own account was a very far cry indeed from the millions that he had inherited just over sixty years before.

Ishbel, too, was born, on March 14, 1857, into privilege and wealth. She was the granddaughter of Queen Victoria's banker, and the daughter of a brewer whose expensive habit of collecting mansions, castles, and rare works of art with which to furnish them, barely dented his vast fortune.

Like many Victorian grandees, Ishbel devoted her life to good works, but hers were on a larger, far more ambitious scale. She was an activist who became one of the great social reformers of the nineteenth century. A woman of prodigious energy and a thinker constantly ahead of her time, she really did transform lives with the campaigns she fought to improve the health, education, and economic circumstances of working people and to win greater equality for women.

"My grandparents lived more regally than royalty," my father-in-law used to say as he struggled to run the Haddo estate on the £2,000 he inherited with it. But could that be the whole explanation? Could Johnny and Ishbel really have frittered away so vast a fortune simply on high living? I wondered about this, as almost every day during our build I passed the House of Cromar. The more I learned about these archetypal Eminent Victorians, the keener I was to unravel their story. But how to do so?

One morning on a walk through the village, I realized that the answer lay right before my eyes. For their bankers, the cost of the House of Cromar had proved the final straw on the back of the Aberdeens' financial camel, but this was only the last of many properties on which the couple had lavished, and invariably lost, large sums. As I looked across at the house that had drained the last dregs of Johnny's fortune, I realized that I could chart their work, lives, and financial downfall through the houses they had lived in, owned, or built. And since Ishbel appeared to have been in charge of this aspect of their affairs, I decided to concentrate upon the ones that she had occupied or commissioned from childhood to old age.

I knew then of only a few of them: there was Haddo, of course, and the viceregal residences the couple had occupied on diplomatic postings to Ireland and Canada. My list of Ishbel's houses soon grew to include a grand mansion apparently transplanted from London's fashionable Mayfair to the wilds of a Scottish glen, cowboy ranches in Texas and North Dakota, a full-sized replica of a medieval castle in Chicago, two fruit farms in British Columbia, a hospital in the Yukon for the typhoid-stricken gold prospectors of the Klondike gold rush, and a stately "weekend cottage" once owned by a notorious courtesan.

But the story of Ishbel's houses, I discovered, began in a more conventional building on the corner of a smart street in central London.

1

A House by a Brook

The stream that gave its name to Upper Brook Street rose in the shade of a mulberry tree in the garden of No. 29, the house where Ishbel was born. This Georgian gentleman's residence stood on the corner of Park Lane in Mayfair, which in 1857, as now, was one of the most fashionable parts of London. Ishbel, in her rather syrupy memoirs, called it "a comfy old house," but this description belies its grandeur and that of its previous owners, who included a duke, an earl, a count, a dowager countess, a baron, a baronet, and enough Members of Parliament to have filled a bench in the newly rebuilt chamber of the House of Commons.

No. 29 stood on the western edge of what had once been a large country estate that, in 1677, had come into the hands of a family from Cheshire, the Grosvenors, as the dowry of a twelve-year-old heiress called Mary Davies. John Phillips, the carpenter who built the house, began work in the 1720s during the construction boom triggered when the Grosvenors finally decided to enter the property market, but he does not seem to have got round to finishing the job until 1746. Over the century that followed, the house was altered and extended several times before it was bought by Ishbel's father, Dudley Coutts Marjoribanks, three years before her birth.

In later life, Ishbel remembered this, her first home, with great affection. It had a frontage of forty-six feet onto Upper Brook Street and extended back to Wood's Mews, where the horses were stabled and the carriages housed. The mulberry tree in the garden had been planted specially for her, as a place to breed silkworms. Inside, there was a nursery with curtains of "flowered blue chintz presided over by a darling little old nurse with silvery curls and pink cheeks," a "Tent Room" with tall windows over-looking the garden, and a "spacious front hall" where the "kindly, portly" under-butler sat in "one of those enormous black leather 'porter's chairs' studded with brass nails," poised to open the door to callers.

The chair proved a useful bolt-hole for the three-and-a-half-year-old Ishbel, who had been forbidden to learn to read too young, "as it was sup-posed this would excite my brain too much." But under its enveloping black hood, she later confessed to her parents, she secretly learned the rudiments of spelling by looking at books of fairy tales, emerging from its depths to ask "one and another of the household what this and that word meant."

Soon enough, she graduated to the schoolroom, where Mlle. Bing-geli from Switzerland, "very much a type of the old-fashioned family governess—very precise and particular," held sway. There, Ishbel learned to write ("always a bugbear to me") and, like every well-bred Victorian young lady, to knit for the poor. Irksome though it seemed at the time, she later saw this early introduction to good works, the first of countless in a lifetime devoted to them, as an important part of her education:

> For my knitting, I was placed in a high baby chair, with a bar across to prevent my getting down or falling out, and I was set to knit garters and cuffs for a set time, with the supposed object of teaching me to sit quiet.

The grand saloons where the grown-ups sat amidst their father's bur-geoning collection of Old Masters and rare Wedgwood ceramics were out of bounds to boisterous children, but Ishbel and her elder sister Mary were sometimes allowed to escape from the nursery and play in their mother's boudoir. It was there that one of those unforgettable childhood "trage-dies" occurred, when Ishbel's dolly's tea set was swept to the floor by the flounces of an aunt's dress, causing, as she put it, "a ghastly wreck." The tea set was made of Sèvres porcelain: this was a family of means.

To all outward appearances, Ishbel's father, Dudley Coutts Marjori-banks, had been born, in 1820, with the shiniest of silver spoons in his mouth. His father, Edward, was Queen Victoria's bank manager and had become fabulously rich as a senior partner at Coutts & Co., reigning over its imposing premises at 59 Strand until he was ninety-two. He also found time to help establish the London Zoo and to enjoy the life of a country squire at Greenlands, a mansion set in parkland on the banks of the River Thames. But Edward had eleven children, and Dudley, the youngest of his three boys, assumed that he would have to make his own way in the world in an era when the eldest son stood to inherit most of his father's worldly goods.[*]

Dudley got off to a rocky start, for he found that there was no room for him at Coutts. Perhaps it was his ill-concealed lack of interest in the charms of his cousin, the future "richest heiress in all England," Angela Burdett-Coutts,[†] that stymied his application for the job; but it is also clear, in retrospect, that the partners at the bank underestimated both his acumen and his ambition. They deemed the young man to be "totally unacquainted with business habits." But Dudley, who was, according to an obituary, always conscious of "how difficult it would be for fortune seriously to injure him," shrugged off this small obstacle on the road to riches and, like the canny businessman that he actually was, looked for an opportunity elsewhere.

He found it at the Horseshoe Brewery in London's Tottenham Court Road,[‡] the showpiece of the Meux family, a long-established but troubled brewing dynasty. Fortunately for Dudley, its founder, Richard Meux, *did* have sons who were "totally unacquainted with business habits." Soon after they had taken over the management of the family's main brewery, the Griffin, in the aptly named Liquorpond Road in Clerkenwell in the 1760s, the three brothers fell out. As things went from bad to worse, the eldest, also called Richard, was pronounced insane. Then Henry, the middle son, was revealed in a court case to have been embezzling funds from the company's coffers: he had pocketed at least £163,000. He had also been running a secret distillery with a rogue named James Deady, right under the noses of his fellow directors.

The judge ordered the sale of the Griffin—whereupon the shameless

---

[*] In fact, Edward left the largest share of his huge £2,600,000 fortune to Dudley to compensate him for not landing a job at Coutts Bank. Dudley also benefited from the will of his uncle, Stewart Marjoribanks, who left him half his £33,000 estate in 1863.

[†] Miss Burdett-Coutts was awarded the consolation prize of being chosen as Ishbel's godmother, but had to wait until she was sixty-seven to acquire a husband—one who, to the horror of all London society, was only twenty-nine.

[‡] The Dominion Theatre now stands on the site.

Henry immediately used his ill-gotten gains to buy the Horseshoe Brewery. But things went no better there. One October night in 1814, George Crick, Meux's storehouse clerk, heard a loud crash. The hoops of a vat containing more than three and a half thousand gallons of porter had, according to an astonished eyewitness, "given way as completely as if a quart pot had been turned up on the table." A wall of the brewhouse was swept away as a tsunami of beer rushed into the surrounding streets. Eight women and children from the slums nearby were drowned, suffocated by fumes, or, as one reporter put it, "poisoned by drunkenness." The jury at the inquest into what became known as the "Great London Beer Flood" decided that they had met their deaths "casually, accidentally, and by misfortune."*

For a time, the business struggled: not only had beer worth £23,000 flowed off down the streets, but the brewery's scrupulous accountants had already paid the £7,000 duty owed on it. Yet somehow Henry Meux's reputation survived unscathed: so much so, that a few years later, a useful relation, the Lord Chancellor Lord Brougham, arranged for him to be granted a baronetcy. Henry promptly retired to a former royal estate in Hertfordshire.

Henry's son, the second Sir Henry, was made of less stern stuff: indeed, he was rumored to visit the brewery only four times a year, on the days when the profits were shared out. The gossips said that he was too fond of country sports and "the pleasures of the table" to dirty his hands with the business of making beer or even with politics, although he had somehow managed to get elected to Parliament.

---

*Lurid descriptions of the fate of those caught up in the beer tsunami filled the columns of the newspapers. A rather more restrained and oddly *distrait* eyewitness account appeared in the New York *Knickerbocker Magazine* in 1835. It came from an anonymous American, then living in London. He wrote: "On a dismal night in October, I was passing along New-street, on my way to Great Russell-street, when, all at once, I found myself borne onwards with great velocity by a torrent, which burst upon me so suddenly as almost to deprive me of breath. A roar, as of falling buildings at a distance, and suffocating fumes, were in my ears and nostrils. I was rescued with great difficulty, by the people who immediately collected around me, and from whom I learned the nature of the disaster which had befallen me. . . . Whole dwellings were literally *riddled* by the flood,—numbers were killed,—and from among the crowds which filled the narrow passages in every direction, came the groans of sufferers. Though but just rescued, as it were, from the jaws of Death,—my clothes heavy with the hot malt liquor which had saturated them,—I can truly say, that fifteen minutes had not elapsed, before I had entirely forgotten the late disastrous occurrence, in the emotions excited by perusing in the Admiralty Bulletin an exaggerated account of a most brilliant victory gained over the American army before Baltimore."

By the time Ishbel was born on March 14, 1857, Marjoribanks and an-other partner, Richard Berridge, an entrepreneur who, with 160,152 acres to his name, was reputed to be Ireland's greatest landowner, had taken over the management of the Horseshoe Brewery. They were joined by a distinguished judge, William Arabin, Sir Henry's brother-in-law: his job was to protect Henry's interests, because the Second Baronet's behavior had become increasingly erratic.* He had begun to talk nonsense, although this, and other weird aspects of his demeanor, did not seem to disqualify him from remaining an MP. But when he managed to wound six people during a shoot in 1856, he was finally taken to court and declared insane.

This seems to have had no effect whatsoever on the brewery's profits. When Henry eventually died in 1883, he left "upwards of £605,000," about £40,000,000 in today's money.† His partners' coffers, it is safe to assume, were filling at a similarly spectacular rate, and Marjoribanks, who did even better than Sir Henry and left the equivalent of £50,000,000 a decade later, could well afford to set up home in some style.

Brewers loved Upper Brook Street, not least because it was a long way from their breweries. Marjoribanks's neighbors included the "insane" Sir Henry Meux at No. 41, and later, at the same address, Octavius Coope, who, with his brother George and partner Edward Ind, produced beer at a safe distance from their elegant retreats in London, at Romford, Essex, and Burton-on-Trent in Staffordshire.

The street was also the London home of many of the leading lights of Victorian high society. Thanks to his father's job at Coutts and his mother's own rather more exotic pedigree—she was the daughter of a banker and merchant whose family had fled France after the revolution to

---

* "Erratic" was also how Arabin's pronouncements in court were often described. He once said of the townspeople of Uxbridge: "They will steal the very teeth out of your mouth as you walk along the streets. I know it from experience." A poultry thief was given this famous talking to: "Prisoner, God has given you good abilities, instead of which you go about the country stealing ducks." And an otherwise dry summing-up was enlivened with this mystifying assertion: "If ever there was a case of clearer evidence than this of persons acting together, this case is that case."

† Converting "old" money into "new" is an art rather than a science and my figures are simply indicative. I have used the online Currency Converter of the National Archives in London, but even that authoritative institution is careful to point out that its figures are "intended to be a general guide to historical values, rather than a categorical statement of fact." Another approach is to calculate what Henry could have bought for his £605,000 at the time. He could, for example, have purchased 22,000 horses or a gigantic herd of 62,435 cows.

make their fortune in India—Marjoribanks had long moved in its upper echelons. In 1848, he burnished both his social and political credentials by marrying Isabel Hogg, the eldest of the fourteen children of Sir James Weir Hogg, deputy chairman of the East India Company and possessor of great wealth accumulated from running a law firm in Calcutta. The newspapers reported that the wedding at St. George's, Hanover Square, had been celebrated "in the presence of a numerous circle of the nobility," and that it had been followed by a "sumptuous *déjeuner*" at the "family mansion in Grosvenor-square."

Nine months later, almost to the day, Isabel dutifully provided her husband with a son and heir, Edward; and then, the following September, with a daughter, Polly, or Mary Georgiana, as she was formally known. Edward and Polly were playmates, with little time, Ishbel later remembered, for their younger brothers and sisters:

> My elder brother, Edward, was eight years older than myself, and therefore to all intents and purposes I saw but little of him till he was grown up, for he was always away at school, or with tutors, or travelling, and when at home during holidays was out shooting or deer stalking all the time.
>
> My sister Mary . . . came next—a year and a quarter younger than Edward, and six and a half years older than me. Till she came out* at eighteen, we used to be dressed alike, and rode together and used the same schoolroom, but the difference in age necessarily prevented our having common interests.

Ishbel was closest to Stewart, born in 1852. Although he was almost five years older than her, she looked upon "Stewtie" as "my own particular brother":

---

*Young ladies of a marriageable age "came out" into society after being presented to Queen Victoria at Buckingham Palace. When it was Ishbel's turn in February 1875, she found it a "terrible event," since she had to "tackle not only an elaborate evening dress sweeping the ground, but also a long and solid train of some three yards in length, which had to be carried on the left arm" as she approached the Queen. All went "very well" for her, though, and she was flattered when "Her Majesty unexpectedly bent forward and kissed me on the cheek, a quite exceptional favour to anyone below the rank of a peeress."

It was he who gave me two of those much-loved fairy books; it was he who used to come up to the nursery to teach me to draw; it was he who intervened if play became too rough.

But by 1857, the harsh realities of Victorian life had begun to cast dark shadows over the glamorous and successful family at 29 Upper Brook Street. Annie, the Marjoribanks' fourth child, had lived for barely a year, and although Ishbel's birth seven months after her death was duly celebrated, the mood in the house had changed. And the gloom intensified when, in January 1864, eleven-year-old Stewart died suddenly of scarlet fever at school in Brighton. Ishbel was only six, but seventy years later, the shock and pain of Stewart's death seemed as raw to her as ever:

> I remember the blank misery of those days and the questioning in my heart as to the right of the others to mourn as they did when it was *I* who was the one who had lost far more than any one else—my own particular brother and protector.

Even as a toddler, she seems to have sensed the cheerless atmosphere and the unrelenting sadness of her parents. Her dead sister seemed ever present. Annie's portrait, displayed as reverently as an icon in her mother's dressing room, prompted unsettling thoughts: it "made her the angel of the family to us and heaven a reality, for was not Annie there?" And Stewtie's death had dealt her father an even more bitter blow, one from which he never recovered.

The births of two more brothers did little to raise Ishbel's spirits:

> There were two more boys, Coutts and Archie, three or four years younger than me, who seemed to occupy a separate division of the family in early years, having their own nursery governess and separate schoolroom till they went to school, and afterwards their own tutor in the holidays. . . . I always regarded them as another generation which had to be mothered.

Many years later and thousands of miles from No. 29, Ishbel proved true to her word, but in her early childhood she had to find her friends

8 SIMON WELFARE

outside, among the other inhabitants of the street. The crossing-sweeper was one of her favorites. Another was a "white-haired park keeper . . . who entered very heartily into my efforts to put salt on the sparrows' tails." There were games of Tom Tiddler's Ground and Puss in the Corner in the garden and rides on her black pony Filbert, supervised by Ballard the coachman who often found himself enlisted "to play the part of a highway robber" in wild chases "over all sorts of rough places, across fords, and over ditches, and so forth."

Ishbel's picture of her solitary childhood, however, is more romantic than true, for Dudley's ward, Henry Meux Jr., the son of the "mad" Second Baronet, had joined the household. His father, who, it is now thought, was suffering from syphilis, had become incapacitated, and his mother had deserted him while she enjoyed a long and drunken odyssey through Europe. The children's first meeting took place in a railway carriage at Euston Station before the family set off on a journey to Scotland in the summer of 1865:

> We eyed one another silently for some time, and then I ventured, 'How old are you?' 'Eight,' was the laconic reply. 'That is strange—I am eight too.' 'Do you collect butterflies and moths?' Wonderful to say, I had hit on my contemporary's special hobby, and so, much to the amusement of our elders, we were found presently in close confab over the habits and haunts of 'Peacock' and 'Brown Argus' and 'Sulphur' butterflies. . . . The ice was fairly broken, and this common pursuit was to be a great bond in the years that were to come.*

Her parents' marriage was under strain. The couple had always seemed incompatible. Isabel was pious and gave herself airs: she claimed "an

---

* Ishbel was circumspect about Harry in her memoirs, no doubt because, by the time she published them in the 1920s, his pleasures had become far less innocent. When he came of age, he set about spending his vast income of £28,000 ($36,000) a year on louche living: the gossips said he "ran wild . . . with low people." His marriage to a woman who carefully concealed her age and origins, and was said to have been employed as a banjo-playing hostess in a disreputable London casino, caused the eyebrows of society ladies to rise to stratospheric heights. She spent his fortune on a swimming pool and an indoor roller skating rink at their country house, a string of racehorses, and a zebra to draw her phaeton. But Valerie, a great beauty painted several times by Whistler, finally redeemed herself by paying for twelve huge guns for the defense of Ladysmith in the Boer War.

unbroken descent from Edward I, King of England." Dudley was self-indulgent, extravagant, and crafty, a man on the make who was said to have had little time for ethics in his relentless pursuit of profit. The house in Upper Grosvenor Street echoed with their rows.

The real problem seems to have been Dudley's volcanic temper, which, according to his granddaughter Marjorie, "grew more frequent and unrestrained," especially after the death of Stewart who, Ishbel remembered, "dared to laugh and joke when he was cross and the rest of us slunk away."

In "The Mother's Anger with her children," a curious story written when she was seven, Ishbel was surely drawing upon her own experience of parental fury:

> Four children was round the rose singing: 'O beautiful rose, why do thee not close thy leaves?' . . . At this point in the song their mother pounced out and said, very angrily, to her children who were trembling with fright and anxiety: 'Come in, children; you ought to be in bed long ago!!' 'Mamma, Mamma,' said the poor children, half weeping, 'we did not know the time, Mamma, don't be angry with us, we will rush into the house this minute.'

Her father's outbursts disturbed Ishbel:

> Few would guess the desperate miseries of those years, how the terror hanging over me, the fear of always being wrong, the conviction that I was too naughty, and ugly, and 'potato-nosed' to be cared for, have ever followed me.

She cast herself as her "adored mother's protector," but when Isabel became seriously ill with rheumatic fever, Ishbel was unnerved by the confusion she felt:

> I thought that to me was given the mission of saving her from some dreadful fate. Yet I learned to pray for her death, so miserable did my father's tempers make her life seem even to a child. And now as the fever rose and the doctors warned me there could be no hope, how I thanked God that the misery was over for her.

Though her prayers went unanswered and her mother survived, Ishbel, made ever more anxious by her father's behavior, took out her frustration on her governesses, particularly Mlle. Binggeli's successor, "another Swiss instructress." The schoolroom became a battleground:

I am sure that I must have been a terrible trial to that poor lady, for I never seemed to do anything right, whilst she was in command, and I found myself in perpetual disgrace.

But eventually the "secret voices" that urged Ishbel on "became less and less frequent," and when "yet another Swiss lady took over the reins of the schoolroom," they fell silent.

Yet no clue of Ishbel's fear of her father emerges from the loving, playful letters that she wrote to him throughout her childhood. One, from Ramsgate, where she was on holiday, ends:

With much love to all. Believe me my dear naughty Diddlems,
Ever your affectionate and dutiful daughter
Ishbel M. Marjoribanks.

Often, they were mischievous, sometimes conspiratorial:

My dear Papa,

I am writing to you to-night because I don't want Madame to have anything to do with me and my letters, my reason is because I like to do it all alone.

I am very sorry you are not coming tomorrow and I still hope to see a galloping coach come up with you and my brothers.

Are you feeling well my dear darling Papa? I wish I could see bright weather come in our country. You are very kind to send me your message. I pray you thank aunt Laura for her kisses.

Goodbye my dear Papa and I hope you will come home soon to your affectionate little

Ishbel Maria Marjoribanks.

Another pressure weighed upon her, albeit a little less heavily. Financially and socially, the Marjoribanks family was on the up, and throughout their childhoods, Ishbel and her siblings had to endure the success stories of their Coutts, Hogg, and Marjoribanks ancestors. Ishbel took them to heart and later remembered how "an abiding terror of bringing the name of my parents and their forbears into disgrace by my inadequacy to rise to the level of their attainments" hung over her childhood.

Quite who those forbears were was the subject of some controversy among genealogists at the time—Dudley Marjoribanks was suspected of "improving" the family tree—but Ishbel was unconcerned by such niceties. Predictably, she identified with a supposed ancestor named Grizel Cochrane and loved to tell the tale of how this "notable Scottish heroine," a "tall, handsome girl of eighteen," saved her father from execution by disguising herself as a highwayman. "Clad in a coarse jerkin and riding breeches, with a loose cloak thrown around her, and a hat drawn over her face, pistols at her belt, and a staff in her hand," she twice waylaid the messengers carrying her father's death warrants as they rode north from London to Edinburgh, where he faced execution for his part in an insurrection. This brave and cunning plan, Ishbel explained admiringly, won Grizel's family enough time to win a pardon for her by "some means or other."

Another tale that caught her imagination was of her maternal grandparents' escape from France after the revolution; on hearing it, she resolved to work harder at her French. In fact, she had little choice, since the children's daily regime at 29 Upper Brook Street was already "pretty severe":

> My mother did not believe in holidays, and no holidays did we have, not even the regulation Saturday half-holiday, nor summer holidays, the only exceptions being whole holidays on the birthdays of the children when at home.

And when the governess took time off, Ishbel's mother hired another to stand in for her:

> So it was an hour and a half's walk in the morning, and an hour and a half's ride in the afternoon, and the rest of the day mapped out in

work. . . . Those free hours out riding were salvation for us, and it was well that my mother should have made them a necessary item in our daily regime.

But there was a place for this anxious little girl to escape to. Like other Victorians flush with the new money of the Industrial Revolution, Dudley Marjoribanks had discovered the sporting delights of the Highlands of Scotland. There, amidst the rugged splendor of Glen Affric, he had built an extraordinary mansion. Of all Ishbel's houses, this was the one that meant the most to her; the one to which she compared all others; the one she harked back to all her life; but it was also the one that sowed the toxic seeds of her financial downfall.

2

A Mansion in a Glen

*G*uisachan* means "the place of the firs" in Gaelic, an apt name for a house surrounded by the last vestiges of the deep and ancient forests of the Scottish Highlands.

The twenty-thousand-acre estate† lay in Glen Affric in Inverness-shire, and for Ishbel's family and its large retinue of servants, nursery nurses, and governesses, the journey from London took at least twenty-three hours. In later years, tiring of the rigors of travel, Dudley Marjoribanks and his friends simply arranged for a new branch of the railway line to be built closer to their homes.

Even in old age, Ishbel remembered vividly the hardships and joys of the final few miles through the glen in a horse-drawn bus "crowded up with innumerable people and packages":

> By that time we were rather tired, and disposed to be very irritable, and it was an immense trial to small arms and legs to keep quiet for the three hours or more which it took us to get over the hilly roads to our destination, in spite of four horses and of their being changed half-way.

---

* There seems to be no agreement about the pronunciation of Guisachan. I have heard it called "Gweesican," "Joosican," "Goochigan," and "KUSH-g'n," but Ishbel's descendants say "Goos-ee-kun."

† No one ever knew exactly how big the estate was. Marjoribanks thought he had bought 25,000 acres, the Ordnance Survey measured it at 19,186, and a local surveyor roughly split the difference at 21,944.

Eventually, they reached the village:

At last we felt the old bus rumbling over the white bridge near our home, and in a few minutes there was a rush of released prisoners out of the prison van, sniffing the sweet Highland air, rejoicing in reunion with beloved dog friends who were no less excited than ourselves, and receiving the welcome that only Highlanders know how to give.

For Ishbel, every visit to Guisachan seems to have been a spiritual experience. On arrival she always felt

a great wave of Divine power which sometimes seemed to make one's physical body quiver all over. . . . The deep calm and peacefulness that reign here are far beyond description and make one's whole body thrill with the enjoyment of life.

All around there were "hills and woods, and lochs, and streams, and wonderful waterfalls." The slopes were alive with sheep, deer, and wild mountain ponies. She had a pet grouse and a dog called Fairy. Most days, her father took her to see the animals on the farm, especially his prize-winning herd of Aberdeen Angus cattle.* In high summer, on the few red-letter days that their mother was persuaded to relax her strict "no holidays" rule, Ishbel and her sister and brothers rode off on their ponies into the forest, where they measured how much the trees had grown since their last stay. There were treks over the hills on paths newly made by the ghillies in the close season; moth hunts at dusk; and long, quiet hours on the riverbanks spent sketching or fishing.

Ishbel delighted in life at Guisachan from an early age, as the estate's head stalker, Duncan MacLennan, noticed when he played the bagpipes at a Christmas Eve reel party in the servants' hall in 1861:

---

* Such was Marjoribanks's pride in his prize beasts that he commissioned one of Queen Victoria's favorite artists, Gourlay Steell, to paint their portraits as they grazed in the shade of the Caledonian Forest.

I mind of your ladyship dancing by yourself; you were dressed in white, your hair was like flax, in long screw Curls. I would say you would be about four years of age.

Ishbel, too, remembered that little jig: it was, she used to say, her earliest memory.

Guisachan was a true Victorian pleasure dome. For generations, the land had been owned by the Frasers of Culbokie, a successful family of soldiers, sailors, and businessmen. One of its scions became a noted explorer, penetrating the virtually untouched wilderness of British Columbia, later to become one of Ishbel's favorite stamping grounds. There, Simon Fraser traced the length of the "Great Golden River" that bears his name. Despite their reputation for canniness, however, some members of the family made expensive mistakes.

None more so than William Fraser, the eleventh laird of Guisachan: he inherited the estate and its mansion house in 1843, when he was just sixteen, but quickly tired of it. In 1846, he let the shooting rights to Dudley Marjoribanks, only to find himself outsmarted by his tenant, thanks to an astute and typically ruthless piece of opportunism.

According to family legend, the young laird was at dinner with the shooting party when he chanced to remark: "If anyone gave me sixty thousand pounds for Guisachan, I would sell it tomorrow."

"Done!" said Marjoribanks from the other end of the table, and despite Fraser's panic-stricken attempts to back out the next day, the deal was done. After all, an agreement between gentlemen had to be honored, even if it had been made impetuously, and, no doubt, under the influence of the strong liquor habitually served up at dinners for shooting folk after a day on the hill. In fact, in the negotiations that followed, the shrewd Marjoribanks even improved on his bargain by paying only £52,000 for the estate. In July 1854, the *Inverness Courier* duly reported:

We understand that the beautiful Highland Estate of Guisachan, in Strathglass, Inverness-shire, has just been purchased by Dudley Coutts Marjoribanks, Esq., M.P.

Thus, Marjoribanks became a Highland laird, a position that, according to Ishbel, he had long aspired to:

My father belonged to an old Berwickshire family, and so did my mother on her mother's side . . . and both had the liveliest sympathies with the Highland folk.

No one knew better than his youngest daughter how deep those sympathies lay:

One result which came to me is the Gaelic name of 'Ishbel' (pronounced 'Shebail'), by which I was always called, and of which I was extraordinarily proud.

Marjoribanks moved fast to make the place his own and hired a local firm of architects, A. & W. Reid & Mackenzie of Inverness. The Reid brothers had inherited their practice from an uncle, and repairing and extending lairds' houses and designing utilitarian estate buildings was their usual stock-in-trade. Mackenzie is thought to have specialized in building branches of the Aberdeen Town and County Bank. Now they found themselves with the grandest of designs on their drawing boards: a huge and luxuriously appointed mansion more appropriate to a smart street in London than to a bosky glen in the Scottish Highlands.

The handsome but plain old eighteenth-century house was rebuilt "in the French Château style" as an imposing granite edifice, bulbous with bay windows and resplendent with glass. The huge quadrangular Home Farm steading was rather more beautiful, but the architects and builders were asked to raise their sights even higher to create an elegant dairy "in an attractively mannered Alpine style" and fit to rival Queen Victoria's at Windsor Castle. With its stained-glass windows to filter the sunlight, gray marble fountain, and mosaic floor tiles, it was a veritable temple to milk. Kennels, stables, a meal mill, and a school all followed, as well as Tomich, an entire village of ornate cottages, with an inn and a post office as picture-perfect as anything dreamt up by the designers of *Brigadoon*.

Marjoribanks's Highland building spree was as relentless as it was expensive: then, as now, a passion for field sports was a drain on even the deepest of pockets. In 1864, the Reids were also commissioned to design a shooting lodge on a little promontory jutting out into Loch Affric. This Scottish Baronial extravaganza boasted not only a drum tower, a pyramidal roof, and drainpipes supported by ornate brackets, but also a room said to have been decorated with murals by the darling of the Victorian art world, Sir Edwin Landseer, who some years earlier had painted his shortbread-tin masterpiece *The Monarch of the Glen* nearby.

It takes some nerve to presume to improve upon a place as naturally beautiful as Glen Affric, but Marjoribanks wanted to live in a landscape as winsomely romantic as those in the Fragonards and Bouchers he so avidly collected. In the parkland surrounding the "Big House" the Scottish wilderness was tamed and trimmed: paths were laid out and rare trees planted. Here, the pièce de résistance was an ingeniously engineered waterfall that could be turned into a mini-Niagara at the touch of a lever. An ornate iron bridge was built over the Falls of Plodda, a spectacular natural cascade nearby, although only those with a head for heights or a bottle of smelling salts dared to venture on to it.

And it was at Guisachan that Marjoribanks secured a surprising place in history. Although he served as a Member of Parliament for Berwick-upon-Tweed for fifteen years, there was nothing distinguished about his political career, the highlights of which seem to have been winning his seat by exceptionally narrow margins—once by two votes and a second time by a single vote—and a single speech in the House of Commons. Nor is he widely remembered as a great collector and a key figure in the history of British decorative arts, although he certainly was. In the world of dog breeding, however, his is still a household name, revered throughout the world.

Towards the end of the 1860s, he and his son Edward bought a yellow dog for their canine stud. Where it came from has never been clear. According to rumor at the time, it had been spotted in a Russian circus on tour in England, while another account says that the dog, called Nous, came from a cobbler in Brighton. But Edward's story was that he had come across Nous being walked by one of the Earl of Chichester's gamekeepers in the Sussex countryside. He immediately offered to buy him, but the gamekeeper, a religious soul, refused to do business on a

Sunday and made him wait until the next day to clinch the deal. However he was acquired, once at Guisachan, Nous was mated to a bitch from a breed known only around Marjoribanks's parliamentary constituency. Belle was a Tweed Water Spaniel, and over several generations, the puppies descended from this union were recognized as the first true Golden Retrievers.*

As Marjoribanks's program of works intensified, advertisements appeared in the *Inverness Courier* for contractors "for the FORMATION and metalling of a ROAD of APPROACH to the MANSION-HOUSE of GUISACHAN." The contract was won by a Mr. G. G. Mackay from Inverness. Many years later, his path and Ishbel's were to cross again in another country with most unfortunate consequences.†

Ishbel was effusive in her praise for the enterprising way in which her father went about creating this, his own sanitized Scotch Eden:

He delighted . . . in opening up the beauties of the district by making numberless roads and bridle-paths through the woods and over the bogs and mountains, throwing light wooden bridges across the streams, thus giving work to ghillies in the close season and enabling the visitors to these regions to see glorious views of mountains and water which, as a rule, are reserved for those only who can tramp through high heather, wade through torrential streams, and scale rocky heights.

But she was sensitive enough, even as a child, to see that the people of the glen resented one key change to their way of life forced upon them

---

* According to a 1952 article in *Country Life* magazine by the Earl of Ilchester, who was Dudley Marjoribanks's great-nephew, it is possible that the story of Nous's origins was confused with that of Sancho, another dog in the Guisachan kennels at the time and more likely to have come from a circus. But since Sancho sired no puppies, the Earl concludes that "Russian dogs can be dismissed from the problem for good and all." Dudley and Edward Marjoribanks named Belle's first puppies Cowslip, Primrose, Crocus, and Ada, and called them "yellow retrievers." The breed was renamed "Golden Retriever" after another breeder, Lord Harcourt, compared the color of his dogs to a gold sovereign in 1911. A statue of a Golden Retriever, cast more pragmatically in bronze, was unveiled at Guisachan in 2014.

† One of the beneficiaries of Mackay's handiwork was Winston Churchill, who learned to drive on the estate roads while staying at Guisachan with his aunt Fanny, the wife of Marjoribanks's son Edward.

by this metropolitan outsider. Scottish lairds exercised near total power over the lives of the people who lived on their estates. Not only did they have to provide their tenants with housing and fuel for their fires,* but their responsibilities, as one of them noted, also included "almost all public works, the making of roads, the building of bridges, the building and maintenance of churches, schools and manses, the relief of the poor." They could also tell farmers what crops to grow and even when to put dung on their fields. And they could exact a substantial fine, in the form of a rent increase, for any breach of the rules they imposed.† While many lairds used these powers benevolently, others pursued their own interests, indifferent to the effects of their whims or greed upon their tenants. Thus, when Dudley Marjoribanks decided to corral the crofters occupying the estate's best shooting land into a single village, he brooked no opposition, although their covert protests did not escape Ishbel's beady eye:

> Every year a sad little procession of ancient dames in their white mutches‡ and plaid shawls used to wind their way up from the tidy slate-roofed stone cottages in the new village, built by my father . . . to the tumbledown ruins of the old chimneyless cottages with earthen floors and tiny windows and loose stone walls, and there join in a dirge of lamentation, which evoked the liveliest sympathy on the part of us children who heartily agreed with our old friends that the little old thatched, weather-beaten huts were infinitely more attractive than the prosaic row of trim, wooden-floored houses provided with chimneys and stoves and all the other hateful appurtenances of civilization.

---

* Even in the mid-twentieth century, my father-in-law gave his estate workers at Haddo the fuel with which to heat their tied houses. They were not well paid and he did not begrudge them it, although he did raise an eyebrow when the head gardener found a lucky ticket in a bag of coal he had paid for and failed to offer to share the prize, a free holiday in the Channel Islands, with him. The head gardener and his wife enjoyed the trip but forgot to send my father-in-law a postcard: that did annoy him.

† One typical Aberdeenshire landowner dispensed justice at the front door of his mansion every Saturday at noon in the early nineteenth century. Tenants could also bring him complaints and ask him to adjudicate in disputes. On most estates, "sitting at the gate" was abandoned by 1850: by then, most tenants could read and write well enough to send in their grievances or receive the laird's judgment by post.

‡ A "mutch" was a close-fitting muslin or linen headdress worn by old married women.

Dudley Marjoribanks never hid his reason for acquiring the estate. His admission to the Napier Commission of Inquiry into the living conditions of crofters in 1883 that the scenery was "very fine, but it was the game that induced me to purchase it," earned a vituperative riposte from a local man who denounced him as someone who "sees no harm in dispossessing and scattering a whole community of respectable Highland tenantry, and perchance replace them with wild beasts and wild birds."

The next day, Marjoribanks hastened to Kingussie, where the Commission was sitting, to point out that most of the tenants he was accused of evicting were, in fact, dead before he acquired the estate. A few had moved out voluntarily, and the only person he could be said to have sent packing was the innkeeper, whose ramshackle premises were the scene of "constant rows and constant brawls" among the laborers he was employing to modernize the estate.

Marjoribanks added that he had been aghast at the poverty of the local people when he bought Guisachan. He had spent at least £100,000 on improvements and made sure that his workers were well housed and generously paid, so that they would not be tempted to join the growing exodus to the towns and cities. He even offered his own bizarrely impractical solution to the problem of the depopulation of the Highlands:

> Should it be thought right that the straths and glens should again be thickly populated as they were once said to have been, Government should make either a railroad or a tramway in each strath or glen.*

In most respects, Marjoribanks was a conscientious laird. A journalist who visited the estate two years earlier admired his improvements:

> Everything is cleanly and in order about Tomich and Guisachan. The few houses constituting the village are neat and trim, the roads are well kept, and everything indicates a careful supervision.

---

* Both words mean "valley": the difference is in their size. A glen is smaller, and longer and narrower than a strath, which is large and broad.

Marjoribanks's fellow Old Harrovian, the writer Anthony Trollope, offered this, rather more lyrical, description of the grounds of "Loughlinter," a thinly disguised Guisachan, in his novel *Phineas Finn*:

> There was waterfall over waterfall, and there were little bridges here and there which looked to be half natural and half artificial, and a path which required that you should climb, but which was yet a path, and all was so arranged that not a pleasant splashing rush of the waters was lost to the visitor.

And Louisa Knightley was so enraptured by what she found on joining the house party in September 1874 that her husband, Sir Rainald, a long-serving Conservative Member of Parliament, virtually had to drag her away:

> We ride and ride. I long to be alone and listen to what Nature has to say in these wonderful solitudes. . . . Every day we take rides in new directions through these beautiful hills and get exquisite views of blue peaks and sunny lochs and far-away mountains standing out against the clean green of the evening sky. Altogether I am very sorry to turn my back on beautiful Guisachan.

Ishbel's mother threw herself with enthusiasm into the duties that the wife of a laird was expected to perform on an isolated estate. In an age where care for the poor and sick of the countryside was provided, if they were lucky, by churches and a thin scattering of doctors, many people depended upon the "Lady from the Big Hoose" to keep them out of the workhouse and the graveyard. There was one duty, in particular, for which she enlisted her children's help:

> It was far too expensive to send for a doctor twenty-three miles . . . and so my mother prevailed upon her doctor, Dr Stone, in London, to teach her the elements of First Aid and simple doctoring and pharmacy.

A cupboard in Isabel's boudoir contained "an endless array of bottles and pots and strong-coloured fluids," and, Ishbel remembered, "when my mother had concocted her remedies, we used to convey them on our ponies to various destinations, along with sundry broths."

But Dr. Stone's prescriptions were not the only trappings of metropolitan life that Dudley Marjoribanks imported from London to his wild and distant Highland glen. When it came to designing the interior of his mansion, he was most particular. He sent for a cabinetmaker Alfred Wright and his business partner George Mansfield, a builder and decorator. These notable and fashionable craftsmen were based six hundred miles away in the West End of London, but no one in Scotland could match them for their "high class work" in the neoclassical style of the great eighteenth-century architects and designers William, Robert, and James Adam. To their pilasters, swags, pastel paint schemes, and ornate furniture, their patron added the treasures of a collection of Wedgwood ceramics that, Ishbel boasted, was "the envy of many art connoisseurs."

Marjoribanks had acquired many of these pieces in 1856 from the great theorist of evolution Charles Darwin, whose wife Emma was a Wedgwood. They included a rare group of wax models for Wedgwood designs made in Rome by some of the leading Italian sculptors of the late eighteenth century, but Darwin seems to have had no qualms about selling them, for he was greatly in need of a billiard table. Marjoribanks ordered that the décor of Guisachan's main rooms should be designed to harmonize with, and set off, a display of blue jasperware. Thus, in the drawing room, an especially fine vase ornamented with a masterly relief, *The Apotheosis of Homer*, by the sculptor John Flaxman, was artfully positioned on a commode between two windows to catch the eye: one such vase cost Marjoribanks £735 in 1887, the equivalent of more than £50,000 today.

But these were far from the only *objets* carted to Glen Affric from the workshops, salesrooms, and galleries of the south, as Ishbel noted:

> In addition to these larger vases etc., there were innumerable little boxes, writing-table accessories, and ornaments, each of which had a story. They had either belonged to some historic personage, or to a member of the family, or had been found by my father in some obscure shop and purchased because of some particular beauty.

Guisachan was also stuffed with fine furniture. Marjoribanks seems to have been especially fond of English and French commodes: there were at least twenty in the house.*

At the beginning of each holiday, Ishbel had to help her mother "in taking all the treasures from their cupboards, washing them, and putting them in their places." Though she did so with due care, she sometimes harbored "iconoclastic desires":

> The vases had a wicked attraction for me, and I used to look at them and wonder what would happen if I swept them all from their places in a general smash.

When the "magnificent sporting and residential estate" was offered for sale many years later, the brochure waxed lyrical about the luxurious showpiece Marjoribanks created:

> The arrangement of the House cannot be excelled for accommoda-
> tion and comfort. It contains an outer Entrance hall, an Inner Hall,
> Dining Room, Boudoir, Drawing-room, Business-room, Library,
> and a very large Banqueting Hall or Ballroom, with polished floor.
> Opening off this room is a very fine Conservatory. There is also a
> well-fitted Gun-room with Ammunition Cupboards; [and a] large
> Schoolroom.

Downstairs was just as extensive:

> A fine Kitchen, Serving-room, Scullery, Baking-room, Box-room,
> Large Servants' Hall, Housekeeper's Room, Stillroom, Beer Cellar,
> Larder, Boot, Knife and Lamp Room, large Pantry, fitted with 10 Cup-
> boards and Iron Safe; 2 Wine Cellars; a Large Room with 4 Linen
> Cupboards, Coal-room, and 4 or 5 miscellaneous Cupboards.

---

* One particularly beautiful example made by the eighteenth-century furniture designers and cabinetmakers Ince & Mayhew, which stood in the dining room, is now a cherished exhibit at the Metropolitan Museum of Art in New York.

And on the upper floors there was plenty of space for the Marjoribanks' guests to live in the style to which they were accustomed in their
own mansions and country houses in London and the English shires:

> 15 family bedrooms, five of which have Dressing-rooms; 14 servants'
> Bedrooms, giving accommodation for about 30 servants; 3 Bathrooms.

Ishbel enjoyed the house parties, where archbishops and Prime Ministers mingled with dukes and duchesses, clan chiefs and fashionable painters.
But none of them impressed her as much as a young man who, one morning
in the hot summer of 1869, rode into Glen Affric in search of shelter.

A note arrived at Guisachan. The writer said that he was on a riding
tour and had been unable to find anywhere to stay on this leg of his
journey. Could he possibly, he wondered, put up in the lodge down in
the neighboring glen? A card attached to the note revealed the traveler's
name: the Honorable John Campbell Hamilton-Gordon,* the brother of
the Earl of Aberdeen. The etiquette was clear: a man from such a good
family could never be allowed to fend for himself in a shooting box. An
invitation to stay at Guisachan itself was immediately issued, and, just as
promptly, accepted.

Almost sixty years later, Ishbel relished every remembered detail of
the visit:

> Presently he appeared, mounted on a good-looking chestnut horse,
> and carrying all his travelling equipment in a small valise strapped
> behind his saddle. It may be imagined what excitement such an event
> would cause up and down the glen, where the passing of any stranger
> was always reported to my father, and discussed and commented on in
> every cottage in the strath.

Inside the big house, "the children, the housekeeper, and the maiden
aunts, staying on a visit, were all agog." The twelve-year-old Ishbel, how-

---

* Johnny later dropped the "Hamilton" from his name. It had been added by his grandfather, the
4th Earl of Aberdeen, in 1820, in tribute to his father-in-law and friend, John James Hamilton,
1st Marquess of Abercorn.

ever, was unable to welcome or even meet the visitor. She had been confined to bed with sunstroke after a butterfly hunt along the banks of the river. When news about the dashing Oxford undergraduate reached her sickroom from downstairs, her curiosity was whetted:

> I determined to have a look at the intruder, and managed to elude the vigilance of my guardians when the family was going into dinner, and, leaning over the balustrades, I just caught sight of a very black head. That was all I was to see of him on that occasion . . .

Johnny's version was, characteristically, less sugary. It appears in We Twa, a joint autobiography written by the couple in the 1920s. By this time, the tale of the meeting that never quite happened had become embroidered. He dismisses

> the more picturesque versions of the episode, which have, from time to time, appeared; for example—how I was discovered wandering through the woods with a gun, trespassing in pursuit of game; and how I was suddenly confronted by the proprietor, whose demands for an explanation were followed by an invitation to be a guest, with the result that, in this way, I was enabled to win the youngest daughter of my host. . . . As a matter of fact, during this first visit I did not even see my future bride.

Nearly two years were to pass before Ishbel and Johnny met face-to-face, but this encounter took place in London, where Dudley Marjoribanks, the man of property and now a baronet, had built himself another, even more palatial residence.

3

A Palace in Mayfair

Ishbel disliked "the new and lordly" Brook House, the vast edifice in the "French style" that her father built on the corner of Park Lane in 1867. To make way for it, the elegant old family home at 29 Upper Brook Street was demolished, along with No. 28 next door.

Marjoribanks, like the owners of Britain's first great country houses, wanted a showcase for his ever-expanding collection of art, and in Thomas Henry Wyatt he chose just the man to design this monument to his refined taste and success. Wyatt's portfolio of public buildings included the assize courts in Cambridge, the railway station at Florence, and the Wiltshire County Asylum for the Insane (the latter in the "Italian style"). Thanks to his uncle, who was the agent to the Duke of Beaufort, Wyatt's practice was also the first port of call for the aristocracy and the landed gentry.

He came up with a suitably grandiose scheme, although a plan to top off the building with a tower seems to have been left on the drawing board. But this did little to water down the ostentatious splendor of the place: its red brick facade, dressed with Portland stone, was festooned with balconies, balustrades, ornamental crestings, and bay windows. The roof was flat, so that the family could watch "reviews and other displays" in Hyde Park below. The servants lived at the bottom of the garden, in an imposing building of their own, complete with billiard room.*

---

* Marjoribanks's concern for the welfare of his servants outlived him. In his will he left £100 (£8,000 or $10,000 today) each to his butler and his valet and £250 (£20,000 or $25,000 today) to John Rennie, "whose conduct and cooking during many years have given great satisfaction."

Before the building was even complete, however, a passing critic from the arbiter of Victorian architectural taste, *Building News*, had damned it with faint praise, describing it as "a remarkable rather than a handsome building." But, he added, "the iron cresting is not what we should wish to see, and no amount of gilding or colour will improve it," and the contrast between the red brick and the stone dressings was "too strong." Two years later, the magazine had not changed its mind, calling Brook House "unobjectionable in mass, but not so in detail." Another critic sniffed that it was "rebarbatively French."

Ishbel's chief complaint was that "in spite of its large and beautiful rooms, and its fine position overlooking Hyde Park, it was undoubtedly a noisy place." But visitors were more enthusiastic. In the summer of 1870, Louisa Knightley was one of a group of friends who dropped in on Brook House after dinner to find "all the world" gathered there. She applauded Marjoribanks's good taste in her journal:

> It is very handsome certainly, especially the staircase, and I think the public ought to be much obliged to him for adding a really fine house to the few there are in this monotonous city of ours.

She was not alone in being impressed by the interior, which, like Guisachan's, had been decorated by Wright and Mansfield. The entrance from Upper Brook Street led into a cavernous hallway dominated by a sweeping mahogany staircase lined with marble of variegated hues. On the first floor there was a library built of cherrywood with a chimney piece copied from one made for the Master of the Dublin Mint in 1785, set with a rare Wedgwood plaque. Its shelves groaned with precious books, including a Shakespeare first folio: the catalogue ran to almost three hundred pages.* The dining room was bedecked with carvings salvaged from the Drapers' Hall down the road in the City of London and paneling said to have come from the Maison de la Poste in Paris. Upstairs, there was a suite of opulent

---

* Today, the catalogue is itself a rare book, presumably because it was published by Charles Whittingham II, the top printer of the day. One copy, recently offered for sale at a price of more that £1,000 ($1,279), bears the bookplate of Marjoribanks's son Coutts, who became a cowboy in North Central Dakota and presumably leafed through it between cattle drives in his log cabin by the Mouse River.

drawing rooms crowned with gilded ceilings where exquisite French furniture jostled for space with prime pieces from Sir Dudley's Wedgwood collection.

On the walls hung masterpieces by Boucher and Fragonard, Gainsborough and Reynolds, Canaletto and Hogarth, Ramsay, Landseer and Stubbs. Marjoribanks was an obsessive and highly discerning collector. "He had a passion for perfection," his granddaughter Marjorie wrote, "and if he set his heart on anything it must be his." Why own just one portrait by the Scottish artist Sir Henry Raeburn when he could own seven? Or only Reynolds's portrait of Viscount Ligonier, when he could have those of Emilia, Countess of Bellamont; Miss Theophila Gwatkin; and Miss Anne Dutton too? Marjoribanks never stopped wheeling and dealing in the finest galleries and salesrooms of London right up to his death in 1894. He took pains to keep the true cost of his acquisitions from the rest of the family, as Ishbel later discovered:

> My grandfather, Edward Marjoribanks, senior partner of Coutts' bank, did not approve of this hobby, and thought it led to extravagance. So on one occasion when my father, under an assumed name, bought a very valuable collection of Derby vases at Christie's, and set all the London art world's tongues wagging as to the identity of the purchaser, he dared not reveal the secret, but hid away the vases for a number of years till the new "Brook House" was built, and then sold half the collection for more than double the sum he gave for the original, and adorned the drawing room mantelpieces with the remainder.

One wag said,

> There is no need for dwellers in Brook House to dream that they live in marble halls. They do dwell in them. They realize what the poet* merely imagined.

---

* More accurately, the librettist: the reference is to a famous aria, "I Dreamt I Dwelt in Marbled Halls," written in 1843 for an opera, *The Bohemian Girl*, by Alfred Bunn, manager of Drury Lane Theatre. While singers as diverse as Joan Sutherland and Enya have recorded it, actors are wary of whistling the tune for fear it will bring them bad luck.

While Sir Dudley busied himself in salesrooms, galleries, and anti-quarian bookshops acquiring further treasures for Brook House, Isabel, as was expected of a society wife, was already setting about preparing her daughters for marriage, preferably to the heir to a grand and ancient title, a stately home or two, and a substantial fortune.

A new governess, Mlle. Baux, was hired to ensure that Ishbel would acquire the polish and social skills and the modicum of education a young lady would need to attract such a husband. When Ishbel was thirteen, she was occasionally allowed to escape from the Brook House schoolroom to attend the classes held by high society's favorite French teacher, M. Antonin Roche. She later joined an English language and literature course run by John Meiklejohn, a prolific writer of school textbooks with an exotic past as a spy in the Schleswig War of 1864. "Under his tuition," she later wrote, "a whole fairyland of literature was opened up to me, and it began to dawn upon me what education might mean." Now the once reluctant pupil could barely contain her enthusi-asm for study, developing a love of learning and a way of working that never left her:

> Unknown to parents and governesses, I used to get up at night when
> all was quiet and my elder sister was out at a ball, and pore over a
> book which might furnish me with the necessary armoury to meet the
> shower of unexpected questions.

But when Professor Meiklejohn, who believed that women should be allowed to study at university, suggested to Dudley Marjoribanks that Ishbel should try for Oxford or Cambridge, he met with "an absolute iron door refusal to entertain any such wild-cat proposition."

Perhaps by way of compensation, or perhaps because it served most conveniently her mother's stratagem for finding her a husband, Ishbel was allowed to have a little job while she was still a teenager. After the minister of their regular place of worship died in 1873, the socially op-portunistic Marjoribanks had lost no time in transferring to the Quebec Chapel, a much more exclusive and fashionable church where "perma-nent sittings . . . were difficult to obtain." When the minister, Canon

Francis Holland, suggested she should help run its Sunday school, Ishbel was ecstatic:

> I felt the colour rush to the roots of my hair, so overcome was I with joy at the very thought.

Like a suspect suitor, the virtuous Canon was summoned to Brook House to be interrogated by Sir Dudley, and, to Ishbel's relief, "consent was finally given, though not too graciously." But for a young unmarried woman there were still a few logistics to be overcome:

> In the morning I was actually allowed to walk to the Sunday school ... by myself, but in the afternoon I had to be guarded by a footman walking behind me.

She was also allowed to open a Sunday school at Guisachan, as long as she obeyed the strict conditions laid down by her father:

> I was not to start till after the dining-room breakfast ... and provided that I did not need any extra vehicle to transport me the one and three-quarter miles between the house and the school.

Here, too, there was a problem. The Free Church would not countenance the use of a musical instrument, such as a harmonium or an organ, to accompany the singing of hymns. But the ingenious Ishbel got around that one by learning to play the concertina.

At about the same time, Lady Frederick Cavendish, a prominent social and educational reformer who had taken a shine to Ishbel, called on Sir Dudley "and dragged out of him permission" for her to help with her work among the poor of London's East End.

For Ishbel these worthy, yet exciting, missions were a taste of things to come, but to her mother they were tiresome diversions: Isabel Marjoribanks had long been busy matchmaking, with conspicuous success. In 1873, Edward, her eldest son, had married the belle of every ball and house party, Fanny Spencer-Churchill, daughter of the 7th Duke of Marlborough. And that same year, a most eligible husband was found for Polly:

Matthew White Ridley, heir to 10,200 acres in Northumberland and a fellow of All Souls College, Oxford. A cousin described him as "rather handsome and exceedingly clever."[*]

Ishbel presented her mother with quite a different dilemma. She had needed no help in choosing the man she wanted as a husband, but tying him down was far from plain sailing. After her first glimpse of Johnny Gordon from the upstairs landing at Guisachan, she had had to wait many months before she was formally introduced to him. The meeting took place on a wet February morning in 1871 while she was exercising her pony, Crotchet, in the mud of Rotten Row in London's Hyde Park. Johnny was twenty-three; Ishbel was thirteen—and instantly smitten.

The man Ishbel now set her heart upon had not had the easy life usually enjoyed by the children of rich and landed aristocrats, nor had he been given, by the standards of the time, a conventional upbringing. Johnny's father, George, the 5th Earl of Aberdeen, had a reputation for being a lugubrious and irritable fellow, no doubt because he suffered from a strange and debilitating illness. Described in his lifetime as "a wasting atrophy" or "dyspepsia in an aggravated form," modern historians have suggested that it may have been a rare type of tuberculosis or even motor neurone disease[†].

Yet behind what his biographer called George's "extreme reserve and shyness" lay a man of kindness, humility, and winning eccentricity. He was also a talented artist and twice exhibited at the Royal Academy.[‡] But it was not until he was thirty-one that he found his true vocation. It came in a flash one night in 1847 as he was changing for dinner:

> I felt the imperative necessity of preparing for death at any cost, and any sacrifice. I mentally abandoned, without hesitation, everything; and resolved to make an entire change in my life; to spend the whole

---

[*] Rather more flattering than a later assessment: "fairly stuffy and a huge eater."

[†] Also known as Lou Gehrig's disease, after the renowned star of the New York Yankees baseball team of the 1920s and '30s, and more clinically, as amyotrophic lateral sclerosis (ALS).

[‡] Several of his paintings still hang at Haddo. One, showing two figures in a landscape, labeled *Lord Haddo after Claude [Lorrain]*, confused my wife when she was five. "What's Lord Haddo doing running after Claude?" she asked. The oddest depicts a dead piebald pheasant that secured its immortality because it was shot by Prince Albert.

day in the service of God, and devote myself entirely to the promotion
of His glory.

His wife Mary, he admitted, "fairly thought that I had lost my senses,"
but "after a few days she herself embraced the same sentiments." The
couple were mocked for their fanatical evangelism, and George, who
was also a Member of Parliament, did not greatly help their cause when,
in one of his rare speeches in the House of Commons, he blamed most
of humanity's ills upon the fact that art schools were given government
grants to pay models to pose nude in life classes.

Hansard noted drily:

> It was, in his opinion, impossible for young men to visit those schools
> of art, where nude figures were presented, without being led into acts
> of great debauchery.

George soon resolved to give up painting and most of the luxurious
trappings of the aristocratic life in favor of good deeds great and small. He
sold his own art collection at Christie's to fund them. When a ship with a
hundred Prussian emigrants aboard went down in the Firth of Forth, he
arranged a dinner of roast beef and plum pudding to cheer up "the poor
forlorn creatures." In Brighton, where he lived for a time, he built a school
for boys "from one of the worst streets" of a run-down district. In the
East End of London he went much further, paying £10,000—more than
£800,000 in today's money—for the construction of an imposing church,
St. Mary's, Cable Street, again in a slum area. Though he laid its foundation stone, he played down his generosity, according to his biographer:

> The church having been finished, it was seldom that he alluded to
> it. Very few of his friends ever heard of it during his life. He was very
> watchful over his motives; and greatly feared lest the desire of human
> praise should mar the free-will offering, which he wished it to be, to
> the glory of God.

In the streets near his home in Blackheath, George was a familiar sight,
"carrying little comforts in his own hand to the sick," or driving in his car-

riage, with a "hair-mattress, or arm chair on top of it, on the way to some invalid." He encouraged Sunday schools to hold picnics in his garden and issued a special invitation to the Greenwich Brigade of Shoeblacks ("a useful and deserving class of little gentry," his father remarked).*

At Haddo, he started classes for his tenants and designed comfortable cottages for them to live in. But he had to be dissuaded from turning the family's mansion in the West End of London into an "industrial school, where poor boys should be fed, as well as taught."† He was kind, too, to his own children: he loved spending time with them, sharing their interests and rejoicing in their achievements, while instilling in them the virtues of frugality, generosity, and concern for those whose lives were far less privileged than theirs. In his selfless and sometimes reckless Christian charity, he set his son an example that he never forgot, although ultimately it did not serve Johnny well.

George finally gave up the good fight in 1864 after struggling to swallow a light supper of a mutton chop and a cup of milk, but not before he had thoroughly checked a religious tract for publication. Presciently, and typically, it was a meditation on death, entitled *It May Be Soon*.‡ He was forty-seven years old.

At least the succession seemed safe. He had left three sons: an heir, also named George; a "spare," James, known as "Jem"; and Johnny, the "spare

---

* Shoeblack brigades were formed initially to provide boys from "ragged schools" with employment. During the 1851 Great Exhibition in London, a brigade of twenty-five boys polished, it is thought, more than one hundred thousand pairs of shoes.

† Actually, turning Argyll House, which the 4th Earl had bought in 1808, into a school was not such a bad idea. Its layout was eccentric: the 3rd Duke of Argyll had designed it himself to accommodate his vast library of books. The *Survey of London* was critical of its "rambling arrangement and accretive character," calling it "a house of little beauty and less convenience," a sentiment echoed by the 6th Duke's mistress, the notorious courtesan and society blackmailer Harriette Wilson who thought it "a dismal château." But the 4th Earl liked Argyll House well enough, staying on long after "the neighbourhood had ceased to be fashionable or even respectable." He died there in December 1860. Two years later, the 5th Earl sold it at auction for £18,500 ($24,000). But he kept the stables in Marlborough Mews and established a "ragged school" there instead. He noted proudly that 274 girls had passed through its doors, along with 326 boys, "many of the worst possible character." The house and mews were demolished in 1864–65, and its replacement did welcome children, albeit in a way the 5th Earl never expected. Charles Hengler, one of the most successful impresarios of the Victorian era, opened a circus there. The London Palladium now stands on the site.

‡ The pamphlet with its urgent message—"Death *may* be near at hand; *how near* thou knowest not. It might be this hour, this moment; but, *should it be this moment, where would thy soul be?*"—was distributed at his funeral.

spare," who could have had no expectations. But neither George nor Jem survived for long. Both brothers loved what would nowadays be called extreme sports. In their early twenties, they rowed across the English Channel in a small dinghy. The decision, which, like the boat, was taken on the spur of the moment while on holiday at St. Leonards-on-Sea in Sussex, left them woefully ill-prepared for the rigors of the journey, and they were lucky to avoid drowning in the rough seas or being mown down by much larger vessels.

Not long afterwards, acting again on a whim that had come to him only that morning, Jem, who had rowed for Cambridge in the University Boat Race in 1867, embarked upon another perilous escapade: a solo voyage in a tiny canoe from Dover to Boulogne, and then home via Mâcon, the Rhône, the Mediterranean Sea, and Rotterdam. Later, after a trip to visit his uncle, Arthur Gordon, then Governor of New Brunswick, George severed an artery in his ankle, ironically while demonstrating what North American lumberjacks had taught him about how *not* to use a broadaxe.

This accident seemed only to encourage the brothers, and soon, according to one shocked eyewitness, George and Jem invented an even more dangerous game:

> James often stood at the further end of the room, holding out a small book, while his brother fired at it from his bed with a pistol. When remonstrated with, on account of the danger in case of his brother missing, his answer was, 'George could not miss.'

Predictably, Jem's love of firearms proved his undoing, and on February 12, 1868, he was found shot dead in his university lodgings. The coroner recorded a verdict of "accidental death," after one of Jem's friends had described him as "one of the most careless men in handling his rifle I ever met"—a judgment echoed with much hand-wringing by other eyewitnesses. But the coroner was almost certainly being kind to spare the feelings of a grief-stricken family and to keep the true story out of the press: everyone knew that Jem had killed himself in a moment of regret and panic after being persuaded to seek election as a Member of Parliament, a job to which he felt he was decidedly unsuited.

George met his fate almost two years later, in circumstances that mystified his family. With the hindsight afforded by a hundred and fifty years, it is now quite obvious that he, like his brother, was driven to desperate measures to avoid responsibility. He was an unwilling Earl of Aberdeen, and he had taken up his new position with acute discomfort upon inheriting his lands and title in 1864. Although he dutifully took his oath at the House of Lords and did his best to apply himself to the complex details of the management of his estates, he was secretly planning his escape.

In February 1866, George set sail for North America again, this time with two friends. By the late spring, however, he had disappeared. He left his traveling companions in New York, telling them that he intended to make his way back to New Brunswick via a stop for some sightseeing at Niagara Falls. A week later, he had assumed a false surname and begun a new and far humbler life as a sailor.

"George Osborne" covered his tracks with meticulous—even devious— care. He managed to conceal his origins from his shipmates, and was equally concerned that his mother, waiting anxiously for news back at Haddo, should not realize how completely he had embraced his new station in life. Months of silence, punctuated by the occasional letter containing only the vaguest of details, turned into years. George repeatedly fobbed off his mother's increasingly urgent entreaties with the excuse that his travels were good for his health. He "surfaced" only twice: once to cash two checks in New York, and once to retrieve a favorite rifle and a revolver from Uncle Arthur, who was now the Governor of Trinidad.

By 1870 the family had become alarmed, and his devoted former tutor, the Reverend W. B. Alexander, was persuaded to go to the United States to search for him. The hunt proved frustrating, as the clergyman doggedly followed an ever-cooling trail from New England, south to Texas and Florida. He was about to give up and set sail for Australia, where it had been suggested the elusive Mr. Osborne might have made landfall, when he was shown a letter Captain James H. Kent, skipper of the schooner *Hera*, which had set sail from Boston in January 1870, had written to James Erastus Green, one of the friends "Osborne" had made in Richmond, Maine. Kent asked Green to pass on some "sad news" to people in the town: only six days into the voyage, the ship's mate, "G.F. Osborne," had fallen into the sea while lowering the ship's mainsail and drowned.

The news of George's death reached Haddo on August 30, 1870. Only five days earlier, in a speech at the opening ceremony of the new church at Tarland, which George had promised to pay for as his father lay dying, Johnny had glossed over the family's worries. His brother, he assured the congregation, "had accomplished a voyage nearly all round the world," so there was "reason to trust" that he would soon be home.

But the family now knew for certain that, of the three brothers, only the youngest, most cautious one, had survived. They summoned their lawyer and financial advisor, George Auldjo Jamieson,* from Edinburgh for a meeting and agreed to recognize Johnny as the new Earl of Aberdeen. They knew that there would be many questions† to answer before his status could be officially endorsed—and that two of these might prove particularly awkward. Had the secretive George ever married? And if he had, could there be a son and heir waiting somewhere in Scotland or even in a fishing town in New England?

The family made sure that George's obituaries stated firmly that he had never married, but they could not, in those first days, be sure. They were well aware that George had had girlfriends, most notably Jane Ogilvie, a seamstress he had met in the first days of 1862 in the Aberdeenshire fishing village of Boddam, where his grandfather had built a "marine villa" for his holidays. They also probably knew that, barely nine months later, Jane had given birth to a son, whose father's identity she did not reveal, but perhaps hinted at, in naming the baby Charles Gordon. If there was a scandal, it was efficiently hushed up. When, later that year, George enrolled at the University at St. Andrews, only forty miles from where Jane was living, his redoubtable tutor, the Reverend Alexander, seems to have been sent there, too: presumably with instructions to keep an eye upon his errant pupil.

From across the Atlantic, after George's death, came rumors of a dalliance with a certain Miss Rook of Bath in Maine. These grew stronger after

---

*Johnny was lucky to have his advice. According to the *Oxford Dictionary of National Biography*, which deems the lives of only forty-four accountants worthy of inclusion in its parade of the most notable figures in British history, Jamieson was "undoubtedly one of the most successful and influential Scottish accountants in the late nineteenth century." Jamieson had begun his career as an accountant but later studied as a lawyer too.

†Johnny's uncle, the diplomat Arthur Hamilton-Gordon, later Baron Stanmore, was present at the meeting and went along with the decision, "although," he confided to his diary, "in my mind some doubt lingered."

it became known that she had sent George's mother, Mary, a photograph of her sailor son sporting a luxuriant beard; but no doubt to the family's relief, Sewell Small, one of his shipmates, was allowed the last word:

> George was an unmarried man. He often spoke of himself as such. I used to joke him about getting married and he would say he would marry when he found the right one.

Captain Small was one of many witnesses whose evidence was submitted to the two official hearings into George's death. The first, in 1871, by John McLaren, the Sheriff of Chancery in Edinburgh, followed a diligent investigation on both sides of the Atlantic by an advocate, Henry Stone Smith, who, rather more forensically than the Reverend Alexander, had taken depositions from people who had encountered George during his adventures on land and sea. When Smith showed the Americans photographs taken before he left Scotland, they all agreed that "George Osborne" and the "Right Honourable George Gordon, Earl of Aberdeen in the Lands and Barony of Haddo and others" were one and the same. Smith also brought back a sad little bundle of possessions—two toothbrushes, a razor, some sheets of music, a commonplace book, and a Bible—some of which George's mother was able to recognize. She provided letters written to her by her son for comparison with "a large number of documents bearing the signature of George H. Osborne," and events mentioned in their pages, such as "a great storm of thunder and lightning" on the day of a devastating earthquake off the Caribbean island of St. Thomas in November 1867 and "the capture of a shark" a year earlier, were corroborated by his former shipmates. Crucially, a rifle sold by "Osborne" to a man in Richmond, Maine, just before embarking on his last voyage, was "identified by Mr Henry* of Edinburgh, the maker, as having been sold to Lord Aberdeen on October 20, 1863": this was more

---

* This would have been a work of real craftsmanship. Alexander Henry (1818–1894), one of the inventors of the then revolutionary Martini-Henry rifle used by the British Army at the end of the nineteenth century, was appointed "gun and rifle manufacturer to His Royal Highness the Prince of Wales." In 1873, Queen Victoria commissioned a .450 double-barreled hammer rifle from him, which she gave to her ghillie John Brown for Christmas. This "extremely rare and fine" gun, complete with its case inscribed "J. Brown Esq. H.M.P. Attendant, Balmoral," was sold at Bonham's in London in 2016 for £35,000 ($45,000).

than two years before his disappearance. In his judgment, the sheriff, who admitted that he had "considered this case with some anxiety," ruled that despite "the improbability of the history . . . the facts on which this claim is founded are proved."

The following year, after the Attorney General had assured Queen Victoria that "sufficient evidence" had been laid before him to support Johnny's claim, and the Queen had given her assent for the Committee of Privileges of the House of Lords to review the evidence in the case, Johnny was at last allowed to claim his inheritance.

The tragedies had shaped him: devout and sensitive, serious and moody to the point of melancholy and depression, "Gentle Johnny," as the family called him, was determined, nonetheless, to rise to the challenge of his new responsibilities and to continue in his father's philanthropic footsteps. He vowed to improve the lives of the tenants on his Scottish estates, those of seafarers like his lost brother, and those of the poor in the cities chaotically spawned by the Industrial Revolution.

The problem was that he was woefully ill-equipped to handle the business of running his estates: even more so than George, who, according to his mother, "had never been accustomed to great expenditure, nor to hear large sums of money spoken of and had not turned his attention to business matters." Soon after his dash to Haddo when the news of the "Sailor Earl's" death reached the family, Jamieson wrote to Johnny urging him to get to grips with his new responsibilities. He was now, on paper, a very rich man, but his income would come almost exclusively from the rents paid by more than a thousand tenants and from the yields of his own farming operations. At the same time, his outgoings would be considerable: there was land to improve and fields to drain, tenants' houses and farm buildings to maintain and repair, the latest agricultural equipment to buy, and ever-higher taxes to pay to governments that had come to see landowners as easy game. A run of bad weather and failed harvests could quickly, and disastrously, deplete the coffers, and Jamieson was concerned that Johnny should be thrifty and save for the inevitable rainy day.

But this was the first of many warnings from his cautious Edinburgh advisor that the unworldly new Earl was to ignore over the coming years, and Johnny's first attempt to manage his affairs prefigured the problems to come. Generously, and perhaps euphorically—the long investigation into his brother's disappearance had wearied and frustrated him—Johnny waived his right to a share of the £118,728* that George had left in Britain and the $600 discovered in his American account, so that it could be divided among his three sisters, Mary, Harriet, and Katherine.

As their acquaintance grew, Ishbel thought him "my ideal of all that a man should be," and it is not hard to see why Johnny appealed so much to her. With his dark and slightly feminine good looks, he cut a striking figure: many a mother anxious to marry off a daughter bemoaned his reluctance to attend society balls. To Ishbel, though, his impeccable manners, his Christian faith, and his easy, if diffident, way with people counted for just as much. She never forgot how, at that first encounter in Rotten Row,

> he found a ready road to my heart by treating me as if I was a rational being, and a grown-up young lady, instead of chaffing me, as was the fashion with most of my sister's friends.

Ishbel's journals record the highlights and setbacks of what, for the first few years, was to prove a painfully one-sided adoration. Her mother had presented her with a notebook in September 1870 in the hope that she would record and reflect upon the sermons she heard on Sundays, but the pages of the volume for 1875, the year she turned eighteen and made her entry into London Society, contain some decidedly secular observations:

> Tonight I went to my first dance at Lady Adelaide Cadogan's†—it was considered a very good one—no crowd, plenty of men etc. I got on well enough but did not find where the wonderful enjoyment lay— hopping round a room and talking about the floor, the weather and such like.

Aided and abetted by her socially ambitious mother, Ishbel never wavered in her devotion to Johnny, but the rules and routines of London

---

* About £7,500,000 ($9,600,000) in today's money.

† Despite her then fame as a society hostess, Lady Adelaide is known today for her espousal of a much less gregarious activity: she is thought to have written the first book about Solitaire and Patience.

Society in the 1870s were rigidly laid down, often making it difficult for young aristocratic men and women to follow their hearts and pursue the object of their affections. They could meet at the garden parties held by the Prince and Princess of Wales at Marlborough House, at balls at Buckingham Palace, and in the residences of the grandes dames of London society—Lady Holland, the Countess of Jersey, and the Duchesses of Argyll and Northumberland—or at government receptions at the Foreign Office, where Ishbel loved to watch the arrival of "all the leading personages of the time, in full uniform and decorations, and the ladies in a blaze of jewels and splendour."

But since Johnny was a reluctant social butterfly, Ishbel soon realized that the best way to pursue the man she was determined to marry would be to engineer regular "chance encounters" at church. Young ladies were less closely chaperoned than usual while visiting such obviously respectable places, and a conversation struck up in the porch could be continued on the way home without a reputation being compromised. Thus, every Sunday, she would try to guess which of London's most fashionable places of worship would be graced with Johnny's presence. Then she would head to St. George's, Hanover Square, or to the Quebec Chapel, where she hoped to run her quarry to ground.

On February 14 she struck lucky:

8.30 Sacrament service; met Lord Aberdeen just at the door of the church (the 1st man I met with the exception of an old policeman— St Valentine). Lord Aberdeen walked home from church with us & came into luncheon having written to propose himself—how nice he was! He is going to dine with us on Saturday week. D.V.

Ishbel's wish was granted. Johnny duly came to dinner on the 27th and stayed to hear her give a little recital on the piano:

Such a delightful evening—played all the while after dinner & he sat by the side of me & talked and chatted so warmly between the pieces.

In page after page of the diary, Ishbel records a romantic campaign that becomes increasingly relentless. Worldly and religious devotion are soon intertwined, and God's help in bringing them together is repeatedly invoked:

> He knows the desires, hopes & fears of my heart concerning my earthly life & He will do what is best for us—only that He may glorify Himself in us both!

Johnny's every word and deed are analyzed for signs of love. One day in March when they met out riding on Rotten Row, "he was as warm and unconstrained as possible," only to seem cool and distant a few days later:

> Rode this morning—Lord Aberdeen joined me for a few minutes at the end but seemed shy & confused.

Through London's streets, salons, ballrooms, parks, and churches, Ishbel charted Johnny's trail:

> I only caught a glimpse of Lord Aberdeen at the morning service today—otherwise he has not come near me. Strange boy. Faith and Patience! If I did not feel the deep assurance that the Lord is undertaking for me, I think this suspense would drive me mad—as it is, all is right, for the best, I know.

When, in the spring, Johnny was nowhere to be found, Ishbel feared that he had deserted her:

> It has been a sad four weeks. For a few days I have scarcely ever felt so ill & done in body & as to mind and soul, a sort of agony swept over [me] almost to more than I could bear.

Yet whenever they did meet, Johnny gave her little encouragement:

> I have not had the heart to write anything the last few days—the ups and downs have been too much. I prayed that if it was the Lord's will that I should have the wondrous blessing of having Lord Aberdeen—

for my own, my very own, that he should either come to tea or show some particular civility—if not, that I should see nothing of him . . .

Johnny failed to call at Brook House that afternoon, but he did offer his greetings to Ishbel when they bumped into each other in the street. The problem was that he never showed his feelings and clearly enjoyed his bachelor routine, attending the House of Lords and chairing the Royal Commission on Railway Accidents: heaven to a passionate lover of trains, whose party piece was to imitate the whistles of famous locomotives.* Emotionally, however, he seemed to blow hot and cold, sometimes paying Ishbel close attention, at others appearing indifferent and remote.

In the summer of 1877, however, crisis struck. Towards the end of the London Season, rumors of an engagement began to spread. Ishbel was aghast: the real situation was quite different.

One Sunday, when they had met after a service at the Quebec Chapel, Johnny seemed to be in a disconcertingly pensive mood:

We walked home together but he spoke enough to let me feel that only friendship was his feeling towards me & the next day Monday, when he came and spent an hour with Mamma & she made up her mind to tell him exactly how I felt for him, he told her plainly he had not that feeling for me which he felt he must have for the woman who was to be his wife—only the warmest friendship must continue between us. . . .

Johnny fled to Aberdeenshire. At her desk, the heartbroken Ishbel continued her tale of woe:

Mamma wrote to him on Saturday to tell him that Papa didn't know of the conversation & to tell him she thought he was deceiving himself as to his feelings. The past week has been trying to the last degree— wherever I went, nothing but congratulations & questions as to

*When Ishbel and Johnny paid a last visit to their dying friend Lord Rosebery in 1928, he "remembered old associations," asking Johnny "to give him a performance of an imitation of the sounds of a locomotive engine which he and Mr Gladstone used to call for in the old days." Johnny could also produce a startlingly lifelike imitation of a cuckoo's call to amuse his grandchildren.

whether it was true—sickening & people won't believe me when I
deny it. . . . The Queen wrote to the Duchess of Roxburghe to tell her
to find out whether it was true.

All Ishbel's plans seemed to have gone awry:

The one dream of my life for the last six years has dissolved and I must
face life without him.

Perhaps they would never become a couple in this world, although
"nothing can prevent our being united in Christ anyway," she added de-
fiantly. But Lady Marjoribanks came to the rescue with a firm letter that
brought Johnny to his senses:

For your own sake I would not have you throw away a priceless blessing,

she wrote.

A reply arrived by return. Johnny was coming back to London to ask
for the hand of the woman he thenceforth called his "priceless blessing."
Family tradition has it that, after posting his letter, Johnny panicked and
tried to fish it out of the postbox—but in vain. Although it was late at
night, he sent an urgent message to his friend the postmaster general, asking him to help get the letter back. But such was the efficiency of the Royal
Mail in those days that even the government minister in charge failed to
have it intercepted before it reached the butler's salver at Brook House.

Ishbel was talking to her mother when

a letter came, the handwriting of which made one tremble from head
to foot but when it was opened! He says he finds his feelings are not
those of mere friendship for me—that he wants to return to London.

Ishbel was ecstatic, counting the miles from Aberdeenshire:

Now I cannot, cannot realise that it is really true, It is too good—too
great a blessing & is a miracle—it is an answer to prayer. . . . I keep on
thinking—I can never, never doubt about prayer again.

Two days later, Johnny called on Sir Dudley to ask for his daughter's hand.

Suddenly, with a wedding to plan, there was much to do. The church, St. George's Hanover Square, had to be booked, a guest list of more than two hundred drawn up, the menu for the lavish wedding breakfast discussed with the Brook House kitchen staff, and a date found in the Archbishop of Canterbury's calendar so that he could conduct the service. The organist, William Pinney, set about composing a celebratory march, and a dress of white satin trimmed with Brussels lace and orange blossoms was ordered from Miss Stratton of Piccadilly. Johnny called at the jeweler's and bought his bride a diamond-and-pearl necklace and matching bracelet. Typically, his future father-in-law outdid him with "a magnificent tiara."

The customary complex marriage settlement was drafted, negotiated, and signed.* Although no one would have imagined then the financial problems that Ishbel would have to face in later life, Marjoribanks dutifully agreed to place £10,000 in trust for his daughter and to provide her with an income of £3,000† a year.

Three weeks passed before Ishbel found time to describe all these events in her diary:

It is as well perhaps that I have not written about it all, day by day there was something so intensely deep, intensely sacred & special about everything that passed between us two that first week in London—it was between us two & all is graven on my heart for ever. His love is such as

---

* This was in line with the advice offered by *The Guide to the Unprotected in Every-day Matters relating to Property and Income* published three years before. In it, the author, "A Banker's Daughter," offered this sage counsel: "No prudent woman should marry without this provision, as, if it is made before her marriage, however much in debt her husband may become, from extravagance or misfortune, her settlement money cannot be made liable. The friends of the lady should *insist* upon a proper marriage settlement to the satisfaction of her Lawyer being signed *before the marriage*. On her return *from* church, the husband's will should also be signed. It would not be valid if signed *before* marriage."

† With a trust fund equivalent to about £600,000 ($800,000) today and an annual income equivalent to more than £150,000 ($200,000), Ishbel was a rich woman in her own right. The accusation that she gave away most of Johnny's fortune is not entirely misplaced, but she spent her own, too, on good works.

one would only have dreamt of—so deep, holy, deferential, tender, so heavenly; it humbles me to the dust to think of my having been given that love—& my own utter unworthiness.

The highs and lows of their courtship, while not forgotten, had been worth enduring:

It has not been a scrap too long as a preparation for such Paradisiacal happiness. . . . I have still 3 months, as we are not to be married till Nov., as that proved most convenient to all—it is too long, but we shall be kept and guided day by day.

The night before the wedding, Johnny sent his bride a note:

My darling, sacredly given gift; shall we take as a text for tomorrow, "the Lord shall give strength to His people—the Lord shall give His people the blessing of peace"—

I am, now and always hereafter
Your own Johnny, who loves
you very much.

In London on the morning of November 7, 1877, as the crowds gathered outside St. George's, heavy rain was falling, but no one seemed to mind. The church was full an hour before the service and the carriages of the guests who, the newspapers reported, included "a large number of members of the aristocracy," were double-parked right back to the far end of Hanover Square.

After the marriage ceremony and a homily from the Archbishop on "the reciprocal duties of husband and wife," the congregation repaired to Brook House, where a "sumptuous" wedding breakfast was served in the dining room. The bride of course enjoyed "a day consecrated for me by wonderful memories," although that part of her heart that was not taken up with her adoration of a man "who has often been described as realizing Chaucer's ideal of 'a very perfect knight' " was, as ever, at Guisachan:

We had a lovely wedding, even though it took place in dull old St George's Church, Hanover Square, instead of at my dear beautiful Highland home, as was at first intended.

There were parties, too, for tenants and local worthies on the family estates. Sir Dudley had made yet another addition to his property portfolio by buying, a year earlier, Hutton Hall, a tumbledown sixteenth-century castle in the heart of his Berwick on Tweed constituency. In the nearby town, Mr. Thompson the Mayor, the Sheriff James Allan, and the town's aldermen gathered to toast the health and happiness of "the noble Earl and his Countess" and to enjoy "a magnificent brides-cake sent down from London." Flags flew and the bells of the Town Hall rang out at noon in celebration. After dark, "a company numbering between 30 and 40" was reported to have done "ample justice to an ample dinner" at the Pack Horse Inn, while outside a magnificent display of fireworks lit up the sky. In the Highlands, bonfires blazed from the high hills of Strathglass above Ishbel's beloved Guisachan amidst "much rejoicing."

On Johnny's estates across the Aberdeenshire countryside, the tenants celebrated far into the night. At a dinner at Haddo, "500 gentlemen" drank no fewer than fifteen toasts: to the happy couple, of course, but also, mysteriously, to "the Clergy of All Denominations" and "the Medical Faculty." At Tarland, where the children had already feasted on cake delivered from Gunter's Tea Shop in London's Berkeley Square, the minister of the parish, the Reverend William Skinner, regaled the fifty Cromar Estate tenants who sat down to a banquet in the village hall with a character sketch of the bridegroom:

> The Earl is a man of intellect and of goodness. His public speeches and his private conversation are always sensible, temperate, and shrewd. . . . He is no extreme man, no crotchetee, no hobbyist. . . . Then he is a good man, a man of high moral principles, of a most blameless life.

In the next-door village of Logie Coldstone, John Grant Michie, the schoolmaster, confidently drew on hearsay for a word portrait of the laird's new wife:

I can assure you that from all I have heard of her she is in every way worthy of him, and every way qualified to make him happy. She was lately described to me as 'a bonnie, sweet, fair-haired lassie.'

The next day, newspapers the length and breadth of Britain devoted many column inches to what had undoubtedly been one of the society events of the year. They described the music played at the service, the bride's gown, her eight bridesmaids, the "blue velvet costume trimmed with white lace" worn by her mother, and even the "drab silk bonnet, with a dress to match, and a white cashmere shawl" sported by her godmother, Baroness Burdett-Coutts.

But most of the space was devoted to a long list of the presents lavished upon the couple: among them a "turquoise, pearl and diamond bracelet" from the Earl of Dudley, "sapphire and diamond ear-rings" from Ishbel's brother Edward and his wife, a "thin double band of diamonds with ruby centre bracelet" from Lord and Lady Ilchester, and a "trellis-work necklace set with pearls and diamonds, pearl heart-shaped locket and ear-rings, and bracelet to match" bought with the proceeds of a collection among the tenants of the Haddo estate.

Ishbel was so thrilled with the jewelry that, "heedless of warnings," as she later confessed, she decided to take most of her "lovely wedding presents" with her on honeymoon.

4

A House for a Honeymoon

Thirty miles from Brook House, near the small town of Sevenoaks in Kent, stood Halstead Place, the eighteenth-century home of Ishbel's maiden aunts, Emma and Laura. Like all Marjoribanks houses, it was grand and imposing. Christopher Greenwood, one of the foremost architectural writers of the time, vaunted its charms:

> The house is of modern architecture, handsome and spacious, the interior is very elegant and decorated with some valuable paintings by Corregio, Salvator Rosa, Caravaggio, Vandervelde, Breughel, Marcenay, Clevely, Wyche, Cuyp, etc. The grounds here are beautiful and well adorned with shrubberies.

Ishbel and Johnny reached Halstead Place late in the afternoon of their wedding day in another of Sir Dudley's presents, an open barouche driven by two postilions and drawn by his four finest horses. Fifty years later, one of the Marjoribanks' neighbors, writing to congratulate the couple on their Golden Wedding, still remembered their departure from Brook House:

> The postilions with their lovely blue jackets was a sight that one never forgot. We do not see it now. The grandeur has gone.

Ishbel added a postscript to the "thank-you" note she sent back with the coach to her father:

We have just arrived—a very nice drive; delightfully mild, such a sunset, and the barouche rolled along so smoothly. . . . A beautiful archway of flowers was erected for us at the lodge here and a band is playing for us below the house.

Before them lay the prospect of a long and idyllic honeymoon, but, as Ishbel recalled in her memoirs, things soon took a dramatic and unwelcome turn:

We might have been allowed to retire into decent obscurity during our honeymoon and wedding trip, but this was not to be our lot, for unhappily we attained unsought and most unpleasant notoriety through an experience which we suffered at Halstead.

She and Johnny were just sitting down to tea on the afternoon of Monday, November 19, when her "German maid rushed into the room, wringing her hands and uttering inchoate ejaculations, '*Ach, gnädige Frau—Ach! ach!*'"

A., very unperturbed, asked chaffingly, 'What is the matter; have the pipes burst?'
    But in a moment it flashed upon my mind what must be the cause of the trouble, and I asked, 'Are the jewels stolen?' . . .
    '*Ach ya—ya—kommen sie doch—ich kann nicht herein,*' wailed my maid, and we rushed upstairs after her to find my dressing-room literally strewn with the contents of drawers, which the thieves had evidently dragged out one after another in wild search for their booty. The marks of their boots were on some of the clothes; chains of beads and such like things of no value had been thrown around the room in evident disgust, until they at last found the locked drawers and burst them open, and made off with the contents.

The thieves, the shocked couple realized, might still be on the premises, for they discovered that the door of the room opposite was locked from the inside. To Ishbel's horror, Johnny grabbed a poker from the fireplace and tried to break it down; a task not helped by the "maid now hanging on to his coat tails and entreating him to desist or he might be murdered, and his valet standing behind him shaking like an aspen leaf."

But all they found on the other side was an open window through which the thieves had clearly made their escape. The police were summoned, with crime reporters, scenting a story ripe for serialization in the "penny dreadfuls," hot on their heels. One wrote:

> Superintendent Okill, of Sevenoaks, on making an examination of the place, found that a ladder had been placed against the balcony and an entrance had been made through a window above into a spare room, whence the thieves had no difficulty in making their way into the dressing room, where they appear to have carried on their operations unmolested, and they got clear away with their booty without leaving the slightest trace behind.

The hunt quickly intensified. More detectives arrived to question the servants; the villagers reported that strangers had been spotted lurking in the area from the day of the newlyweds' arrival; the gardener's boy confessed that he had seen two men climbing a ladder and entering the house through a window, but had said nothing because he had assumed they were workmen; a trail of empty jewel cases on the way to a nearby railway station suggested that the thieves had escaped to London with their swag; and a reward of £500 was offered for its safe return. Emma and Laura, the "irate aunts," bustled home, but having made sure that their own jewels were safe, "they could offer no enlightenment."

A disconsolate Ishbel sat down to make a list of the stolen jewelry:

> When we began going over the list of missing articles, it was heartbreaking to realize our losses, and not only the precious pearl and diamond necklace, and the big sapphire and diamond locket, given me by A.

Gone, too, were many of the other treasures so gloatingly described in the newspapers: the sapphire and diamond earrings from her brother Edward and his wife, the Ilchesters' diamond-and-ruby bracelet, and the beautiful collection of gems from the Haddo tenants. The thieves' haul was worth at least £5,000, equivalent to £300,000 today.

Hopes rose when, within three days, Superintendent Okill proclaimed a breakthrough: an old soldier turned ne'er-do-well called William Todd had confessed to the police at Maidstone. But when Todd came up for trial at the County Police Court at Sevenoaks, the prosecution witnesses, a clothier named Benjamin Barnett and his son Benjamin William, were unconvincing. They testified that although Todd had offered to sell them the jewelry from the Halstead robbery, they had not actually seen any of it. Soon afterwards, disappointed journalists reported that Todd had been cleared of any involvement:

> With regard to the statement he made to the police and others at Maidstone, he now says that he had read an account of the robbery, and he then concocted the story of his connection with it, but that there was not the slightest foundation for it, and he cannot tell what made him accuse himself.

The crime was never solved, nor was any of the jewelry recovered, and in any case, the honeymooners were, Ishbel claimed, "far too much engrossed in our new-found happiness to be much perturbed by even such a misadventure as our burglary."

The police shrugged off accusations that they had been incompetent with a neat counterattack:

> We had to submit with as good grace as we could muster to the reproaches of the county police for not having notified them of our arrival, so that the place might be guarded, and to being held up as a warning to other young couples.

But Ishbel had the last word, claiming that Superintendent Okill and Kent's finest had failed to pursue the most obvious suspect:

> Many years after, an uncle of mine, who was a visiting magistrate, had the duty of visiting the celebrated burglar and murderer, Charles Peace,

in his cell, and from admissions made by the latter was convinced that he was personally concerned in the Halstead burglary, which certainly corroborated the detectives' opinion that we were lucky in not having personally met our unwelcome visitors.

Charles Peace was the most colorful and prolific cat burglar of the Victorian era: a man to be feared. Born in Sheffield, the son of a wild animal tamer who traveled the country with a fairground attraction called Wombwell's Wild Beast Show, he embarked on his sensational life of crime after a sliver of red-hot steel flew into his leg, bringing a respectable career at a rolling mill to a painful end. In 1877, Peace was a fugitive, accused of murder and with a trail of burglaries in Yorkshire, Manchester, and London behind him. He masqueraded as a musical instrument dealer—his talent as a fiddler had earned him the nickname of "the modern Paganini" in the pubs where he played—but, in proto-mafioso-style, he used his violin case for a more sinister purpose: to hide his tools for cracking open doors, windows, and safes in the houses of the rich.

While the Halstead Place robbery did indeed have many of the hallmarks of Peace's infamous modus operandi, the master criminal's involvement was never proved. When he went to the gallows in 1879 for killing a civil engineer named Dyson, Peace was more concerned to secure a pardon for one of his associates wrongly convicted for a murder *he* had committed than to confess to his lesser crimes. But, if nothing else, this accusation against a cat burglar who had caught the public imagination and had inspired a Sherlock Holmes story added a touch of spice to Ishbel's memoirs.

Suitably chastened, the couple traveled on to Egypt for a voyage down the River Nile and a honeymoon of sightseeing, reading, and sketching, but for a couple brought up to do good works and help the poor there were other, less frivolous, diversions. Johnny, in particular, was conscious that they were following in the footsteps of his father, who had twice traveled to Egypt in the hope that the climate there would restore his failing health.

On his first trip in 1854 and 1855, George's letters home to the 4th Earl describe "indolent days," "basking like a crocodile" on the deck of a riverboat as it drifts down the River Nile, watching mirages shimmering over the desert sands, resting in the lush gardens of Cairo and Alexandria and fantasizing about bringing his father "a gigantic leg of polished red granite" from an ancient statue to adorn the garden at Haddo.

His second visit in 1860 was quite different. Although his illness had returned with a vengeance and he knew that the "death-warrant" issued by his doctor six years earlier was about to be executed, he had God's work to do. Thus, before he left England, George stocked up with copies of the Bible in Arabic and tracts on miracles and the parables that, with the help of an American missionary couple, Dr. and Mrs. Lansing, he sold "at a very reduced prices" to Christians who lived on the banks of the Nile.

Seventeen years on, Johnny and Ishbel embarked on their trip down the river with their own cargo of "nicely bound Testaments and Bibles for sale or distribution." As they made their stately progress in a large dahabeah called the *Nubia*, the villagers soon cottoned on to the presence of generous foreigners and "seemed pleased to receive a neatly-bound book as a souvenir." No doubt remembering the days when she had ridden through Glen Affric delivering the "potions" concocted in her mother's boudoir to ailing tenants on the Guisachan estate, Ishbel had also brought "simple medicines and ointments" to "treat any patients who applied."

When, in old age, they looked back at their life together in their joint memoirs, Ishbel and Johnny chuckled at the comically earnest figures they had cut on the banks of the Nile:

> We laugh now at the remembrance of the picture we must have made,
> when with all due care and solemnity we dealt out pills and quinine,
> soothing lotions and ointments, and applied bandages and plasters to
> the crowd of poor wretches suffering from various troubles who heard
> of our practices.

But the pattern was set: these impromptu clinics were the first of countless enlightened, innovative, and often expensive ways in which, over nearly sixty years, Johnny and Ishbel worked to improve social conditions wherever they went. And they cared not a hoot if they risked the contempt of their peers by taking their campaigns to the slum dwellers of London, to the servants who skivvied below stairs in Scotland's great houses, to the starving people of the Irish countryside, and far beyond to lonely settlers on the prairies of Canada and the sick of the goldfields in the Yukon.

Even on honeymoon, Ishbel and Johnny ventured where most of their fellow travelers feared to tread. Appalled by stories that the slave trade was still flourishing in Egypt, they made it known that they wanted to hire some children as servants. The bait was quickly taken, and four boys aged eight, nine, eleven, and sixteen were paraded before them:

> We found the children on the deck, and we listened whilst all their good points of strength and beauty were exhibited. Then A. called together the crew, and . . . explained that these boys having come to a boat flying the Union Jack were not slaves, and could not be slaves. . . . But, A. added, as the men who brought them had some trouble, some compensation would be given them, after which they had better get away as quickly as they could.

These "most terrified small beings" were kitted out in red shirts and blue trousers and were immediately adopted by Johnny and Ishbel: a ruse to ensure that they could be baptised into the Presbyterian Church and freed from the shackles of their masters. Though they then left the three youngest, now incongruously renamed Abdeen, Gordon, and Haddo, to be cared for at the mission school at Asyut, their new parents kept in touch with them for the rest of their lives. These proved to be distressingly short: Abdeen and Haddo did not survive their childhood, both succumbing to tuberculosis, and Gordon, who became a professor at a college in Khartoum, died "when not much over thirty." The older boy, now named Campbell, was found a job as a cabin boy, and when, like the others, Campbell later decided to further his education, he wrote to Johnny to thank him on behalf of their adopted sons:

> To His Excellency our Revered and Honoured Parent Lord Aberdeen, may he be continually preserved. I cease not to feel grateful for your kindness in placing me in school-orchards to pluck the fruit of knowledge and good breeding under the care of virtuous Christian people.

As to our news, we—thank God—are happy to the highest degree and we are progressing in our studies.

And so, after leaving "the poor little fellows . . . scrubbing their eyes with their new pocket handkerchiefs," the couple drifted on down the Nile on their dahabeah, innocents abroad. Both their guide and the captain of the boat had realized that they were a soft touch and spun out the voyage: the dragoman by taking them on long excursions to dull villages ashore and the captain by engineering "many delays."

Eventually the charms of the Nile began to pall, not least because Ishbel had proved to be a fussy traveler, chronicling the disagreeable rigors of the honeymoon journey in her diary in rather more detail than the sights of ancient Egypt: from the "v. bad eggs" served for breakfast at an English ferry port hotel to her "three days of misery" on the steamer to Alexandria. And on the waters of the Nile, their dahabeah was alarmingly unstable when a strong wind blew:

> As the gale grew stronger, the crew found it impossible to manage the boat & frantic efforts were made to furl the sail & bring her to shore. All attempts to do this were unavailing . . . & J gave me full directions as we sat on the stern how, where to jump over should we capsize altogether & how to lay hold of him.

Johnny finally lost patience with the dawdling crew: the hot season was approaching and he wanted to take his bride to the Holy Land. Meanwhile, Ishbel was making no secret of her yearning to return to the more comfortable, more "civilised," delights of Cairo. They urgently needed a tow along the river. By chance, help was at hand from a kinsman, the legendary General Charles "Chinese" Gordon, the Governor-General of Sudan, who was due to pass by on his way to Cairo, where the khedive had asked him to help sort out his finances.

Ishbel was excited as the great man's boat approached on March 4, 1878:

> At about 11 a steamer was seen. The cannon was made ready, & with eager expectation we awaited the longed for approach of GORDON PACHA.

Johnny whiled away the time by loading his gun:

When at last the signal of the rapidly-travelling vessel was given, A. was on deck in a trice, firing off shots of distress. 'Would she stop?' was now the anxious question, but before the echo of the last shot could be heard, the steamer slowed down and a boat was sent alongside, inquiring whether this was Lord Aberdeen's *dahabeah*, and asking him to come over to see Gordon Pasha.

The general knew what was expected of him:

'You are a chief of the Gordons and I am a clansman, whose duty it is to come to the assistance of his chief; so we'll hitch you on and take you within sight of Assiout at any rate.'

After reading the Bible with them, Gordon presented the couple with a late wedding present, a set of Egyptian filigree coffee holders crafted from the finest silver. Ishbel was delighted that a "fast friendship was set up, and we, too, came under the fascination of that keen blue eye and that single-minded heroic character." But Gordon, as poisonous as he was pious and with little affection for women, was less captivated. "Aberdeen has married a great fat girl," he told his sister.

Towards the end of their honeymoon, the couple was enlisted in another, far riskier, rescue operation. A young man called Ahmed Fahmy had fled the clutches of his family who were furious with him for converting to Christianity. They threatened murderous retribution. Dr. and Mrs. Lansing, the missionaries who had given him refuge, were desperate to help him flee Egypt, and thus a plan was hatched and executed. Fahmy joined Johnny and Ishbel's retinue—they were traveling with their maid and valet—and, after a stormy voyage to Europe, he was sent to Edinburgh University "for the necessary training for a medical missionary." Johnny stumped up the fees from his ever-open wallet, but in this case, at least, his investment was triumphantly justified: Fahmy went on to spend thirty years as a revered evangelist and surgeon in China, and the hospital he founded in Zhangzhou was "famous for its popularity."

When she wrote to her father at the end of the trip, Ishbel concealed her true feelings—but only just:

> We have found 'Nile life' enchanting, delightful—no drawbacks at all to perfect enjoyment. Nevertheless we shall not shed many tears on leaving Egypt.

On the way home, the couple stopped off at "some favourite haunts of A." At one of them, Mendrisio in the Swiss Alps, they toyed with the idea of building a cottage, but only briefly. In any case, there were more than enough houses in London and Scotland for Johnny, with the assistance of a new wife whose upbringing had given her decided views on architecture and interior design, to lavish his vast inheritance upon.

5

The Family Seat

Even today, the heir to an ancestral seat in the North East of Scotland does well to think hard about how best to introduce his new bride to the family home. Haddo House, some twenty miles north of the fishing port of Aberdeen, was more refined than the rough-hewn castles that covered the dour coastal plain: there was one of those, it was said, to every square mile. Nonetheless, when Johnny brought Ishbel to his mansion in the summer of 1878, he had every reason to fear that she would find becoming its chatelaine a daunting, uncomfortable, and perhaps unwelcome prospect.

In the 1730s, Johnny's ancestor, the 2nd Earl, had set out to build a showpiece. After taking the "many good advises" of Scotland's greatest arbiter of taste, Sir John Clerk of Penicuik, he hired the fashionable architect William Adam to draw up a very grand design; demolished what was left of the old family seat, the crumbling House of Kellie; and employed the country's most skillful mason, John Baxter, to carry out the "longsom work" of hammering the local whinstone into shape.

The result of their labors was a Palladian mansion with an imposing central block and adjoining pavilions. An elegant wrought-iron staircase swept up to the entrance on the first-floor piano nobile. Baxter was pleased with his handiwork, noting that the house "stanes weill without crack or flau or the least symptom of a sitle in any pairt of the whoall," while the local lairds were amazed by its splendor and impressed by the amount of money that had so ostentatiously been lavished upon it.

Johnny had planned their first visit to "H.H.," as Ishbel called it, with great care, spinning out their honeymoon and the weeks after their return to London until summer arrived and, with it, he hoped, good weather. His canny wife knew exactly what he was up to:

He had guarded it jealously from my view during the unfriendly spring months, and decided that we must wander in distant lands, until June had clothed the woods and policies of Haddo House with beauties sufficient to equal those of the Highland glen from which he had brought me.

But Haddo did not measure up to Guisachan:

Alas for human plans! The 1st of June dawned as bleak and forbidding as a March day, and a persistent north-east wind faced us all the twenty miles from Aberdeen in our barouche and four horses with postilions; my face must have matched my blue velvet dress by the time I was submitted for inspection to the big escort of mounted tenantry which awaited us on the road, several miles before we reached our destination.

According to a grandson, who heard it from her own lips sixty years later, Ishbel turned to Johnny as their barouche rounded the last bend of the drive and asked, "Why have you brought me to this horrible house?"

In 1804, when he was almost twenty-one, Johnny's grandfather, the 4th Earl, had felt the same when he traveled to Haddo to claim his inheritance. The condition of the place, which he had not visited since his childhood, shocked him. He wrote to a friend:

The desolation of the exterior is only equalled by the appalling badness of the house.... Alas! This is not my Paradise: this is not Vall' Ombrosa of which you have heard so much, but a real Siberian waste.

He consoled himself with the thought that "there is a sensible pleasure at standing to look around one and being able to see nothing but one's own," and stoically claimed that he did not find the "country so horrible as I imagined." But he later confided his true thoughts to his youngest son Arthur, who wrote:

> The scene before him was certainly cold and cheerless. The short lime avenue before the house terminated in a dreary and extensive peat moss, which lay stretched between it and the grim high walls of a distant deer park. Snipe were to be shot in the marshy swamp which reached to the foot of the garden terrace. Stacks of fuel and sheds of lumber were piled against the walls of the house itself. . . . Three o'clock in the afternoon was the ordinary hour of dinner, at which every gentleman present was expected to propose a toast and every lady a sentiment. A particular small kind of raw turnip appeared on the table as the winter dessert.

The 4th Earl despaired at the harsh conditions in which his tenants had to live:

> Women habitually assisted to draw the plough; and the houses of the peasantry, and even the smaller farmers, were of the poorest description.

The simplest advances of the modern world seemed to have passed them by. Even his umbrella was a source of wonder. It was, according to one account, "the first ever seen in the parishes of Methlick or Tarves, and on going out with it, he was repeatedly stopped by curious persons, who asked him to put it up and close it again."

For the rest of his life, the 4th Earl struggled to shake off these grim first impressions and confessed that he had only been able to get through his twenty-first birthday party there, soon after his arrival, by becoming "completely immersed" in the wine he provided for an "elegant dinner." But Aberdeen was a man who took his duties seriously, and he quickly banished any thoughts of selling up and retreating to "the olive groves of academe," where, as a scholar, antiquarian, and art connoisseur, he would have been far more at ease.

His wife Catherine, the lively and clever daughter of the Marquess of Abercorn, whom he married in 1805, took a different view of the place on her first visit, telling her father:

You need not believe a word of what Ld. Aberdeen says about this place, for I can assure you that there is nothing to complain of. I was never so surprised in my life as when I first saw it, for I had been told so much about it by every body, that I expected a thing not fit for a human being to live in, placed in the middle of a barren, bleak, moor, without a Tree, or anything near it but a bog, instead of that I saw a great many good trees about the House which is not regularly beautiful on the outside, but very comfortable in the inside. . . . With a good chair and Sopha or two, and new curtains to the Drawing Room I do not wish for anything better.

The 4th Earl set about improving the estate, planting no fewer than fourteen million trees* on the "barren, bleak, moor," creating avenues and vistas with the help of a local artist, James Giles, and digging out two large ornamental lakes. A few years later, in the hope of persuading his second wife Harriet to visit Haddo—unlike Catherine, she thoroughly disliked the place—he commissioned two Aberdeen architects, John Smith and Archibald Simpson, to design, among other improvements, a new kitchen wing and a flight of stone steps up to the drawing room. But the tetchy, hypochondriac Harriet was not won over and obdurately refused to join him on his journeys north.

Queen Victoria, who visited Haddo with Prince Albert in October 1857, found the country surrounding the house "frightful," and noted grumpily:

The air very different from the dear Highlands & one sadly missed the mountains.

But she found the inside, which Aberdeen had had spruced up and again altered for the occasion, perfectly adequate. The bedrooms were

---

* This figure may sound preposterous, but in 1808 the 4th Earl sent his father-in-law a list of trees that he had planted between January and September that year alone. There were no fewer than 698,610 of them, mostly Scotch firs (440,000), but a huge number of deciduous ones too. The 4th Earl loved trees and noted down interesting specimens in a book he carried with him on his travels. His herculean labors at Haddo not only transformed the bleak bogs surrounding the house into a bosky park, but also provided a cash crop for the future.

"small but comfortable, consisting of a sitting room, and a dressing room for us each, and a bedroom," but the dining room was "very narrow, reminding me somewhat of the one at Frogmore*—it contains some fine pictures."

Ishbel's dislike of the "horrible house" was only gradually dispelled:

Everything has gone very well so far & J says he has never seen the Aberdonians show so much enthusiasm, for as a rule they are supposed to look on gloomily without even touching their hats,

she wrote to her father soon after her arrival. A few days later, she confided:

I am being gradually introduced to all the old people about—it is amusing to see them place themselves before me and inspect me thoroughly and then turn to Johnnie & express their opinion of me in some quaint way or other. They are all wonderfully hearty and nice.

The weather was rather less welcoming:

It is raining today for the first time since we arrived . . . but I do not expect to be frightened by the Aberdeenshire cold, as the people about seem to expect me to be. It is very sheltered within the grounds & it is altogether a much prettier and dear old house than I expected. I know I shall get very fond of it—& am already. Still I dare not yet think much of Guisachan and its mountains.

---

*This may not have been a criticism. Queen Victoria had a soft spot for Frogmore House, which stands in Windsor Great Park. "All is peace and quiet and you only hear the hum of the bees, the singing of the birds and the occasional crowing and cackling from the Poultry Yard!" she wrote. Significantly, perhaps, she confined her praise to its surroundings, since James Wyatt's remodeling of the building as an English Petit Trianon at the beginning of the nineteenth century was not a success. Although King George VI and Queen Elizabeth spent some of their honeymoon there in 1923, the house does not seem to have had a permanent resident in recent times. Today this inconvenient rabbit warren of interlocking rooms is sometimes used for royal occasions, and Queen Mary, wife of George V, a canny connoisseur and collector of art and antiques, used some of the space to establish what she called "a family souvenir museum, as well as a museum of bygones and of interesting odds and ends." Frogmore Cottage, refurbished in 2019 for the Duke and Duchess of Sussex, stands nearby.

And she signed off one letter to her "dearest Papa" with a poignant little confession:

I don't feel as if I knew exactly what I was saying for I still feel rather unlike myself & inside out.

But it came as no surprise to Dudley Marjoribanks that the elaborate welcoming ceremonies—a dinner for nine hundred tenants and their wives, another for the people who worked on the estate, and "a school treat" for the children—had barely been cleared away before Ishbel went to work:

The first business which engaged us at home was the renovating of Haddo House. A's grandfather had been wont to say that he must leave the overhauling of the *inside* of the house to his successor—*he* had devoted himself to the transformation of the 1700 acres of policies from the bare, neglected state in which he found them into a demesne of varied beauty and charm.

She realized at once that Haddo was desperately in need of improvement, pronouncing that it was "not suitable to the Scottish climate." Guests, she discovered, were forced to enter the house through "what appeared to be a window," and "14 cesspools were found in the vicinity of the house."

The 4th Earl had done his best, but in his last years he had spent less and less time at Haddo, preferring his smaller and plainer villa twenty miles away, overlooking the North Sea at Boddam. Both his private and public lives had brought him much unhappiness, and the frowsy, echoing rooms of the family seat conjured up memories too painful to bear. He had never recovered from the loss of his first wife, Catherine. When she died in 1812, his son said that "the sunshine went out of his life for ever." In the months following her death he saw visions of her, which he recorded in his diary in Latin—*Verissima tristissima imago . . . Verrissima dulcissima imago*"*—and for the rest of his life he dressed in mourning black.

The children Catherine had borne him had all died young: a son and

---

* "The truest, saddest apparition . . . the truest, sweetest apparition."

longed-for heir had lived for less than a day, and his beloved daughters Jane, Caroline, and Alice, did not survive into adulthood, despite his agonized efforts to find doctors who could cure them of the diseases that struck them down. And his failure as Prime Minister to prevent the Crimean War had brought his once glittering political career to a sour and guilt-ridden end.

When he refused, uncharacteristically, to rebuild the parish church at Methlick, the nearest village to Haddo, his family put it down to the cantankerousness of old age, but there was another, sadder reason: the deaths of more than twenty thousand soldiers from the British Empire in the Crimea haunted him. After he died in December 1860, scraps of paper were found hidden all over the house. On each of them he had written a verse from the first Book of Chronicles in the Bible:

> And David said to Solomon, My Son, as for me, it was in my mind to build an house unto the name of the Lord, my God: but the word of the Lord came to me, saying, Thou hast shed blood abundantly, and hast made great wars: thou shalt not build an house unto my name, because thou hast shed much blood upon the earth in my sight.

The gloom of those days, Ishbel sensed, had lingered in the family quarters:

> I remember my dismay when the old housekeeper showed me round the house, and when the dank atmosphere of these rooms met me on entering, and when I felt the dampness of the curtains. I resolved on the spot that if ever children were given to us *they* should not be brought up in these rooms. Yet when I went over the house I could find no others which would lend themselves for the purpose.

Thus, a new family wing* was added to her list of necessary improvements, which also included

---

* My father-in-law, David Gordon, later 4th Marquess, remembered arriving at Dover after a trip to France in April 1930 and seeing newspaper placards proclaiming "Stately Home Burns." It was Haddo. The family wing was gutted, but my father-in-law less so: Ishbel had gone too far, and David, his wife, and four children lived happily in the hundred rooms that remained.

the introduction of bathrooms (a matter of no little difficulty when some of the walls were four or five feet thick), the provision of servants' quarters adequate for a modern household, a front hall, and a central inside staircase, the original architect having adopted the Italian idea of approaching the reception rooms on the first floor by means of stone staircases outside, providing small staircases within.

Johnny had made a start improving the house before his marriage, commissioning a chapel at its north end from G. E. Street, the industrious master of "High Victorian" gothic architecture, whose work on the Law Courts in London is thought to have driven him to an early death. Street's design for Haddo was far less exuberant than the buildings that had made his name: they ranged from the church of St. James the Less in Westminster, London, ablaze with colorful tiles and paintings, to the towering Crimea Memorial Church in Constantinople with its more somber, but still richly ornate, interior. The devout Johnny preferred to keep things more austere, but he did allow himself some expensive indulgences, commissioning a stained-glass east window with angel-filled upper lights from the studio of the pre-Raphaelite artist Edward Burne-Jones and a fine organ by "Father" Henry Willis, whose instruments graced the Royal Albert Hall and cathedrals throughout the country.[*]

Refurbishing the living quarters was a far greater challenge, especially for a twenty-one-year-old, but Ishbel did not shrink from it. Help was at hand in the shape of her father, the mastermind of Guisachan and Brook House, and a man, she believed, of "rare judgement and knowledge" in all aspects of building and interior decoration. Marjoribanks, whose signature appears on the first page of Haddo's new visitors' book, undoubtedly gave her advice, but Ishbel was firmly in charge.

She drew adroitly upon his contacts, for Marjoribanks had employed the best in the land. Thus, James Sant, Queen Victoria's Principal Painter in Ordinary, probably won the commission to paint large, romanticized

---

[*] While the chapel was under construction, Willis, who was a keen sailor, suffered an unfortunate loss when his yacht, the inaptly named *Vigilant*, was run down by a German tramp steamer in the Solent. Not all his customers were as satisfied as Johnny: a letter of complaint from the organist of a hall in Bristol is thought to have brought about Willis's death from heart failure in 1901, even though the instrument in question had been made by his son.

portraits of the youthful Earl and Countess for the library because Ishbel's mother had sat for him. It is likely that Ishbel hired the Edinburgh architects Wardrop and Reid to carry out the building work because Charles Reid was the younger brother of the architects of Guisachan, although Wardrop's work on Methlick Church and the firm being the darlings of other improvers of grand Scottish houses would also have helped their cause. And there was no contest for the contract for decorating Haddo's upper floors: her father's favorites, Wright and Mansfield, were briskly imported to Aberdeenshire from their headquarters in the West End of London.*

The harsh Aberdeenshire climate had taken its toll on the house over a hundred and fifty years: the roof was riddled with dry rot, and one of Wardrop and Reid's first tasks was to rebuild it. They also remodeled the entrance to the house so that visitors no longer had to enter it through that "window": instead, they passed beneath a balustraded terrace supported by sturdy granite columns into a cavernous oak-paneled hallway. This was decorated with paintings of scenes from *Aesop's Fables* by John Russell, a housepainter turned artist from Aberdeen, and dominated by an ornate fire surround cunningly cobbled together from several pieces of dark carved oak to give it an "olde worlde" look. The south wing was altered to provide a new kitchen and better quarters for the servants, and a magnificent new library was installed in the north wing. An inscription in Ishbel's hand on a photograph she took of it explains that it was constructed "by combining Billiard Room and Prayer Room and two corridors." An airy and comfortable morning room, suffused with light from a deep bay window, was created from two pokey apartments. The family wing was duly built: this was good timing, since Ishbel and Johnny's first child was soon on its way.

Wright and Mansfield's job was to transform the interior of Haddo into what one perceptive architectural historian has called "the decorative background against which [Ishbel's] childhood had been passed." Indeed, from photographs taken at the time, it is hard to tell Haddo's morning room and Guisachan's drawing room apart.

---

*Winning a contract at Haddo was no guarantee of future prosperity: Street died a few weeks after the chapel was completed in 1881, James Maitland Wardrop died in 1882, and Charles Reid survived him by barely a year. Wright and Mansfield went bust in 1884. Sant was the exception: he died in 1916 aged ninety-six.

Although some craftsmen who met Wardrop and Reid's rigorous standards could be found in the locality—carpentry, glazing, and iron-mongery from Messrs. Watt and Clark of Aberdeen and plasterwork from Messrs. Hutcheon of Methlick—Wright and Mansfield imported the fittings for whole rooms from London.

Thus, the library arrived by the train and cart, mostly prefabricated.* With its shelves made of cedar of Lebanon and embellished with ebony, and its chenille carpet—one of the largest in Europe—specially made by Templeton's of Glasgow, this room is Wright and Mansfield's surviving masterpiece. In the middle stood a remarkable desk, also made of ebony, decorated with rams' heads and a Doric frieze. And everywhere there were Ishbel's father's favorite Wedgwood plaques: not just on the desk, but on the chimneypieces, and even adorning the coal scuttles. Though the shelves were crammed with the 4th Earl's books on archaeology, gar-den design, travel, geography, religious thinking, and the classical world, this room, with its deep blue leather chairs, has the atmosphere of a gen-tleman's club rather than of a place of learning or contemplation. This was where the men would gather after dinner, while along the corridor their ladies sat and chattered in the drawing room, which had been given a lighter, more exuberant look. The brown and rather folksy Georgian paneling was replaced, but the prospect to the Upper Lake and the Deer Park beyond it was carefully preserved. And Ishbel was quite content that access to the terrace below should be through the kind of window she had thought so unsuitable for the front of the building. The dining room, which Queen Victoria had pronounced "very narrow" during her visit in 1857, was also remodeled, with a large bay window to let light in from the terrace.

---

* In using this sort of proto-Ikea operation, Ishbel and Wright and Mansfield were ahead of their time, according to Ian Gow, the distinguished former Head of Collections at the National Trust for Scotland: "[Haddo] is beautiful because it was conceived as an aesthetic whole with a sure sense of colour and harmony. The refitting is technically ingenious and you can see how the William Adam bones were enhanced through miles and miles of railway-borne composition ornament and every single element is of a simply breathtaking quality. This kind of contracting was to become the norm c. 1900 in America with entire French rooms going out from Paris and Georgian rooms from London." Ishbel resorted to many stratagems to stave off financial disaster at the beginning of the twentieth century, but we should be grateful that she did not resort to exporting Haddo's rooms, for America's gain would certainly have been Scotland's grievous loss.

As her working notebooks* show, Ishbel was a perfectionist like her father: no detail escaped her. Each room has its own page, listing the alterations to be made—a "new grate with tiled fire-place" for the Rose Room, a "new mantel-piece (wooden)" for the Minerva Room, "window seats lowered etc" in the Terrace Room—and the furniture required. She notes that every bedroom needs a coal scuttle; that "5 new iron bedsteads and 5 new white and blue painted chests of drawers" are on order for the ladies' maids' quarters in the attics of the Center Block; and that "wash-stands and tables" used at their weekend "cottage" outside London are on their way. She has chosen the paintwork: "all the walls of small passages to be painted with a brown dado and green above"; "ceiling and walls [of the vestibule] to be somewhat decorated by Wright & Mansfield's man." Curtains are being recycled and new covers are being sewn for chairs and sofas; the engravings to be hung on the walls of the Dowager Lady Aberdeen's bedroom are due to "come in a separate box." She wants "a small two-shelved book-case for nailing up on wall to be made for every room in the house and a small round table."

There are lists of furniture "which will come with Wright & Mansfield's van" from London. One note stipulates that "the yellow parts of Swiss beds [are] to be covered with chintz"; another requires the billiard table for the smoking room to be "small size—not more than 14 ft. long"; and in another she warns that "furniture for Lady A's bedroom from Baird† had better come out as soon as the room is at all ready for it, so as to wear the smell off."

Many pages have a swatch of wallpaper pasted to them: she chose a red-and-white pattern for the "W.C.s" in the north wing; one, naturally, with blue flowers for the Blue Room; and a riot of pink blooms was presumably

---

* These turned up hidden in a pile of old kilt socks and starched collars as we were clearing out the last and highest shelf of my father-in-law's wardrobe after my mother-in-law's death in 2009, and finally gave the lie to the idea, subscribed to by both the family and architectural historians, that Ishbel's father "directed" the works.

† The more workaday furniture and carpets were supplied by Thomas Baird, an upholsterer and cabinetmaker from 181 Union Street, Aberdeen. For him, as for Street, Wardrop, and Wright and Mansfield, this Haddo contract proved to be one of his last. He died in 1884. His obituarist said he was "possessed of excellent taste, [and] his workmanship was of an artistic and substantial character" and that "there were few men better known on the streets of Aberdeen, his tall and portly presence, marking him out for notice." Which suggests Ishbel will not have found him hard to find when she was chasing the delivery of the Dowager Countess's furniture.

meant to brighten up the ladies' maids' bedrooms in the gloomy attics. These are working notebooks, full of ideas hastily jotted down and often crossed out after a change of mind. The reader can picture Ishbel keeping a watchful eye as work went on around her in the corridors of Haddo, and almost smell the new furniture that Mr. Baird was so slow to deliver.

Despite Ishbel's vigilance, she faced at least one spectacular and potentially disastrous crisis during the build. On August 4, 1881, the *Aberdeen Journal* reported that a fire, which had broken out in the attics, had damaged the Aberdeens' "splendid modern mansion." The workmen on-site—more than a hundred of them—successfully doused the flames, but the *Journal* added:

> On examining the drawing and dining room, which are immediately below, it was seen that the water was beginning to ooze through the roof and down the walls; and we understand that, for the purpose of saving the finely gilded and painted roof of the drawing room, it was found necessary to cut holes in it, through which the water might run, large vessels being placed on the floor to catch it. Not withstanding these efforts, however, a large portion of the decorations was damaged; and the roof and walls of the dining room were also injured. . . . The fire is supposed to have accidentally originated in the operations of some plumbers who had a fire in the attic for the purpose of heating their bolts.

Two days later, after assessing the damage, Thomas Wright wrote to his partner George Mansfield:

Dear Mr Mansfield,

I paid a visit yesterday to Haddo, to see the state of affairs.

There is not as much damage apparent as might be expected; but I apprehend a great deal more will develop itself when the water has had time sufficient to percolate from its present lodgements. It is so far fortunate that it broke out during the day, and moreover, that there was plenty of help upon the spot; all the water had to be carried up a narrow winding stair, the hydrants when fired were useless, as the water would not even dribble from them.

I believe Souter* was mainly instrumental in saving the property, but all worked with a will under his instructions. He was very much excited when I saw him the next day, and also yesterday, when he was pointing out, and relating to me the circumstances. From the deeply charred state of the beams the fire had been smouldering for some time, and I infer that the violent gale which blew on Wednesday fanned it into a flame.

The plasterer was so prostrate with grief that he was quite ill and could not rise from his bed; Wales the House carpenter fainted in the height of the turmoil, and as I before said, I believe it was Souter's presence which mainly contributed to the saving of Haddo House. I have to meet the Fire Office Agent (Nth. British) on Tuesday.

As far as I can form an opinion at present the Dining room ceiling is very much damaged, the Drawing room partially and several Bed-rooms. I will write you further particulars next week.

Very kind regards,
Believe me,
Very sincerely yours,
A. Wright.

Ishbel had been in London and missed the drama, learning of it only by telegram. But she pushed on regardless, the blow softened by a generous insurance payout of £500.

Ishbel had already found that she no longer had to pretend to enjoy her visits to Haddo, calling it "this lovely place," and confiding to her diary in December 1879, after a walk to the frozen lake on the day of the "fearful Tay Bridge disaster"[†]:

---

* Probably William Souter, a painter and decorator connected with an Aberdeen firm, Slaker and Souter, "painters, glaziers and paper hangers," that had worked for the Gordon family before: notably on the building of Tarland Church in 1870.

† Seventy-five people are thought to have died when a bridge over the River Tay outside Dundee in Scotland collapsed while a train was crossing it on the night of December 28, 1879. Although it is still one of the greatest bridge disasters of all time, the tragedy is chiefly remembered today because it inspired the weirdly named William Topaz McGonagall, justly renowned as the "worst poet in British history," to write a so-bad-it's-a-must-read lamentation, which begins "Beautiful Railway Bridge of the Silv'ry Tay!/Alas! I am very sorry to say/That ninety lives have been taken away". . . and continues in that vein for another fifty-six lines.

J does skate so beautifully and looks so graceful when doing it & goes
at such a pace.

The house was now fit for family living, which was just as well, since
Ishbel had provided Johnny with an heir in January 1879. The birth of
George, or "Doddie," as he was nicknamed in the Scottish manner, was
greeted with bonfires and peals of bells in the villages on the Aberdeenshire estates, but within the family the celebrations were muted. Doddie
was sickly and prone to fits and did not thrive.

We know now that he suffered from epilepsy, a condition that was
little understood and greatly stigmatized by Victorian society. Many
sufferers were consigned to asylums for the insane, while others were
feared because they were thought to have violent criminal tendencies.
But Ishbel cherished her firstborn and was determined that he should
survive to live a happy and fulfilling life. The parliamentarian and orator
John Bright was touched by the couple's devotion to their small son,
noting in his diary:

> They have one child, a boy of eight months old, somewhat delicate I
> fear, and receiving and having great care shown to him.

Marjorie, born without fanfare less than two years later, in December
1880, proved sturdier, but Dorothea, who arrived in March 1882, lived
for less than nine months. She died on November 25, her death certificate
said delphically, of "debility from dyspepsias since birth." Her funeral was
held in Haddo's new chapel, which had been formally opened with "a very
bright, refreshing service" the year before, almost to the day: poignantly,
the order of this sad and somber service was only the second one posted
in the chapel register.

Ishbel, the sister of Annie and Stewart, had seen for herself that no loving parent ever recovers from the death of a child. Consolation was hard
to find for the couple, even from the Bible that they studied so assiduously
together; even from the funeral prayer that exhorted them "to rejoice in
the blessedness of this child" through their tears; even from the letters that
poured in from friends like Lucy Cavendish. She wrote:

Dear, Dear Ishbel,—I have only this morning seen in the paper that
you have lost your little darling, 'God-given' baby—at the age when
I know they begin to have real little ways and characters of their own.
O how I grieve for you, dear Ishbel!—yet you will not wonder that
I could almost envy you this most gentle and tender stroke of God's
Hand.* You now have a 'Holy Innocent' to link you to Heaven, as well
as your two darlings to love on earth, and to train for the Happy Land
where their little sister has flown.

Ishbel reprinted this letter in her memoirs, but otherwise she kept her
feelings to herself, mentioning Dorothea only in passing in her writings
and once vaguely claiming that her lost infant had inspired her efforts to
improve the lot of young women and children. In private, though, she
ensured that "our little Dorothy's" memory stayed alive among the family,
and when, in 1927, she and Johnny published a booklet to mark their
Golden Wedding, they duly gave a portrait of her pride of place.

Yet in the midst of death, new life was stirring: Ishbel was pregnant
again and "another little laddie," Dudley Gladstone, named after his Marjoribanks grandfather and his godfather the Prime Minister, was born
in May 1883. Marjorie, who became the chronicler of the family at an
early age, remembered the birth of Archie, the last of Ishbel's children, on
October 3, 1884:

He was the first Gordon born at Haddo for many years, and we always
envied him for being really a Scot, and not a Cockney like the rest of
us. . . . Archie with his big blue eyes and golden curls was a particular
pet with everybody, at home or with strangers. When he was a little
older, he rather resented the demonstrations of some of the ladies who
came to Haddo, and especially when they chucked him under the chin.
People often said he looked like an angel.†

* God had certainly not administered a tender stroke to Lucy Cavendish or to her husband,
Lord Frederick, who had been brutally murdered by members of an Irish National Group a
few months earlier in Phoenix Park, Dublin, on his first day as Chief Secretary to the Lord
Lieutenant of Ireland. Ishbel was particularly moved by the way that Lady Frederick, "whilst
giving us a beautiful thought, so touchingly referred to her own sorrow."
† According to Marjorie, "on the night of his arrival an owl flew in at the window, an omen of
good luck and wisdom for the newcomer." Fate was to prove otherwise.

By then, Ishbel was twenty-seven, and with the nurseries built and her family complete, she and Johnny could devote themselves to the upbringing of their children. Characteristically, they chose to do so in a way that was unconventional, both for their era and for their position in society. Although the children's needs were catered for by their own retinue of nursery maids, nannies, and governesses, they had loving parents who, despite the demands of house parties, good works, and politics, enjoyed their company and, as Marjorie remembered, kept them close:

> Once at Sunday evening service in the Chapel at Haddo, Archie aged three or four, fell asleep leaning against Mother's shoulder. At the end of the service she carried him out without waking him, and his curls and pink cheeks on her arm made a pretty picture.

Earnest and open to new ideas, as ever, they found their own views on child-rearing chimed with the precepts advocated by Charlotte Mason, a British educationalist.* These were a far cry indeed from the strict and narrow classical regimes usually practiced in the grim educational establishments of Victorian Britain. Parents, Mason ordained, should encourage their children to be "active agents" of their own education, assimilating information and the rules of grammar from "living" literature rather than from textbooks; moral principles from examples set at home; knowledge of the world by spending time in the open air studying nature; writing and spelling skills from taking dictation from the works of great authors and thinkers; and culture from looking at and discussing great works of art.

Thus, Ishbel made sure to install a schoolroom in her houses,† and in 1887, she wrote to Mason thanking her for a copy of her book *Home Education* and asking:

---

*When Mason founded the Parents' National Educational Union with Emeline Petrie Steinthal in 1888, Johnny and Ishbel became joint presidents. They would have found it easy, in their stately home, finely decorated and hung with Old Masters, to follow Steinthal's advice on how children should learn to draw: "To begin with, the surroundings of a child ought to be beautiful: the nursery ought to be one of the most harmonious in the house, for a child should be accustomed to see and appreciate only good colours from the first."

† Ishbel and Johnny did not stick rigidly to Charlotte Mason's guidelines. In the summer of 1888, for example, the children went to a kindergarten in Baker Street, London. Later, while Marjorie was privately tutored, they sent Doddie and Dudley to Harrow and Archie to Winchester.

If you know of any governess either foreign or English who is imbued
with the ideas about children expressed in this book & whom you
could recommend for three children, two boys, one of nine, the other
of nearly 5 & a very quick little girl of 7—one who would wish to work
with the mother.

Thus, every afternoon, wherever they were, the children were sent outside to ride their ponies. She and Johnny seized on another of Charlotte
Mason's suggestions and reveled in taking part in the "dramatic entertainments" organized for the children by her secretary, Miss Wilson. Marjorie
remembered how Archie,

at two or three, in some scenes at Haddo . . . was Little Miss Muffet,
but in spite of previous rehearsals and adjurations from behind, when
the large spider was lowered over a screen, he did not run away but sat
and smiled sweetly, to the delight of the audience.

When Ishbel looked back on her transformation of Haddo, her feelings
were mixed. Though Wright and Mansfield had carried out the commission "with great skill and perfection," their bills had been "scandalously
high":

Whether we would have undertaken this vast transformation had we
known our own future, and the times that were coming, is another
matter.

But in the hills far to the west of Haddo in 1878, there was another
house to be visited, altered, and furnished, and in the first busy and exciting months of her marriage, no shadow fell of the financial nemesis to
come.

6

A House for the Shooting, a House for Good Works

Just after half-past three on the afternoon of Tuesday August 20, 1878, a cry of welcome went up from a group of horsemen as an open carriage approached the narrow pass, or "slack," above the village of Tarland, some forty miles to the southwest of Haddo on the road to Queen Victoria's home at Balmoral.* This was the gateway to a wide and shallow valley called the Howe of Cromar and to Johnny's other Aberdeenshire estate.

The view that greeted Ishbel when she reached the top of the hill struck straight to her heart:

I found myself once more amongst the hills and heather of my childhood.

---

*Prince Albert had acquired the lease of the castle from Johnny's grandfather the 4th Earl, who had unexpectedly inherited it from his younger brother, Sir Robert Gordon, in 1847. As a diplomat, Sir Robert witnessed the aftermath of Napoleon's retreat from Moscow and helped to establish the Greek state in 1830, but his most lasting contribution to the history of Britain and its monarchy was to have died from choking on a fish bone over breakfast just when Queen Victoria was looking for a Highland retreat.

Here Johnny had planned another ceremonial welcome, carefully stage-managed and generously catered, hoping that the gloomy debacle of their arrival at Haddo a few weeks earlier would not be repeated. The horsemen had been waiting for two hours to lead them to the modest farmhouse where Johnny now stayed on his regular visits, after tiring of the family's traditional pied-à-terre, the village inn. All around them, the hills stood purple in the hazy sunshine: Morven, Mount Keen, Clachnaben, and the long wall of Lochnagar.

Curiously, Ishbel mentioned none of the day's events in her diary, but the *Aberdeen Journal*'s reporter assiduously recorded the scene. Although "the cavalcade was not a large one," he wrote, "it was, almost without exception, a well mounted one, and an entirely enthusiastic one." The doctor and the church minister were among the riders, along with tenant farmers and the senior tradesmen of the village: Mr. Bey the blacksmith and Mr. Hay the general merchant; the saddler; and the landlords of Tarland's two inns. Flags "of various colours" flew, and messages bearing greetings had been painted on banners. In the village below, the houses had been decorated with "bundles of heather in abundance."

Across the narrow road, on the crest of the hill, an elaborate gothic arch had been erected by Mr. Smith, the local joiner. More heather and boughs of evergreen had been wound round its timbers and a coronet swung gently from its apex in the summer breeze. Small fir trees, a freshly culled deer's head, and "the inscription 'Welcome,' . . . affixed in very tasteful lettering," completed the bizarre design. The *Aberdeen Journal*'s man remarked that "it had a most striking effect."

The procession rode off down the steep road with their laird and his bride at its head and the tenants following, past the farms of Craskins, Hillocks, and Easter and Wester Knowehead, and the mysterious prehistoric underground storehouse at Culsh. The hills of Pittenderich and Pressendye loomed to their right, while, on the left, the fields fell away to the wide valley floor.

Two miles on, "a large company of spectators" had gathered at the gates of Tarland Lodge, hoping to catch a glimpse of the new Countess. The cavalcade slowed for waves and cheers, before sweeping up the sloping avenue to the house. The place was a contrast to Haddo, little more than a cottage and far from grand, despite its name: until 1874 it had been more modestly called Indego.*

Dr. Andrew Robertson, the previous tenant, was a man of many parts and considerable energy: he farmed the two hundred and fifty acres around the house while running a medical practice that covered a huge area from Blairgowrie in Perthshire to Banchory in West Aberdeenshire. And he combined these jobs with a third: as Commissioner (or manager) of the Balmoral and Birkhall Estates for Queen Victoria and the Prince of Wales, he supervised the building of the castle and the laying out of the grounds. He was said to have been a particular favorite of the Queen, who often called on him at Indego. After one visit, made on her way to see the 4th Earl at Haddo in 1857, she described the house as "very small, but so neat, & prettily arranged" and admired its "pretty garden, & well cultivated land."

The royal party stayed for only fifteen minutes with Dr. Robertson, but for Johnny and Ishbel on their visit in August 1878 a long afternoon lay ahead. There were speeches of welcome, a musical promenade accompanied by the village's own brass band, and countless hands to shake. Tea was served in a large tent on the lawn: naturally, all the elaborate trappings of the aristocratic dining room—porcelain, cut glass, and silver—had been brought outside for the occasion.

At first, Ishbel felt daunted by "those welcoming crowds, that strangely assorted mounted guard of honour, those long rows of kindly, weather-beaten faces round the festive tables," but she later looked back with affection on her first encounter with Tarland and its "strange-speaking people":

> I cannot recall that day without thinking of all the rich experiences and wonderful friendships to which it was a prelude.

Ishbel was not the first to fall in love with the Howe of Cromar. Visitors to Tillypronie, a country house built by Sir John Clark, the son of Queen

---

* This old and odd name is thought to mean "the brow of Ego's hill." Ego was a fairly common surname, apparently, in medieval times and the first name of the son of Fergus, Earl of Mar. Indego may indeed have been his hill, since he was granted the lands of "Huchtirerne" in 1364, and these lie just across the fields from Tarland Lodge.

Victoria's physician, Sir James Clark, were particularly taken with the area. The Queen had laid the lintel stone over the main door in 1867, "smiling pleasantly at her own handiwork,"* and later called there often, accompanied, as ever, by her cherished servant John Brown.† Brown, being a member of the lower orders, was never allowed to share the same table as Her Majesty in public, but equally was not prepared to take his meals with the servants. A compromise was reached: he dined in a specially constructed gazebo outside the front door. Once these domestic arrangements had been sorted out, the Queen loved nothing better than to settle down to enjoy the view.

The American writer Henry James, who rated visiting Scotland "a pastime second to none," was a guest in September 1878 and wrote to his close friend, the Harvard literary critic and editor Thomas Sergeant Perry:

> I am perched on a great hillside in Aberdeenshire with brown and purple moors rolling away behind me, & in front a wonderful view of tumbling hills & gleaming lochs, stretching away to Balmoral. I have just been to see some very picturesque Highland sports—I am going this afternoon to ride across the moors to an ancient Scottish castle & this evening I am going to a ball, ten miles away, where I shall behold the divine Langtrey,‡ the great English beauty of the day. So you see I

---

* The newspaper report of this little ceremony, which required the Queen to stand on "a small raised platform and spread a bed of lime," noted that it was "the first of its 'Royal' kind recorded in the annals of masonry."

† Before entering service with Queen Victoria and acquiring such airs and graces, Brown is said to have worked along the hillside from Tillypronie for Dr. Robertson of Indego, making the people he now looked down upon virtually his "ain folk."

‡ Lillie Langtry was the mistress of the Prince of Wales, later Edward VII. She and her husband were staying with the merchant banker and politician Sir William Cunliffe Brooks at Glen Tanar House. The newspapers reported that she "attracted a great deal of attention when her presence became known" at the "Highland sports" in Aboyne that James refers to. This paled in comparison to her visit to Inverness a few days later, as the Aberdeen *Press & Journal* reported: "Many people behaved quite ludicrously in rushing about, almost shouting 'Where is she?' and actually passing her by over and over again. At the hall in the evening she wore a black satin dress, which the furious antics that passed for waltzing with some of her partners nearly tore from her body, and may have accounted for her early departure." Sadly, although the "Jersey Lily," Henry James, and Ishbel were all in Aberdeenshire at the same time, there is no record of their having met. Lillie Langtry, in particular, might have appreciated it. Left alone at Glen Tanar while the rest of the house party went shooting, she is said to have relieved the boredom by commandeering a silver tray from the butler and tobogganing down the stairs.

am amply entertained; & if I only had a taste for grouse & partridge, like most of the rest of the world here, I should be still more so. But the air, the views, the walks on the moors & the lounges on the autumnal heather are balm to the soul.

Throughout that first visit, Ishbel thrived on meeting the tenants and touring their farms and cottages. Her determination to live among them quickly crystallized. The problem was that the existing Lodge was far too small to accommodate a house party. In the short term, she realized that she and Johnny would have to make the best of it, but, in time, a proper new country house would have to be built.

She wasted no time in finding a site: a patch of ground less than a mile due south of the Lodge, looking out onto the tumbled remains of one of the prehistoric stone circles that abound in Aberdeenshire, and, beyond it, to the hills. Thus, in the summer of 1879, barely a year after her first visit to the valley, Ishbel persuaded her father to break his journey to Inverness-shire to show him the spot she had chosen and to help her decide what the house should be like. Marjoribanks prescribed a villa, with a dining room, a drawing room, and a writing room, bedrooms above and cellars below. But since Ishbel knew she had enough on her hands with the rebuilding of Haddo, she settled for extending Tarland Lodge, adding bunkhouses and, as her children grew up, a large sitting room for the young.

A way of life was soon established: Tarland Lodge for the shooting in the autumn, Guisachan for summer holidays,* and London for the parliamentary and social seasons. But Haddo, where they lived in the winter and summer, was no mere pleasure-dome, for there Ishbel and Johnny were about to launch a social revolution.

---

* According to her daughter Marjorie, Ishbel found it impossible to recapture the idyll of her own childhood at Guisachan on these visits. She took her own children there only "dutifully" because "the fear of her father's overbearing tempers made the stay an ordeal for her." But Marjorie herself echoed her mother's devotion to "our Highland home": "How we looked forward to the well-known marks and the changing of horses on that beautiful twenty-three miles drive, and to the familiar Guisachan smell of the hall, with its stags' heads at the end. We looked on it as a kind of paradise, with the ponies, the herd of cattle, the dairy, the yellow retrievers in the foreground, and a background of mountains, waterfalls, bridlepaths and dark brown water in your bath."

They began with conventional good works designed to "make the life of the community better and happier" in the villages surrounding the "Big Hoose":

Our efforts chiefly concentrated on starting a district nurse and cottage hospital at Tarves; a hall and recreation room at Methlick; hot penny dinners for school children at several schools on the estate; a number of working parties where the wives and daughters of farmers and others met to make garments for the poor of each district.

But Ishbel realized there were deeper, more awkward issues to be addressed. Social reformers were busy in the cities, trying to improve the lives of the poor, but the teenaged girls in service in the houses of Aberdeenshire's landowners and the adolescent boys who worked on their farms, living hugger-mugger in primitive, freezing stone cottages, had no such help. They were allowed only one brief respite from the harshness of their lives: a few days' annual holiday, which, one scandalized clergyman protested, were usually devoted to "drunken horseplay that many hitherto innocent young servant-girls would, in due course, have life-long cause to regret." Ishbel, who preferred action to moralizing, decided to find them something better to do, and she did so on an extraordinary scale.

In August 1879, Johnny bought a huge tent, which Mr. Edgington its maker confided had been originally "constructed for the King of the Netherlands," and had it erected on the lawn in front of Haddo. The *Aberdeen Journal* described how mountains of food—"something like 7000 bundles of rolls and 700 plumcakes"—were laid out on long tables inside and out. A brass band had been hired from Aberdeen, the Haddo skating rink was pressed into service as a dance floor, and a boat floated on the Upper Lake "for the use of any inclined to enjoy themselves on the smooth surface of the water."

By noon everything was ready, but torrential rain had been falling for hours. Everyone waited—the Methlick and Tarves Volunteers who were acting as stewards, James Wood the bandmaster, the suitably named Mr. Cheeseman who was in charge of the catering—full of "earnest hopes" that the weather would improve. Johnny and Ishbel put on brave faces so as to bring "an appearance of cheerfulness to the scene," but they had chosen a day that was "wet to a disheartening degree—the wettest indeed of a disagreeably wet week." And to add to the grim picture, there was no sign of anyone from "the very large body of the tenantry on the Haddo estate."

But as the opening time grew closer, the guests began to arrive "in numberless gigs and other conveyances," and by half-past two, six thousand people were blithely disporting themselves beneath "the leaden-hued sky [that was] still sending down its torrents." The ever-vigilant *Journal* reporter noticed that there was more on offer than bread, tea, and cakes and a chance to admire Baby Doddie: the crowds were allowed into the house for a taste of high culture:

> Opportunity was afforded to the guests of visiting the magnificent picture gallery of Haddo House, where among other gems of art are to be seen 'The Nativity' by Paolo Veronese; Murillo's 'Good Shepherd,' Tomenicho's 'David and the Head of Goliath'; while claiming equal attention are Sir Thomas Lawrence's portrait of the fourth earl, and Sir Philip Kemble's painting of Viscount Melville, both fine specimens of portraiture.*

The invitation was repeated the following year. In a field near the house, Johnny combined two traditional local events, a Highland Games and the village flower show, with a bazaar. And the reporter from the *Aberdeen Journal* was back, even more impressed than before by the beauty of the surroundings and the generosity of the Earl and Countess:

> On a level spot at the foot of a gentle slope towards the south side of the field the ring in which the sports took place was staked in, and on the slope itself the large marquees for the accommodation of the bazaar and flower show, with the various tents for the sale of temperance refreshments, were pitched. On each side the scene was bordered by a

---

*Let us hope that the other visitors paid more attention to the pictures than the *Aberdeen Journal*'s correspondent. The picture of David and Goliath is by the Italian baroque master Domenichino, and Philip Kemble was an actor and friend of the 4th Earl. His portrait by "the circle of Sir Thomas Lawrence" now hangs in the dining room.

fringe of dark firs, and visible from the summit of the declivity a large portion of the policies* was spread out to view.

This time, the weather was fine and there was no holding back the eager guests:

At an early hour the grounds began to assume a stirring aspect, and by about one o'clock it was calculated that from eight to ten thousand persons were present.

Johnny and Ishbel were doing nothing new in opening their house to the public: it was the way they went about it that set them apart. Until the 1770s, the British aristocracy had lived unostentatiously in their ancestors' castles and manors, but now they needed space to show off the art they had brought home from the Grand Tour. Stowe, the seat of the Dukes of Buckingham and Chandos, was typical: more a gallery than a house, it boasted huge rooms where treasures could be displayed, and even had a guidebook. At first, only friends whom the owners wished to impress were invited to look round such palatial residences, but gradually ordinary people were allowed in too, as the railways and works holidays made day trips possible. Warwick Castle became a favorite in the 1820s and Hampton Court recorded two hundred thousand visitors a year.

As country houses became businesses, competition between their owners intensified and the high-born were not averse to stooping to the low trick of embellishing the family history to boost trade. But the gentry made sure that they did not sully their own hands with the pennies of tourists. Instead, household staff served as guides and often grew rich on the proceeds: the housekeeper from Warwick Castle is said to have amassed £30,000 in tips† before she died in 1834.

Making money was far from the thoughts of Johnny and Ishbel. Indeed, they spent lavishly on their open days. The welcoming parties at Haddo and Cromar in the summer of 1878 had cost the then staggering

---

* A Scottish term for the parkland around a stately home.
† More than £2,000,000 ($2,600,000) in today's money.

sum of £7,500,* and the King of the Netherlands' tent and the rolls and plum cakes would not have come cheap in the years that followed. By mingling with their tenants and happily leading the tours of the house themselves, they were conducting a radical experiment in philanthropy, which an editorial in the *Scotsman* commended for being "notable in its novelty and success in these days of conflict between classes."

But there was much snobbish whispering in castle corridors about how the Aberdeens were letting the side down, especially when the couple decided to go further, appointing themselves as teachers to their staff of a hundred servants. In this, once again, they were following the example set by Johnny's father, the saintly and enlightened 5th Earl. He had set up "evening schools" for the men and women who worked on his farms in 1862. The women met once a week during the summer and studied Scripture, needlework, reading, and writing under the supervision of the wives of the "principal farmers." Two hundred and seventy men paid a penny a week to learn from tutors paid for by the Earl, but the scheme soon collapsed, perhaps because they were not allowed to skip the compulsory ten minutes of Bible study. The women were more stoical, and thirteen of their schools were still going in 1865.†

Ishbel was determined to try again, and drew upon her experience at Guisachan and the Quebec Chapel to organize a Sunday school for children from the estate. Meanwhile, Johnny was deputed to organize classes for his farm laborers and for the builders working on the chapel and the house.

The "astonishing success" of the scheme surprised Ishbel, for she knew "how shy the farm servants are, as a rule, of co-operation with persons of other classes." Her masterstroke was to keep her distance. She enlisted the help of the farmers to persuade the men themselves to take charge by

---

* Around £500,000 ($650,000) today.

† The 5th Earl's educational mission was not the first in Aberdeenshire. In 1846, twenty-year-old Robert Harvey Smith of Rhynie, thirty miles from Haddo, gathered together eleven young men from the village to form a Mutual Instruction Society. An upper room at the village hall served as a "classroom" where members met to hear and criticize essays read out by one of their number. The society's strictest rule was that any member who came in ten minutes late would be fined one penny, "unless an excuse satisfactory to the majority were given." The movement spread rapidly across the county and beyond, and grew in influence. In 1849, the Rhynie society published *An Address to Farm Servants, on their Intellectual Condition*, which stimulated widespread public debate and may well have inspired the 5th Earl to take action.

"inducing them to realise how important it was for their own future to follow up their school education." But she faced greater resistance to her plan
to improve the lives of young women, for their mistresses, who, in many
cases, subjected their servants to a nine o'clock curfew, were reluctant to
allow them to be out at night to attend classes.

Ishbel's solution was simple, ingenious, and far ahead of its time: she
founded the Haddo House Association. This acted as a virtual school, allowing housemaids and cooks to study at home in their quarters or in the
servants' hall. The ladies of the county were cajoled into acting as tutors.
Their overt task was to make sure that the "Associates" in their employ
followed the prescribed syllabus and read the set books, but Ishbel and
Johnny also charged them with a heavier responsibility:

> We desired to reach mistresses as well as servants and to bind both
> together by common interests. We wanted to make our aim elevation
> of women materially, mentally, morally—to help all who joined us
> 'Onward and Upward.'

The Association's rule book asked its members to do their "daily
work as in God's sight" and to "endeavour to lead a life of temperance,
of truthfulness, of purity and love." Virtue was rewarded with "a set of
clothes or a cot to the first child of every associate who marries and on
whose former life there is no blemish." But Ishbel understood human
failings and, in declaring that no one, whatever their status or behavior,
would be refused membership,* she took a swipe at other, more priggish,
social reformers:

> All are made welcome. The 'Scotch Girls Friendly Society' is doing a
> noble work to uphold the standard of purity. But I think that it needs

---

*This was typical of Johnny and Ishbel's ecumenical approach to life. They decided against
having a formal consecration of the chapel at Haddo "as this would involve its being under
the authority of some one church." For more than a century, preachers of many faiths have
held services there. Few have turned down the invitation, although my mother-in-law was
disappointed when Pope John Paul II did so during his arduous tour of Scotland in 1984.
"He needs some peace and quiet," she announced to a member of that year's large and noisy
summer house party. "Well if that's what he wants," the guest replied, "he'd do better to try the
clocktower in the courtyard."

by its side another Society which has no rule qualifying for admission and in which a member who loses her character is not required to forfeit her card.

"Married Associates" were recruited to set an example and "raise the concept of womanhood amongst the young women." Mothers, especially, were encouraged to join, for, Ishbel argued, "it is her words and ways which must be the main influence in the lives of the little children."

When word reached Johnny and Ishbel from the villages surrounding Haddo that the classes were flourishing, with those on mathematics, biology, and reading the particular favorites, they seized the opportunity to expand the scheme to areas far beyond their own estates. Soon, 115 branches of the H.H.A. had been set up throughout Scotland, and a new name had to be found. After much debate, the eight thousand members decided to call it the Onward and Upward Association, because the phrase neatly encapsulated their aims. "ONWARD AND UPWARD," Ishbel explained, "is obviously the opposite of Backward and Downward."

Almost unwittingly, as her daughter Marjorie observed, Ishbel had hit upon a modus operandi that was to serve her well in the years that followed:

> Ishbel's first thought in all schemes was to make them start running on self-governing lines; their members had to elect committees, decide programmes, pay fees, all by their own choice. The benevolent rulers who provided suggestions and means kept well in the background.

This was not always true. In 1891, Ishbel launched an *Onward and Upward* magazine and installed herself as editor. The opening page of the first issue set its tone:

> We are such a large family now that we cannot get on any longer without some means of talking with one another. And we know that all our Mothers and Girls, all our Members and friends, will heartily welcome the little stranger, and will be very kind to it, especially during the earlier months of its life.

Behind the chatty style and the coy protestations about her own role, the editor's strong moral purpose is clear. There are articles on "Health in the Home," stories about "the Old Saints" and other religious topics, a "Mother's Corner," advice for housekeepers ("To kill rats—pounded glass mixed with flour into a paste should be placed near the rat-holes"), "hints as to how we may best profit from our reading," guidance about etiquette in the sick room ("If the invalid asks you to read the newspaper aloud to him, omit the death list and *In Memoriam*"), and a page "where Home-makers of all degrees can discuss the means which will help them in their vocation." Gourlay Steell, painter of the Guisachan herd, was one of the many prominent artists who were prevailed upon to provide the illustrations. Contributors of articles included Ishbel's sister-in-law Fanny Marjoribanks, her friend and fellow doer-of-good-deeds the Marchioness of Tavistock,* as well as other grandes dames, professors, and prominent clergymen.

W. T. Stead, the editor of the *Pall Mall Gazette* whose investigations into the plight of child prostitutes gave him common cause with Ishbel, was another willing and admiring recruit to the editorial team. Stead showed Ishbel how to take advantage of the latest newspaper printing techniques to produce a magazine that domestic servants and farm laborers could afford. He also advised her to find ways of disguising homilies on morality and to avoid discussing the "women's rights movement": neither sold papers.

The ever-willing Johnny turned out articles on the family's amateur dramatics at Haddo and *Sketches Personal and Social*. Other pages were filled with *Bible Notes*, useful recipes,† and *Tiny Sermons*:

---

* Ishbel looked up to Adeline Tavistock, later the Duchess of Bedford, who had been "one of the reigning beauties of London" in her youth, for "in addition to physical beauty, she possessed great personal charm, and was endowed with many intellectual and artistic gifts." They worked closely together between 1879 and the Aberdeens' departure to Canada in 1893, organizing meetings and founding charitable schemes. "In later years our paths led us apart from one another," Ishbel wrote, "but there was that between us which could never die." Yet die it did, almost as soon as the friendship was renewed in 1920. Much to her distress, Ishbel discovered that Adeline "was on her way to see me on the day when she caught the chill which was the precursor of a fatal illness."

† Today's gourmets may relish Ox-Cheek Soup ("First clean a whole ox-cheek carefully with warm water; then soak it for twelve hours in two gallons of warm water; then stew for six hours...") and even High Church Pudding ("½lb suet shred fine, ½lb flour, teacupful of black currant jam, teacupful of milk, teaspoonful carbonate of soda. Mix all *thoroughly* together, stirring for a few minutes . . . boil 2½ hours"). The recipe for Herring Pancakes, though simple—"Skin, bone, and cut up a couple of dried herrings, make a light batter of flour, eggs, and milk, drop in the pieces of herring, and fry in boiling butter sufficient of the mixture to form a thick pancake"—may have less obvious appeal despite its omega-3 potential.

Do not say one word or entertain one thought that you cannot repeat to your Mother, nor do anything which, when the golden day comes you cannot tell to your sweetheart.

Ishbel herself provided a window to the wider world with articles about her travels, illustrated with her own photographs, while fiction, in the form of a serial entitled *Her Day of Service*, came from the pen of Mrs. Isabella Fyvie Mayo, an Aberdonian author.

Mayo's story is romantic, well written, and enjoyably cozy, but it is none too subtle: the moral improvement of her readers is her aim. From the moment Margaret Ede, the protagonist, takes her leave of her widowed mother before leaving home for a new life in domestic service, everyone converses in pious proverbs:

'Oh Margaret!' sobbed the widow. 'Remember what your dear Father used to say—that life comes to us as we take it and goes with us as we make it.'

In the train, Margaret never misses an opportunity to do good: she gives a bunch of flowers to a disabled girl and shares "the best of her sandwiches" with some poor children. When she reaches London, Kenneth Fraser, a young man who has been sharing the carriage and covertly admiring her benevolence and discreet manner, helps her with her luggage before explaining that he would be "continuing his journey, far across the sea."

Margaret finds work with Mrs. Foster, an old lady whose homespun philosophy inspires her to more acts of kindness. She then moves on to another family and becomes a civilizing influence not only on their "rather unruly children," but also upon a young man employed in their shop. Thanks to her advice, he renounces his gambling habit, confesses to having stolen from the till to fund it, and emigrates to Tasmania to begin a new and more virtuous life. Soon Margaret is swept off there herself, after the reformed gambler bumps into Kenneth Fraser, the helpful young man from the train, and sings her praises.

Margaret and Kenneth marry and set up home on a farm where Margaret, now surrounded by children of her own, performs many more good deeds. And then, like every *Onward and Upward* story, this one ends with a moral to inspire its readers to dream of higher things:

> Surely if one had a world full of people like those one finds there, the Kingdom of God for which we pray would be set up at once, and all the world would be one great home, so that there would be no more 'strangers' within the gates.

Wee Willie Winkie soon followed. Once again Ishbel was breaking new ground, for this charming spin-off from *Onward and Upward*, printed on pages small enough to fit comfortably into a child's hand, was one of the world's first magazines for children. According to its masthead, ten-year-old Marjorie—hailed in other organs of the press as "the world's youngest editor"—was in charge, contributing tales of her travels in Canada and accounts of her adventures at home in Scotland. Much was made of the recruitment of Marjorie's siblings to the "Editorial Board," which was photographed meeting in the boudoir at Haddo, but the guiding hands were undoubtedly those of Ishbel and Stead.

> Lady Marjorie is an interesting child, somewhat tall for her age, but still a child at her lessons. She does her editing in the intervals of play time. Like all the rest of the family she is devoted to her mother, who is naturally very anxious that such a child should not be unduly forced into prominent activity,

wrote Stead, somewhat disingenuously. But the former Sunday School teacher and the wily journalist understood their young readers and produced a sparky magazine that spoke directly to them with a real sense of fun and wonder. "Marjorie" offered something for everyone: educational articles about tadpoles and other wriggly creatures, mini-sermons for the goody-goodies, and surely the liveliest and most surprising correspondence column in the Victorian press: even the farm dogs wrote in. A Highland Collie called Oscar complained that he was forced to live in "a smoky town with nasty streets and bad smells" and confessed that he longed to be "away, away among the hills where the pure breezes blow."

There were puzzles and riddles and competitions galore: one offered a prize for the best design of "a cosy home"; another invited readers to submit their best pet stories. Exciting features were devoted to the adventures of true-life child heroes, such as "Arthur Stuart Houston, the twelve-year-old Niagara hero." Arthur had won a medal from the Royal Humane Society in London after rescuing his mother and six-year-old brother from the waters on the edge of the Falls just in the nick of time. He also happened to be "a reader of 'Wee Willie Winkie,'" the editor proudly noted.

There were bedtime stories too. Many of these, like their counterparts in *Onward and Upward*, were illustrated by the finest painters of the day, cajoled into doing so by Ishbel on her social rounds. Johnny Millais, son of the more famous Sir John Everett and a well-known artist in his own right, provided two portraits of the fearsome protagonists of "The Prairie Wolf and the Locust." Another morality tale, "Tried in the Cat's Court," featured pictures by Louis Wain, of whom H. G. Wells said:

> He has made the cat his own. He invented a cat style, a cat society, a whole cat world.... Cats that do not look and live like Louis Wain cats are ashamed of themselves.

As the Onward and Upward Association grew, hidden social problems could be addressed. Ishbel recognized that "the life of a working man's wife is a very hard one," and that many mothers of small children found themselves as housebound and isolated as their servants. The problem was not hard to solve:

> We find that an occasional tea-meeting, to which babies may be brought, is a great pleasure to the mothers, who are seldom asked out. At our first tea-meeting, a mother told me she has not been out to tea for twenty years, for she could never leave the babies. Then, in some of our branches, Cottage Meetings are held fortnightly, to which the mothers from a group of cottages near together go as they are, without arraying themselves in their Sunday dress, meeting alternately in different cottages. These meetings for reading and conversation have been much enjoyed.

But in high society the mutterings about the Aberdeens grew louder. It was said that the Prime Minister himself had been summoned to the Queen who demanded to know whether there was any truth in the rumors that the Earl and Countess sat down to dinner with their servants. He reassured her, but he did acknowledge that they had created a club for their own household and that, as president and vice-president (the hierarchical niceties were, of course, observed), they attended its meetings in the servants' hall.* This did nothing to still the tut-tutting of the gossipmongers, and later, to the couple's evident exasperation, the stories followed them around the world and seemed to have "a perennial life."

They were lampooned by J. M. Barrie in his comedy *The Admirable Crichton*, in which a peer of the realm, Lord Loam, in the interests of breaking down the class system, allows his staff to mingle with his aristocratic friends at tea parties. This did hurt Johnny and Ishbel's feelings† and stiff letters followed. Barrie denied the charge in a rather slippery reply to Johnny:

> I am very sorry indeed to learn from you, whom I so greatly esteem, that any person has ever thought that my many years old play, *The Admirable Crichton* was aimed at you or your manner of running your household. I can assure you that this was not the case.

But by then Johnny and Ishbel had long since risen above the rest of the gossip, for they knew that they had been right to treat their servants as fellow human beings and that the bold Onward and Upward experiment had changed many lives:

> Of one thing we are very sure, and that is that the existence of our Household Club in no way tended to deteriorate the service rendered

---

* Queen Victoria herself, many thought, had "form" when it came to inappropriate relationships with servants. Her reliance on the ghillie John Brown, in particular, set tongues wagging and the satirists of the humorous magazine *Punch* to work. In 1866, they published a spoof Court Circular: "Mr Brown walked on the Slopes. He subsequently partook of a haggis. In the evening Mr John Brown was pleased to listen to a bag-pipe. Mr John Brown retired early."

† Three-quarters of a century later, the Haddo House Choral & Operatic Society presented *The Admirable Crichton*, with June, wife of one of Ishbel's grandsons, the 4th Marquess, in the role of the formidable Countess of Brocklehurst. All was forgiven, but not forgotten, particularly by the production's publicist.

either to ourselves or to our guests, nor did it interfere with the discipline which must exist in every well-ordered household. But it did introduce the element of deep, mutual regard and understanding and sympathy for one another's lives, and a basis on which to build a common fellowship for all true and noble purposes, which should surely be the aim and desire of every thoughtful householder.

At a public meeting held to mark the tenth anniversary of the founding of the association, Dr. James Brebner, a local clergyman who served as the Haddo chaplain, looked back with satisfaction on the help that it had given to young female servants in particular. It had, he believed, "raised them up to a higher life, and to a purer, happier life, too."

Many years later, among the letters that Johnny and Ishbel received when they celebrated their Golden Wedding, there were several from women who wanted them to know how much their lives had been transformed by the association. Margaret Thorburn, who had been in service in Glasgow and still treasured the prizes she had won for "scripture knowledge," clearly spoke for many:

> Thanking you heartily for the Onward & Upward Association. It gave me high ideals just as I was starting out in life, when I needed guidance more than I knew.

Meanwhile, Johnny set about improving his estates. Before his disappearance, his brother George had honored his father's dying wishes and paid for two new churches at Tarland and Methlick, but he had otherwise carefully husbanded his capital, and further funds had built up in his absence. Johnny eschewed such thrift, embarking, in 1879, upon an extravagant plan to construct a railway line across his land at Haddo. He professed that his aim was to bring prosperity to his tenants, but there was undoubtedly an element of self-indulgence in this madcap project. He loved trains, and in his younger days he had brazenly buttonholed Sir James Elphinstone, the chairman of the Great North of Scotland Railway Company, when he turned up at Haddo to have lunch with his father, to ask him for permission "to travel occasionally on the engines." But Johnny gave a whole new meaning to the word "occasionally" as soon as he had wheedled a letter out of Sir James, allowing him to ride on the footplate of any train in Aberdeenshire. Thenceforth, hardly a locomotive chugged along the branch lines of the county without the aristocratic apprentice on board.

His expertise and passion were of no avail, however, when he tried to set up his own "light railway" in 1879. This, he proposed, would branch off the main line from Aberdeen to the fishing port of Fraserburgh and run for "10 miles, 3 furlongs and six chains" (roughly ten-and-a-half miles) across his estate to the outskirts of Methlick, the nearest village to Haddo. To the astonishment of railway officials, he promised to bear all the construction costs himself, even though the budget was £55,000, around £4,000,000 today. The parliamentary act that would have allowed it to go ahead passed its second reading, but Johnny's grand plan was stymied by vehement opposition from the people of the nearby town of Oldmeldrum, situated on a different line, who feared they would lose business. The directors of the Great North of Scotland Railway were also unconvinced: their shareholders had become restive about the cost of the lines they were already financing and were unlikely to welcome a railway, however "light," with a terminus in a field outside a small village. When the projected costs rose dramatically and the G.N.S.R. stipulated that he would have to make good any losses from his own funds, Johnny ordered the white flags marking the line's route to be cleared from the fields and gave up the fight. He told his tenants in February 1880:

> The estimated cost of construction, and also the difficulty of making terms of agreement with the Great North of Scotland Railway Company, are so much greater than could have been anticipated, that I have come to the conclusion that the project must be abandoned.*

But he immediately softened the blow by announcing that he would "relieve" them from paying rent for the next six months to help them weather the "unfavourable circumstances by which agriculture has for some time been affected."

---

* Neither Johnny nor the directors of the Great North of Scotland Railway seem to have harbored hard feelings. He was appointed to the company's board in 1886 and served as its deputy chairman from 1890 until his retirement six years later.

The tenants had, indeed, been struggling to scratch out a living, thanks, principally, to a succession of poor harvests, caused by rainy summers and harsh winters. The winter of 1878–79 was especially cold: twenty trains were stuck for days in deep snowdrifts in the countryside; in Aberdeen "wheel traffic" was "conducted with great difficulty"; and, after seven weeks of snow, a report from Johnny's Cromar estate on February 1 told a sorry tale:

> Man and beast are suffering in various degrees of discomfort and loss. All the wild animals are in pinching want. Sheep flocks are becoming greatly reduced in condition, and the deaths are already numerous, and will, by-and-by, increase to a serious degree. Turnips, where bare, are becoming much deteriorated in feeding properties, and will soon be frosted almost useless.

When a farm laborer wrote to a newspaper to complain that, in cutting the rents of the farmers, the plight of his other estate workers had been overlooked, a tenant sprang to Johnny's defense, arguing that "in some cases the remission of half a year's rent will do no more than cover the loss incurred on a fractional part of this season's grain crop." Johnny and Ishbel, he continued, were setting an example that others should follow:

> If landlords would take the same interest in the welfare of their tenants as Lord and Lady Aberdeen do, not keeping aloof from them, but treating them as beings 'of that same mould, from that same maker's hand,' as they, then the relation of landlord and tenant would be relieved of much of the hardness and bitterness which in general marks it. In this deed of princely generosity we see just the crowning act of a course of kindly sympathy, as well as a practical illustration of the principles they profess.

But Johnny's timing could not have been worse. These were the first years of the Agricultural Depression that brought poverty and often bankruptcy to the people of the British countryside for a quarter of a century. Johnny's "deed of princely generosity" cost him the equivalent of a million pounds today. Even when the period of grace ended, the tenants found that they were paying less rent than before, yet their softhearted landlord had not reneged on his obligations to pay for new buildings, equipment, and repairs. And, although they were careful never to reveal the exact costs of building the new chapel and refurbishing the rest of Haddo, the cash reserves built up in the "Sailor Earl's" absence must have been largely, if not entirely, dissipated.

In fact, as their daughter Marjorie later wrote, the seeds of Johnny and Ishbel's financial problems had already been sown in the first months of their marriage:

> They set aside, in the estimate they drew up for the first year's budget, £2,000 to be spent on cottages, to cost £100 each; another £2,000 for charities; £6,000 was to cover all other outgoings, and savings to be put by where possible. They did not know that their income would fall from that very year, and savings never begin.

A more worldly man might by now have thought that he had spent enough on others and put away his well-thumbed checkbook. Not Johnny. The estate, after all, was still bringing in more than £40,000 a year and was, for the moment, in the black: more than enough, surely, to pay the mounting bills for their smart new residence in London.

7

A House in Town and
Cottages in the Country

In London, where Johnny attended the House of Lords between January and August,* Ishbel found herself mistress of 37 Grosvenor Square, which stood only a few hundred yards from her parents' home at Brook House. Johnny had managed to buy it amidst the commotion that had followed the theft of her jewelry during their honeymoon at Halstead Place. As the maid screamed and Ishbel gave orders to summon the policeman from the village, a bewildered messenger boy arrived with the unwelcome news that a rival bidder had emerged. Somehow, the unflappable Johnny managed to dictate a reply, upping his offer. And soon, for £43,500, the place was his.

Unlike most of the houses nearby, No. 37 had not been built by the Grosvenor estate, although its surveyor, Thomas Cundy II, seems to have intervened to insist that its stucco facade matched those of its neighbors.

---

*Before the parliamentary timetable was reformed in the 1920s, sessions ran from the beginning of January until early August, with the opening of the grouse shooting season on the "Glorious Twelfth" the unofficial deadline for getting business done. Writing in 1844, the Irish satirist John Fisher Murray sketched the scene in the Palace of Westminster as the recess loomed: "The surplus talk of both Houses is bottled up for another session; as much business as can be huddled through both Houses is 'lumped,' and 'read a third time,' and 'passed,' with astonishing rapidity; clerks, and gun-makers, are much hurried; and, about the beginning of August, the collective wisdom, their dogs, guns, and gamekeepers, set out together for the moors." In Johnny's day, to the frustration of both the Lords and the Commons, this target date was rarely met.

Instead, it was the largest of the many projects carried out in Mayfair in the 1850s by a property speculator called Wright Ingle. He commissioned the interior from a fashionable architect named Henry Harrison, who was conveniently based nearby, as were the builders, Messrs. Higgs and Cullingford. Even so, by the time the house was finished in 1855, the budget of £7,564 had been exceeded.

The final cost, Ingle calculated, was nearer £10,000,* but his creation, with its grand sweeping staircase and excellent sanitary arrangements (water closets on every floor, two on the top one; a bathroom on both the first and second), was seen by the lords and ladies who visited it as the height of luxury and an enviable improvement upon their stately homes in the shires, with their drafts and primitive plumbing.

No. 37 also boasted a huge basement: the domain of the servants. There were suites for the housekeeper and the butler; bedrooms for the cook and the housemaids; a larder, a scullery, a laundry, a wash house, a servants' hall; cellars for beer, wine, and coal; a cubbyhole for sharpening knives; and, of course, a huge kitchen. In the stables behind, there were four rooms where seven menservants could sleep, and there was a comfortable loose box for any horse that fell ill.

The Duke of Buccleuch pronounced it "the nicest and best arranged house in London," and he, as the owner of a portfolio of opulent stately homes that included Boughton House in Northamptonshire, Drumlanrig Castle in Dumfries and Galloway, Dalkeith Palace in Midlothian, and Montagu House in Whitehall, will have known a thing or two about property. But Ishbel was less impressed by what she saw on her return from her honeymoon, especially when Mr. Eassie, a surveyor summoned to inspect the drains, reported that "some incredible things" had been found in them.

While those were being disposed of, another problem arose: Ishbel was disappointed to find that the house was too small to accommodate meetings of "societies formed to wake up the social conscience." Her daughter Marjorie remembered her saying that "drawing rooms were not meant for meetings, nor housemaids for cleaning front stairs after audiences had gone up them from unpaved streets and 'indescribable slosh.'"

---

* Equivalent to around £800,000 ($1,000,000) today.

There was enough space for her old tutor Professor John Meiklejohn of the University of St. Andrews to give five afternoon lectures about Victorian poets, and even to accommodate a "fancy fair" at which the band of the London Scottish Rifles played. But there were complaints when "the heads of representative drapery establishments from all parts of London" were forced to squash into the drawing room to discuss the "provision of spring seats behind the counter for young women, who found themselves kept standing from eight a.m. to ten p.m., with very short intermissions for their meals."

Knitting for the poor as a child, and her father's insistence that his children should make charitable donations from their own pocket money, had prepared Ishbel well for a life of campaigning and good works. And Johnny, she asserted, "was looked upon as a sort of assistant and successor to the great Lord Shaftesbury* and was in great demand as chairman or speaker at all kinds of charitable and philanthropic meetings."

Their calendars were always full, particularly in the summer when they looked like "a list of the principal charitable and philanthropic societies." The list was long indeed: it included the Parents' National Education Union, Homes for Working Girls and Homes for Little Boys, the Homes for Orphan Girls at Ilford, George Holland's Mission in Whitechapel, and the Canning Town Women's Settlements. They were particularly fond of the Mission to Costermongers, whose beneficiaries "presented us with a donkey, bringing it on to the platform for our little girl to ride," and the Omnibus Men's Suppers, despite their being

---

* This was quite a claim by Ishbel. Anthony Ashley Cooper, 7th Earl of Shaftesbury, was the most revered social reformer of the Victorian age. He espoused many causes (many of which were indeed taken up by Johnny and Ishbel, who were his neighbors in Grosvenor Square), campaigning against the exploitation of young children as chimney sweeps and as factory workers, for the "ragged schools" that provided them with an education, for cleaner water supplies for London to prevent the spread of cholera, for more compassionate care of the insane and better lives for flower girls and street traders, for the suppression of the opium trade and for the abolition of slavery. On his death in 1885, his friend, the barnstorming Baptist preacher Charles Spurgeon, declared: "We have, in my judgment, lost the best man of the age. I do not know whom I should place second, but I certainly should put him first—far beyond all other servants of God within my knowledge—for usefulness and influence." A more recent biographer was only marginally more measured in her praise: "No man has . . . ever done more to lessen the extent of human misery or to add to the sum total of human happiness."

held between 12 midnight and 2 a.m., "partly because we were well acquainted, by sight, with many of the drivers frequenting the Edgware Road, as we passed them so often."*

Ishbel flourished, as her neighbor Louisa Knightley, an older, more experienced activist for women's causes, noted in May 1879:

> I went to Ishbel Aberdeen, whom it is delightful to find so full of enthusiasm for all good works.

Ishbel was never afraid to go where angels feared to tread. Despite the raised eyebrows of her neighbors in Mayfair, she took herself off to the darkest corners of the Strand on Friday evenings, where she invited the "ladies of the night" to join her in a nearby shop for a cup of tea and some gentle words of moral improvement. In a bid to dissuade her from what they saw as a reckless course of action for a woman so young, her alarmed parents sought the support of an old friend and pillar of Victorian society, the Prime Minister, Mr. Gladstone. But the plan backfired, perhaps because he was himself engaged in his own much-gossiped-about mission to rehabilitate "fallen women."

"If she hears a call to do this, she should go," he told her disapproving, disappointed, parents.

It was not until half a century later, on her Golden Wedding day in 1927, that Ishbel discovered how much her small act of rebellion had meant to at least one of the women she tried to help. She had seen Ishbel's photograph in a newspaper and wrote:

> When I look at your picture I see again your sweet face as on that first night we met. How lovely you were to me then—when few can

---

*The rich aristocrats, bankers, and businessmen of Mayfair had had a soft spot for drivers of horse-drawn omnibuses ever since, it was said, one of them stopped his vehicle to help a female member of the Rothschild family to cross Hamilton Place at the height of the rush hour. He and his fellow members of the Victoria Station Association were rewarded with five shillings and a brace of pheasants every Christmas (three thousand brace, it was said, were distributed every year), while the busmen expressed their thanks by tying ribbons in the Rothschilds' blue and gold racing colors to their whips and bellpulls. In 1897, businessman Morris Abrahams raised funds for an even more far-reaching initiative, the Omnibus Men's Superannuation Fund, which provided pensions for drivers and conductors who were old or down on their luck.

understand the torture of the struggle that has to be borne—and have been ever since.

Only at weekends did the couple allow themselves to relax a little. Johnny rented Littleberries, a fine eighteenth-century country house at Mill Hill. Today Mill Hill is a prosperous North London suburb, but in 1880 it felt a long way from the stink and smoke of the city. Littleberries was hardly a weekend cottage: it was even larger than Dudley Marjoribanks's equally rural bolt-hole at Dollis Hill to the west of the capital, and although it lacked the modern conveniences of 37 Grosvenor Square, it was far more extravagantly decorated.

The former hunting lodge got its name from George Littlebury, a bookseller, who bought it in 1691. By the 1750s, according to a map drawn up by the garden designer and surveyor John Rocque, the grounds, approached along a wide avenue, had been laid out in the grandest style with ponds, grass terraces, and even an Ionic temple, described as a "banqueting house." Johnny and Ishbel's landlord, J. F. Pawson, a city merchant who'd bought the house and its forty acres in 1847, had made substantial improvements, adding a new staircase and a second storey to the building and, like every well-heeled Victorian follower of horticultural fashion, a couple of monkey puzzle trees to the garden.

Littleberries was reputed to have had a racy past: two of British history's most colorful women, Nell Gwyn, the mistress of Charles II, and an eighteenth-century courtesan named Mrs. Margaret Caroline Rudd were said to have lived there. While a bishop remembered Nell Gwyn fondly as "the indiscreetest and wildest creature that ever was in [the royal] court," Mrs. Rudd was a more sinister character. In 1775, she appeared at the Old Bailey accused, with Daniel Perreau and his twin brother Robert, of attempting to defraud Henry Drummond, a prominent banker.* She was held by the court of public opinion to have masterminded the

---

* By coincidence, Ishbel's descendants are now linked to both Nell Gwyn and Henry Drummond through Cecile Drummond, who married Ishbel's son Dudley. The Nell Gwyn connection has led to invitations to commemorative dinners for recent Marquesses, but having a family bank has not always proved so palatable. In the 1930s, Ishbel's grandson Archie Gordon, later 5th Marquess, found himself pursued by Drummonds' solicitors after running up an overdraft of £4. His grandfather was chairman at the time.

crime, but the jurors at her trial were said to have fallen for her charms—
she had dressed for the occasion in "a striped Night Gown, with a Pink
and ermine cloak, and a black laced bonnet"—and they seem to have been
especially taken with "the tremulous flutter and rustle of her elbow laces."
She was duly acquitted, while the Perreau twins were hanged at Tyburn.

Ishbel enjoyed historical gossip, but she was more interested in the
design of Littleberries than in tales of its previous chatelaines. Outside,
the three-storey red brick house had an elegant Doric porch with four
columns forming a loggia, but it was the "Gilt Room" inside that really
caught her eye, with its fine gold-encrusted plasterwork and medallion
portraits of King George I and other members of the Royal Family. She
wanted to know more about it, but who could satisfy her curiosity? The
answer came to her during a weekend at Mentmore Towers, the home of
the heiress Hannah de Rothschild, who had become the wife of the 5th
Earl of Rosebery.

One of the other guests, Sir Andrew Clark, was W. E. Gladstone's personal physician, famous for keeping the Prime Minister calm at moments
of crisis and notorious for his garrulousness. When he confided to Ishbel
that he had prescribed weekends in the country for his distinguished
patient,* who was suffering from a persistently sore throat and a number
of other ailments caused by exhaustion, but that Gladstone was unwilling
to leave the city during the parliamentary season, she came to the rescue:

> Happily we had a special plea to offer for his coming to us because
> we happened to have taken a house that summer near Hendon called
> 'Littleberries' which contained some very interesting pictures and dec-
> orations. . . . So we told Mr Gladstone that we wanted him very much
> to come and give an opinion on these debated art questions,† and so
> he said he would come for one weekend; and he became so interested

---

* British Prime Ministers did not have an official country residence until Lord Lee of Fareham
presented Chequers in Buckinghamshire to the nation in 1921 as "a thank-offering for her
deliverance in the great war of 1914–1918" and ordained that it should be "a place of rest and
recreation for her Prime Ministers for ever."

† Gladstone was well qualified to pronounce on questions of art. He had a library of more than
twenty thousand books and a fine collection of pictures. Ishbel remembered how he and her
father "used to meet in the old bookshops and old china and antique shops, where they would
discuss the rival merits of the art treasures that both loved to collect."

that he came the next and the next, bringing with him various learned persons with whom he discussed the points at issue.

By the end of that summer, Gladstone had permanently "contracted the weekend habit" and his eagerness to escape from Westminster early on Fridays soon led to dark mutterings from members of the cabinet that he was neglecting his parliamentary duties.

Gladstone's niece, Lady Frederick Cavendish, was also invited to stay at Littleberries in the summer of 1880. She had mixed feelings about the house:

> A most elegant little white and gold drawing-room has Charles and Nell's medallions in plaster-work set round the cornice; and there is a quaint little succession of grassy terraces, one below the other, ending in a gazebo summer-house, also most prettily decorated with medallions, 2 different ladies occurring here!

But she thought the copy of Rubens's *Neptune and Cybele* in the drawing room "inaccurate"* and "rather horrid."

Lady Frederick was most struck by Gladstone's transformation from workaholic to relaxed country gentleman. She "found Uncle W. casting care to the wind in the excitement of finding it was a villa built by Charles II for Nell Gwynne!" And she was amused that, while a few miles to the south in Westminster, the House of Commons sat debating the "Irish Question" right through until Sunday morning, "the Prime Minister picked strawberries, went a good quick walk with us . . . and enjoyed himself hugely."

Many young married couples might have complained about having so permanent a weekend guest, but for Johnny and Ishbel the Gladstones had long been part of the family:

---

* Lady Frederick spoke with authority. She had grown up at Hagley Hall in Worcestershire, the seat of her father, the 4th Baron Lyttleton, where the original of "our dear old Neptune and Cybele" used to hang in the salon before "Papa sold [it] for £500, to my grief." Gladstone, too, will have been familiar with the picture, since Lyttleton asked his brother-in-law to consign it for sale. It was bought for £525 by John Niewenhuys, a noted art dealer from Brussels, in about 1860.

We both knew Mr and Mrs Gladstone very well personally, for there had been an hereditary friendship between them and both our families, and they had always shown much cordiality to us both.

Gladstone had been a protégé of Johnny's grandfather, the 4th Earl, who was Prime Minister between 1852 and 1855, and he had served as Chancellor of the Exchequer in his cabinet. The two statesmen were, according to one observer, "on terms of the utmost intimacy, friendship and affection." This was something of an understatement. "He is the man in public life of all others whom I have *loved*," Gladstone once said. "I say emphatically *loved*."

Ishbel had known Gladstone all her life because her father was a leading Liberal. Like the artists Landseer and Millais; John Thadeus Delane, the editor of *The Times*; and "any number of members of Parliament," Gladstone had even made the epic journey to visit Guisachan, where he stayed for six days. So it was perhaps not surprising that Ishbel was a staunch Liberal from the cradle and fiercely resisted the attempts of her mother, who came from a family of true-blue Conservatives, to persuade her to see any virtues at all in anyone whose political views she disagreed with. When Gladstone's rival Benjamin Disraeli came to dinner one evening, she refused to shake his hand, until the grown-ups stepped in with a stern reminder about good manners.

Given the ferocity of her political loyalties, Ishbel's friends were surprised that she married a man who did not share them. But, determined though she was to convert him to the Liberal cause, she thought it wise to bide her time.

Johnny had begun attending the House of Lords in 1873 after the Committee for Privileges had ruled that his errant brother George was dead. But deciding which party to join was not easy, because his "hereditary political bearings were of a somewhat mixed sort." The 4th Earl had been a Tory before joining a breakaway faction of the party known as the Peelites, after its leader Sir Robert Peel. But this small group flourished only briefly on its own before joining up with the Whigs, the Radicals, and the Independent Irish Party to defeat the Conservative government in 1859. Many members of this alliance went on to form the Liberal Party, and it was this party that Johnny's father, the 5th Earl, had represented in the House of Commons as a member for Aberdeenshire. While Johnny hesitated, he sat on the cross benches in the House of Lords, which, he said, "provided a sort of 'No Man's Land,' with the advantage also of securing time for consideration."

In fact, it took him only "a short time" to make up his mind to join the Conservatives. He chose his ground carefully for his maiden speech in a debate about railway safety: it drew on his own experiences of riding on the footplates of Aberdeenshire trains as a young man. The result was gratifying: he found himself elected to a "Special Committee" charged with deciding whether the country's railway companies should adopt a universal signaling system for their ever-expanding networks. Other appointments followed: to an inquiry into whether the Midland Railway should run into London, and to another into the practicalities of building the Manchester Ship Canal. His speeches, which carefully weighed the interests of the entrepreneurs behind these ambitious and often risky engineering projects with the need to ensure the safety of the men who worked on them, impressed his fellow peers. Thus, when a Royal Commission on Railway Accidents was set up in 1874, Johnny was a natural choice as member.* He worked hard, often late into the night, to absorb the "vast amount of evidence" submitted to the inquiry. Much of it was dry, abstruse, and technical, but the bleak and graphic testimony given by many of the "railway servants" struck a chord with the budding social reformer that still resonated when, half a century later, he wrote his memoirs. Many accidents, the commissioners heard, were caused by fatigue, and Johnny was shocked when one engine driver revealed the effect of the "excessive hours" he was expected to work. His record was more than a hundred in six days. He described how

sometimes his wife and his wife's sister would sit, one on each side of him, 'Holding me up and shaking me, and trying to get me to eat my

---

*Johnny again made a good impression, and when, a few years later, another Royal Commission was set up to inquire into "Loss of Life at Sea," he was made its chairman: no easy task because discussions sometimes became heated. He "found that an adjournment for luncheon was often helpful," but less so the meal itself, which was "somewhat spartan," thanks to the Treasury's allowance of only one shilling and sixpence a head. Once again, Johnny brought out his checkbook and secretly "entered into a private arrangement" with the caterers. This was probably the first time he subsidized affairs of state—but it was not to be the last.

supper.' He also mentioned that sometimes the call boy would come to bid him come out when he had only been about two hours in bed.

But by 1876, when the Prime Minister, Benjamin Disraeli, picked Johnny out to make the Address in Answer to the Queen's Speech, disaffection and disillusionment were already creeping in:

I soon discovered that though *in* the Conservative Party, I was not altogether of it, my convictions leading me from time to time to deviate from the recognised party lines.

Things came to a head two years later when Disraeli sent troops into Afghanistan. Johnny, outraged, broke off a visit to Edinburgh and rushed back to Westminster to speak against the expedition. Ishbel, swaddled in an ample cloak to conceal her pregnancy (Doddie's birth was imminent), waited in the Peeresses' Gallery for three uncomfortable days to hear him. Johnny's speech, when at last he rose, was short but cutting. He refused to believe that the policy the government had adopted was "the only one they could have pursued," and defended himself against accusations of disloyalty to the party. The matter, he declared, "involved great political principles" and his conscience would not allow him to blindly toe the Conservative line.

Ishbel and her allies now went to work on Johnny. In October 1879, she persuaded the veteran Liberal politician John Bright to include a visit to Haddo in a tour of Scotland. Bright, the greatest orator and radical of the Victorian age, had cast his spell over her when, aged seventeen, she had sat next to him at one of her parents' dinner parties.* Now she hoped that Johnny, too, would become a disciple.

Bright, though, spent much of his time at Haddo fishing and seems to have confined his evangelism to a "pleasant conversation" about "farming affairs" over tea with some of Johnny's tenants and a more heated late-

---

* Half a century later, Ishbel could remember the conversation almost word by word. When she confided to Bright that she hoped to become a public speaker, he advised her to "have a peroration ready to which you can have quick recourse if you think your audience is beginning to weary." He also instructed her to prepare herself by reading famous political speeches, including his own. He gave her a three-volume set of them as a wedding present.

night discussion on the "Land Question" in the smoking room. He left impressed with his young hosts:

> Our visit to Haddo has been very pleasant. Lord and Lady Aberdeen most kind. They are religious, good—everything about them shows the influence of good. They have prayers twice daily—9 a.m. and 7 p.m. Lord Aberdeen reads a portion of Scripture and a prayer, and in the evening a hymn is sung by those present, servants included.

A month later, another less obvious trap was laid for the still swithering Johnny. The bait was an invitation from Lord Rosebery to join the house party at Dalmeny, his flamboyant and luxurious Tudor-Gothic-style mansion a few miles from Edinburgh. When Johnny and Ishbel arrived there, they found their host in the thick of overseeing Gladstone's Midlothian Campaign. This was to be the former Prime Minister's comeback after five years in the political wilderness. Rosebery had planned an innovative meet-the-people tour of the cumbersomely named Edinburghshire constituency that he hoped would not only ensure that Gladstone was reelected to Parliament but also restore him to office. Rosebery had entrusted much of the day-to-day work, Johnny soon discovered, to a reassuringly familiar figure: John McLaren, the sheriff who had conducted the hearings into the disappearance of his sailor brother in 1871 and who was now an aspiring politician.

There had never been an election campaign like it, not least because Rosebery used crowd-pulling methods gleaned from watching campaigns in the United States a few years earlier. Though Midlothian could only muster a few thousand voters, huge throngs descended on the halls where Gladstone was billed to speak. Other "ardent Liberals," as the *Scotsman* called them, who had come by bus and train from all over Scotland, stood outside for hours waiting to catch a glimpse of their idol and to cheer him as he passed by.

Rosebery made sure that Johnny missed nothing of the extraordinary spectacle that unfolded, positioning his two-horse landau in the forefront of the processions that, often three carriages abreast, slowly picked their way through the streets. He made sure, too, that he had a seat on the podium almost at Gladstone's elbow. Like everyone else, Johnny was caught up in the excitement, especially on December 1, the day when Gladstone made two rousing speeches, first to five thousand people at the Edinburgh Corn Exchange and then to twenty thousand at the Waverley Market. He certainly won over the *Scotsman*'s reporter, who, breathlessly nailing his own political colors to the mast, reported that Gladstone's enthusiastic reception at the Corn Exchange "was inspired not merely by the wish to see a blow struck at unrighteous Tory electioneering, but by a feeling of profound gratitude for great public services in the past." And at Waverley Market, "the veteran statesman was profoundly moved as the acclamations of that mighty multitude rose around him like the roar of a storm-tossed sea."*

Though Johnny's own description of the campaign was rather more low-key—he found his stay at Dalmeny "memorable and intensely interesting"—Gladstone's "silver tongue" had won him over to the Liberal cause. A few weeks later, at what the *Aberdeen Free Press* called "a great Liberal demonstration" in Aberdeen, Johnny was on the platform again, this time to speak in support of "resolutions condemnatory of the Govern- ment and of their domestic and foreign policy." Soon afterwards, Johnny told Lord Granville, leader of the Opposition in the House of Lords, that he was ready to join the "Liberal flock." The decision came as a relief, and, he wrote later, "never since that time, have I for one moment regretted my enrolment, nor has there ever been even an inclination to deviate from the central path of Liberalism." His marriage to Ishbel was now, as she had hoped, a marriage of Liberal minds.

But it was at Littleberries that Johnny and Ishbel really came to know the Gladstones, and a mutual admiration society was immediately formed. Gladstone described the Aberdeens as an "edifying couple," while his starstruck weekend hostess gushed that he and his wife Catherine were "the most delightful and considerate of guests" and was impressed that the great man was "revered in Bulgaria."

Johnny and Ishbel's tenancy of Littleberries lasted for only one summer—their landlord had put it up for sale—but the arrangement

---

* Gladstone, who calculated in his diaries (with curious precision) that he spoke to 86,930 people in the course of the fifteen-day campaign, was particularly astonished by the way that people who fainted in the tightly packed crowd were "continually handed out over [people's] heads . . . and were as if dead."

with the Gladstones continued when, in 1881, they took over Dollis Hill House, a five-hundred-acre farm that had been Ishbel's father's weekend retreat. Built in 1825 on the very northwestern outskirts of London, the house was architecturally undistinguished and, Ishbel noted, "much more modest," but it was famous for its views over fields and hills. There was no better place for jaded city-dwellers to take the air. The mercurial Rosebery, unnerved by tales of an infamous eighteenth-century murder there,* refused to visit, but, to Ishbel's relief, Gladstone found it even more to his liking than Littleberries:

> It was indeed extraordinary that a drive of forty minutes from Downing Street could transfer one into absolutely rural surroundings, delightful country lanes with high hedges, along which we had many a ride in early summer mornings. There was an old blacksmith of our acquaintance in the neighbourhood who could boast that he had never been to London!

A later visitor, the American writer Samuel Langhorne Clemens, Mark Twain, also waxed whimsical about the place's charms. "Dollis Hill comes nearer to being a paradise than any other home I ever occupied," he wrote. Nothing could equal the vista spread out beneath it:

> The rolling sea of grass still stretches away on every hand, splotches with shadows of spreading oaks in whose black coolness flocks of sheep lie peacefully dreaming. Dreaming of what? That they are in London, the metropolis of the world. Post-office District, N.W.? Indeed no. They are not. For there is no suggestion of city here; it is

---

* Ishbel herself had put the rumors about. Not for her, though, any run-of-the-mill criminals: only the most dastardly rascals, like Charles Peace at Halstead Place and Mrs. Rudd at Littleberries, were allowed to figure in the histories of her houses. The villain whose deeds terrified Rosebery was Jack Sheppard, whose exploits in the first years of the eighteenth century had been embroidered by popular dramatists and novelists such as William Harrison Ainsworth. Sheppard was indeed a colorful character, though he was more famous for his ingenious escapes from prison than for the crimes he committed. The *Oxford Dictionary of National Biography* says Sheppard's robberies "were characterized by adroitness and skill rather than by violence," suggesting that Rosebery was easily spooked or that, tactfully, he wanted to hide his preference for weekends in the far greater luxury of his wife's vast country house, Mentmore Towers, over the simpler, more rustic charms of Dollis Hill.

country, pure and simple, & as still and reposeful as is the bottom of the sea.

Ishbel, according to her daughter, had always loved the idyllic charm of Dudley Marjoribanks's own *Hameau de la Reine*:

On summer afternoons D.C.M. would drive his children down to look at the little Swiss cows which with cow-herd and cow-bells he had brought from Switzerland; then they would play in the hay and eat strawberries in the old walled garden.

At Dollis Hill, in the most literal sense, Gladstone made himself at home. He was not a demanding houseguest, and, in any case, his hosts were happy to indulge him. Whatever the hour, Johnny always made sure to greet him with a cup of tea on his arrival. The Gladstones returned the Aberdeens' hospitality, by inviting them to their much grander pile, the gothic eighteenth-century Hawarden Castle in Wales, and there, too, Johnny always showed himself ready to help the great man out, especially when a crisis arose.

One dark winter's night, ten years before Johnny and Ishbel were married, the Gladstones had been invited to visit some friends nine miles away, but the head coachman was off with a chill and his deputy could not drive because he had hurt his hand. And the police had received intelligence that an assassination attempt was about to be made on the Prime Minister's life by members of the Fenian Brotherhood, rebels against British rule in Ireland. But Johnny, who was then twenty, stepped forward and, with a brisk crack of the whip, rescued the couple's night out.

Inevitably, Ishbel decided to use the grounds of Dollis Hill House for what Gladstone called "your good works." Whether it was a gathering of a "political character," a haymaking party for city children, or a Punch-and-Judy show, her recipe was simple: food, fresh air, and fun. Thus one afternoon, according to admiring newspaper reports, two hundred and fifty "persons engaged in Ragged School work" enjoyed "an excellent tea," and the children invited on another occasion "testified that no other sauce was required than that of the invigorating air of Dollis Hill to enable them to empty the large basketfuls of bread and butter, cake, &c, provided for them."

But those gatherings were dwarfed when Ishbel, the former Sunday School teacher at Guisachan and the Quebec Chapel, welcomed a thousand delegates to the World's Sunday-school Convention to the lawns of Dollis Hill. The conference *Proceedings*, an otherwise dour account of church services and debates, enthused about "the very favourable weather," "the admirable selection of inspiring airs" played by the "military band of the Homes for Little Boys," "the vigorous music which thrills the heart of Scotsmen" from the pipers and drummers of the Royal Caledonian Asylum,* and the "gentler strains" of the hand bells swung by ringers "attired in the period costumes of the period of Edward the Fourth." The refreshments, especially the "cooling ices," the "luscious strawberries," and the "deliciously cold" water, also won praise, and the guests "felt so much at home" that they "seemed to share the feeling expressed openly by one, who said he would like to stay there always."

Invariably, her family and houseguests joined in the fun, and Ishbel and Johnny later chuckled over the memory of "Mr Gladstone and Sir William Harcourt† and other grave statesmen as care-free as any schoolboys, gleefully watching Mr Punch's outrageous proceedings." But when Gladstone was in residence, Ishbel, conscious that curious crowds tended

---

* The Royal Caledonian Asylum, which had impressive buildings in Copenhagen Fields in North London, was initially set up to help orphans of Scottish soldiers who had died in the Napoleonic Wars, but it later expanded its remit to include "the children of soldiers, sailors, and marines, natives of Scotland, who have died or been disabled in the service of their country; and also the children of indigent and deserving Scotch parents resident in London, upon whom poverty has fallen or by whose death they have been left unbefriended and helpless orphans."

† Sir William Harcourt, a leading Liberal politician, lawyer, and journalist, was notorious for his abrasiveness and tactlessness. Johnny used to tell the story of Sir William's encounter with Sir Rainald Knightley, who was rather too proud of his family's ancient lineage and prone to boring fellow guests at dinner parties with the details. "One evening during a visit to a country house, he was narrating some of the facts of his genealogy; but before he had finished, it was time to join the ladies. Next evening, however, he resumed the subject; but Sir William Harcourt soon intervened by remarking, 'Ah yes, most interesting; and one cannot help recalling a passage in that fine poem by Addison: "And Nightly, to the listening earth / Repeats the story of his birth."'" Nor was Harcourt famed for letting his hair down in public. Perhaps at Dollis Hill, he was making up for lost time after enduring what a biographer described as "an austere childhood" in various grim rectories in the north of England.

to gather when he went out and about in London,* took care to protect his wish for peace and quiet. She issued an edict that her guests should not ask for, or expect him to make, a speech, but he often did appear at the picnics and garden parties and even presided over some of them. At one, Mrs. Gladstone, perhaps embracing with a little too much enthusiasm Johnny's call, at an earlier event, for guests to "make a free use of everything," handed out "large numbers of flowers from the beds on the lawns." No one was surprised when "the distinguished visitors were enthusiastically cheered."

At quieter times, the Prime Minister was often found swinging gently in a hammock reading Homer on Sunday afternoons. He and his wife stayed at the house so often that many people found it hard to believe that the house did not actually belong to them.† Gladstone claimed to enjoy every minute of his country weekends: even the journey out of London that he occupied by counting every passing bus. But the eagle-eyed Samuel Clemens was not convinced that he truly found the peace and relaxation there that his doctor had prescribed or that his dreams were as peaceful as those that he attributed to those ruminative sheep:

> Was he always really tranquil within, or was he only externally so—for effect? We cannot know: we only know that his rustic bench under his favourite oak has no bark on its arms. Facts like this speak louder than words.

Johnny and Ishbel's friendship with Gladstone took them to the heart of British politics, but it was Rosebery, the Svengali of the Liberal Party, who guided them as they took their first steps into public life: steps that led them to a royal palace and a very curious encounter.

---

* Even the journey from Westminster to Dollis Hill could be fraught. The *Pall Mall Gazette* reported what happened when Gladstone dropped in on a bookshop in the Edgware Road: "His entrance into the shop being observed, in a short time a crowd assembled outside, and when Mr Gladstone attempted to leave the thoroughfare had become blocked, some 3,000 persons being present." He had to be rescued by "a gentleman at hand" who drove him safely to his carriage.

† The "Grand Old Man" became so inextricably linked to the house that, many years later, in the days when London telephone exchanges had names, the one for the area surrounding Dollis Hill was called GLAdstone.

8

A Royal Residence in Edinburgh

When "Granny," famous throughout the kingdom as the "world's oldest sea anemone," finally expired on August 4, 1887, at the grand old age of sixty-six, newspaper editors kept back the news of her passing for two months so as not to cast a pall of gloom over Queen Victoria's Golden Jubilee.

The Scotsman's obituary, when it was finally published, ran to no fewer than 108 lines, although the writer provided only scant details of "Granny's" life story. In any case, everyone knew how she had been found by Sir John Graham Dalyell, an aristocratic naturalist and antiquarian, and some had even braved his pioneering scientific tome, *Rare and Remarkable Animals of Scotland Represented from Living Subjects: with Practical Observations on Their Nature*, to read his own account of his discovery of the remarkable creature:

> I took a specimen of *Actinia mesembryanthemum* in August 1828, at North Berwick, where the species is abundant among the crevices of the rocks, and in the pools remaining still replenished after the recess of the tide. It was originally very fine, though not of the largest size; and I computed from comparison with those bred in my possession, that it must have been at least seven years old.

Some remembered, too, that for many of the years that followed, "Granny" had lived quietly in a jar "made of the very finest, clearest glass, wide at the top, just the same width as at the bottom," beneath the window of Sir

John's study in Great King Street in Edinburgh; that the seawater in which she dwelt was changed every morning by "a person specially employed for the purpose"; and that she had produced hundreds of offspring, even in old age: her record was 240 little anemones on a single night in 1851.

But sitting at the bottom of a glass can be uneventful even for a celebrity cnidarian, and the obituarist clearly struggled to identify many milestones in the "career" of "the leathery-rounded mass, not two inches in height and breadth." After Sir John's death, "Granny" passed through several hands, and her new owners showed her at meetings of scientific societies in Edinburgh and Aberdeen and at the International Fisheries Exhibition in London.* But the only other event of note that her obituarist could unearth was a visit from Johnny and Ishbel Aberdeen.

This almost surreal encounter came about in 1881 when Johnny was appointed Lord High Commissioner of the Church of Scotland. He had already taken his first step into public life a year earlier when he was appointed as Lord Lieutenant of Aberdeenshire, Queen Victoria's representative in the county. This came as no real surprise, since the job was by custom given to the county's largest landowner,† but in an ingratiating

---

* In an age in which international expositions flourished, this was one of the most successful. Held between May and October 1883 in the Royal Horticultural Society's gardens in South Kensington, London, more than two hundred thousand visitors (including Johnny Aberdeen, who was among the dignitaries on the platform at the opening ceremony) crammed into the pavilions in the first week alone. The critic of the *Spectator* complained that "only a superficial view is possible on a first visit to this gigantic Exhibition," which may explain why he made no mention of "Granny" in his decidedly mixed review of some of the thousands of wonders on show: "Lady Brassey's wonderful collection of coral, madrepore, carved shells, feather and shell ornaments, and other objects from the Southern Seas, is surrounded all day long by an admiring crowd. Curiosity, rather than admiration, is aroused by a stand containing articles of use and ornament, cunningly contrived from crab and lobster-shells mounted in silver and gold. These are ingenious, but ugly: knives and forks with handles formed of lobster-claws are objects which every gentleman's dinner-table is better without, so far as comfort is concerned. Equally uncongenial is the notion of a toilet mirror framed in the distended jaw of a shark. Death and the Lady, indeed! The force of eccentricity and bad taste could hardly go farther."

† The appointment of the Queen's representative was by no means automatic. The 3rd Earl of Aberdeen was passed over for the job because his behavior was thought too scandalous, even for an eighteenth-century rake. After marrying the cook at the Strafford Arms near Wakefield in Yorkshire, who had presented him with the finest mutton chops he had ever eaten and then, when he pursued her, forced him to propose at the point of a loaded pistol, he embarked on a life of unbridled licentiousness. Though he is known today in the family as the "Wicked Earl," he was kind to his many mistresses and their numerous offspring and billeted some of them comfortably in the castle at Ellon, far enough from Haddo for discretion but close enough for visiting. But he was fond, too, of his wife Catherine, and does not seem to have regretted being forced into a true shotgun marriage.

letter to Ishbel, their friend Lord Rosebery now proposed that both she and Johnny should move onto the national stage:

> It appears to me that Aberdeen could make a most excellent Lord High Commissioner to the Church of Scotland: not the least of his qualifications being the Lady High Commissioner.

The Lord High Commissioner's main job was to preside over the General Assembly, the annual meeting of the Church's governing body. As Rosebery had expected, his invitation proved irresistible to a couple as devout and sociable as the Aberdeens, although Johnny professed later that they reacted cautiously to their friend's inquiry and only agreed to take the job after discussing "the nature and scope" of the duties they would be expected to perform.

In fact, they knew perfectly well what these were. The post had a long history, dating from the years after 1603 when King James VI of Scotland moved south to assume the throne of England and appointed a number of Lord High Commissioners to protect his interests at home. In return for their loyalty, the King allowed his representatives to enjoy all the trappings of the monarchy, as Johnny explained to readers of the couple's joint autobiography:

> The Lord High Commissioner is the Sovereign's appointed Representative and Deputy. His official prefix is therefore that of the former Kings of Scotland, namely "His Grace" ... Not only is the annual meeting of the Assembly officially opened by him in State, but the proceedings of each day commence only when the Lord High Commissioner takes his seat in the "Throne Gallery," all the members present rising when he enters.[*]

Thus, in May 1881, Ishbel, at the age of only twenty-four, found herself living like the Queen herself as the temporary chatelaine of the Palace of Holyroodhouse, one of the most magnificent edifices in Britain.

---

[*] Only the post of Lord High Commissioner to the Church of Scotland survived the 1707 Act of Union, and even today, he or she is treated with the respect due to the monarch, heralded everywhere by Scotland's Royal Banner and the National Anthem.

There had been a royal residence in Edinburgh since the sixteenth century, but by 1881, the original Tudor palace where Mary, Queen of Scots, had married twice and witnessed the grisly murder of her secretary and alleged lover, David Rizzio, in 1566, had been almost entirely replaced. This far grander building was, for the most part, designed in the late seventeenth century by Sir William Bruce of Kinross, a "gentleman architect," described by the author Daniel Defoe as the "Christopher Wren of North Britain." Bruce's lack of technical knowledge was more than made up for by his ability to find craftsmen he could trust, and no one was more assiduous in cultivating rich and influential clients: in this case King Charles II himself, who became his patron. Though the palace's exterior is said to have been influenced by that of Amsterdam Town Hall, itself an extravagant lowlands version of a classical Roman building, Johnny and Ishbel will have felt at home there, for the rooms inside were decorated, like those at Haddo, in the Adams style.

Rosebery confessed to Johnny that he had an ulterior motive for recommending him for a job that involved not only ceremony but also a great deal of entertaining. Traditionally, the Lord High Commissioner and his lady kept open house during their fortnight in residence, but their guests were always drawn from the same elite group: members of the General Assembly, judges and senior lawyers, and "leading personages in Edinburgh, and some of the adjacent counties."

Rosebery felt that the time had now come to spread the net more widely and that the guest list "should extend beyond the Assembly, and strictly official circles" to include "representative members of the various sections of the community." Johnny and Ishbel, he was sure, would bring the common touch to the most old-fashioned of institutions, and he knew, as her daughter Marjorie* later put it, that "Ishbel could not accept conventions without herself looking in to them and adding any improvements she thought required."

There were plenty to be made, and not just in the arrangements for the entertainment of the delegates. The Church of Scotland had long been riven with bitter arguments about the relationship between church

---

*Marjorie was six months old when Johnny first became Lord High Commissioner, and her brother Doddie was two.

Ishbel aged three, by Eden Upton Eddis, a fashionable London artist whose portraits of children graced many a society lady's boudoir in the mid-nineteenth century. Some of Eddis's other sitters were rather less winsome: he also specialized in portraits of crusty Victorian schoolmasters.

Brook House, Dudley Marjoribanks's flashy mansion on London's Park Lane, in a superior "architect's drawing" by its designer, Thomas Henry Wyatt. Wyatt is forgotten today: partly because he so indulged his clients' whims (Marjoribanks demanded a "French château") that he had no distinctive style of his own; partly because most of the four hundred buildings he designed have been demolished, Brook House among them.

Ishbel commissioned this romantic portrait of herself from James Sant, "Painter in Ordinary" to Queen Victoria, for the library at Haddo in 1879. But she disliked his matching one of a gloomy-looking Johnny with his equally lugubrious dog and banished it to a shadowy spot above the stairs.

Haddo, Johnny's ancestral home in Aberdeenshire: the "horrible house" transformed by Ishbel into one of Scotland's finest stately homes.

The drawing room at Haddo: dark and dowdy when the 4th Earl lived there, between 1801 and 1860 . . .

. . . bright, elegant, light, exuberant, and, as Ishbel put it, "marvellously fresh" after her renovations in the 1880s.

W. E. Gladstone sits on Ishbel's right and the 5th Earl of Rosebery, then Scotland's most influential politician, on her left in Alfred Emslie's *Dinner at Haddo House*, commissioned by Johnny and Ishbel to commemorate the Prime Minister's visit to Haddo in September 1884. Family and friends, including Johnny's sister Lady Harriet Lindsay (on Rosebery's left) and Henry Drummond (framed by the candelabra farther down the table), make up the rest of the party in this iconic Victorian "conversation piece."

Ishbel had no qualms about using her children in her campaigns, but they did not always cooperate willingly: Dudley and Archie had to be rewarded for sitting still in an uncomfortable position on a heap of potatoes while Louisa Starr Canziani painted *Two Little Home Rulers* in 1890. The picture, captioned *Brought up on stirabout* [porridge] *and milk,* was used by their mother's Women's National Health Association to promote healthy living in Ireland.

and state and the right to appoint ministers, and in 1843 around a third of its members had broken away to form the Free Church. But this "Great Disruption" did not calm the storm, and Rosebery was well aware that he was inviting Johnny to preside over a battleground: the Christian soldiers at the General Assembly would be more eager to debate church politics, break into factions, and make personal attacks on their fellow delegates than to parse any fine points of theology. He hoped that the young, enthusiastic, and emollient Aberdeens, with their ecumenical approach to life, would begin to heal old rifts and settle long-running feuds.

Thus, change was in the damp Edinburgh air on Thursday May 19, 1881, although the ceremonial that marked the opening of the General Assembly appeared to be as full of pomp and circumstance as ever. Johnny's day began with a levee,* a stiffly formal reception for men only that had become a centerpiece of Court ritual during the reign of Charles II. Dapper in his Lord Lieutenant's uniform, he sat on a throne and received churchmen, military commanders, provosts, councillors, diplomats, and aristocrats: four hundred members of the Great and the Good of Scotland. Yet the more relaxed atmosphere—the "lengthening of the cords and a straightening of the stakes" that Rosebery had asked the couple to create—was already evident to the *Scotsman*'s reporter:

> With the exception of the municipal bodies, who appeared in their official robes, and were presented according to their respective corporations, the company passed to the Throne Room without regard to rank or precedence, and the ceremony occupied little more than twenty minutes.

But the procession from the palace to the opening service at St. Giles' Cathedral was as stately and flamboyant as it had always been, to the

---

* This was the first of many levees held by Johnny, who again assumed most of the trappings of monarchy when he was Viceroy of Ireland and Governor General of Canada. In Canada, where the ceremony grew out of the tradition of fur trappers paying their respects at the forts of their local government representatives on New Year's Day, levees are still held, although they are now family events and far less formal. The last levee held in Britain took place at St. James's Palace in July 1939. Doddie went to it.

obvious delight of the "vast surging throng" that had gathered to cheer as Johnny's carriage, "resplendent in scarlet hammercloth* and drawn by four splendid horses" passed by:

> The approach of his Grace was heralded by a flourish of trumpets, the guard of honour at the same time presenting arms, the colours being lowered and the band playing a bar of the National Anthem. Simultaneously with the departure from the Palace, at five minutes to twelve o'clock, the guard of honour and band marched up Canongate in order to receive his Grace on arrival at St Giles'.

Although Ishbel was used to life in large and luxurious mansions, Holyroodhouse, with almost three hundred rooms, including fourteen state apartments, was on quite a different scale to Haddo, Guisachan, and Brook House, and now, Johnny realized, she faced a challenge that would have daunted even the most experienced hostess:

> Every member of the Assembly was entitled to be invited, singly, to dinner at the Palace. . . . The invitation cards were placed in a room in the Assembly hall building, where the members for whom they were intended could pick out their cards at convenience. In theory an answer was expected, at any rate in the event of non-acceptance. But, of course, the method was liable to result in some uncertainty as to how many were to be expected.

Johnny, however, had prudently arranged for their own household staff to be imported from London and Aberdeenshire, and Ishbel was relieved when their "excellent house steward," Mr. Cheeseman, "managed admirably, especially when many more came to dinners, etc., than we expected." On May 22, for instance, Cheeseman and his team laid the table

---

* An embroidered cloth, often ornamented with gemstones and a coat of arms, that decorated the coachman's seat. The word's origin is obscure. One authority says the cloth was originally used to conceal the tools coachmen used to repair "broken wheels and shivered panels"; another that "hammer" is a corruption of "hamper" and that it was a cover for a basket containing food for the journey; yet another that the term derives from the flexible, hammock-like seats optimistically designed to protect passengers from the worst of the potholes on the road.

for 111 people, and once that was over, set about organizing an even more elaborate reception in honor of the Queen's birthday the next day.

But the pressure on Ishbel was no less unrelenting. She was just as involved in all the ceremonial as Johnny, and unlike the real monarch, skulking at Balmoral in her widow's weeds, she was determined to put on a show. The press exulted in her eye-catching ensembles:

> The Countess of Aberdeen wore a sage-green velvet dress, with tablier of white corded silk embroidered with garniture of cherries and leaves, the body surmounted with a wreath and bouquet of the same, and a rivière of diamonds with brooch. The necklace was of Oriental pearls set in large diamonds, with earrings *en suite*; and the headdress a tiara of brilliants, surmounted with five large diamond stars, with feather.

Ishbel had supervised the decoration of the palace, which, suitably for such a theatrical and precisely choreographed occasion, had been adorned like the set for a grand opera:

> The entrance corridor was illuminated with small coloured lamps, arranged so as to form a large crown with the letters V.R.; and the principal passages were lined with beautiful palms and green-house plants from the Botanic Garden, while in the Picture Gallery and other apartments were choice collections of cut flowers and plants in flower from Haddo House, and from the nurseries of Messrs. Methven and sons.*

Wherever they went, they were surrounded by a cut-down version of Queen Victoria's court: a retinue that included a purse bearer, a chaplain, aides-de-camp, and ladies-in-waiting. Johnny's equerry was the preposterous social gadfly Augustus Hare, author of ghost stories, guidebooks, and hagiographies of noble ladies, and a shameless plagiarist. Many years earlier, in 1865, he had "made rather friends" with Johnny, who was then

---

* Thomas Methven & Sons of Leith Walk and Princes Street, Edinburgh, held the contract to supply flowers to Holyroodhouse and advertised themselves as "Nurserymen & Seedsmen to the Queen."

only eighteen, while they were staying with Lady Ruthven, one of the aristocratic old ladies Hare made it his business to cultivate:

> I have seldom seen any one I liked as well on short acquaintance. His family are all said to be dreadfully shy, but he seems to be an exception.

But although his lifestyle plainly did not accord with the austere values of the members of the General Assembly, Hare was an inspired choice, vividly, if not always kindly, capturing the atmosphere of the Lord High Commissioner's brief "reign" in his diary* from the moment he arrived late on a Friday night:

> I joined the party [of ninety guests], in the reception rooms, where I entered at once upon my duties, which, for the most part, seem to be to talk right and left to every one I see. Each evening the Synods of the different districts dine, some eighty or a hundred clergymen, and I have generally found from my clerical neighbours that they regard it as their carnival, looked forward to throughout the whole year and giving them much to talk of when they return home.

He loved "the moving diorama of people, with varying lights and shades of character which they display, the old-world aspect of how this should be done, with the pages in their crimson and white liveries, the chaplain and the purse-bearer in their court dresses, and the mounted guard." But the days were long and the strict formalities often irksome:

> It is an interesting life here, but a very fatiguing one—the hours and hours of standing, as for real royalty; the etiquette of always address-ing Aberdeen as 'Your Grace', and getting up when he comes into the

---

* Hare would have been in seventh heaven at Holyroodhouse, for as his obituary in *The Times* put it, "he was much given to society," although the *New York Times* added that "Mr. Hare's ghosts are rather more interesting than his lords or his middle-class people." The pages of his memoirs thud with dropped names, and they were ridiculed by critics who complained that "he gave way to his besetting sin of long-windedness, and dwelt at unmerciful length upon trifles, or upon facts and places familiar already." Many believed that the *Oxford Dictionary of National Biography* had not gone far enough in suggesting that his six-volume autobiography "might have had some chance of permanence if it had been cut down to two."

room; the whirlpool of invitations to be sent, in which one is always being swallowed up.

And keeping up with Johnny and Ishbel's punishing schedule could be a struggle:

> Now we are just off to a luncheon, then to visit the castle in state, then a soldiers' home, a sculptor's studio, an artist's studio, a dinner of a hundred, and the Assembly again in state at 10 P.M.

It was on one of these afternoon tours of the great and the good of Edinburgh that Johnny and Ishbel went to call upon "Granny," the sea anemone, then living at the house of John Sadler of the Botanic Garden.* Along with the rest of the Lord High Commissioner's party, Hare signed her own little visitors' book,† but the oddity of the encounter seems to have been lost on him. He was far more amused to see Johnny, who had made his stint as Lord High Commissioner a family affair, "being followed everywhere by his mother and his aunt . . . two charming old sisters."

But not everything went well for Ishbel. In the eyes of some of the stuffier delegates to the Assembly, she demeaned the office of Lord High Commissioner when she did even more than Rosebery had asked and extended the guest list to "many out-of-the-way and literary people." And eyebrows were raised to the heavens when she took it upon herself to forge links with the breakaway Free Church of Scotland that was holding its own rather fractious assembly down the road. She invited its leading lights to Holyrood in the hope that she could persuade its members to return to the body of the established kirk. And then she went even further by cajoling

---

* Sadler was a good choice as custodian of such a wonder. An enthusiastic collector, he was prepared to risk his life in pursuit of curiosities. At the height of pteridomania, the Victorian craze for exotic ferns, he toppled over a cliff near Moffat in southern Scotland while trying to gather a particularly rare specimen. Sadler survived, unlike William Williams, a guide who took "a lady and a gentleman" up to the summit of Snowdon, the highest mountain in Wales, in 1861. He then, according to the newspapers, "left them in order to gather some ferns . . . when his foot must have slipped, and [he] was precipitated down a declivity of 300 yards, and of course, killed."

† It is still preserved and treasured in the library at the Botanic Garden.

church leaders into allowing "a kind of surreptitious visit by the Lord High Commissioner's wife" to hear a debate at the Free Church's Assembly.

To the surprise of many, Ishbel and Johnny's strategy paid off. Almost forty years on from the "Great Disruption," they had dared to think the unthinkable, and a start was made on mending fences, with the Moderators of the Assemblies agreeing to exchange visits and the Lord High Commissioner officially calling in on the Free Church. An editorial in the *Scotsman* welcomed their efforts:

> If there is no change for the better, the fault will not be with the Lord High Commissioner and with Lady Aberdeen. What winning courtesy, graceful hospitality, wide sympathies, and indefatigable attention to all the duties of the high position could do, have been done.

Success, however, came at a price. The Lord High Commissioner was paid an allowance of £2,000. This was meant to cover his expenses, but Johnny and Ishbel found even this large sum* inadequate to pay for the clergy's "carnival" and had to dip into their own pockets for half as much again. They did try to cut back during Johnny's third year in the job, but because they increased the pay of their servants and pipers, the saving amounted to a mere £25. Gladstone himself had to be brought in to persuade them to return for a fourth year. He wrote suggesting, not very helpfully, that they could reduce the "pecuniary burden" by cutting back on "the free and large current of entertainment," because they had successfully "changed the character" of the Lord High Commissioner's role.

Johnny and Ishbel had never said no to Gladstone, and they immediately caved in, despite the warnings about the state of Johnny's bank balance that were beginning to flow from their accountant's office in Edinburgh.

> I hope and feel sure that you will never have reason to regret this step of yours, so unselfishly taken,

wrote Gladstone's Principal Private Secretary, Sir Edward Hamilton, in reply to Johnny's letter of acceptance. If they did, they never said so, and

---

*About £130,000 ($170,000) in today's money.

were grateful instead that Johnny's fourth term as Lord High Commissioner brought them, in 1884, a friendship that they believed transformed their lives.

Ten years earlier, at one of the meetings held across Britain by the charismatic evangelist Dwight Moody and his associate, the singer Ira Sankey, Johnny had been riveted by the preaching of a young Scot who had joined the Americans on a tour that, at every stop, saw the "sudden conversion" of fervent and excited crowds. On Sundays, admission to their services had to be by ticket only, so great was the crush. People traveled miles to see and hear them, sometimes in the worst of weathers. In Tyneside alone in the autumn of 1873, "nearly 2,000 persons" stepped forward to profess, as one reporter quaintly put it, that they had "got good." Johnny's attendance at one of these extraordinary meetings was not unusual, for, as one onlooker noted, "these audiences were composed of all classes, including, strange to say, many of the most fashionable families."

But there was another charismatic figure on the platform that night. Henry Drummond, the son of a prosperous seed merchant from Stirling, was only in his twenties, but he was already a legendary figure in church circles. Moody recruited him not only to speak at his meetings, but also to follow up his work among young people when the evangelical circus had left town. Drummond was a clever choice. His biographer noted his "boundless energy," and many agreed that "he thrilled his audiences with the remarkable *timbre* and soft cadences of his voice." Moody was struck by his natural goodness:

> Some men take an occasional journey into the thirteenth of 1st Corinthians, but Henry Drummond was a man who lived these constantly, appropriating its blessings and exemplifying its teachings.

Others said—and they meant it as a compliment—that he was "utterly unconventional in everything that he did." To the frustration of many churchmen, he rejoiced in his independence, firmly resisting their countless attempts to persuade him to become a parish minister, dismissing ordination as "a mere matter of worldly position." In any case, his interests ranged beyond the theological. He studied geology and, like others at the time, was fascinated by science and its darker fringes. He taught at the Free

Church College in Glasgow, where a chair in Natural Science was created especially for him. His thoughts on the relationship between science and religion and on less orthodox subjects like hypnotism were eagerly sought after, and he traveled widely in Africa, Europe, and North America.

Ishbel, too, had been alerted to Drummond's growing reputation, by her uncle Quintin Hogg, but although both she and Johnny had admired him from afar, the three of them did not meet until Drummond was persuaded to take up an invitation to dine with Johnny and Ishbel at Holyrood. By then, as the author of *Natural Law in the Spiritual World*, he was famous beyond the meeting halls in which he held his audiences in thrall. This bestselling book neatly linked his preoccupations, opening with the questions that he hoped to try to answer in the pages that followed:

> Is there not reason to believe that many of the Laws of the Spiritual World, hitherto regarded as occupying an entirely separate province, are simply the Laws of the Natural World? Can we identify the Natural Laws, or any one of them, in the Spiritual sphere? That vague lines everywhere run through the Spiritual World is already beginning to be recognized. Is it possible to link them with those great lines running through the visible universe which we call the Natural Laws, or are they fundamentally distinct? In a word, is the Supernatural natural or unnatural?

Drummond was a member of the Free Church, and Ishbel was keen to recruit this glamorous celebrity author to her mission to mend the schism between the warring assemblies:

> I therefore wrote a personal letter to him, saying how we desired to join with others in thanking him for the inspiring message of his book, and asking if he would come and dine with us one evening.

But, according to Ishbel, when the letter landed on the doorstep of the Drummond family's home in Stirling,

> Henry showed his father the invitation with some amusement, saying, 'Fancy *my* being asked to dinner by a Lord High Commissioner!'
> 'Well,' said his father, 'of course you are going to accept.' 'Indeed I

am not,' answered Henry; 'what have I to do with Court life at Holy-rood?' 'But indeed you *are* going,' rejoined his father, 'this invitation is a compliment to you as a Free Church man, and it is your duty to go.'

So it came about that on a certain evening in May 1884, when we were receiving our guests, 'Mr. Henry Drummond' was announced, and instead of the mature, bearded professor whom we expected, there stepped up to us a handsome young man of distinguished bearing, and intellectual aspect, and a glint of humour in his keen brown eyes. On his side he was surprised to find his host and hostess his contemporaries in age instead of the ancient dignitaries he expected.

Johnny and Ishbel were not alone in succumbing to what one historian has described as Drummond's "peculiar power."[*] Another wrote:

For Ishbel and many others, Drummond's creed[†] ultimately revitalized religious faith, justified activism, armoured them against critics, and helped them cope with illness, death and disappointment. Such benefits were far from inconsequential.

Drummond's career became another cause for Ishbel to promote. Her first step was to introduce him to London society by persuading the Duke of Westminster to lend her his huge ballroom at Grosvenor House for a series of meetings at which Drummond would preach. She and Johnny may have regretted their decision to keep the "distribution of tickets in our own hands," for their "house was simply besieged for tickets, and many had to be refused."

---

[*] Drummond's influence on Ishbel lasted long after his death in 1897. She presented my father-in-law, David Gordon, with a copy of Drummond's *Baxter's Second Innings*, an evangelical allegory disguised as a ripping yarn for children, for his fourteenth birthday in 1922.

[†] Not everyone was dazzled. In 1897, Ernest Newman, a stalwart of the National Secular Society, pulled no punches in his denunciation of Drummond's philosophy in his book *Pseudo-philosophy at the End of the Nineteenth Century*: "He has simply taken the oldest and crudest arguments of the professional theologian, and by a little manipulation of them, and a little infusion of the jargon of second-hand science and philosophy, has fitted them into the frame of evolution. His facts are just the facts every one has known for years past; his interpretation of them is either hopelessly fallacious or altogether grotesque; and his philosophy is the sentimental rhetoric of the street-preacher. As one of his critics remarked, whatever is true in the book is not new, and whatever is new in it is not true. Let us then leave him in peace, and devote ourselves to the consideration of a more intelligent man."

Friends like the Duke of Argyll and Johnny's best man, Arthur Balfour, were, of course, admitted to the glittering congregation, along with some of the greatest thinkers of the Victorian age. They included Frederic Harrison, the historian, jurist, and advocate of "positivism"; "Darwin's Bulldog," the biologist Thomas Henry Huxley; and Matthew Arnold, the poet and scholar.

The ballroom was crammed: almost five hundred people had managed to wangle a coveted ticket and Drummond held them spellbound. "One only had to watch the faces to see the interest aroused," wrote Ishbel, but then she had long since been smitten. She had wasted no time in taking Drummond under her wing after their first meeting at Holyroodhouse:

> He joined our immediate house party that evening, lunched with us next day, accompanied us soon after on a boating trip on the Thames, came to stay at Haddo in the autumn and thenceforth became the closest of our friends and comrades, the playmate and boon companion of our children.

She sang his praises at every opportunity:

> Henry Drummond's power as a speaker was of a very exceptional character, and was essentially of the Spirit. Of course, the personal charm of the man, and his clear, musical voice predisposed an audience to listen, but there was always an originality of ideas, clothed in exquisitely chosen words, with a latent pathos and humour, and charged with a simple intensity which made all feel that this man was speaking of that of which he had personal and irrefutable knowledge.

Drummond, in his turn, according to one of his biographers, averred that this "lasting friendship was one of the great joys of [his] life." With his droopy mustache and piercing eyes, he cut a striking figure in the salons of Mayfair; his dandified appearance contrasting intriguingly with his grave demeanor. Soon tongues were wagging. What, the gossips wondered, was going on between the charismatic young preacher and the apparently pious Countess?

Historians disagree: one has asserted, on the flimsiest of evidence, that they were lovers and that Drummond was the father of Ishbel's youngest son, Archie; another cites Drummond's own description of his mind as "celibate"; yet another says "he was thought to be indifferent to women." Even the family was puzzled. One of Ishbel's grandsons wrote:

> He became such an overpoweringly close friend that one wonders, with his somewhat untouchable beauty, what were her real feelings towards him.

But this does not mean, of course, that Ishbel and Drummond really were lovers as the society gossips alleged. The whispering campaign that had begun with the rumors that the Aberdeens were too familiar with their servants gathered new momentum from what was certainly an unusually intense friendship, and inevitably some of the accusations stuck.

Unwittingly, Marjorie fueled prurient speculation about an affair. Although copies of Drummond's many playful and affectionate letters to Ishbel can still be found among the family papers, Ishbel's side of the correspondence and her diaries covering that period of her life have disappeared. Just as Princess Beatrice bowdlerized Queen Victoria's diaries to exclude her most private thoughts, acts, and opinions, so Marjorie, ever the devoted daughter and keen to protect her mother's privacy and reputation, seems to have destroyed all the evidence of what was undoubtedly, on Ishbel's part, a tendresse. And when Ishbel did venture an oblique comment on the relationship by quoting from one of the "lost" diaries, she simply encouraged the gossips:

> Our first great friendship with a contemporary was with Henry Drummond, and in more recent years too, some of our men friends have become real comrades and have taught me more about 'the joy of living' than ever I knew in my youth. I do not suppose that any woman can have enjoyed the satisfaction of such friendships more fully than I have, and though to some they may seem dangerous they are worth it: I am sorry for those who have no such opportunities. A. has rejoiced so much in this that for me all has been plain sailing. Of course, I owe it to the blessed lack of jealousy in his composition, and I believe that he too has reaped benefit from his generosity.

More thoughtful observers believed something other than sexual attraction or even normal friendship lay behind Ishbel's devotion to Drummond, which was shared by Johnny. He had come into their lives at an acutely painful moment: when they were mourning the death of their baby daughter Dorothea. His message of Christian love would have brought the distressed and deeply religious couple much-needed comfort and consolation: to them, he was what the psalmist called a "refuge and strength, a very present help in trouble."

Whatever the truth about his friendship with Ishbel, Drummond became a constant presence in the Aberdeens' life. He joined them on their travels and they kept a special room for him in their houses. The family's photograph albums contain pictures of him lounging next to Ishbel in the gardens of Haddo and Dollis Hill. And he appears, appropriately, perhaps, in the shadows, in a painting of an event that confirmed how securely, by the autumn of 1884, Johnny and Ishbel had established themselves at the heart of British political life.

In *Dinner at Haddo House 1884,*[*] the now virtually forgotten Victorian artist Alfred Emslie[†] has captured the last moments of a grand party in the dining room at Haddo—just before the ladies leave the room and the gentlemen turn to serious talk and the liqueurs. The guests are in full evening dress: white tie for the men, sleek, slinky gowns and the biggest and brightest of the family jewels for the women. Everywhere on the table, silver gleams: candelabra, finely fretted dishes piled with grapes, and wine pails by the Georgian master craftsman and silversmith to the royal families of Europe Philip Rundell. A piper, resplendent in kilt and

---

[*] The original title of the picture, which is now in the collection of the National Portrait Gallery in London, was *Dinner at the Earl of Aberdeen's*.

[†] Alfred Edward Emslie (1848–1918) was the son of an engraver from Croydon, Surrey. Van Gogh admired and collected his pictures, including a dramatic scene of rescuers at a colliery explosion in 1882. But Emslie's ambition was to paint High Society portraits. He achieved this after becoming a protégé of the rich industrialist Sir William Mather, one of the couple's coterie of Liberal Party politicians and social reformers, who commissioned him to paint Ishbel. According to family legend, Emslie originally went to Haddo to paint a portrait of Johnny, but someone suggested he should also record the 1884 dinner for posterity. At once, Emslie stepped forward, pencil, brush, and oils at the ready, but there was a problem. "Alas," he said, "I don't have a spare canvas." Whereupon, he was told to take one off the wall. History does not relate who had originally painted it: perhaps it was by one of the Old Masters like Titian or Annibale Carracci whose work the 4th Earl had bought in the early nineteenth century.

bonnet, is playing.* In the foreground, at the head of a long table lined with politicians, local dignitaries, and members of the family, sits Ishbel, with the Prime Minister, Mr. Gladstone, on her right, and on her left Lord Rosebery.

Hoping to repeat the success of his barnstorming Midlothian campaign, Gladstone had decided to make a progress through Aberdeenshire to hear the vox populi about a law, fiercely opposed by the House of Lords, that would, for the first time, allow men who did not live in towns to vote if they owned land worth more than £10 or paid an annual rent of the same amount. Queen Victoria was decidedly unamused, grumbling to her Private Secretary, from nearby Balmoral:

> The Queen is *utterly* disgusted with his *stump* oratory so unworthy of his position—almost under her very nose.

By now, the Grand Old Man was seventy-four: breaking his journey at Haddo was a chance to rest and regain his strength after long days of delivering speeches on station platforms and receiving loyal addresses. But his schedule for September 15 would have been demanding even for a much younger man. He and his wife had stayed the night at Mar Lodge, in the farthest southwest of the county, and, after lunch at Birkhall† with

---

* Andrew Cant was Johnny's personal piper and a legend throughout Scotland. Many years later, when he was working for another laird, Sir Charles Forbes, the elder brother of the novelist Henry Rider Haggard came across him. Cant was now a gamekeeper, but his fame as a piper lived on. "There was nothing he could not play," wrote Haggard. "Indeed, it is of Andrew that the celebrated 'Lord's Prayer' story was first, and truly told. There having been some festivities among the gillies and tenantry overnight, Andrew, forgetting the day of the week, started off very early one Sunday morning marching round and round the castle blowing away as though his bellows would burst. Suddenly up goes a window and out comes a head. 'Confound you, Andrew, do you know this day, man—is that the Lord's Prayer you are playing?' 'No, Sir Charles,' replied the imperturbable piper, 'but if you can whistle it, I'll play it.'"

† Birkhall, now a much-extended eighteenth-century house near Balmoral, has been used as a Scottish residence and holiday home by members of the Royal Family since Prince Albert acquired it in 1849. Queen Victoria gave it to her son the Prince of Wales, later Edward VII, but, since he preferred to stay at Abergeldie Castle, she bought it back in the year of Gladstone's visit. In the twentieth century, the Duke and Duchess of York, later King George VI and Queen Elizabeth, spent summer holidays there with Princesses Elizabeth and Margaret. After the death of Queen Elizabeth, the Queen Mother, who loved her "little, big house," it passed to Prince Charles.

the Duke and Duchess of Edinburgh,* they had continued their progress by coach and then train to Oldmeldrum, the nearest station to Haddo.

The Gladstones reached the house in the early evening, escorted by a cavalcade of Johnny's tenants. There, on the front lawn, according to one reporter, they found "an immense assemblage of 3000 to 4000 people" who watched as the Prime Minister, accompanied by Johnny, climbed the steps to the balcony to be greeted by Ishbel. The children, Doddie, Dudley, and Marjorie, all neatly squeezed into their best bibs and tuckers by their nurse, had been waiting, too, along with Storm the dog and two tenants who had been chosen to deliver an address of welcome.

> We are proud indeed, Sir, to see our worthy proprietor the Earl of Aberdeen have this day as his guest the trusted colleague and friend of his grandfather,

they said. Gladstone, remembering his manners rather than the instruction to rest, could not resist making a long speech, mixing reminiscences of an earlier visit to the 4th Earl in 1836 with his political message about voting reform. And then with the cheers ringing in his ears and his campaigning temporarily done, he was conducted inside to the library for tea.

Later that evening, Ishbel gave the first of two large dinner parties. She made sure that the guest list reflected the interests of the guest of honor by inviting academics, churchmen, politicians, social reformers like Sir Kenneth Mackenzie of Gairloch, admired for taking "an active part in every movement to promote the social welfare of his fellow countrymen," entrepreneurs like James White, the fabulously rich proprietor of Balruddery near Dundee, the first large house in Scotland to have electric light,† and landowners including Ronald Munro Ferguson of Novar, who had

---

* The Duke of Edinburgh was Prince Alfred, second son of Queen Victoria, known as the Duke of Saxe-Coburg and Gotha from 1893, when, through his descent from Prince Albert, he became ruler of the eponymous duchy of the German Empire. The Duchess of Edinburgh, Maria Alexandrovna, was the daughter of Tsar Alexander II of Russia, and is best remembered for giving her name to the Marie or Maria biscuit: first baked by Peek Freans' bakery in London in 1874 to celebrate the couple's wedding.

† Haddo did not get electric light for another sixty years. Doddie, Johnny and Ishbel's eldest son, had refused to install such a newfangled invention while he lived there, and it was left to his nephew David to replace the gas lamps in 1946.

inherited his estate thanks to an unhappy chapter of accidents suffered by his ancestors in the service of the British Empire: one was mauled by a tiger, another dispatched by a shark.

Some guests had been imported to enliven the party: not least Lord Young, a judge known for being "humorous and very Scotch," and seventeen-year-old Rachel Gurney, a noted beauty who "played the harp divinely" and later married, amidst "a great deal of feeling of jealousy and envy," the most eligible of bachelors, the young, rich, and dashing Earl of Dudley. In contrast, Victor Alexander Bruce, 9th Earl of Elgin, was, according to his biographer, "notoriously silent," and "disdained equally smartness (whether social or sartorial), [and] conspicuous consumption." He earned his place at the table because he was chairman of the Scottish Liberal Association and much admired by Rosebery.

And there were two outsiders. In the published guest lists one was mysteriously, and confusingly, simply named "Mr. Anderson." In 1884, as today, many people of that name lived in the North East of Scotland, but this "Mr. Anderson" may well have had an interest in keeping his true identity quiet. His first name was Robert and he was born in Dublin in 1841. Three months before Gladstone's visit, he had lost his job "as adviser in matters relating to political crime at the Home Office," cover for his real role as a secret serviceman, with a mission to track down Fenians, the militant Irish republicans. A few years later, the now Sir Robert Anderson would earn his place in history as the Assistant Commissioner of the Metropolitan Police in charge of the hunt for Jack the Ripper. A useful man, then, for the Prime Minister to have at his side on a meet-the-people-tour, but he was also, oddly, something of a theologian, and would certainly have been able to hold his own with the clergymen round the Haddo dinner table.

The other outsider was also keeping a watchful eye. George Washburn Smalley was the London correspondent of the *New York Tribune*. He had made his name in the United States with a dramatic report on the Battle of Antietam in the Civil War in 1862. His ride through the night from a scene of dreadful carnage to a telegraph office in Frederick, Maryland, was the stuff of legend and his prose that day was of the deepest purple. To get his scoop, Smalley had wormed his way onto General "Fighting Joe" Hooker's staff, and later, when posted to London, he seems to have used similar techniques to ingratiate himself with the owners of all the best houses, such as "Lord Salisbury's London palace with hall and galleries and great apartments, brilliant with stuff" and Lady Rothschild's mansion "with its matchless Gainsboroughs and lovely Murillos."

Smalley's description of his trip to Haddo also verges on the saccharine, but he does vividly evoke the curious mixture of politics, philanthropy, populism, piety, and eccentricity that marked even the informal moments of Gladstone's progress. At the opening of an orphanage in Methlick, Smalley was impressed by the lack of ceremony:

> Mr. Gladstone and his party walked through the rooms, beautifully clean and well arranged. The Hon. and Rev. Edward Glyn . . . began with a prayer in the little room on the right of the entrance. Down went Mr. Gladstone on his knees in the middle of the room on the bare floor.

And when, before leaving for Brechin the next morning, Gladstone planted a tree, Smalley's practiced pen conjured up the scene with just a few vivid details:

> A group of people had collected; guests, laborers and others. The day was hot, the sun blazing. Mr. Gladstone took off his soft gray felt hat. . . . plying his spade with an energy at which the professionals looked amazed.

A few weeks later, someone—no doubt an opponent of the Liberals—lopped the top off the tree. Another one had to be planted. Though Smalley missed this part of the story, the tree planting and its sorry aftermath certainly impressed themselves on Marjorie, who was almost four: these, she used to say, were her earliest memories.

It is hardly surprising that Johnny and Ishbel were keen to commission a souvenir* of such a milestone in the history of Haddo, and in *Dinner at Haddo House 1884*, Alfred Emslie has brilliantly captured the Victorian

---

*They took many of their pictures with them on their travels, for the walls of their various homes, but not *Dinner*, which they lent to an exhibition soon after it was painted and then forgot about. It was lost until 1927, when it turned up, still in the art gallery's packaging, in the attics at Haddo.

"establishment" at play. The guests round the table are rich, important, aristocratic: glamorous people. The surroundings are luxurious and elaborately decorated: this is a place dedicated to pleasure and the finest things in life. But the picture is a confection. Perhaps because it was painted some five years after the event, Emslie has exercised his artistic license to the utmost: half the guests are missing, and Ishbel boasts a svelte figure, although, in reality, she was days away from giving birth to Archie.

On that autumn night in 1884, Ishbel, her gaze fixed adoringly on Mr. Gladstone, and Johnny, quietly listening to the happy chatter at the other end of the table, seem not to have a care in the world. But they and their accountant, Mr. Jamieson, knew otherwise, as did keen-eyed readers of the newspapers. For a few months earlier, on April 22, 1884, *The Times* had published a long advertisement for the public sale of Johnny's Cromar estate. Despite the high "upset price," or reserve, of £145,000,* the offer was beguiling: more than ten thousand acres, half of them "choice arable land"; the village of Tarland, "where there are two churches, a postal and telegraph office, and two hotels"; "dry and healthy sheep pasture, and first-rate cattle grazing"; "excellent shootings" and "industrious" tenants who paid their rents "with the utmost punctuality."

But when, on July 2, the auctioneer from Dowell's Salerooms in Edinburgh invited bids, there was silence. Until they found a buyer or until, somewhere in Cromar's rolling acres, Mr. Jamieson chanced upon a cash cow that would restore their ebbing fortunes, Johnny and Ishbel would have to keep up appearances, as they had done so triumphantly during Gladstone's visit to Haddo.

Four years passed before Johnny got round to speaking about the debacle to the people most affected, the farmers of the Howe of Cromar. He chose a dinner on the night before the annual agricultural show in Tarland to explain his reasons, and the local press, long starved of information, seized upon this mea culpa.

He realized, Johnny said, that, he was *"aiblins nae sae pop'lar* ["perhaps not so popular"] in the parish as might be desired," but in putting the estate on the market, he "had always had the interests of his tenants in mind." He had been, he confessed, an absentee landlord, preoccupied

---

* More than £11,000,000 ($14,000,000) today.

with his responsibilities at Haddo and in Parliament, and so had hoped "that the estate might pass into the hands of a proprietor of means, and one who would be in a position to take a practical and beneficial interest in his property." He added that he would never allow the estate "to pass into the hands of a rack-renting proprietor, and he desired still more that the proprietor should not be an absentee proprietor."

When that plan came to nothing, he had tried an experiment in "peasant proprietorship," offering to sell the land to the tenants themselves. But this, too, had failed due to the "unfortunate depression of the times and the consequent absence of capital and means among the majority of the farmers." Nonetheless, "he felt himself obliged to adhere to the steps which had already been taken with reference to putting up the estate for sale."

That these were the words of a man with a guilty conscience would not have been lost upon the worried men gathered that night in the smoky dining room of Mr. Skene's Hotel. Johnny's speech, which contained no hint of his financial predicament, was evasive, but at least his excuse that he had become an absentee landlord, though thin when he first put the estate on the market, was now justifiable, thanks to an extraordinary and unexpected turn of events in the first weeks of 1886.

9

A Castle in Dublin City and
a Lodge in Phoenix Park

On February 5, 1886, Ishbel escaped from the thick smog enveloping London to spend the day with her friend Lady Rosebery at Mentmore Towers. While she was there, a telegram arrived from Johnny summoning her home: he had, he said, "something to mention."

When she stepped off the train at Euston Station, she found Johnny waiting for her on the platform. Both were tense: Ishbel because of the urgency of his puzzling message; Johnny because he had news that he knew she would not welcome.

That morning, he told her, Gladstone, who had just become Prime Minister for the third time, had sent him a note, asking to see him urgently:

> As soon as I arrived, Mr Gladstone, without preface, said, 'I want you to go to Ireland as Lord-Lieutenant.'*
>
> For a moment I remained silent; and he then said, 'A pretty large order, eh?'
>
> 'Yes,' I replied, 'and I would like to have a little time to consider it; and especially to consult Lady Aberdeen.'
>
> Mr. G.: 'Where is she?'

---

* This was the official title of the Governor, or Viceroy, of Ireland between the end of the seventeenth century and 1922, when the post was abolished with the creation of the Irish Free State.

Lord A.: 'At Mentmore for the day.'

Mr G.: 'Ah; but that won't do: I must really ask for your reply at once.'

Lord A: 'Very well; I accept; and I'll tell you, sir, why I do so with confidence; it is because of the help I shall get from Lady Aberdeen.'

As Johnny had predicted, Ishbel "was taken aback, as I had been." And so was everyone else. Ireland had long been a political hot potato, and the campaigns for land reform and Home Rule increasingly challenged the authority of the British Crown and its representative, the Lord Lieutenant. At Westminster, the Irish Parliamentary Party, which called for self-government for Ireland within the United Kingdom, was gaining in influence under its leader, the charismatic Charles Stewart Parnell, and outside, the Irish Republican Brotherhood had been trying to foment rebellion.

Yet for this most testing of roles and with no clear solution to the Home Rule problem in sight, Gladstone had chosen a thirty-eight-year-old with no diplomatic experience, whose career at Westminster had largely consisted of membership in a handful of commissions of inquiry. The reaction of the London *Times*, more accustomed to chronicling the far more illustrious political career of Johnny's grandfather the 4th Earl, was typical:

His name is familiar to all who remember the Coalition Cabinet of which the late earl was the head, but his own part in politics has been little, if at all, distinguishable in the ranks of Liberal peers.

Gladstone's first choice, Lord Northbrook, a former Viceroy of India and thus a far more seasoned diplomat, had turned down the job: partly because he had qualms about Home Rule, something he regarded as a "dangerous" political experiment, but principally because the new Lord Lieutenant would not be a member of the cabinet.* Nonetheless, the Prime Minister insisted, Johnny would be playing a vital role in bringing

---

* Northbrook sulked for years, and as his career went into decline, he denounced Gladstone, describing him as "the most eloquent and, I am afraid, the most conscientiously unscrupulous leader . . . in the history of English politics" and the man responsible "more than any other" for the unrest in Ireland.

about a new order in Ireland. "You will look after administration; we will deal with policy at home," he said.

Johnny soon realized that he would be walking a tightrope: the Lord Lieutenant was a member of the government, and yet, at the same time, like the Queen he represented, he had to be seen to be impartial and above politics. The correspondent of *The Times* wondered whether Johnny would find his toothless and almost entirely ceremonial role frustrating, and whether he would be content to take "little more than a formal part in political affairs." The true power now lay in the hands of the man actually responsible for governing the country, the Chief Secretary for Ireland, John Morley; and since he, unlike Johnny, was a minister with a seat in the cabinet, he had, perforce, the Prime Minister's ear.

When the news of Gladstone's appointments reached Queen Victoria at Osborne House, her residence on the Isle of Wight, the 5th Earl Spencer, a former Lord Lieutenant,* happened to be there. Neither he nor the Queen, who afterwards recorded their conversation in her journal, minced their words:

> I said I thought the new Govt. must be very explicit as to their inten-
> tions & that they must be very careful in what they did,—that I con-
> sidered Ld. Aberdeen, who had been appointed Ld. Lieut of Ireland,
> a very weak man, which Ld. Spencer answered was better, as then all
> could be left in the hands of Mr Morley.

Johnny and Morley made an odd couple. While Johnny enjoyed addressing the practicalities of preventing accidents on the railways or saving lives at sea, Morley was an intellectual, a friend of philosophers, writers, and aesthetes like John Stuart Mill, George Meredith, and Dante Gabriel Rossetti. In sharp contrast to the affable aristocrat, who prided himself on his skills as a joke-teller, Morley had spent many years editing the *Fortnightly Review*, a magazine described by the novelist Anthony Trollope as "the most serious, the most earnest, the least devoted to amusement, the

---

*According to a biographer, Spencer's two stints as Lord Lieutenant had proved, as Johnny was soon to discover, "a severe financial drain." His Althorp estate, like Johnny's at Haddo and Cromar, had been hit by the Agricultural Depression, and "by late 1885 Spencer calculated that his net income was 40 per cent less than it had been ten years previously."

least jocose" of the Victorian age. Morley was fastidious in his habits and would not pick up his pen until he had put on a clean shirt and made sure that his desk was perfectly tidy. And while Johnny had far more difficulty holding on to his money than acquiring it, Morley's health had suffered from the long hours that he had to put in at his desk to earn a living. Johnny had had to make no effort to enter politics—once he had proved his claim to the earldom, he had simply assumed his seat in the House of Lords— but it took many years before, as a fellow-journalist put it, Morley's "indefatigable industry and seriousness brought him into the grand circle of Victorian Liberals."

And then there was Morley's marriage, about which there was much speculation in political and high society circles. He never spoke of it. Perhaps because she had given birth to two children before she met her husband, the mysterious Mrs. Morley never attended public events or even the dinner parties at which Home Rule was discussed. According to Lord Rosebery in an unpublished memoir found among his papers after his death, this "slight cloud on her" prevented Morley from becoming Foreign Secretary. It would have been "an impossible appointment, partly because his wife could not have received ambassadors' wives." But the thing that both men had in common was an unswerving commitment to Home Rule and to Gladstone's bold and risky campaign to persuade Parliament to pass, at long last, the bill that would bring it about.

While Johnny and Morley went off to Ireland to be sworn in, Ishbel, who had been rather more than "taken aback" by Johnny's revelation on the platform at Euston, let her true feelings run free in an angry letter to Henry Drummond:

> Don't you think that I ought to be very much offended at not being consulted. I who have registered a solemn vow never to set foot in Ireland?

Ishbel had made that vow in the aftermath of the grisly assassination of Lord Frederick Cavendish, the husband of Lucy, her friend and mentor, less than four years before. The brutal crime had been committed by members of the Irish National Invincibles, a splinter group of the Irish Republican Brotherhood dedicated to assassinating British government officials, known to them as "Castle rats." The memory of the atrocity was all too fresh, although, she claimed, "we are not dwelling on the danger—we do not think of it." But behind Ishbel's bravado lay a grim truth: security would be tight, perhaps suffocatingly so. Lord Spencer had had to be protected by a force of eight hussars, eight mounted police, two detectives, and two police constables whenever he ventured beyond the confines of his homes at Dublin Castle and the Viceregal Lodge. Would she, Johnny, and their four small children have to live that way too?

And she had discovered that there was something else that would constrict their freedom: the rigid etiquette that pervaded every aspect of the life of the Lord Lieutenant's court. Ishbel had rebelled against such "flummery" all her life, but Lady Spencer, who lost no time in offering her the benefit of her own experience, was aghast when she announced that she was looking forward to exploring the city on her own:

My dear Lady Aberdeen, you don't know what you are talking about. You must *never* take a walk in Dublin except in the Pound—the enclosure behind the Castle; you must not take a drive without an aide-de-camp; you must not go to a shop without telling them, so that they can put down the red cloth.

This provoked another outburst in her letter to Drummond:

It is giving up all of one's liberty to be like State prisoners and how we shall ever be able to endure months of this, I know not. All seems dark ahead and I just feel overwhelmed. Perhaps it is partly because of the perpetual gloomy yellow fog, and the poor mobs of unemployed rioters,* and my having been maddened with neuralgia. . . . Certainly the idea of our going there had never occurred to us and

---

* The riots, described by the *Illustrated London News* as "a deplorable outbreak of silly and mischievous mob violence, attended with wanton destruction of property in some of the most fashionable streets of the West-End," were sparked by "the exciting and provocatory speeches of certain fanatical orators" at "an open-air meeting of the unemployed and distressed men of the labouring classes, improperly convened in Trafalgar-square." The rioters had come very close to Ishbel's home, rampaging through Grosvenor Square "throwing at the windows of several large private houses as they passed."

it was the very last post one would have chosen. So that one feels it all the more a direct call which one can only obey blindly, plunging into the unknown.

And then there were sensitivities peculiar to the place and time to learn about. Ishbel did so the hard way. Marjorie, who was five, later remembered how they even percolated down to the nursery:

> For her children to wear on their arrival in the Emerald isle, Ishbel ordered velvet coats in the national colour. Some advisor got wind of this and cried, 'Quite impossible!' So the green coats were sent to be dyed blue, and cream poplin ones hurriedly put in hand. They were finished only just in time for the State Entry on February 20th.

By then, after hours of interviews and much fending off of friends from the landed gentry eager to secure prestigious sinecures for their second sons, Johnny had put together his household: a private secretary, a state steward, a comptroller, a chamberlain, a gentleman usher, two aides-de-camp, five extra aides-de-camp, a librarian, a master of the horse, a dean of the Chapel Royal, and a medical team consisting of a surgeon-in-ordinary, a surgeon to the household, a dentist-in-ordinary, a surgeon dentist, and a surgeon oculist. Henry Drummond, whom both Ishbel and Gladstone had been urging to seek a position in public life, airily turned down the offer of an official post, declaring that he wanted no such distractions from his "real work and mission in life."

Meanwhile, the Irish newspapers had been diligently gathering every scrap of information about Johnny and Ishbel that they could find. Though the nationalist *Freeman's Journal* asserted confidently that the Irish viceroyalty "stands out pre-eminently among the doomed institutions of the country," and that Johnny was "fated to be the last who in quasi-state shall represent the royalty of Great Britain in Dublin Castle," it did concede that his stints as Lord High Commissioner to the General Assembly had been "distinguished by a broadly general and liberal spirit far in advance of that of any of his predecessors in the same office." In a barely concealed swipe at his own country's reviled landowners, the writer praised "the policy of the Earl of Aberdeen as a Scotch landlord." Johnny had set an example to others with his generosity to his tenant farmers as they struggled to survive in the hardest of times:

> Very early in the depression Lord Aberdeen invited his tenants to a conference on the subject of the agricultural situation and the possible remedies; and he followed that up by an act of munificence scarcely equalled by any landlord great or small in any part of the United Kingdom, viz, the remission not of a percentage of the rentals due, but of the whole half year's rental on the estates.

Ishbel, too, was praised for her efforts to improve the lives of agricultural laborers, a "useful class" that had been "badly neglected":

> Their debased moral and social condition has been the theme of frequent consideration and discussion amongst the ministers of different denominations and others, but no useful practical steps were taken until the Earl and Countess of Aberdeen took the matter in hand by the establishment of winter evening classes for young male servants on the Haddo House estates, and a Young Women's Improvement Association for the females, of which the Countess of Aberdeen is both founder and president.

By February 19, everyone was ready. Johnny's last task in London was to take his formal farewell of Gladstone: they talked for almost two hours. Then he hurried to Euston Station, where he had broken the news of his appointment to Ishbel exactly two weeks before. And it was here, as they stepped into the ornate saloon carriages hitched onto the workaday Irish mail train, that he and Ishbel assumed the mantle of royalty.

The next morning, even before he had disembarked from their chartered steamer at Kingstown,* Johnny was reminded of the fractious and often hostile political climate in which he would have to govern. At the

---

* The town, originally called Dunleary but renamed in honor of a visit by King George IV in 1821, is now called Dún Laoghaire.

Town Hall, the *Freeman's Journal* gleefully reported, tempers were running high as the commissioners argued over the wording of an address of welcome—or even whether one should be presented to the new Lord Lieutenant at all. Only after countless points of order, about whether enough notice had been given for the meeting, did they get down to business:

> Mr North proposed, and Mr Burke seconded—That an address be presented. Mr Begg moved as an amendment—That the consideration of the question of presenting an address to the Lord Lieutenant be postponed until the intentions of the Government regarding Ireland are definitely known, inasmuch as no Viceroy is entitled to an address unless [he is] a member of a Government prepared to concede the just demand of the Irish people for Legislative Independence.

Mr. Begg was soundly defeated, but the argument about what the address would say was so long-drawn-out that the viceregal train steamed off without it.

In Dublin itself, crowds lined the route to the Castle, but perhaps because there had been so many comings and goings of Lord Lieutenants in recent months (Earl Spencer had been briefly and unhappily succeeded by the Earl of Carnarvon), the press reported that the couple's welcome was "cordial, if not enthusiastic." Amidst the intimidating display of pomp and power, many noted the appearance of the children, excitedly waving and blowing kisses as they rode with Ishbel in the state barouche, and wondered whether this heralded a softer, less "coercive" viceroyalty that really would help to fulfill Gladstone's promise of Home Rule. For Johnny, too, the sight of the children's moment in the bright spring sunshine was the highlight of an unforgettable day:

> We always attributed much of the subsequent kindly feeling shown to us by the Dublin public to the impression created on the first day by the little folks' spontaneous delight in the gay show, which they evidently thought was organised for their special benefit.

Ishbel now found herself mistress of two more houses: Dublin Castle, where they lived in the social season, and the Viceregal Lodge, their home for the rest of the year.*

A local guidebook was lukewarm about the Lodge, which it described as a "large but rather plain and unpretentious edifice," but it was enthusiastic about its setting, Phoenix Park, "a magnificent and delightful recreation ground and admirably well kept . . . considered by many to be unequalled in beauty by any inclosure or pleasure ground in the British Islands." The Lodge was built in the mid-eighteenth century by Nathaniel Clements, whose multifarious talents and lucrative job as Teller (or cashier) of the Exchequer, the organization responsible for collecting revenue for the Crown, allowed him to enjoy several other careers at the same time. As a property developer, he built several houses in Henrietta and Sackville Streets, Dublin's most elegant and fashionable thoroughfares, and acquired eighty-five thousand acres of land spread across three counties. But it was not until he had contrived to become Chief Ranger and Master of Game of Phoenix Park in 1751 that he embarked upon replacing the house that came with the position with a splendiferous villa of his own. Though he was not a trained architect, he designed it himself with the help, it was said, of pattern books. The result was an imposing red brick mansion, its central block flanked by single-storey wings.

Soon after Clements's death in 1777, the government decided to provide the Lord Lieutenant with an "occasional residence" away from the Castle and bought the Lodge from Clements's son for £10,000. But when the Duke of Portland, who became Lord Lieutenant in 1782, refused to move in, the government soon found that it could not even give the house away, and had to refurbish and extend the "white elephant" instead. The place was deemed fit for royal visitors in 1821 when George IV rolled in, almost literally, after staving off seasickness with strong liquor on his journey across the Irish Sea. At the gates of the Lodge, in a speech that one

---

* One of their guests said that Johnny and Ishbel "much preferred the Viceregal Lodge to the Castle and only occupied the Castle for a week or so in the year; often they merely came down from the Viceregal Lodge for the Banquets and Balls and went back to sleep."

observer said was like that "of a popular candidate come down upon an electioneering trip" he proclaimed:

> Rank, station and honour are nothing; to feel that I live in the hearts of my Irish subjects is to me the most exalted happiness.

But it was not until long after the 1830s, when a whole army of architects, including the talented Francis Johnston of the Board of Works, and Decimus Burton, the planner of London's grandest royal parks, was called in, that the *Dublin Penny Journal* was able to describe the Lodge as "a fair architectural ornament in the Park."

Since the social season was in full swing, it was in Dublin Castle, just over two miles away in the city, that Johnny and Ishbel began their tour of duty. The new Lord Lieutenant and his Vicereine were expected at every ball and soirée and since they also had to meet a stream of organizations offering elaborate addresses of welcome, there was little time to get used to, or even to take in, their new surroundings.

Dublin Castle was first constructed as a fortress by Vikings in around 930, but in the thirteenth century their original wooden buildings were replaced by a stronghold with stone walls, fifteen feet thick. Long before Ishbel and Johnny's time, this, too, had been superseded, and their temporary home was now a Georgian palace, incorporating only one survival from medieval times: the tall and bulbous Record, or Wardrobe, Tower, designed to house King Henry III's treasure and his vast collection of clothes. This was now a library for government papers and the files of the Lord Lieutenants.

Work on a complex of state apartments had begun in the mid-eighteenth century, and by 1886, the Castle boasted a lavishly decorated drawing room, a Privy Council chamber, a grand staircase, a throne room, and a state corridor along which the Viceroy and his court walked in solemn procession to levees and other ceremonial events. Four rooms were set aside for the family: the state bedchamber, a study and a dressing room for the Viceroy, and a boudoir for the Vicereine.

Inevitably, George Washburn Smalley, the *New York Tribune* journalist and more persistent haunter of stately homes than any ghostly "Green Lady," wasted no time in booking himself in for a visit. And he was not impressed by Johnny and Ishbel's new home. His expectations had been high:

> The name of Dublin Castle is famous in two hemispheres, and con-
> jures up visions of towers and battlements, of drawbridge and portcul-
> lis, and all the manifold magnificence of medieval architecture.

But instead he found "brick buildings, nowhere more than three stories high and everywhere singularly dingy and even dirty": the place was a "third-rate barracks." "Of the interior of the Castle," he sniffed, "the most one can say is that it is comfortable." Saint Patrick's Hall was "the only room with pretensions to splendor." The drawing room was "long and narrow" and "not much better furnished than the sitting-room of a good English hotel, which seldom approaches the standard of opulence common to second-rate hotels in America. This, however, is all that the Government of Great Britain thinks itself able to afford for the represen-tative of the Queen."

But then, as Smalley conceded, Dublin Castle was not a hotel but a seat of government and a theater for royal ceremonies:

> From the moment you enter to the moment you quit the Castle you
> are never allowed to forget that you breathe the atmosphere of a Court.

The American regaled his readers with deadpan descriptions of some of the stranger rituals. One in particular, enacted with the greatest solem-nity in the throne room before the St. Patrick's Day ball, caught his eye. Etiquette decreed that none of the women guests, whatever their age or rank in society, could so much as set a toe upon the dance floor unless they had been formally "presented at court," and there were many that evening who had never been to the Castle before. The rule was so rigid, Smalley marveled, that even Johnny's sister-in-law, Fanny Marjoribanks, had to join the procession of "trembling maidens and matrons" to where Johnny stood in all his pomp by the throne:

> Arrived in front of His Excellency, the *debutante* sank to the floor in
> the lowest curtsey she could manage, the Lord Lieutenant held out

his hand to raise her—a support which to some of them was plainly welcome, and even needful—and, as she came up, kissed her lightly on the cheek. Blushes came and went on the faces thus touched by the Viceregal lips or moustache, and I even thought I saw a faint flicker of color on Lord Aberdeen's face as he bestowed this salute on the ladies best known to him. But it had to be done.

Although Johnny's first week in office saw two elaborate ceremonial set pieces of this kind—a levee and a Drawing Room—he found that the civil servants, whose offices were also in the Castle, did defer to him on some matters of government policy, despite Gladstone's ruling that he should stick to "administration." With John Morley preoccupied with the Home Rule Bill in London,* much of the day-to-day work fell onto the shoulders of the Permanent Undersecretary, Sir Robert Hamilton,† and Johnny was gratified that he called in to see him every morning to discuss "whatever needed attention." And when, soon after his arrival, an opportunity arose to blur the line between politics and the good works expected of a Lord Lieutenant, he seized upon it.

Johnny had already secretly stepped in to avert a crisis caused by the government's failure to deliver seed potatoes to the destitute farmers in the west of Ireland. Once again, he had dipped into his own pocket and provided the very considerable sum—£1,500‡—that they needed to get the crop planted in time. But this extraordinary act of generosity was only the start: there were problems to sort out on his doorstep too. Dublin was in decline, no longer the fair city of legend but a crumbling, stinking, over-crowded slum where disease was rife and jobs were scarce. Smalley was shocked when Ishbel took him out for a drive through the city streets and he saw "a grim squalor and a blank hopeless poverty which beats anything I ever saw in London."

---

* Morley made frequent visits to Dublin, which was decidedly not his habit when, in the final years of his career, he was Secretary of State for India: he never once visited the subcontinent.

† Hamilton was a supporter of Home Rule and later lost his job after writers of letters to the London *Times* claimed that he was too partisan and under Gladstone's thumb. One wrote: "Sir Robert Hamilton's sympathies were too much with the Irish people, and what we want now are men without this absurd affection and sympathy for the people they are set over to govern." Compensation came a few weeks later when he was made Governor of Tasmania.

‡ About £100,000 ($130,000) today.

Johnny asked the Lord Mayor, T. D. Sullivan, a writer of rousing nationalist songs but an ardent advocate of achieving Home Rule by peaceful
means, to organize an emergency meeting to discuss how the "distress" in
Dublin could be relieved. If he did so, Johnny added, he would take part.
His subsequent appearance at the Mansion House caused a sensation. All
communications between City Hall and the Castle had ceased abruptly
after an earlier Lord Lieutenant, the Duke of Marlborough, a staunch
opponent of Home Rule, had, in the eyes of the city's councillors and the
press, "snuffily" declined the Lord Mayor's invitation to dinner, "with the
air of a potentate who was dealing a mortal thrust at a presuming parish
beadle."

Now the Lord Lieutenant was on the platform supporting the Lord
Mayor's plan of action and handing over a princely donation of one
hundred guineas* to his relief fund. Before he left, Johnny caused an even
greater frisson by making a point of speaking, and, even more significantly, shaking hands, with Michael Davitt, a former member of the Irish
Republican Brotherhood who had served several spells in prison for his
campaigns against British rule and the country's landowners.

Opponents of Home Rule were quick to express their outrage, although Johnny was unrepentant. This "simple interchange of courtesy"
between the two men was, he argued, "of a decidedly beneficial sort from
the point of view of promoting confidence in the purpose of the British
Government to pursue a policy of conciliation in regard to Ireland." And
the press, though still wary of the newcomer, welcomed Johnny's surprising gesture of reconciliation:

We take his unassuming and straightforward conduct at the Mansion House to portend that the Lord Lieutenancy in its old unreal
and mock-royal state is about to disappear, and that whatever the
Governor-General of the future is to be, or whatever his duties, he
must have no airs that will conflict with plain-dealing Irish democracy.

Ishbel, who turned twenty-nine three days after the meeting, became
patron of the Ladies' Committee for the Relief of Distress, but she had also

* Around £7,000 ($9,000) in today's money.

found herself, on the day after her arrival, another, even more absorbing cause. Would she, an official had asked, take over from her predecessor, Lady Carnarvon, as president of a committee that was preparing a small showcase of Irish crafts for the Edinburgh International Exhibition of Industry, Science, and Art that was due to open in May?

Ishbel did not hesitate, for she knew that preparations for the exhibition were well underway: Johnny had been elected a vice president of the show, and she was one of the four conveners of the Women's Industries section. Earlier that month, the *Illustrated London News* had offered its readers a glimpse of what would be on display in the vast, cathedral-like Main Hall going up on the Meadows, "one of the finest and most accessible parks" in the Scottish capital. The exhibits would range from "minerals, mining, quarrying and metallurgy" to "steam-engines and other 'prime-movers,'" to "fishery and fish-curing" and "reproductions of the streets and architecture of 'Old Edinburgh.'"

Lady Carnarvon's plans for the Irish showcase, Ishbel at once decided, did not match the ambitions of so great an exhibition, but, with its opening just three months away, how would she find the craftwork she needed in time? She soon discovered that she could draw upon the experience of a philanthropic Englishwoman, Alice Hart. Like Ishbel, she was the daughter of a rich businessman: Alexander Rowland, manufacturer of the Macassar Oil* used by fashionable gentlemen to slick down their hair. A love of good works ran in the family: Alice's younger sister was Henrietta Barnett, who, by the 1880s, was already gaining a name for herself as a social reformer. But Alice's husband Ernest, a brilliant doctor, enjoyed a more controversial reputation: he was rumored to have been responsible for the "accidental poisoning" of his first wife and to have embezzled funds earmarked for contributors to the *British Medical Journal*, which he edited.

If Ernest was in need of redemption, he certainly earned it when, on hearing news of a new famine in Ireland in 1883, the couple traveled to

---

* Rowland's advertisements promised that Macassar Oil would make men more attractive to women, a claim endorsed by the poet Lord Byron, who called it "incomparable." But there were many women, especially maids and housekeepers, who found Mr. Rowland's money-spinning unguent less than attractive when they tried to clean off the stains that it left on the upholstery. Hence "antimacassars," the strips of cloth attached to the tops of armchairs in all the best Victorian and Edwardian parlors.

Donegal to investigate. "The destitution was extreme and widespread," Ernest reported in a moving letter to *The Times*:

> I found 14,000 persons in dire destitution and tragic suffering . . . the whole of the children of one district living on two biscuits a day each, distributed at the schools, and no small proportion of the adults kept alive by a daily pennyworth of meal.

He and his wife, he added, had set up a relief fund for "these industrious, sober, pure, and honest tillers of the soil," because "their sufferings make the heart bleed, and can never be forgotten by any who have witnessed them."

But the Harts did not stop there. When the immediate crisis was over, they realized that, in the face of government indifference and the violent hostility of many of their landlords, the people of Donegal should be helped to help themselves, and the best way to do that, Alice suggested, would be to revive traditional cottage industries such as lace-making, weaving, knitting, and embroidery. Thanks to another fund-raising campaign—Alice chipped in the first £50—the Donegal Industrial Fund was soon up and running. Hundreds of local women enrolled at the free classes it provided, and soon their handiwork was on sale in London at fashionable stores like Liberty and the fund's own emporium in New Cavendish Street. The Harts' enterprise and compassion were widely applauded, not least in Donegal itself, as Dinah Craik, author of a travel book on Ireland, discovered when she fell into step with a woman on a country road:

> 'It's been hard times with us for a long time,' she said, 'but things are mending a bit. Many of us have gone to America—there's no starving there. A kind English lady has been helping us in Donegal—the women, I mean—giving us work and paying for it. Maybe ye'll know her?'
>
> 'Mrs Ernest Hart,' I suggested—glad to own that I did know her.
>
> 'Sure, that's the name. I don't work for her myself, but I know them as does. She pays them regularly, ye see. She's brought a little money into the country, and it's money we want; we're all so poor.'

As Ishbel gathered craftwork for the Edinburgh exhibition—lace from the Presentation Convent in Youghal and the Poor Clares in Kenmare, crochet worked by cottar women in Killarney, poplin from Dublin, tweed from Blarney in the south and Inishowen in the north, crimson cloaks from Connaught, flannel from Galway—an idea crystallized. She would create an organization more ambitious than Mrs. Hart's: one that would nurture, promote, and market the work of artisans from all over Ireland. It would bring prosperity to the rural communities that had borne the brunt of the century's devastating famines and empower them to make a real contribution to the country's economy when Gladstone's plans for Home Rule finally came to fruition. Thanks to her habit of working through the night,[*] Ishbel managed to set up her stand just in time for the exhibition's opening on May 6, but she delayed the launch of her new Irish Industries Association until later that month, when she had something special planned.

By then, she and Johnny had settled into the Viceregal Lodge, where, even in the midst of the hectic preparations for the Edinburgh exhibition, she found time to call in the builders to install a small wooden chapel. They had got used to having one on hand at Haddo for prayers twice a day, and incorporating it into the house meant that they could dispense with the hussars and policemen who shadowed them so tiresomely whenever they went out. And the Lodge, with its spacious grounds, was the perfect place for a garden party, although the one that Ishbel organized on May 22 to launch the Irish Industries Association was unlike anything that local high society had seen before, as a report in the *Dublin Daily Express* acknowledged:

> It is not often that the somewhat torpid waters of social life in Dublin receive such a thorough stirring up as they did at the hands of the Earl and Countess of Aberdeen in connection with the garden party given at the Viceregal Lodge on Saturday. Certainly no social event in recent years has been productive of such widespread interest or given birth to such glowing expectations.

---

[*] Although she had begun working into the small hours as a teenager from sheer panic—she had to put in long hours to cram in the knowledge to help her answer the "shower of unexpected questions" she knew she would face from her demanding French tutor, M. Antonin Roche, in class the next morning—this soon became her favored modus operandi. One of her grandchildren marveled that she got by on "only four hours sleep at night, generally from 4 to 8 a.m. Johnny had to follow suit, and so did their faithful secretary."

Ishbel had flouted the conventions of viceregal party-giving, stipulating an unusually informal dress code for her guests. Everything they wore should be made of "materials of Irish manufacture":

> Gentlemen were required to wear suits of Irish tweed or serge, Irish-made hats, gloves and poplin ties of St Patrick's blue; while the ladies were left to devise for themselves the costumes which they would appear in—fancy or otherwise—always provided, of course, that the material was Irish.

The children should look "as like Irish peasants—in miniature, of course—as possible."

Johnny opted for a suit of gray poplin and carried a traditional blackthorn stick, but for herself Ishbel had commissioned a fantastical creation, designed to reflect Ireland's cultural heritage, from Mary Sims, Ireland's leading dress designer. The shape of her costume was inspired by *The Marriage of Strongbow and Aoife*, an epic picture by the historical painter Daniel Maclise, and its overskirt was opulently embroidered in gold thread with designs taken from the Book of Kells, an ornate illuminated manuscript dating from around the ninth century. Just as Ishbel had hoped, the awestruck fashion writers described her "costume of an Irish lady of the eighteenth century" in the minutest detail:

> The skirt looped up by a girdle over a petticoat of gold brocaded poplin, a gold embroidered shoulder piece fastened by a fibula brooch, the sacque* falling behind the puffed sleeves, the cap of soft Irish linen rising out of a head ornament, the long mantle fastened by a Tara brooch, were all typical of the period.

Shamrocks were everywhere: in the huge bouquet she carried and embroidered on her stockings, which, like Queen Victoria's, were woven by Smyth's of Balbriggan, a seaside town north of Dublin. The children were just as colorfully arrayed. Doddie wore a jerkin of gold-brocaded poplin, breeches "puffed with St Patrick blue" and a poplin shoulder

---

* A loose-fitting coat or train.

cape. His siblings, too, had been pressed into service as little clothes-horses:

> Lady Marjorie Gordon representing a Connemara peasant, Hon. Dudley Gordon an Irish peasant, and the Hon. Ian [Archie] Gordon an Egyptian peasant.

Five bands played, the children laughed at the "harrowing tragedies" enacted by Punch and Judy and the antics of a "Professor" who performed his "breaking of the egg" trick to great acclaim, while their elders promenaded through the exhibition of Irish crafts in the racquet court, enjoyed the refreshments laid out in the tents dotted across the lawns, and had their photograph taken by "M. Lafayette"* in his "artistically arranged studio." Like everyone else, the reporter from the *Express* enjoyed every minute, but the message that Ishbel had gone to so much trouble and expense to send out into the world was not lost on him. It was, he wrote, "a *fête* which will long be remembered by all who had the pleasure to participate in it, and which is, no doubt, destined to exercise a most important influence on our country's welfare."

When visits to convents where the nuns made fine lace appeared on Johnny and Ishbel's schedule of a tour to the southwest of the country, no one was surprised. But although Johnny and Ishbel were well received, even in places like Kenmare "where extreme Nationalist influences were rife," it was, in the main, a traditional affair of civic addresses, visits to schools, and sightseeing. The tour was, they promised both themselves and the people of Ireland, the first of many.

Their next journey, though, was back to London, where the Home Rule Bill was being debated in the House of Commons. The Gladstones came to stay at Dollis Hill to escape from the sound and fury at Westminster. For both families, Ishbel noted, "it was a time of tense anxiety." At Brook House, Ishbel's father, angry as ever, accused supporters of the bill of being "steeped up to the lips in treason," and her brother Edward, now a

---

* "M. Lafayette" was not the Parisian avant-garde photographer his name suggested. His real name was James Stack Lauder and he came from Dublin. Thanks to commissions from Johnny and other Viceroys, he was invited to photograph Queen Victoria at Windsor in 1887. Thenceforth, he liked to style himself "Photographer Royal."

government whip, warned of "an awfully bitter feeling" against the Prime Minister. Gladstone said,

> You don't know what a wretched creature I feel, and what a load there
> is on my heart every morning when I wake.

Ishbel watched from a gallery in the House of Commons as the government went down to defeat. Gladstone resigned and a general election was called. The Conservatives, helped by Liberal Unionists, were returned to power. A new Lord Lieutenant was appointed: the 6th Marquess of Londonderry, a staunch opponent of Home Rule. On August 3, Johnny and Ishbel began their journey home. As they left Dublin Castle, Ishbel wrote afterwards, she realized that the streets were filled with "one dense mass of human beings":

> The moment we came in sight there was a sudden mighty roar of voices
> which one could never, never describe, but which could never be forgotten. It was this marvellous crowd, with their wonderful orderliness
> and the expression of their faces, that filled us with emotion. And the
> emotion was largely that of sorrow; for it all seemed to speak of a 'might
> have been'.

In his farewell speech, Timothy Sullivan, the nationalist Lord Mayor of Dublin, agreed:

> While warmly appreciating the personal merits of Lord and Lady
> Aberdeen,* what has evoked this outburst of feeling was the fact that
> he was to us a sign and token of a speedy restoration of the right of
> self-government to our country.†

---

* Sullivan had taken a shine to Ishbel in particular. On the day she left, he sent a letter asking her to give him a portrait of her—"a large one, if possible."

† In the euphoria of the moment, Johnny naively agreed to pass a message from Sullivan to Queen Victoria. The Lord Mayor said that he looked forward to "the happy day, which we trust may not be far distant, when she may be pleased to come among her Irish subjects to return to them their ancient constitutional right of self-government." The Queen was furious, complaining bitterly that "Aberdeen had betrayed her" by behaving as if he was Gladstone's representative, not hers. Thus, "weak" Johnny went down even further in the royal estimation.

But for Ishbel, this was a bitter parting. The young woman who had once vowed never to set foot in Ireland was now heartbroken at having to leave a country she had come to love. Exhausted, disappointed, frustrated that her work was unfinished, and now plagued with migraines, she found little pleasure in anything: not even amidst the woods and hills of Guisachan where she now had to languish for the summer.

10

A Cabin in North Dakota and
a Ranchhouse in Texas

On a fine June morning in 1887, a reporter from the *New York Herald* hitched a ride across the glittering waters of San Francisco Bay. He had talked his way onto the "quarantine boat" carrying the doctor assigned to check on the health of the passengers aboard the S.S. *Alameda*, inbound from Australia and the islands of the South Pacific. Now he hoped to steal a march on his rivals by snatching an interview with Johnny and Ishbel about "the present political conditions in Ireland"—a matter of keen interest to his paper's many Irish-American readers*—before they had even set foot on American soil.

The journalist found the "celebrated 'Home Rule Lord Lieutenant' of Ireland" and his "vigorous-looking wife" on deck "in conversation with a group of friends from the colonies," but he gleaned little from Johnny, who told him:

> I am not prepared, for various reasons, to make any remarks about the situation in Ireland. I have not studied recent events closely enough to warrant me in making any statements whatever. I am travelling more for the purpose of informing myself than to give information to others.

---

*According to a census conducted three years later, there were 190,000 immigrants from Ireland living in New York City.

This was disingenuous, for Ireland had been constantly on the couple's minds—Ishbel's especially—since the day they had left Dublin ten months before. "Ireland is laid on us to do all in our power for her for ever," she had written in her journal. And when she found herself surrounded at Guisachan by people who, like her father, were virulently opposed to Home Rule, she complained to Henry Drummond:

> The mention of Ireland sets me on fire, yet I must drill myself not to speak, not to look. It seems impossible for anyone here to comprehend that one can really *care* about the Irish people, whether they be bad or good.

Ishbel had found it hard to return to the life she had led: a sense of disappointment pervaded everything and her debilitating headaches had become more frequent. When the doctors prescribed a voyage round the world, she took little persuading, rather to her surprise. She was, she convinced herself, no longer a reluctant sailor after discovering that "the Irish Channel was not so terrible an experience after all, provided a horizontal attitude was assumed before the boat started." The children, she reasoned, could be safely left behind with "Baa," their "trustworthy nurse"; and, tantalizingly, Rosebery had dangled the prospect of another viceregal appointment before them. It was, he maintained, "the duty of everyone called upon to take part in public affairs to visit different parts of the Empire personally."

Johnny and Ishbel left Haddo in early December 1886, and on New Year's Eve, as their ship neared Bombay, Ishbel was still struggling to make sense of the events of the past few months:

> It seems strange finishing up this eventful year on the Indian Ocean. All has been so unexpected, we have been so uprooted and turned inside out—that it bewilders one to look back. We have been talking over past and future under these star-lit skies. The phosphorescent waves flying past, their brightness flashing over dark deep relentless waters, seem to remind us of unrevealed depths of life around us, of so much work to be done. We want to make a plan for some definite purpose so as not to be overwhelmed by the possibilities and are very thankful to have this breathing-time away from the feverish rush at home.

She had packed her Irish dresses and showed them off at the dinners and receptions laid on by colonial governors and maharajahs as she and Johnny made a quasi-royal progress through India, traveling by private railcar and dashing up the Khyber Pass on horses borrowed from the Bengal Lancers. But the exotic sights—the ancient cave temples of Elephanta Island in Bombay harbor, an "immense" horse fair at Shikarpur, a durbar at Gwalior presided over by a colonel from back home in Aberdeenshire, the "strange and imposing" gorge at Kuchalari—failed to lift her mood. Even the beauty of the Taj Mahal, she wrote, offered no distraction for her "mingled yearnings and indescribable pain":

> We begin again and again full of enthusiasm for some new duty, for some new way of conquering ourselves and laying down our lives for others' good, but does it not always end in disappointment and discouragement?

It was not until they reached Adelaide in Australia, not long after her thirtieth birthday, that Ishbel's spirits began to rise, thanks to "an unexpected and interesting experience." After a "rather much filled up" day of touring the city, the couple rushed to the station to catch a train. There they found a crowd of two thousand people, most of them Irish, waiting to present them with an address thanking them for their support for Home Rule. This was, Ishbel wrote happily, "the first of a succession of similar manifestations which occurred throughout the remainder of our journey."

More crowds met them in Melbourne and Sydney, although the reaction to their arrival in Tasmania to stay with the island's Governor, Sir Robert Hamilton, who, like Johnny, had lost his job in Dublin for supporting Home Rule, reflected the heat of the arguments still raging at home. A "loyalist" wrote to the *Launceston Examiner* to express his "feelings of indignation and regret at the introduction of old world prejudice and party feeling in the midst of this loyal and orderly community."

There were no such sour notes when they made landfall in San Francisco. At a party in the "reception parlor" of the Palace Hotel, Johnny, his earlier reluctance to discuss politics quite forgotten, replied to an address of welcome from the city's "leading Irishmen" with a speech assuring them that Home Rule would "shortly be accomplished." He added that Ishbel, who was wearing, the newspapers noted, "a beautiful dove colored Irish poplin dress, elaborately trimmed with Irish lace," had been especially touched to find a four-foot-high harp made of flowers waiting for them in their hotel suite. Similar scenes greeted them as they traveled onward through Colorado and Utah, but while Johnny was always happy to linger to preach the Gladstonian gospel of Home Rule, Ishbel was in a hurry to reach Texas for a family reunion.

A few years earlier, her parents had been faced with a quandary. Edward, their eldest son, was making a name for himself as a Member of Parliament and winning praise for what his biographer described as "his engaging manners, assiduity, imperturbable good humour, and devotion to manly sports," but his brothers, Archie and Coutts, did not share his sterling qualities. Coutts, in particular, had earned the displeasure of his father, who had cut off his allowance: Johnny, at Ishbel's urging, had stepped in to provide one. Archie and Coutts showed no aptitude for anything and seemed quite uninterested in pursuing the careers that traditionally kept the younger sons of landed families in funds and out of trouble, in the church, the army (although Coutts did serve briefly as a lieutenant in the Queen's Own Cameron Highlanders), or the imperial diplomatic service. Something would have to be done before they besmirched the family name any further, and soon their father, who had been created Baron Tweedmouth of Edington a few years earlier, came up with a plan. Its benefits, he believed, would be twofold: his wastrel sons could sow their wild oats far from the society salons of Mayfair, and he would make money too.

Down in the counting houses of the City of London, financiers had been devouring a book called *Food from the Far West* by James Macdonald, a Scottish journalist. He had been sent on a tour of North America by the *Scotsman* newspaper to report on the burgeoning cattle businesses said to be flourishing on the myriad wide and empty acres of the prairies.

In some respects, Macdonald offered little of cheer to the cattle breeders at home, who were already coping with the dire effects of the Agricultural Depression. The first freezer ships were plying the Atlantic, their holds full of meat that could be sold at rock-bottom prices in Europe, and he warned that British farmers faced a new and imminent threat to their livelihoods. But between the long lines of statistics in Macdonald's report,

Tweedmouth and his fellow speculators read another, far more beguiling story: of a cattle raisers' utopia, of bonanzas awaiting the canny investor in the grasslands of Texas and Dakota Territory, in Wyoming where the Great Plains met the Rocky Mountains, and far to the west along the gleaming new tracks of the Santa Fe Railway.

Other excited prophets weighed in. The title of a book by a former Civil War general, James Sanks Brisbin, published in 1881, told them all they needed to know. London's investors did not actually have to read *The Beef Bonanza: How to Get Rich on the Plains* to hear, from Sweeting's Alley and Threadneedle Street, the thunder of hooves on the grasslands and, behind it, the even more enticing sound of a cascade of cash.

Stories of overnight fortunes raced across the Atlantic. It was said that Charles Goodnight, a rancher on the Texas Panhandle, had made $600,000 in just a few years. In Montana, according to Walter, Baron von Richthofen,* another European imbued with the zeal of the convert, a hard-up cattle breeder offered to pay his Irish servant girl the $150 he owed her in cattle instead of cash. He would, he promised, repurchase the fifteen cows whenever she wanted to sell them. She took the deal and, ten years later, sold her herd back to him for $25,000.

Even the canny Aberdonian James Macdonald, who wrote scathingly about the quality of American beef and mutton, was enthusiastic about the prospects for British investors if they sent their cattle and expert breeders out to the prairies:

> A gentleman who had been engaged in the stock-trade for many years in the south of Texas assured me that, though he had seen a few reckless Americans go to the wall at cattle-raising, he had never known a Scotchman or an Irishman to fail.

Perhaps it was those get-rich-quick stories that inspired Tweedmouth's plan, or maybe a rallying call from General Brisbin caught his eye:

---

* Cattle-raising was only one of the eccentric baron's many enthusiasms. They included beer from his German homeland (he opened one of the first beer gardens in the West), milk (he believed, mistakenly, that it was a cure for tuberculosis), and a "medieval" castle in Denver that boasted thirty-five rooms and a moat. He was also fond of his nephew and godson Manfred, the World War I flying ace known as the "Red Baron."

No industrious man can make a mistake in moving West, and if I had a son to advise, I should by all means say to him, "Go West as soon as you can; get a good piece of land, and hold on to it."*

All this struck a chord with Dudley Tweedmouth, not least because one of his hobbies was breeding cattle at Guisachan.† His mind was soon made up: he would join in the Great American Beef Rush and send Archie and Coutts out to work on his cattle ranches and keep an eye on his investments.

Buying a ranch was all too easy for anyone with money to spare. Cattle entrepreneurs, rough-mannered but smooth-talking, had taken the long trail east to London armed with tantalizing prospectuses: "little pamphlets of gilded glory," one old-timer called them. Sixty years later, Estelle Tinkler, a Texas historian, drew on the still-fresh memories of the Texan pioneers to paint this picture of prairie fever:

> Through the rosy colored glasses of optimism the capitalists could see only the wealth to be attained from the fat, sleek beef; could smell only the invigorating air of delightful days that was a tonic to body and soul; could envision only the wealth and the ease and the dignity of life on a western cattle ranch. But they seemed to take no cognizance of the other side of the picture—prolonged dry spells that parched the grass to the color of washed-out khaki; biting winds from the north that brought ice and snow, and spelled destruction to man and beast alike.

Despite the acute problems faced by his farming operations at home and his continuing failure to find a buyer for the Cromar estate, Johnny agreed to become Tweedmouth's partner in this highly speculative venture, and soon they had succumbed to the sales talk of John Drew and Earl W. Spencer, the owners of the Rocking Chair Ranch in Wheeler and Collingsworth Counties on the Texas Panhandle. John Clay, an emigrant

---

*While Brisbin urged young men to go west, he was more circumspect about young women doing the same. "It is not a good place," he wrote, "for ladies to come who wish to keep single. There are so many bachelors a young lady finds herself surrounded by suitors, and some of the applicants will not be put off." It is the only note of caution in his book.

† One particularly magnificent beast, the winner of the Queen's Gold Medal at Windsor in 1889, was, appropriately, called "Cash."

Scot and one of the leading stockmen of the time, described both men in his classic memoir, *My Life on the Range*. While Spencer, he wrote, was "cheery, receptive, and had a good knowledge of the cow business," Drew was a "miserable specimen of mankind, a sort of adventurer with an evil tongue, with no sense of honour."

Nonetheless, a deal was done, and in 1883, a consortium led by Tweedmouth, Johnny, and Ishbel's elder brother, Edward, launched the new Rocking Chair Ranch Company Limited. They agreed to pay, in annual installments, $188,000 for the doubtful pair's 150,400 acres of land, and $365,000 for their ranch equipment and stock of 14,745 head of cattle and 150 ponies. They hired Drew as manager at a salary of $2,500 and Archie Marjoribanks was drafted in as his assistant on $1,500.

Archie was in his early twenties when he arrived at the "unpainted" ranch house at North Elm Creek, and he was quite unprepared for the rigors of life in what Estelle Tinkler called a "primitive society in which there were no restrictions save those set by an elemental conscience and a neighbour's six-shooter." The county capital, Mobeetie,* was a far cry from the genteel places where he had grown up: Mayfair, Eton College, Oxford University, and even Glen Affric. It boasted little more than a general store, a courthouse, and rackety cowboy hangouts of the likes of O'Laughlin's Saloon, the Pink Pussy Cat Paradise, and the Buffalo Chip. Charles Goodnight, the pioneer of cattle breeding in the Panhandle, described the town, "patronised by outlaws, thieves, cut-throats and buffalo hunters, with a large per cent of prostitutes," as "the hardest place I saw on the frontier except Cheyenne, Wyoming."

Enough old-timers survived into the 1940s for Estelle Tinkler to compile this slightly implausible description of Archie:

> The Honourable Archibald John looked every inch a Scotsman and he spoke with a decided Scots brogue. He stood at least six feet in height, and was a large raw-boned fellow with a flushed face and habit of never looking one squarely in the eye.

---

* The town's founders wanted to name it "Sweetwater," but legend has it that when the postal authorities pointed out that there was another place of that name in Texas, they asked the local Native Americans to translate it into their own language. Many years passed before the inhabitants discovered that *Mobeetie* actually means "buffalo dung."

According to an article published many years later in the *Fort Worth Star-Telegram*, unkindly headlined "As Manager of the Rocking Chair Ranch Honorable Archie was a Good Dog Fancier," the ranch's cowboys, who nicknamed him "Marshie," were never going to make life easy for a British gentleman:

> They were known to charge down on him at full gallop, yelling like wild Indians, shoot around his feet or head, cursing till the air was blue, for no other reason evidently, than to satisfy themselves that they were as good men as the "Honourable Archie."

No wonder Archie hid away in the ranch house at Elm Creek, writing reports for the shareholders back home and complaining to grocers, feed merchants, and other suppliers about the poor service they were giving him. But this conscientiousness won him no favors: the cowboys dismissed "Old Marshie" as standoffish, and the local press singled him out for censure because of "his connection with titled people across the Atlantic, who have sent him over to speculate and squeeze all he could from the children's grass and bring it away." Like many "remittance men,"* Archie drank heavily, probably out of loneliness, and he was much mocked for his frivolity in buying a pack of hounds and going hunting. In fact, as he pointed out in a letter home, wolves were "killing off quite a number of young calves."

For a couple used to traveling in luxurious private railcars, finding their way to Elm Creek along the still unfinished Southern Kansas Railway to visit Archie was a daunting prospect, but Johnny understood Ishbel's strong attachment to her younger brothers:

---

* Mark Twain provides the most entertaining definition of a breed often encountered in the nineteenth century. On a voyage across the Pacific, he noticed that "the most interesting and most felicitous talker was a young Canadian who was not able to let the whisky bottle alone." When he mentioned him to the other passengers, they said he was a "remittance man" and explained that "dissipated ne'er-do-wells belonging to important families in England and Canada were not cast off by their people while there was any hope of reforming them, but when that last hope perished at last, the ne'er-do-well was sent abroad to get him out of the way. He was shipped off with just enough money in his pocket—no, in the purser's pocket—for the needs of the voyage—and when he reached his destined port he would find a remittance awaiting him there. Not a large one, but just enough to keep him a month. A similar remittance would come monthly thereafter. It was the remittance-man's custom to pay his month's board and lodging straightway—a duty which his landlord did not allow him to forget—then spree away the rest of his money in a single night, then brood and mope and grieve in idleness till the next remittance came. It is a pathetic life."

I was quite aware that Lady Aberdeen would have gone to the utter-most corner of the earth if one of her brothers happened to be there feeling lonely and wishing for a visit from his sister.

In any case, he needed to see the place for himself. By 1887, the consortium had increased its investment by acquiring further leases on land adjoining the ranch. With more than three hundred thousand acres under their control, Johnny and Tweedmouth were living up to the sardonic nickname given them by their Panhandle neighbors: now they were truly "Lords of the Prairies."

From Kansas City, the couple traveled for thirty hours in the railway construction team's train, in temperatures "about ninety-five in the cars," cheek by jowl with cowboys and enduring "tremendous jerks and jolts." At last, at midnight, they found themselves in the middle of nowhere, at the point on the track—"80 miles beyond Buzzard's Roost"—where its builders had knocked off for the day. Archie had ridden across country to meet them, and he and Johnny slept with the navvies in a dormitory tent. Ishbel was dispatched to a freight car where a surprise awaited her: she would have to share it with Mr. Stokes, the train's storekeeper, and his wife. There was, she discovered, no room for modesty in the West, since Stokes "evidently seemed to think that we would all undress and do our toilet together." She "managed v. well," though, "by not undressing."

The next morning, they set off for the ranch in a buckboard wagon. Johnny was impressed with Archie's driving, but not by the track, "which was sometimes all ridges, sometimes heavy sand, up and down steep little hillocks, through vast desolate prairies." The journey took three days, and for Ishbel it was an uncomfortable and nerve-racking adventure:

> The poor horses often had to pull us through wastes of heavy sand, and we were not sure if we could ford the treacherous Canadian River as there had just been a flood but the water only came over the foot-board once. It is full of quicksands and many are the lives both of men & cattle which have been swallowed up there.

When they finally reached Elm Creek and Ishbel had conducted a thorough inspection, she and Johnny pronounced themselves "very much pleased" with the way Archie had done out the "perfectly tidy" ranch headquarters:

> The frame house consists of Archie and Mr Drew's joint bedroom, which they gave up to us and slept on the veranda; the dining-room, cowboys' room, and kitchen. Out-houses are the store-room, tool-house, buckboard shed and fowl house. It was a lovely evening when we arrived, with a feeling of peacefulness and freedom.

Johnny, his eyes belatedly opened to the financial risks that he was carrying, pondered his investment:

> This trip gave us some idea of the difficulties of ranch life, which is sometimes supposed to be a simple affair.

There was certainly nothing simple about the problems confronting the ranchers. Unprecedented bad weather the previous winter, a slump in the price of cattle, repeated invasions by other settlers who claimed they had the right to graze their herds on their land, their transport company's chaotic schedule that led to animals being delivered to the market on the wrong day, and a plague of flies that sapped the health of the beasts, all played their part. And the squatters had cooked up a scheme to defraud Archie of his dwindling funds:

> They drove bunches down, counted them and got their money. Then they drove the cattle over the hill and threw them into the pasture; another outfit took them, drove them around from the other side, sold them, and got their money a second time. This process was sometimes repeated until the same bunch of cattle had been sold four or five times.

Most damagingly of all, the ranch's manager, John Drew, had turned rustler himself: he was secretly shipping trainloads of cattle to market and selling them right under the nose of the unwitting Archie.

Oblivious, Ishbel headed back to Fort Worth, where the by now in-escapable reporter was poised to bring his readers a pen portrait of "Mrs Aberdeen":

The Countess could not be called a strictly beautiful woman, though she is undeniably very fine looking, and has the indefinable air of aristocratic breeding and bearing that marks out the patrician class. . . . In response to the reporter's question of how she liked Texas, her ladyship said with a winning smile that 'it was a most beautiful and charming country, far lovelier than she ever imagined.'

Together they traveled to St. Paul, Minnesota, where Johnny was to be entertained at a banquet given by three hundred Irishmen (no women were invited). Ishbel went on to visit the ranch belonging to her other brother, Coutts.

After a tour of possible sites, Coutts had settled on McHenry County in north-central Dakota Territory. There he bought six parcels of land, amounting to just under a thousand acres, seven miles from Towner, the county capital. The Mouse River ran along the western edge of the new Horseshoe Ranch, which meant there was plenty of water to irrigate the cattle pastures. Though he found himself in alien territory, an innocent abroad among the tough pioneers, the drifters, the displaced Civil War veterans, and the chancers of the frontier, the twenty-four-year-old drove a hard bargain for the land, acquiring it for an average of $3.18 an acre: half the usual price. The initial capital for the purchase, it was rumored, had been provided by Johnny alone, since Coutts was still in disgrace with his father. He would not be paid a salary, the syndicate decreed, and he would have to live on his allowance of £400 a year.

Coutts started well. He appointed an experienced foreman, Bernie Kelly, registered his "Horseshoe V" brand, planted trees, built haystacks, and constructed a house. And to supplement the five carloads of cattle that he had bought locally, he persuaded his parents to send him some breeding stock from the Guisachan herd. He also teamed up with another well-born Englishman, Edmund Thursby, who had a slightly smaller spread to the north. They helped to found the Mouse River Live Stock Protective Association: its principal aim was to stamp out cattle rustling, although Coutts's first decision on taking the chair was to spend its funds on an "oyster supper" for members and distinguished visitors. Away from the ranch, Coutts joined the local school board, worked to improve—or, rather, create in those wild parts—a local infrastructure, and thus, unlike Archie, earned the respect of his neighbors.

But all too soon whispers of unruly behavior reached Brook House: Coutts had fallen into bad company in Towner; he was spending too much time hunting for wolves with his pack of hounds; he was seen too often at the races—why, he was even on the organizing committee!

Coutts had come to meet Ishbel at St. Paul, and they set out on the journey to McHenry County as the fireworks of the Fourth of July set up a "tremendous cannonading" overhead. This, too, was another demanding trek, despite the comforts of a private railroad car lent by James J. Hill, president of the St. Paul, Minneapolis & Manitoba Railway.

At the Horseshoe Ranch, Coutts had built himself a simple cabin. Though it was far more modest than Thursby's, which boasted a billiard room and was elaborately decorated with pictures "without equal in America,"* Ishbel wrote admiringly of her brother's efforts in her journal:

His house here is a nice little log-house with wooden roof painted green and surmounted with a pair of elk horns—has two bedrooms and sitting room with kitchen leading out of it.

But the rigors of the trip did not end there:

An overpoweringly hot day. 104 in shade and 126 in sun—hot wind besides—Coutts took me around his buildings—new barn and old, the garden which is thriving well—then tried to find place for sketch-

---

* Thursby's house, in its turn, was nothing compared to the "château" built by a French aristocrat, Antoine-Amédée-Marie-Vincent Manca Amat de Vallombrosa, Marquis de Morès et de Montemaggiore, who, in the early 1880s, had realized the need for an abattoir and meat-packing plant right on the range. He bought more than forty thousand acres, founded the town of Medora, and built a two-storey "summer lodge" which had twenty-six rooms and was staffed by twenty servants. In this transplanted corner of the *ancien régime*, his guests dined off Sèvres porcelain and drank the finest of French wines. But the Marquis was not as civilized as he appeared and was one of those who put the "bad" into the Badlands. He shot those who crossed him, was rabidly anti-Semitic, and once challenged Theodore Roosevelt to a duel. The meat-packing business—"the worst of all the mad schemes" in the West, John Clay called it—lasted only three years. De Morès then decamped to Indochina, where he tried to build a railway linking China to the Gulf of Tonkin. That, too, came to nothing. He moved on to North Africa, where his efforts to foment insurrection against the British were stymied by Tuareg tribesmen who shot him.

ing and sat and drew a bit, but there was no shade so was obliged to retreat indoors.

Even here, bizarrely, Irish politics dominated Ishbel's thoughts, and she spent most of the day "discussing Home Rule with Mr Thursby and Mr Kelly." Only in the relative cool of the evening did she venture out to tour her brother's domain, although she found herself "much persecuted by very large mosquitos." But this small inconvenience was as nothing to a drama that Ishbel had witnessed a few hours before:

> Great misfortune happened today. A new purebred Polled Aberdeen bull, Baron, which Coutts had just purchased died of heart disease which means a loss of $800.

Others might have taken this as an omen, but Ishbel seems to have gathered no inkling that Coutts's venture, like Archie's, was already beginning to run into trouble. For him, too, the dream of a beef bonanza, promoted so enthusiastically by James Macdonald, General Brisbin, and Walter, Baron von Richthofen, had turned into a nightmare, thanks to the harsh weather of the winter before. The summer had been hot and dry, leaving the once lush, but now chronically overcrowded grasslands of the West barren and the cattle short of food. Then the snows fell early and temperatures plummeted, in some places to minus sixty degrees. There was no way of getting feed to the starving herds across an open range encased in a carapace of ice.

When the thaw came at last, it brought no relief: the corpses of hundreds of thousands of cattle were revealed sprawled across the prairies and in the rivers, creeks, and coulees. One of Coutts's neighbors and fellow ranch owners, Theodore Roosevelt, later the twenty-sixth president of the United States, described it as "a perfect smash-up" that had inflicted "crippling" losses across the cattle country of the Northwest.

The cowboys, laconic as ever, called it the "Great Die-Up." Many of the remittance men went home that summer, but some, like Coutts and Archie, hung on, putting a brave face on things and praying that their backers, far away across the sea, would share their hopes that the boom times would return. Clear-sighted as ever, John Clay, the doyen of cattle breeders, understood why "the story with its flavor of romance" had ended in "hollow failure":

> Three great streams of ill-luck, mismanagement, greed met together— in other words, recklessness, want of foresight, and the weather, which no man can control.

But Johnny and Ishbel traveled on to Chicago and New York unheeding. They had been captivated by their glimpses of life on the ranches, never imagining that a new bout of prairie fever would soon prove even more damaging to Johnny's fortune than the first.

11

A House Near Niagara Falls

As the Cunard steamship *Servia* approached the shores of England in August 1887, Ishbel, reinvigorated and eager to take up her causes once again, signed off her tour diary with a hopeful flourish:

> God has been good to us in these months: not even one's own frailty can stand in the way of His work. I go back without shirking; each day will come right.

There was plenty to keep her busy, not least a new house, 27 Grosvenor Square, where they would live during the week while still enjoying the bucolic delights of Dollis Hill on Saturdays and Sundays. It stood on a site once occupied by the home of Johnny's mentor and fellow philanthropist, the 7th Earl of Shaftesbury. Shaftesbury had refused to spend much money on the eighteenth-century building, partly because he had little cash to spare, but principally because, as he wrote in his diary in 1851, he believed that a time was coming when the rich would have to share their wealth and property, and "what then," he wondered, "will a Palace be worth?"

Johnny, who confessed to no such fears, bought the house in 1885 and sold No. 37, their first marital home, to Edward Levy-Lawson,* managing

---

* A distinguished newspaperman and philanthropist, Levy-Lawson, later 1st Baron Burnham, is also remembered for the activities that went on at another of his houses, Hall Barn in Buckinghamshire. There, on December 18, 1913, King George V and his son the Prince of Wales, later Edward VIII, were members of a shooting party that bagged no fewer than 3,937 pheasants. "Perhaps we overdid it today," the King said on the way home.

proprietor of the *Daily Telegraph*. The Duke of Westminster, the owner of the lease, did not object when Johnny announced that he planned to demolish the existing building, but did balk at his choice of architect for its replacement: a draftsman in the estate office at Haddo. Yet J. T. Wimperis, who had long been on the Grosvenor Estate's "approved" list, sprang a surprise with his design for a house built of red brick, stone, and terracotta. It was, a critic opined, "the most violent departure yet from the original styles of house fronts in the Square."

Inside, the mansion boasted all modern conveniences, including an elevator, electric light, and cutting-edge plumbing. The *Survey of London* listed its more traditional features: "rooms for housekeeper, butler, under-butler, chef, cook, housemaid, valet, and menservants" in the basement, and on the upper floors "fourteen bedrooms, three bathrooms, two large night nurseries, a large day nursery, a large schoolroom, a governess's room, two dressing-rooms, a maid's room, two boudoirs, a sitting-room, two intercommunicating drawing-rooms, Lady Aberdeen's room, two rooms for Lord Aberdeen, a dining-room and a library."

Crucially for Ishbel and the advancement of her causes, the adjoining stable block contained a large hall for public meetings with a separate entrance from the street. She hired the "Furnishing and Decoration Studio" from Arthur Liberty's store in Regent Street to fit it out, because Leonard Wyburd, who had become its director at the age of only eighteen, specialized in "Eastern" designs. She had seen some painted panels on the tour of India and thought that they would create the right ambience.

But although Ishbel knew what she wanted, and Johnny, as usual, had provided a generous and flexible budget, she struggled to get the house built. Progress was frustratingly slow. To spur on the builders (who may have been biding their time because Ishbel had organized a rudimentary canteen on the site and read to them during their lunch breaks from the memoirs of intrepid adventurers*), the couple took to spending the night in the unfinished building. But when even this ploy failed, no less a figure

---

* The builders especially enjoyed stories about an American army officer, Adolphus Greely, who was rumored to have survived a disastrous expedition to the Arctic a few years earlier by eating the bodies of his less fortunate companions.

than their old friend and perennial houseguest at Dollis Hill, Mr. Gladstone, weighed in. He sent the builders this poetic exhortation:

Ye painters! Ye carpenters! greater and less,
Have done with your hammers, have done with your mess;
Go, make yourselves scarce; go, yourselves and your stuff,
This Boxing and Coxing* has lasted enough!
Go! And leave the premises clear and clean
For the Earl and Countess of Aberdeen.

When the house was finally finished, Ishbel waited before allowing a reporter through its doors, and so it was not until April 1889 that "A Lady" revealed to the world the wonders that lay beyond No. 27's striking facade:

Entering, you find yourself in a spacious hall, and then ascend by the broad stairway to the magnificent rooms on the first floor. The handsome balustrade is of carved mahogany, supporting here and there gracefully-wrought iron electric lamps.

But this was just the prelude to an even more impressive scene:

The spacious quaintly-shaped white and gold drawing-room is in Louis Quinze style. The blinds are of blue silk, arranged in festoons and edged with blue ball fringe. The mantel-pieces, of purest white marble, are exquisitely chiselled with floral wreaths. The walls are a mass of white and gold, and I noticed three groups of cupids, or Amorini, as I am told they are correctly styled.

Leonard Wyburd, the prodigy from Liberty's, had triumphed too:

The Indian music-room has carved panels, copied from windows round the tombs of Oriental sovereigns. The corridor along which the

---

* *Box and Cox* was a farce premiered in 1847 about an odd couple who shared rooms so cramped that one had to live there by day and the other by night. Arthur Sullivan's operatic version appeared in 1866.

visitor passes to reach the music-room has a tessellated floor, and the decorations are of distinctly Oriental character, carrying one in imagination away from busy, common-place London to the dreamy, far-off region of 'Araby, the blest'.

In these exotic surroundings, family prayers were said; dinners given for up to ninety guests; concerts, exhibitions, and "Cinderella dances"* held; and causes old and new promoted. These included the Co-operative Movement, the London Playing Fields Society, the National Poultry Council, and, of course, Irish Home Rule. Soon after moving in, Ishbel made the most of the setting for a spectacular "Eastern Bazaar" organized to raise funds for St. Mary's, Cable Street, the church Johnny's father had built. Visitors, who paid a sovereign to enter, could eat "an excellent dinner" served by "his lordship's henchmen," drink champagne for four shillings a pint, buy flowers from Mrs. Gladstone's stall, caricatures of famous actors from Ishbel's, and marvel at tricks performed by a conjuror in "eastern garb." But four-year-old Archie, decked out in "Nubian costume," stole the show as he danced "a curious measure," and everyone was amused by the "earnestness and gravity with which the wee man went through the business."

In what she saw as exile, Ishbel's love affair with Ireland was as ardent as ever, and she threw herself into promoting her Irish Industries Association on the mainland. She commissioned more dresses, trimmed with lace and embroidered with shamrocks and old Celtic symbols, from Dublin and Donegal, and relished the frisson that ran through the startled courtiers when she 'dressed Irish' to Queen Victoria's first Drawing Room of the season in 1888. That same year, Alice Hart drew crowds to an Irish exhibition in London with a full-sized replica of a Donegal village. There, inside one of its twelve cottages, as peat smoke wafted from an open fire, they could watch a young Irishwoman deftly embroidering a new black satin dress for Ishbel with silver thread, and at the "Fancy Fair" that ran alongside the exhibition, the *Illustrated London News* was much taken with her audacious ensemble:

---

* These were balls that, like the one in the fairy tale, ended at the stroke of midnight. Ishbel's, though, invariably went on into the small hours because "our friends enjoyed these little affairs."

The ex-Vicereine of Ireland wore a gown of white Irish poplin made
with a round body, and a narrow belt and hanging reticule of green
poplin. Limerick lace formed a short drapery at the top of the tablier;
Irish moss composed the foundation and the coronet of the bonnet,
the green ribbon strings of which were fixed by three little shamrock
brooches of Irish spar, while a necklace of shamrocks in the green
Connemara marble finished a costume carefully and kindly thought-
out to compliment the country concerned.*

Freed of her duty to remain impartial—something that she had found
irksome in the corridors of Dublin Castle—Ishbel returned, more visibly
than before, to the political fray and to women's causes. After delivering
a lively welcome to delegates at a "Conference of Women for Women's
Work" that she organized as president of the Aberdeen Ladies' Union for
the Protection of Young Girls, she found herself in demand as a speaker at
Liberal Party gatherings. Although the prospect of making her first speech,
to more than five thousand delegates in Birmingham Town Hall, filled her
with "fear and trembling," the reception from the *Leeds Times* to an address
at Bradford some months later, attested to her growing confidence:

> The speech was stateswoman-like and was creditable alike to the head
> and heart of Lady Aberdeen.

Soon, she was having to turn down invitations, which, in the case of
one from the Women's Liberal Association in a northern town, she did
gracefully, if not altogether convincingly:

> I do assure you there is no place in England I would rather go to than
> to Darlington.

But she readily accepted the suggestion from a group of women activists that she should run as a candidate in the election to the first London

---

* Although Ishbel's stall sold lace, embroidered bags, cushions, and "fancy needlework," and a
"beautiful Kerry cow" was raffled, not everything on offer came from Ireland. The wares on
other stalls included kittens, puppies, photographs of leading politicians, and "chips from trees
cut down by Mr Gladstone."

County Council in January 1889. They wanted her to test whether the new Local Government Act, which gave women rate-payers the right to vote, would also allow them to stand for election: the wording was vague. Ironically, having geared herself up for the campaign, Ishbel found herself disqualified because her husband paid all the property taxes on their houses.

She was also hard-pressed at home: new branches of the Onward and Upward Association were opening across Scotland and she had to keep its magazine rolling off the presses. Her mother begged her to slow down:

> As usual you have crowded into 10 days as much good work as would have taken anyone else months to accomplish. . . . But your rushing about quite confuses me and is enough to give you brain fever.

And Henry Drummond, too, was worried by the way she worked "like a tiger, or a hundred tigers," and although he knew she would be "frightfully angry" with him, begged her to "rein in."

As they had noticed, Ishbel was exhausted: not only by the "continuous stream of visitors" to her houses, but also from the stress of having to nurse her mother through an attack of rheumatic fever soon after Ishbel's return from her world trip in 1887. The society columns of the newspapers were filled with lugubrious predictions of Lady Tweedmouth's imminent demise, asserting that "no hopes are now entertained of recovery." Ishbel, too, feared the worst, as she watched her mother "hovering between life and death." But though the family was summoned to her bedside at Guisachan, along with the senior bishop of the Scottish Episcopal Church and an eminent specialist who was brought by special train from Aberdeen, Isabel did recover.

In October 1889, Ishbel was still depressed and confused. Drummond's unorthodox religious beliefs seem to have raised doubts in her about her own faith, causing her an "anguished mental struggle," and a letter from Johnny's uncle, Arthur Gordon, revealing that he had heard "plenty of gossip" that their "extravagance" had landed them in financial trouble, darkened her mood even further. The crisis came when she was hosting a lunch at Haddo:

I struggled through the luncheon as best I could, although the world was swimming around me, but afterwards, when coffee was being handed round on the lawn, I disgraced myself by subsiding in a faint.

In the "general panic" that ensued, the village doctor was summoned, but his only prescription was that Johnny should persuade Ishbel's London physician, Dr. Thomas MacLagan, to make a house call, even though his office was more than five hundred miles away in London. MacLagan was no ordinary family practitioner: as a researcher, he had pioneered the use of thermometers, and his work on the effects of salicin, an extract of willow bark, had been key to the invention of aspirin. But he ordered no pills for Ishbel, insisting instead that she should stay at Haddo and endure what she complained was "an enforced retirement in my own rooms for a couple of months."

Now it was her turn to have her health picked over in the newspapers. One asserted that her illness was "of the nature of a nervous fever," while another put it down to overwork, since there was "hardly a town of importance in the kingdom which her ladyship has not visited in her efforts to better the condition of the working people." Ishbel duly stayed inside, read a few books, devised elaborate games for her children, and soon rebelled. Dr. MacLagan, chiding her for being "bad to circumvent or restrain," tried another prescription: a trip abroad to a place in the sun.

The destination that Johnny and Ishbel chose may have seemed modest to their friends in high society, who, like Queen Victoria, usually set up with a large retinue of servants in grand hotels in Grasse or Menton or in the hills above Nice in the South of France. Bordighera, just a few miles across the border in Italy, was indeed rather less fashionable, but the climate was just as balmy, and it was home to another kindly and philanthropic denizen of Aberdeenshire, George MacDonald, whose villa, the Casa Coraggio, was a beguiling mixture of religious retreat and bohemian health spa. More than one poet* wrote ecstatically of Bordighera's romance and soothing beauty:

---

* Eva Gore-Booth (1870–1926), was also, like Ishbel, a campaigner for peace and women's rights. Bordighera and the Casa Coraggio had a special place in her heart, for it was there that she met Esther Roper, another activist, who became her lifelong companion, and possibly lover, in 1896. W. B. Yeats was one of many admirers of her poetry.

Was it not strange that by the tideless sea
The jar and hurry of our lives should cease?
That under olive boughs we found our peace
And all the world's great song in Italy?

MacDonald was the author of dark and sternly moralistic fantasy novels that kept many a Victorian child awake at night; but Ishbel found solace in his company, like many of his wide range of friends, who included Pre-Raphaelite artists, the poets Robert Browning, Alfred, Lord Tennyson, Henry Wadsworth Longfellow, and Walt Whitman, and writers and thinkers like Charles Dodgson (Lewis Carroll) and Thomas Carlyle. She especially enjoyed MacDonald's informal Sunday evening sermons, delivered from "an armchair by the big open fireplace":

He passes on the thoughts which have been in his mind, never hammering them in, just suggesting. Fancy what it would be like to have a church like that to go to every Sunday!

Meanwhile, even in her absence, the Indian Music Room was earning its keep with an extraordinary variety of events. Ishbel ensured that a newspaper correspondent was always on hand: she knew that her causes would only attract funds and volunteers if they were given publicity. Thus, a conference on women's trades unions, opened with "a forcible speech in favour of combination by women workers" by the theologian and social reformer Canon Henry Scott Holland,* was dutifully reported. But the newspapers were more far more interested in an afternoon talk given in aid of "the cottage work of poor Irish peasants and distressed Irish ladies" by P. T. Barnum, whose "Greatest Show on Earth" was enjoying a sell-out season in London.

Barnum regaled a packed audience, who had each paid half a guinea

---

*Henry Scott Holland (1847–1918) is remembered now for the hymn "Judge Eternal, Throned in Splendor" and for "Death Is Nothing at All," which is often read at funerals. The latter is commonly thought to be a poem, but it was, in fact, part of a sermon preached in 1910 while the body of King Edward VII was lying in state at Westminster. According to a Holland biographer: "He was a gifted if somewhat florid orator, driving home his message by piling up verbal images one on top of another, so that a little girl once commented after one of his sermons, 'My, what a lot of adjectives that man knows.'"

for their ticket, with what he billed, with uncharacteristic modesty, as "a short sketch of his life and adventures." He reminisced about how his tiny protégé General Tom Thumb had cheekily sung "Yankee Doodle Dandy" to Queen Victoria and danced around the room with her at Buckingham Palace; offered "sound advice" to everyone, "enjoining unswerving probity of character and a habit of looking at the bright side of things." He told a story about a dog with two tails and "yarns about Irish pilots, Irish waiters, funny deacons, mean men and all sorts of funny people whom the great showman had met in his travels through life." Everyone was charmed by the entertainment, and one journalist present managed to combine a fashion note with her words of praise for the supporting acts:

> Mr Shortis, the American banjo player,* contributed two clever solos, and Mrs Shaw,† 'the whistling lady,' was as wonderful as ever. She was dressed in grey, and looked very handsome, and it is easy to imagine how thoroughly natural this power must be to her to allow her to be graceful over it, if anyone observes their own face in a glass trying to whistle!

Even Queen Victoria was worried about Ishbel, beckoning Johnny forward when she noticed him among the dignitaries waiting to greet the Queen when she passed through Aberdeen in the royal train "and for a few minutes engaged him in conversation, Her Majesty very kindly making inquiries regarding the health of the Countess of Aberdeen."

---

* "Paddy" Shortis from Halifax, Nova Scotia, was known as the "Father of Ragtime" and the "Banjo Player to Royalty." A gifted musician—he was also a virtuoso on the violin and the piano—he played by ear. When he died in 1935, his obituaries recalled his concerts for the crowned heads of Europe, including the Tsar of Russia. One claimed that after performing in front of Queen Victoria and her son, later Edward VII, Shortis was "entitled to use a crest as banjoist to the court of England."

† Alice Shaw was another novelty act much loved by high society. "She only renders pieces of a high musical order," wrote a captivated New York journalist. "And then she whistles and looks pretty at the same time, which is something few male whistlers can do. Tall, beautiful, a very Juno in figure, she is the last person whom one would suspect of being addicted to an art that once was forbidden to our sex on pain of 'coming to a bad end.' Her tones in whistling are bird like in beauty." At one concert, "she presented her beautiful little five-year-old twins, Ethel and Elsie, who in simple fashion warbled the notes of an easy melody with wonderful facility and accuracy."

In fact, by the summer, Ishbel felt able to appear in public again, although, at first, only on home ground in Aberdeenshire. In June 1890,
she had the King of the Netherlands' tent erected again at Haddo for a
garden party in honor of Henry Morton Stanley, famous for finding the
"lost" explorer David Livingstone in Africa nearly twenty years before.
Stanley, who stayed for a few days, heard an address of welcome from the
tenants, planted a commemorative tree with a silver spade, and was shyly
presented with an admiring letter by eleven-year-old Doddie on behalf of
the pupils at his school.

Soon Ishbel had eased herself back into her charitable work, too, ignoring all the doctors' instructions, except one:

> As a measure of prevention, we were advised to avoid our usual au-
> tumn houseful of visitors, and instead, to go for two or three months
> to a country where none would know us and where we would know
> nobody!

They chose Canada, even though they knew plenty of people there.
Many of the tenants on the Guisachan and Haddo estates had emigrated
to farms on the prairies, as had a large number of "*Onward & Upward
girls,*" and Ishbel had heard worrying stories about the difficulties they
were experiencing as they tried to settle in a land so vast and empty. But
the trip would not be all work and no play, they decided: this time, they
would take the children with them to share the adventure.

In the first of a series of articles in her magazines, Ishbel described how,
in August 1890, she and Johnny sailed for Quebec on the S.S. *Parisian*,
braving the bad weather on the second evening to catch "a last glimpse
of the shores of 'Oold Ireland'" and "some whiffs of a dear familiar peat-
smoke, which sent us happy to our cabins that night."

Typically, once the high winds had dropped and they no longer felt
seasick, Johnny and Ishbel threw themselves into life aboard. Though
she now had "no cares, no responsibilities, no work, no telegrams, no
letters," and the children had been sent ahead with their nurses, Ishbel
did not allow herself to relax entirely. She made it her business to strike
up conversations with her fellow passengers. Some were useful, enabling
them to "pick up a good deal about the country and the people amongst

whom we were going to live for the next three months," and some were disturbing:

> This very ship of ours, the *Parisian*, had a narrow escape in May. In the fog she ran atilt against what was called a small iceberg, but which one of the passengers described to me as having a most alarming appearance . . . a towering white mass, part of which seemed to overshadow the deck.

According to a fellow traveler, Ishbel sought out the women in steerage, the cheapest, most basic accommodation on the ship, and "romped with the little ones, told them stories, and acted towards them all, as an observant sailor remarked, 'as if she had been their sister.' She is, indeed," the passenger concluded, "one of nature's noblewomen, whom to know is to respect and love." Typically, while she was there, Ishbel took a close look round and was shocked by the crowded, insanitary conditions, particularly those endured by her own servants. "As one gentleman said," she complained to Henry Drummond, "he would not put his dog to sleep in such places." She wasted no time in taking up the matter with the captain, who was most displeased. Ishbel, thus unmollified, said: "I should never advise anyone to come by this boat."

At home, as the ship neared the Canadian coast, the newspapers broke some surprising news: "Lord Aberdeen has sold his house in Grosvenor Square." Although the couple had only recently moved into No. 27, there were good reasons for the sale, the story explained:

> Irish Industries and Scotch Industries, and their advancement, occupied a great deal of Lady Aberdeen's time and attention, besides ragged schools, young women's Christian associations, and other movements entailing committee and platform work. The last straw was politics and the Gladstonian propaganda broke down Lady Aberdeen's health.

Mayfair in the London Season was no place for an invalid, so Johnny had first let the house to a "rich Australian to remove any temptation to Lady Aberdeen to mix again in crowds." Soon after, another tycoon, James Mason, who had made his fortune by cleverly reopening some ancient pyrites mines in Portugal, had then come forward with an offer of £65,000 for the house: one that the cash-strapped Johnny, who had spent £48,000 on the building, could not bring himself to refuse.*

Now, free for the moment of immediate financial worries, the family could settle happily into a house that the Governor General's son had found for them in Hamilton, Ontario, an industrial town about forty miles from Niagara Falls. Highfield† was a clever choice—not least because the rent was "decidedly cheap"—and the family felt at home immediately. As Marjorie, who was nine at the time, remembered, it was big enough to accommodate the large household that Johnny and Ishbel had brought with them: "their secretary, doctor, valet, maid, four children, governess, nurse, and as servants for Highfield six young women and two young men who wished to stay in Canada afterwards."

Even the look of the place will have been familiar, for Highfield was built in the "picturesque gothic" style that colonial officials and rich settlers had imported from England. Fifty years earlier, Captain Frederick Marryat, a British naval officer and author of the classic novel for young readers *The Children of the New Forest*, had noted the fashion for designing houses "according to the English taste and the desire for exclusiveness, away from the road and . . . embowered in trees." Highfield's setting conformed to these ideals, although Ishbel was unimpressed by its grounds, which, at only thirteen acres, she deemed too small. But she liked Hamilton itself and the chance to spend time with her family, reverting to her own childhood with Henry Meux Jr. as she and Johnny led their own children on hunts for the butterflies that flitted around the town. At night, they covertly smeared honey and molasses on the lampposts in the street outside to entrap the "magnificent but unwary moths" that swarmed there. Looking back many years later, Ishbel wrote:

---

*At today's values, £65,000 amounts to around £5,500,000 ($7,000,000) and £48,000 to around £4,000,000 ($5,200,000), so Johnny's profit was considerable.

† Though she applauded his philanthropy, Ishbel was wary of their landlord, William Eli Sanford, a clothing tycoon known as the "wool king of Canada." It was not because she thought him or his other house, named "Wesanford" after himself, "vulgar," although, with its fifty-six ornate rooms, elevators, bathroom fittings inlaid with Royal Crown Derby porcelain, and electrical orchestrinas, he and it certainly were. "It is a notorious fact," she wrote, "that when he arrives home Mrs Sanford goes away, & when she comes home, he goes away, & that there are reasons for this in his private life." Sanford drowned in a boating accident in 1899. His "young female companion" was unable to save him.

Our thoughts still linger fondly over the days spent at Highfield, which will always be associated in our memories and those of our children with sunshine and butterflies.

But although she piously advised the young readers of *Onward and Upward,*

if you want really to know something of a country, its customs, and its people, it is a great advantage if you can settle down in some typical place for a few weeks,

she and Johnny were soon heading west, leaving the children in the care of their nurse, governess, and the eight servants. Inevitably, despite Dr. MacLagan's entreaties, Ishbel believed she had work to do. And there was another incentive: Henry Drummond, who had been on a trip to Australia and Japan, had arranged to meet them in Vancouver and join them for the return journey.

They traveled in even more luxury than usual, thanks to Sir Donald Smith, a friend from North East Scotland and one of the founders of the Canadian Pacific Railway, who lent them "a beautiful new [rail]car all to ourselves." "We could shut ourselves off into comfortable little rooms at night," Ishbel wrote, while during the day they sat in the "long sitting-room, panelled with pretty white mahogany, where we read, and wrote, and painted, and where we had many a pleasant little tea party during the four weeks while we inhabited it."

What Ishbel did not enjoy was looking out of the window "at such apparently sterile country":

The trees are stunted, the vegetation allows us to see the stony character of the soil below; some of the telegraph poles even have to be upheld by heaps of stones around them, and the desolation is often rendered greater by many of the trees having been the prey of forest fires.

Both Ishbel and Johnny had been at the forefront of a drive to encourage young Scots to emigrate to Canada. Her Aberdeen Ladies' Union had helped dozens of girls to find "a better future" in the country, which, according to the report of its emigration committee, seemed to have "an almost unlimited capacity for absorbing our surplus population of young women." Thanks to a colonization fund raised from the British government, Highland lairds, and collections at public meetings, a group of crofters from the Hebrides had been helped to settle at a place called Killarney in Manitoba, which was not far off Ishbel and Johnny's route.

Ishbel was curious to see how this experiment was working, but now that she could see for herself what life was really like on the prairies, she was beginning to have her doubts:

> It is difficult for those at home to realise the isolation of such settlers; everything has to be begun and carried out by the work of their own hands, and their whole thoughts are absorbed by the desperately hard work which is an essential for success.

And the sudden appearance at Winnipeg of one of her family's own New World émigrés, her brother Coutts Marjoribanks, pressed the point home. Her mother had warned her: "Coutts has had ill luck with his farming; 'Papa very angry'." Thus, his confession that he had given up the struggle at the Horseshoe Ranch came as no surprise. But Ishbel was, as ever, on Coutts's side: she would have to find a way to rescue him from "the dreary place in Dakota where I visited him a few years before, and where bad luck had dogged his footsteps."

In the meantime, she and Johnny traveled on together to Killarney, enduring the discomfort of "a 'Democrat', a sort of four-wheeled cart, with two seats, one behind the other," on a track that seemed to consist entirely of "bumps and jars and ruts, and roots and hillocks." They found that the crofters had had mixed fortunes. For some, like the Daroughs, the first year's harvest had been disappointing;* others, like John Nicholson, had adjusted well to their harsh new surroundings, piling up hundreds of bushels of wheat in the barns beside their little wooden houses. Ishbel professed to be encouraged:

---

* A year later, Ishbel heard good news from Killarney and wrote in her diary: "Mr Shaughnessy reports wonderful things of the Manitoban and North West harvest this year. I forget the exact numbers he gave me but the result anyway is to give an average of between £300 & £400 into the pockets of 17,000 farmers."

Some who came knew nothing about agricultural work. And that they should have got on so well as they have done is very creditable.

But, in private, she despaired of the settlers' plight:

May Heaven preserve us from ever being fated to banishment to the far-famed wheatlands of Manitoba! Oh the inexpressible dreariness of those everlasting prairies! Wooden shanties, most of the size we would put up for a [game]keeper's shelter at home, but here inhabited by farmers owning some hundreds of acres and some half-dozen children.

And she was appalled when she eavesdropped on a conversation between Johnny and the local government surveyor, John O'Brien:

I heard A. expressing a wish to Mr O'Brien that we could have a house there and Mr O'Brien responding by offering an acre of his own. I did not feel enthusiastic over the project. And A.'s ardour cooled down presently when he discovered that said O'Brien was a newspaper correspondent & was prepared to record the words of wisdom that fell from his lips.

Ishbel, who loved her home comforts, was distressed to see that the people of the prairies had none. This, at least, she realized, was a problem that she could do something about; and when, on her return journey, she was asked to address an audience of fourteen hundred women in Winnipeg, she described her dismay at finding that "there was scarce a flower to be seen about the houses, nor a picture on the walls, and the children seemed utterly unprovided with any literature, save lesson books." She asked "if it would be not be possible to organise a collection of magazines, papers, and books from homes in Winnipeg, and to send them out periodically to settlers' homes."

No one said no to Ishbel after listening to one of her impassioned speeches, and the women of Winnipeg duly rallied round to inaugurate the Aberdeen Association for the Distribution of Good Literature to Settlers in the West. They refined Ishbel's plan, to include not only the families of "settlers who have had a good education," but also "bachelor settlers, ranchers, miners and lumbermen" who were in an "extremely isolated position." The postmaster general agreed to provide free postage for the parcels of books, and the philanthropist Andrew Carnegie, who believed that the "noblest possible use of wealth" was to "contribute to the enlightenment and the joys of the mind, to the things of the spirit," sent $500 to pay for paper, string, and other expenses. Soon the association could report that Ishbel's journalist friend W. T. Stead had donated hundreds of copies of his *Review of Reviews* "besides many thousands of his Penny Books," while Johnny's mother gave two hundred and fifty copies of the 5th Earl's biography, which, Ishbel claimed, "were most heartily appreciated by the families to whom they were sent."

The letters of thanks flowed in from the prairies. One from Solsgirth, Manitoba, was typical:

> I cannot tell you how grateful I am for the reading sent. It is such a boon in the long winter evenings and I have ever been "a book worm."

Others, like this thrifty recipient from Alexander, an isolated halt on the Canadian Pacific, revealed that the magazines supplied them with more than just good reading:

> I must tell you how useful the picture papers are that you send to us. Our house is nearly papered with them from top to bottom and we have made frames for the good ones. We cover the walls with cheap factory cotton and then paste over. It is more durable and warmer than any wall paper besides being pretty to look at and such a pleasure and amusement for winter evenings.

But none struck more sharply to Ishbel's heart than this plea from a mother from Neepawa, whose "four beautiful lads and wee girlie" had drowned in a nearby lake:

> Don't send reading matter for little ones *it breaks my heart*; but I truly thank you for making the last months of my dear ones' lives happy. They were truly delighted with the books.

After the visit to Killarney, Coutts returned home to Dakota Territory. He now had the blessing for his escape plan from his sister, who decided:

> We are going to get Mr Clay* to report on the profitability of selling the place wh[ich] Coutts thinks will be cheap at 20,000 dollars and then try to get Coutts over into Canada into some more civilised part, probably Brit. Columbia.

Johnny and Ishbel set off again for the West, their progress interrupted only when, soon after leaving Winnipeg, their train was derailed after some cattle had strayed onto the unfenced line. No one was hurt, and Ishbel was frustrated that the light was too low to photograph the wreckage with her new Kodak camera† and had to sketch it instead.

At Vancouver, they were contacted, or more accurately ambushed, by "an old friend," G. G. Mackay. "Gee Gee," as he was known, was the engineer from Inverness who had won the contract for making the roads at Guisachan. He had also bought and sold properties in the Scottish Highlands and islands, and was now one of many agents talking up investment opportunities in the virgin acres of British Columbia. Another emigrant from Britain, Charles William Holliday, watched Mackay and his fellow property hucksters going about their business with a mixture of amusement and distaste:

> The real estate men were shouting about the delights of fruit growing—a lotus-eating existence in which you idled away the sunny hours while the dollars grew on the trees—you could actually see them doing this in some of the illustrated circulars that were broadcast all over the world. The main push of this movement was G. G. McKay, a bluff and genial promoter from Vancouver, who thought of and lived for nothing but real estate—it was said of him that when he died, and the gates of

---

* This was John Clay, author of *My Life on the Range*. Known across the West as the "Dean of American Stockman," he enjoyed a lucrative sideline as an advisor to foreign investors. But for once his golden touch escaped him, and Coutts did not manage to sell the Horseshoe Ranch until 1901, and then for less than half his vaunted $20,000.

† Ishbel was a talented artist and an enthusiastic photographer. She included a number of her photographs in both her *Onward and Upward* articles and *Through Canada with a Kodak*, a book about her travels, published three years later.

heaven opened up for him, he would seize St. Peter by the lapel and say to him, 'How are the chances for laying out a townsite here?'

In Johnny, who had spent the journey musing about buying a "shanty," and in Ishbel, desperate to find a job for Coutts in British Columbia, the silver-tongued Gee Gee found willing patsies. And the £17,000 profit that they had made on the sale of the house in Grosvenor Square had been burning a hole in their pockets. Gee Gee extolled the virtues of a plot of land that would suit them perfectly: so fine was it that he was even thinking of stumping up $10,000 for it himself! Ishbel, echoing his sales pitch, wrote excitedly in her journal after the meeting:

Thirty miles down Okanagan Lake by steamer there is a farm [of] 480 acres with a nice house, some 70 head of cattle, horses, wheat, implements etc. . . . The place besides being on a lake is on a plateau surrounded by hills where the most splendid sport can be had.

This most desirable of properties, Gee Gee had gone on to assure them, would be the shrewdest of investments:

Mr Mackay says he is confident of the value of the land and that in a few years it would sell for double if not four times its present value.

There was no time to visit the farm, which lay almost a day's journey away, but Ishbel, as naïve in matters financial as she was in the ways of New World property salesmen, trusted Mackay:

He has proved himself so safe and wise a man that we are safe in his hands.

Soon afterwards, they left Vancouver as the owners, sight unseen, of those 480 acres in the Okanagan Valley. Everyone was happy: Johnny had his "shanty"; Ishbel could now rescue Coutts from the rigors of raising cattle in Dakota Territory; and Mackay wasted no time in using Johnny's name to secure another deal for enough land to build a town on. But on the other side of the Atlantic, the mood was very different. Ishbel's father,

Dudley Tweedmouth, who now knew the risks of investing in ranches, was not impressed when Ishbel tried Gee Gee's sales pitch on him, and wrote her a letter that was curmudgeonly even by his standards:

Well, as usual, you are head over ears in business of your own manufacturing.

Ishbel named the new farm Guisachan and had some seedling firs sent from Glen Affric to be planted there: they would, she thought, neatly link her holiday homes in the Old World and the New. But no one seemed to worry when they died on the land where Gee Gee Mackay had promised that anything and everything would grow; and no one, except in hindsight, saw an omen in their withering.

12

A Fruit Farm in Kelowna and a Fake Castle in Chicago

The months after leaving Canada at the end of 1890 were exhausting as ever. Signs of a Liberal resurgence revived Ishbel's dream of another tour of duty for Johnny in Ireland, and she returned to speaking at meetings of the party's Women's Federation. Almost immediately, those hopes were swept away by the downfall of Charles Parnell, leader of the Irish Parliamentary Party and advocate of Home Rule, whose long-standing affair with the wife of another politician was revealed in a scandalous divorce case. Now Ishbel spoke, with characteristic understanding of human frailty, in defense not so much of Parnell himself, but of the people of Ireland who had put their trust in him:

> Let us show them that we will not join their opponents in railing at the man who is fallen: that we shall stand by them come what will.

Ishbel also campaigned for a law that would require midwives to be trained and registered: a reform that, despite what one doctor called "the terrible mortality that afflicted lying-in women," had long been resisted by the medical associations. But she devoted most of her time and energy to promoting not only Irish cottage industries, but Scottish ones, too, thanks to Millicent, the 4th Duchess of Sutherland, another aristocratic lady with a zeal for good works and a fabulously rich husband to finance her. In

1850, during the Highland potato famine, one of Millicent's predecessors, Harriet, the 2nd Duchess, had organized a "tartan show" to market the tweed, tartan, and plaid blankets produced by the crofters' wives on her husband's Dunrobin estate and thereby supplement their meager incomes. But Harriet was too busy campaigning against slavery, attending court as Mistress of the Robes and close friend of Queen Victoria, and indulging her greatest passion, building and refurbishing some of Britain's grandest stately homes,* to develop the enterprise that she had started. It was not until Millicent organized a series of "Sutherland sales" in Inverness and London forty years later, that a new Scottish Home Industries Association was formed.

Ishbel explained its aims when, as president of the Eastern Counties Branch, she opened an exhibition in Dundee. The plan was to organize the craft workers "and to try to bring their work into the market under best possible circumstances." She declared that the associations also had a moral purpose and that they "sought to lessen or to prevent the mischief, or more than mischief, which growing boys and girls full of spirits were apt to take to if there was not some thoughtful piece of carpentering or painting or embroidery, or some such thing, to do at home."

But the success of this exhibition, and of the earlier Irish ones in Edinburgh and London, had given Ishbel an ambitious idea: she would apply for the Irish Industries Association to display its wares at what promised to be the greatest show on earth, the World's Columbian Exposition, which was due to open in less than two years. It would mark not only the four hundredth anniversary of Christopher Columbus's landing in the Americas, but also the recovery of its host city Chicago from the "Great Fire" of 1871.

The committee of the Irish Industries Association was, as Marjorie later put it, "startled" by Ishbel's proposal that the association's exhibit be a full-sized Irish cabin for a live model bride and her wedding presents.

---

*Harriet far outdid Ishbel in her expenditure on houses, lavishing vast sums on Dunrobin Castle in Scotland and her magnificent English stately homes, Lilleshall Hall in Shropshire, Trentham Hall in Staffordshire, and Cliveden Manor in Buckinghamshire. Queen Victoria, who made the short trip from Buckingham Palace to visit her at her London residence Stafford House, then the most valuable private residence in London, said, "I have come to your palace from my house."

Some members thought it would be too expensive, while others pointed out that the lace makers would not have enough time to produce enough material for the dresses. But they relented when Ishbel told them that the philanthropist Andrew Carnegie had offered to underwrite the venture. Since time was now short—construction of the fair's buildings was already underway—she decided to go to the United States to "interview the Exhibition authorities" and drum up support from businessmen with Irish connections.

Ishbel sailed for America on August 27, after stopping off in Dublin to inspect one of the Irish Industries Association's new shops. A few weeks earlier, she had opened another at a house she had persuaded Johnny to buy at 20 Motcomb Street in Belgravia, then the heart of the London fashion world. Ahead of her time as usual, she had issued a "circular" to the press and held court on the shop floor to reporters. The one from the *Daily Express* was impressed with the goods on offer. They included "five o'clock tea cloths, tray and table cloths, toilet covers, pillow shams, brush and comb bags, hand-sewn and machine-made under-linen, woollen goods, gentlemen's silk stockings (hand knit), gloves etc." And the *Pall Mall Gazette* left full of admiration for the "aristocratic shopkeeper" herself:

> I took my departure, thinking that Lady Aberdeen might well wear a brooch of the shape of a bee with spread wings, for there is no busier woman in the country than the president of the Irish Industries Association.

Ishbel spent the first few weeks of the trip to America touring the country with Johnny and ten-year-old Marjorie. In New York, which she found "v. hot" and "rather exhausting," she checked on the welfare of some girls who had been helped to emigrate to the city by the Aberdeen Ladies' Union, chased butterflies with Marjorie in Central Park, and photographed the "quaint little grown-up overdressed New York children." In New Hampshire, they rode up Mount Washington on the "cog" railway and marveled at a "nice place, right amongst the mountains, called the 'Profile' from one of the rocks hard by having the appearance of a man's face."* At Northfield, Massachusetts, they called in at the retreat set up by the evangelist Dwight L. Moody: an experience, Ishbel said, that "deeply impressed itself on our minds." "Be prepared for a series of notes of exclamation," she warned Henry Drummond when she wrote to thank him for arranging the visit:

> The tone of the whole place is so helpful and earnest, and yet there is no goody-goody talking. . . . I don't think I ever enjoyed two days more in my life, and A. and Marjorie are of the same mind too.

And so they wandered westwards into Canada, lingering at Banff for a holiday of "sketching, riding, driving, and A. swimming in the sulphur lake"; stopping the train that Johnny had chartered, to check on the well-being of a family from the Haddo estate; and finding themselves making the very first trip on the Shuswap & Okanagan Railway to Vernon, British Columbia, "very slowly and often at foot's pace," on track that had been laid down only hours before.

Ishbel wrote later:

> We must have looked a curious crew. There was the engine and tender, our private car, and then a 'caboose,' a sort of guard's van, on the top and inside of which travelled a medley of men, dogs, packages, agricultural machinery, and all sorts of oddments.

Thus, on October 14, 1891, exactly a year to the day since their meeting with Gee Gee Mackay, Johnny, Ishbel, and Marjorie found themselves on the shores of Lake Okanagan, on their way at last to see

---

* Ishbel had wanted to go there ever since reading Nathaniel Hawthorne's folksy moral tale, "The Great Stone Face." This natural geological formation, also known as the Old Man of the Mountain, dominated the Franconia Notch, a pass through the White Mountains, until it crumbled away in May 2003. It was New Hampshire's original tourist attraction, inspiring many a sententious pronouncement from nineteenth-century preachers and politicians. This prize specimen is attributed to the statesman Daniel Webster: "Men hang out their signs indicative of their respective trades; shoemakers hang out a gigantic shoe; jewelers a monster watch, and the dentist hangs out a gold tooth; but in the mountains of New Hampshire, God Almighty has hung out a sign to show that there He makes men."

the Guisachan Ranch for themselves. Marjorie never forgot the romance of their arrival:

> A small ancient launch conveyed us down the lake for four hours in the moonlight; from the landing stage we walked a couple of miles through tall fir-trees, till in a clearing we saw the white frame-house, with hills behind, lake in front, and at the door the manager pointing his gun at us because it was well after midnight.

Ishbel felt at home immediately, for in the darkness she could make out "mountains more like the Inverness-shire mountains of my youth than any others we had seen in Canada," and Marjorie was amused to see how her parents "hurried like gleeful children . . . to see their very own play-house."

Although Coutts had become used to living in a rough-hewn cabin during his years in Dakota Territory, he had decided that the "nice house" that Mackay had promised—actually one of three very basic wooden buildings on the site, all infested with bedbugs and pockmarked by bullets fired off by boisterous farmhands—would not be grand or comfortable enough for a couple who enjoyed the "Adams style" in Scotland and all modern conveniences in Mayfair. He and his assistant, a fellow Scot named Eustace Smith, hastily drew up a design for a curious "oriental" folly that may have been based on a bungalow that had caught Ishbel's eye on her tour of India a few years earlier. Despite the late hour, she embarked on a tour of inspection:

> The hall is especially pretty with a sort of gold Japanese paper & arranged with stag horns found lying here & some of Coutts's own horns and stuffed heads from Dakota. Then there is a large sitting-room & dining room, four good bedrooms, two small ones, an office & kitchen just across a verandah & a verandah running right round the house. This is just perfect and delightful.

But one small pang of conscience marred that delight. The log house built by the previous owner, John McDougall, only five years earlier, was sturdy and substantial.* "It is really a better house than either of my brothers had at their other places," Ishbel (who was unaware of the bedbugs) noted the next morning. It was, she added, "well" that Mr. Jamieson, the family lawyer, whose letters pointing out the parlous state of their finances were becoming ever more insistent, had not seen it, "for he would have suggested that there is no need to build a new house on the present scale."

But Jamieson's concerns were rather different when he visited Guisachan a year later to compile a report on the business:

> The house is a pretty one and contrasts, of course, very favourably with those in the vicinity, but I was informed, and my own observations confirmed the information, that it is badly finished. No architect acquainted with the style of building and the habits of the country was employed—the thick paper generally used for partitions for warmth and deafening was not, I understood, provided.

In fact, the feckless Coutts had allowed the builders to cut corners, and the Japanese wallpaper was simply stuck onto chicken wire nailed to the house's wooden frame. No one noticed, least of all his devoted sister, as the family enjoyed their newfound idyll. They went on a bear hunt, but, as Ishbel admitted with obvious relief, "Mrs Bruin was cleverer than us," and at home enjoyed the food served up by Mr. Foo, the temperamental cook. They explored the surrounding countryside, hitching up the pair of horses that Johnny had bought at the local fair to drive to a church service held at the pretty schoolhouse, and shared "home cured ham, home made jam, home made bread" with the neighbors, although Johnny had to put up with one "dear old Yorkshire lady" remarking that "if he would eat more oatmeal porridge and do less tea drinking he would be a better figure of a man." They called on the priests at the local mission house; "pottered about the garden" amidst "the splendid cabbages"; and marveled that the

---

* The house survives and is, according to Canada's Historic Places organization, "valued as one of the few pre-1890 houses remaining in Kelowna" and for being "a relatively rare log house" in the "Pioneer Vernacular Style."

cows were so wild that to milk them, the cowboys had to chase and lasso them, before throwing them onto their sides. The highlight of the visit was organizing the valley's first "social," at which Marjorie "brought down the house" with three French songs. There was time for a few good works: Johnny gave $400 towards the cost of a new church, and Ishbel fretted that Coutts and the other young men in the area would succumb to the temptations of the local store. It was, she had heard, "a centre of mischief unhappily to the neighbourhood":

> It is the custom to repair to this store every Sunday after church & then to sit & drink all afternoon & evening & night, making a frightful row & disturbance. Men often spend all the week's wages there.

But for Ishbel and Johnny the temptations of Guisachan were of a different kind. To their surprise, they found the dolce far niente of life on the ranch seductive. "I must not weary you with our enthusiasm for our new home," Ishbel confided to a friend, "which A. says he will enjoy possessing much more than he ever did H[addo] H[ouse], (well so far as regards the rented land part certainly)."

After a visit to some neighbors who had made $250 from the apples that they had grown on only one-third of an acre, there was a good chance, she added, that Mr. Jamieson's regular scoldings might soon be replaced with words of praise:

> So please now calculate what about 200 acres planted with apple trees would bring in according to this. Or calculate that they will only bring in half that amount & then say if our farm is not going to pay.

Johnny wanted to go further:

> A. is going to put up a jam factory. . . . It would be nice to see poor old Coutts a rich man after all!

But he did not stop there, and Gee Gee Mackay was soon sounding out neighboring landowners about selling their ranches, even visiting one who was languishing in the local jail.[*] When he named a preposterous price, Ishbel reported,

> A. was not to be baulked. He is enthusiastic about the prospects of this country & is determined to go in for it somehow.

Within days, Mackay wrote to say that he had persuaded the owner of an even better property to sell up. It was, of course, an unmissable bargain:

> I have this day bought from the Hon. F.G. Vernon his ranch containing upwards of 13,000 acres (believed to be 13,500) together with about 2,000 cattle, about 70 horses, implements, pigs, furniture, crop, hay and everything movable on the ranch. I think it is a very reasonable price; he held out hard for $250,000 but I stuck to £50,000, which is only $241,000.

Ishbel was excited, but more than a little nervous about their new property, the Coldstream Ranch, which was near the town of Vernon, some forty-five miles as the crow flies from the farm at Guisachan:

> Will not Mr Jamieson's hair stand on end at A. taking the bit in his teeth like this? But after all, if we choose to give up the idea of buying a London house, this fit of speculation will be quite justifiable.

Johnny found a more worthy justification for his extravagance. He knew that settlers had been trying in vain for years to persuade the cattle farmers who owned most of the land in the area to sell them plots of twenty to fifty acres on which they could make a living growing fruit, hops, and vegetables. There had been little scope to do this at the Guisachan Ranch which, by comparison to Coldstream, was a small holding: but now with thousands of acres at his command, Johnny could give the settlers the opportunities

---

[*] Arthur Knox was accused of setting fire to a rival rancher's haystacks in the hope, it was alleged, of driving him from the area. Many suspected that he had been framed, and after serving three years' hard labor, Knox was welcomed back into the community and soon became president of the Agricultural & Trades Association.

they sought. The ranches would also provide jobs for immigrants, including some from his own estates in Scotland; the fruit farmers would be able to sell their produce direct to the jam factory; and the experts he would employ to advise him on irrigation, marketing, and planting would be available to help his neighbors too. He hoped that his expensive vote of confidence in the region would attract investors from the Old World, even those whose financial fingers, like his, had been burnt on the cattle ranges of the United States. The time was right for the "fruit rush" to begin.

Though they stayed only nine days at the Guisachan Ranch, Ishbel left relaxed and happy:

> We have enjoyed a more real holiday than we have ever had before. . . . We have found it, too, a remarkably healthy place—I have never had a vestige of a headache and we have all been furiously hungry.

There was no danger of Johnny and Ishbel starving in Chicago, where the city's socialites vied with one another to lionize their aristocratic visitors. Ishbel made the most of it as she presented her plans for an Irish Industries Association showcase at the World's Fair to members of the organizing committee, local politicians, and potential sponsors. After awkward encounters, on their earlier trips, with journalists far less deferential than their British counterparts, she had learned the importance of public relations, and now decided to "endeavour to inspire them with enthusiasm for Irish laces, embroideries, and tweeds." Her strategy worked all too well, and she spent the day "devoured by interviewers."

The *Chicago Tribune* duly described her plan for an exhibit that would fill two rooms:

> The carpets and furniture, the hangings and portières* are to be entirely the work of Irish people, and as far as possible that made by Irish women and girls. There will be shown samples of all the beautiful laces, embroideries, linen and cambric articles, and the coarser kinds of cloth, such as homespuns and friezes.

---

* A curtain designed to hang over a door: an essential draft-prevention measure in all castles and even Mayfair mansions in the Victorian era.

Even more importantly, her search for "prominent wealthy Irishmen" who might fund it was immediately successful, thanks to introductions to the president of the Chicago National Bank and the proprietor of the *Chicago Herald* from John V. Farwell, a local merchant and philanthropist. Farwell had two things in common with Johnny and Ishbel: he was a follower of Dwight L. Moody and a partner in a ranch on the Texas Panhandle* that was hemorrhaging money. Soon, Ishbel could report that "Marshall Field, the biggest dry goods man in America, whose place is a sight in itself, has ordered the bride's wedding dress and has undertaken to make all the arrangements for us for wax figures, glass cases etc."

At least one of the ladies—the most important of all, from Ishbel's point of view—was already on board. Bertha Palmer, the wife of another of Chicago's store tycoons, was renowned as a collector of impressionist art (she had twenty-nine Monets and eleven Renoirs), as a philanthropist who paid for kindergartens for the city's children, and as the owner of jewelry so fabulous that when she arrived late at a concert aboard an ocean liner, a star of the Metropolitan Opera stopped in mid-aria to admire her. She was also clever and a formidable organizer, which made her the obvious choice for president of the Board of Lady Managers of the fair. After a dinner given for Ishbel at the Palmer Mansion, an extraordinary ersatz gothic Germanic castle festooned with turrets and minarets, Ishbel wrote admiringly that she had "conceived a very high opinion of Mrs Palmer's business capacity & of her tact & wisdom in managing people." But Mrs. Palmer and the Chicago store tycoons made the couple work hard for their support, as Ishbel wrote in her diary at the end of the visit:

> Horridly ungrateful is it not to say this when people are so kind? But it is a veritable mystery to us how these people, especially the women, survive, with their heated rooms into which not a breath of air is allowed to wander, their spun out unwholesome meals & their want of

---

* The XIT Ranch, made over to Farwell and his brother Charles by the Texas Legislature as part-payment for construction of the state capitol in 1879, was, at three million acres, the largest fenced ranch in the world. It ran in a strip up to thirty miles wide for two hundred miles along the border with New Mexico. Johnny was a trustee of the Capitol Freehold Land and Investment Company which the Farwells set up to pay for its running expenses.

exercise. For these four days we have done as Rome does, for the sake
of attaining the end.

Ishbel left not only with the sponsorship she needed but with relief,
for she had not told the committee back home in London that Andrew
Carnegie had written to her with second thoughts about the plan he had
earlier agreed to back:

A facsimile cottage may not appeal to people.... If I were you, I should
drop it, but then I am not an irrepressible genius who can win victory
from any—even the most discouraging—conditions. If, however, you
decide to go on and Aberdeen risks £500, I shall gladly go jointly with
him for an equal amount.

They meandered to New York and the ship that was to take them
home, stopping in Hamilton, Ontario, to see the friends they had made
the year before. They dropped in on a conference of the Women's Christian Temperance Union, where Ishbel was so shocked by the "more or
less violent temperance harangues" that when called upon to speak, she
changed the subject to Irish Home Rule, to the general mystification of the
delegates. They toured Wellesley College, where Johnny was "absolutely
captivated" with the "fresh delightful maidens," prompting Ishbel to note
that "certainly there was 'safety in numbers,'" and they extracted several
more generous checks from businessmen for the Chicago exhibit on the
way. But due to a scheduling slipup, they failed to meet with President
Harrison, who, in any case, Ishbel opined, did "not appear to count for
much either in politics or in society."

But the highlight of this last stage of the journey was "a very pleasant
evening" with the venerable writer and medical reformer Oliver Wendell
Holmes in his study overlooking "a glorious view of the Charles River in
Boston." "We all three fell in love with him," wrote Ishbel to Henry Drum-
mond, after hearing the eighty-two-year-old's views on their mutual friend
W. E. Gladstone ("That Gladstone, what business has he to be so vigorous at
his age?") and enjoying "a great deal of chat about America past & present."
When they left, Holmes gave each of them a copy of one of his books, and
Marjorie returned the favor, as another visitor discovered a few years later:

Around me on mantel and table and shelf and stand, were the treasured gifts of nearly sixty years. He directed my attention specially to a model of Grandfather Harrison's white hat* made from redeemed Treasury notes. 'That,' said he, 'was given to me by the daughter of Lord Aberdeen.'

But even as she sailed home, her mission accomplished, from the trip designed to "benefit her health," Ishbel did not allow herself to relax, signing off her diary in typical fashion:

And now Good-bye. Au revoir—to work, to work.

On their return to Haddo, while Ishbel set about organizing the Chicago exhibit, Johnny was occupied with enterprises of his own, drawing yet again upon the apparently inexhaustible profit from the sale of 27 Grosvenor Square. In Canada, work began on planting fruit trees on the ranches under the watchful eye of Gee Gee Mackay, who, despite having secretly taken commissions for the sale of the Coldstream Ranch from both Johnny and the vendor Forbes George Vernon, otherwise proved to be a dependable ally.

All went well at first, particularly at Guisachan, as the local newspapers reported:

This year only slightly in excess of 100 acres will be planted to fruit, 100 being put in oats and 100 in wheat, the remainder (80 acres) in hops, vegetables and small fruit gardens. A large irrigation ditch lately made, by which 600 inches of water are taken from Mission creek, runs through the estate, from which branch ditches have been made, so that every portion of the land can be well watered.

---

*Benjamin Harrison, the twenty-third president of the United States, was the grandson of William Henry Harrison, ninth president. Though he did his best to avoid comparisons with his forebear, Benjamin's campaign managers thought they might help him win the presidency and coined the slogan "Grandfather's Hat Fits Ben." No one could actually remember what Grandfather Harrison's hat looked like or whether he even had one. If he did, not wearing it may have proved fatal. According to popular legend, he caught a chill in a torrential downpour and died of pneumonia exactly one month after taking the oath of office. On the other hand, if his final illness was caused by pollution of the White House water supply from a nearby public sewer, as researchers have recently suggested, no headgear could have protected him.

At the local agricultural show, Coutts and his comanager Eustace Smith proved to be surprisingly green-fingered, showing gigantic pumpkins, each weighing one hundred pounds, "sugar beets weighing 25 and 30lbs each, and extra large heads of cauliflowers." Even these were outclassed by their hops that ran "fully 18 feet up the poles, hanging in large clusters." At Coldstream, Coutts oversaw the digging of three miles of irrigation channels, planning for a dairy, the opening of a butcher shop, and the construction of the new jam factory.

At Haddo, Johnny had commissioned two more buildings. The first, "Holiday Cottage," was a grand playhouse for the children, as Marjorie remembered:

> We four were made joint tenants in 1891, on condition that it was kept in proper repair and a rent of four ivy leaves paid annually on Christmas Day. The boys were supposed to look after the outside, and they did do a certain amount of gardening, especially when the raspberries were in season. They also dug the graves when we buried birds there, put up the flag for tea parties, and then handed round the boiled potatoes, lettuce, strawberries, oatcake and shortbread which we offered our visitors on state occasions. We used to drive a pair of goats in a cart up with the milk and provisions from the house.

The second was a community hall erected between the south wing of the house and the stables. The designer of this imposing pavilion, the estate architect Charles Sleigh, cleverly combined the traditional wooden architecture of the Aberdeenshire countryside with materials that Ishbel had seen on her travels: in this case the shingled roofs and clapboard of North American buildings. The hall's most striking feature was its sweeping roof, reminiscent of the great tent that Johnny had bought from the King of the Netherlands for his garden parties. Inside, a tennis court was marked out with dark slips of wood set into the floor; gas lamps supplemented the light from forty-six windows; there were seats for a thousand people; and heating was provided by a system of steam pipes that ran around the building.

A local reporter understood, from experience, what lay behind this latest example of Johnny's benevolence:

Of late years some inconvenience has been felt when large parties have assembled on the invitation of Lord and Lady Aberdeen ... and found that the weather breaks down, rain falls, and except by the invasion of Haddo House there was very sparse shelter for them. Now, however, the weather will no longer be an element, as the hall is fitted to contain almost for any purpose—short of a cricket match—any company which will be likely to assemble.

By chance, Johnny and Ishbel's new friends, the evangelists Moody and Sankey, were on a tour of Scotland in January 1892, and, although their schedule was tight, they were easily persuaded to open the hall. Despite a very heavy fall of snow that a gang of estate workers labored all night to clear from the seven-mile road to the railway station, more than a thousand people reached Haddo before eleven o'clock that morning. But by the time Moody had finished his sermon, which was based on no fewer than three texts from the Bible, conditions had worsened and special trains had to be laid on, at Johnny's expense, to get everyone back to Aberdeen in time for a special meeting for women that afternoon in the South Church, followed by an evening session in the city's Music Hall and the third huge audience of salvation-seekers for the day.

Johnny was still finding new charitable causes to support: most notably an appeal launched by Squire Bancroft, an actor-manager who had made a fortune producing the first "drawing room comedies" in London's West End. Bancroft had read *In Darkest England and the Way Out*, a polemic by William Booth, the founder of the Salvation Army. Booth claimed that in the East End of London alone, where the population was "sodden with drink, steeped in vice, eaten up by every social and physical malady," more than a hundred thousand people were homeless and starving and seventeen thousand more were crammed into workhouses, and he summoned "all that is best in the manhood and womanhood of our land" to come to their rescue. Bancroft, whose "income was fixed and ample," wrote to *The Times* with a challenge: "If 99 other men will do the same for the cause, I will give General Booth £1,000 towards it." Johnny responded immediately, writing directly to Booth to say that he would be "happy to become one of the 100 contributors." The problem was that, unlike Bancroft's, Johnny's income was far from being "fixed and ample," not least because of the costs of the new Canadian ranches. Indeed, when George Jamieson provided the accounts for 1891 and 1892, he described them as "full of menace": in the first year, Johnny had overspent by £13,740 and in the second by £19,930.

Ishbel, on the other hand, had raised enough money to press ahead with her arrangements for the Chicago World's Fair, and by March 1892 had formed committees on both sides of the Atlantic. She chose her helpers astutely, and not only from her coterie of aristocratic ladies who, like her, arrayed themselves in tweeds, lace, and poplin and manned stalls at the sales that the Irish Industries Association now held regularly in the palatial London homes of friendly millionaires such as William Waldorf Astor, then "the richest man in America." One of her key recruits was Horace Plunkett, the son of Lord Dunsany, an Irish peer. His qualifications for the job were unusually well suited to the task. He had spent a decade as a rancher in Wyoming and thus was used to negotiating with the most hard-bitten of American businessmen. But he also understood the people and problems of the Irish countryside better than anyone, for he had returned home to set up agricultural cooperatives to provide its farmers, as his slogan put it, with "better farming, better business, better living."

Plunkett was just the man, Ishbel decided, to persuade Alice Hart of the Donegal Industrial Fund to fall in with her mission, for, emboldened by the interest she had stoked up on her tour, she now wanted to replace her modest wedding tableau and cabin with a bigger and better version of the Irish village that Mrs. Hart had created for the London exhibition four years earlier. Plunkett, who peppered his diaries with acid thumbnail character sketches, admired Ishbel (although he dismissed Johnny as a "good amicable creature but physically weak"). But he was not at all enamored with Mrs. Hart, whom, after a difficult meeting in January 1892, he described as "an active useful vulgar egotistic woman." Mrs. Hart had good reason to be touchy. At the exhibition in Edinburgh and even at the Fancy Fair in London, Ishbel had stolen the show, and now she wanted to make off with her big idea. Although Plunkett claimed a few weeks later that he had persuaded her to join forces with Ishbel, Mrs. Hart was not content to be sidelined again, as everyone was later to discover.

Peter White was another clever choice for Ishbel's committee. He was a successful businessman in his early forties and a man after her heart, since, according to the *Irish Times*, he was already a successful exporter of Irish cloth to the United States and "never overlooked the interests of decaying industries in his native country, the revival of which he regarded as the most potent means of national regeneration." White was, they all agreed, "admirably qualified" to manage the Irish village, and, inevitably, Johnny was called upon to stump up £500 a year for his services.

With Mrs. White also on the payroll—her job was to look after the young craftswomen, musicians, and dancers who would "populate" the village—and a young architect, Laurence Aloysius McDonnell of Dublin, touring the Irish countryside in search of quaint cottages and picturesque ruins to replicate, Ishbel's team was now in place. But it was then that Ishbel's problems began.

She was dismayed to find that Bertha Palmer's backing counted for little when negotiations began with the exposition's organizers. White and Plunkett, she complained, "had a terrible time before the final concession was given for the village." The deal was only clinched when Johnny, Plunkett, and four other members of the committee agreed to make an immediate down payment of £6,000. The demand was so urgent that they virtually had to turn out their pockets to find the cash. Then Alice Hart took her revenge by announcing that she was planning to build an Irish village of her own, rubbing salt in Ishbel's wounds by obtaining a better deal from the organizers than she had.

But the biggest blow came just weeks before the opening of the World's Fair. In February 1893, despite suffering from a heavy cold, White had toured Ireland with Ishbel to gather exhibits and sign up craftspeople. The trip had shocking consequences, as she later recalled:

> Alas! The visit to Ireland cost Mr White his life. . . . Unhappily he caught a chill, pneumonia developed, and after seven weeks of ups and downs he passed away.

Ishbel, who thrived in a crisis, took immediate action: in Chicago work on the village was far from finished, and the spinners, lace-makers, weavers, and dairymaids, who had been issued with "pretty travelling dresses" and "cloaks of Irish navy blue serge, lined with crimson satin," were about to embark on the White Star liner *Britannic* from Queenstown. Despite being newly widowed and with six small children* to care for, White's wife, Annie, agreed to take over his job. And while she and Ishbel chivvied the plasterers and fussed over the "villagers" as they settled into their quarters in McDonnell's replica of Blarney Castle, Johnny, not to be left out, appointed himself the odd-job man and spent many happy hours "wandering amongst miles of freight train cars on the side tracks, searching for consignments for the Irish Village," because the railwaymen would not unload the cars without a bribe.

Although the London *Times* grumbled that the World's Fair had opened in "an incomplete condition" thanks to "outrageous weather" and disorganized exhibitors, Ishbel's Irish Village was finished in time, albeit only on the night before the exposition began. But all skepticism vanished when the crowds saw the spectacular "White City" that had arisen on the southwestern shore of Lake Michigan and discovered that it offered, over the course of a few hours, an eye-opening virtual tour of the wonders of the world.

Every nation and American state, it seemed, had risen to the occasion with its own eccentric temple of culture. The *Times* correspondent admired Britain's "English half-timber house of the 16th century" with its "wall panelling and elaborate ceilings like some of the best English country houses"; Germany's "magnificent structure" which boasted "high roofs and gables and conical turrets, with a clock and chimes that are heard from a long distance"; and France's equally "magnificent hall in the Renaissance style," flanked by two pavilions packed with art treasures. Florida had contributed "the oldest structure in America, the ancient Spanish fort San Marco of St. Augustine"; Pennsylvania had built an independence hall "containing her precious relic, the 'Liberty Bell'"; and Idaho had sent a "mammoth log house." But the exhibit that really caught the reporter's

---

*One of Mrs. White's children, her daughter Carmel Snow, became a leading arbiter of twentieth-century fashion as editor in chief of *Harper's Bazaar*, her interest having been piqued by childhood trips to the Paris collections with her mother, who, after managing the Irish Industries Association's depot in Chicago, moved to New York, where she ran a leading dressmaking company, T.M. & J.M. Fox. Carmel transformed the ailing magazine by aiming it not just at the "well-dressed woman" but also at the "well-dressed mind." She coined the term "New Look" for the fashion revolution sparked by Christian Dior's innovative couture collection in 1947. Her brother Thomas and her sister Christine also had distinguished careers in publishing, at Hearst and as editor of *Better Homes and Gardens* respectively, while her brother Victor was an artist who painted the ceiling of the Roof Ballroom of New York's St. Regis Hotel.

eye was the "Corn Palace" from Iowa, which contained "a mass of most artistic decoration made entirely of grains and grasses wrought into beautiful designs" and a "fine model of the Iowa State Capitol composed of grain and seeds."

Both Ishbel's and Mrs. Hart's Irish villages loomed over a wide thoroughfare, the Midway Pleasance. One observer called it "the preferred destination of thrill- and pleasure-seekers" and the exhibits there were far more entertaining, if rather less worthy, than those in the solemn temples of engineering and industry of the official exposition. The guidebook dubbed the Pleasance "the highway of the nations," and, for once, the writer could not be accused of hyperbole. Mrs. Hart's Irish Village stood alongside the Japanese Bazaar, the Pompeii Panorama, an "Electric Scenic Theater" featuring a show called "A Day in the Alps," a French cider press, and a model of St. Peter's Basilica in Rome; but it was overshadowed, literally and figuratively, by a huge novelty, the Ferris Wheel, designed to "out-Eiffel" the landmark symbol of the Paris Exposition Universelle of 1899 and erected at the staggering cost of $400,000.

Ishbel's village occupied a much more prominent site, since it stood at the entrance to the Pleasance and caught the eye of visitors before they could be lured into the Orange Judd Farmer Weed Exhibit,* the Wisconsin Cranberry Marsh, or the Colorado Gold Mine. This mattered, because both villages offered similar experiences for the same ticket price of 25 cents (although Ishbel charged a few cents more to those who wanted to kiss the Blarney Stone).

Fairgoers entered Mrs. Hart's through a replica of the St. Lawrence Gate in Drogheda, originally built in the thirteenth century, and found themselves in the village's main street where, as the guidebook put it, "the scene is quaint, picturesque, and uniquely Irish." In the whitewashed cottages, spinners, weavers, woodcarvers, lace-makers, handkerchief "spriggers" and other embroiderers sewing the ancient "Kells" designs that were Mrs. Hart's trademark could be seen at work. At the equally olde-worlde smithy, where "McGloughlin of Dublin" was busy "making things of beauty," one visitor described how "the clang of the hammer on

---

* Orange Judd was a prominent editor and publisher of agricultural journals who believed it was important to make scientific information accessible to farmers.

the anvil is heard all day long, except when the smith leaves his work to take part in a concert or his apprentice joins O'Hara, the weaver, in dancing the Irish jig on the village green." Inside the Great Hall of the replica of Donegal Castle, which was half the size of the original, paintings by Irish artists and, incongruously, a "colossal bronze stature of Gladstone" were on display, and the building also contained an auditorium where Mrs. Hart and a harpist took turns to entertain visitors with lectures and concerts. Outside, dreamers could sit in a reproduction of the "Wishing Chair" rock formation from the Giant's Causeway, and "Mac Sweeney, the Piper, one of the characters of the village," played music that "gives motion to longing feet."

The guidebook waxed just as folksy in its description of Ishbel's rival attraction. Its entrance had been copied from a doorway built by "Cormac, the bishop king of Munster, in the early part of the twelfth century"; a replica of Muckross Abbey was "surrounded by the graves of its heroes of bygone days"; and at the mock-up of Blarney Castle, a "winding staircase" was provided for anyone wanting to "kiss the Magic Stone and to get 'a view of all Ireland' from the battlements." In the Dairy, three young women demonstrated "all the delights of a well-trained dairy-maid's profession"; the cottages housed lace-makers, knitters, carvers of bog-wood, and weavers of "those delightful homespuns whose merits have been found out of late years by the fashionable world, as well as by the sportsman and athlete"; and at the Village Music Hall, a "youthful professor of the harp" and a piper accompanied "sweet singers of Ireland's national airs." Photographs and replicas of Irish antiquities and Celtic jewelry were displayed in the Village Museum and Tara's Hall, and Ishbel had a cottage of her own called Lyra-ne-Grena (the Sunny Nook), a copy of one at Rushbrooke, near Queenstown in southern Ireland, where she had spent weekends. It was filled with "specimens of old Irish furniture" and books given to her by aristocratic friends.

Where Ishbel scored most over Mrs. Hart was in attracting attention. Her name, plastered all over the village, made her, Horace Plunkett acidly noted, "the best advertised lady in the world," but it drew in the crowds. Ishbel also knew how to appeal to the hearts of Irish expatriates, invoking, in speeches, magazine articles, and the ceaseless round of newspaper interviews, her own Irish ancestry and her feelings for a country that she had come to love. A few days after the World's Fair opened, she held a huge audience of them in thrall at the city's Central Music Hall with an emotional speech in which she asked "for their whole-hearted and enthusiastic" support for the work of the Irish Industries Association:

> Are these industries needed? Why are they needed? There are hundreds here who can answer that question better than I can, who could speak of the little cottages nestling on the bare hillsides, of the little piece of land to which the families look for their support, and how bare and dreary is the outlook when a bad season comes, when any difficulty arises, how there seems no alternative but starvation or for some of the family to go over the sea.
>
> This is a good country to come to, but you know well the wrench that it costs to leave the old home, the old country, and you know how sad it is for the young men and maidens to leave their native shores because there is no room for them there.

Not all Ishbel's efforts to drum up publicity succeeded. Her plan to make a presentation to President Cleveland, who opened the fair, was frustrated when his aides prevented him from visiting any of the exhibits on the Midway Pleasance. Instead, she and Johnny had to jump into a carriage along with "six of our best-looking girls" and follow the president and his wife to the station, where the gifts of a blackthorn stick and a lace handkerchief were hurriedly handed over as the train was leaving.

When its six-month run was over, its organizers boasted that the World's Fair had attracted twenty-seven million visitors, almost half the population of the United States. Certainly, huge numbers bought tickets for Ishbel's village, which, unusually for one of her enterprises, made a profit, of £50,000. Johnny got his money back, and so did Horace Plunkett, who immediately forgave Ishbel for sometimes having been "most difficult" while he was trying to help her.

The Irish Industries Association was now on a firm footing, but throughout all the preparations for the World's Fair Ishbel had felt frustrated and unfulfilled. She had never concealed her hope that, if and when the Liberals were returned to government, Johnny would be reappointed as Lord Lieutenant. But when, in August 1892, Gladstone scraped back into power, John Morley, back in his old job as Chief Secretary for Ireland, had other ideas, as the influential Liberal MP Lewis "Loulou" Harcourt waspishly revealed:

> J. Morley has had an interview with Aberdeen in which he told him that [he] could not be Lord Lieut of Ireland. . . . Lady Aberdeen had better take care how she behaves to me in future about Female Suffrage—or I am d——d if they shall have Canada either, which they want very much.

Gladstone, who was then eighty-two, thought it best to defer to his younger colleague and give the job to Lord Houghton, a gloomy stuffed shirt who would give Morley no trouble. To Ishbel it was "a stunning blow," Marjorie remembered, and although an embarrassed Gladstone offered Johnny "his choice of other posts"—Secretary for Scotland, Lord Chamberlain, Viceroy of India, Governor General of Canada—"none was any consolation."

Johnny liked the idea of Canada, but the choice was academic: the current Governor General, Lord Stanley, was popular and, in any case, he was only halfway through his term of office. So when, soon after the opening of the Irish Village, the British consul general in Chicago asked Johnny to meet him urgently, as he had "a secret message of great importance to deliver from the Foreign Secretary," Ishbel wondered what lay in store for them.

13

A Chapel in Ottawa

The message came from Lord Rosebery, and he told them that they would be going to Canada after all. The British aristocracy's wheel of fortune had turned once more: the impecunious Lord Stanley had wasted no time in claiming the title of Earl of Derby and the riches that came with it, when his brother died suddenly from influenza in April 1893. Ishbel was not displeased: she had reconciled herself to not returning to Ireland, at least for the time being. And she had made her peace with John Morley, although she had found it hard to bring herself to do so. They had talked for an hour over lunch at Dublin's Shelbourne Hotel. He was emollient and evasive, assuring her that he had nothing against Johnny, "but that he felt *himself* responsible for this Home Rule policy, that it was a desperate venture, and that he and he alone must lead." Though he was "very nice," Ishbel found it hard to control her temper, and afterwards worried that "I showed my feelings* but too plainly— indeed I could not help it, and I wrote afterwards to tell him I was sorry for this, and that he must not mind, that all would be well, that we could well bear it."

---

*Very few women at the time would have felt empowered even to think of taking on a senior government minister in the male-dominated world of Victorian politics, but Ishbel had grown up in the company of statesmen, notably Gladstone and Rosebery, and through holding her own with them in debating the issues of the day had earned their respect. She would never have heeded the advice given by Queen Victoria to the Countess of Minto, her successor as Vicereine of Canada: "You must never be persuaded to give your name to any new venture which might be criticized."

Ishbel and Johnny left Chicago immediately for a summer of farewells. Two were especially important to them. Johnny called a meeting in Tarland where he spoke to the tenants of his Cromar estate. Many of them, he knew, had lived in a state of anxiety since 1884, when he had announced that the lands they farmed were for sale. But since he had only managed to dispose of a few acres and a handful of houses, he had concluded, he told them, that things should "remain as at present." And there was, he added, "another little matter": he had "decided to take an early opportunity of erecting a new mansion house for the estate." Commissioning an architect had been another task for Ishbel before setting off for Canada: the job of designing what would eventually be their retirement home went to the obvious candidate, Laurence Aloysius McDonnell, the architect of the Chicago Irish village.

On their way south to catch their ship, they called on the Gladstones, who, conveniently, were staying at a castle in Perthshire. After they had said their goodbyes, Ishbel took a last poignant photograph of her "beloved old friends . . . standing at the door of the Castle as we left with their 'God bless you and yours' on their lips," but she was happy to be "starting on our new quest with their benediction."

Not everyone welcomed their appointment, however, and even before they had left Liverpool for Quebec, Ishbel was aware of mocking comments in North American newspapers:

> The people of Canada were warned that they would have to put up with a lady at Government House who had a bee in her bonnet with regard to the servant question, one who would never allow her servants to wear caps, and who was in the habit of playing hide-and-seek and other such games with the housemaids and footmen, at all sorts of odd hours of the day.

And in private, even the people who had met the couple on their earlier trips to Canada were wary of them: particularly, it turned out, of the thirty-six-year-old Ishbel. Donald Smith, the éminence grise of the Canadian Pacific Railway, who had lent them his private railcar on their first visit to the country, wrote to his friend, the soldier and explorer Sir William Butler:

As to Lord Aberdeen's appointment we can only hope for the best. We have so far been especially favoured by Providence in the matter of Governors-General. In this case the fact of Lord Aberdeen's being a great favourite with Mr. Gladstone will not predispose many in his favour; but I believe he is earnest and industrious and a Scotsman of rank and lineage, which in itself signifies a great deal. Then, as I hardly need remind you, there is her ladyship!

A well-meaning article by Mrs. Isabella Fyvie Mayo, a contributor to Ishbel's *Onward and Upward* magazine, made some Canadians wonder whether they were being sent not one Governor General, but two. "It has been said of them," she wrote, "that 'never, perhaps, were husband and wife more thoroughly in sympathy with each other.'"

Johnny and Ishbel reached Quebec on a Sunday in mid-September 1893 in rain so heavy that the usual arrival ceremonies were abandoned. But they still had to "plunge," as Ishbel put it, into a relentless schedule of official visits, dinners, speeches, and travels from the moment they walked down the gangplank of the S.S. *Sardinian*. There was barely time for her to gather her thoughts, although a sermon by the ever-present Henry Drummond, at "a little evening service" in the Citadel where they were staying, did prompt a pious diary entry:

It is not so much what is done, or what is said, but it will be the *tone* which will make itself felt, & in this every member of this household down to the smallest child will have a share. And so with this in mind, it is a great joy to be gathered together on this our first evening to prepare for our new work in a new land.

They lingered in Quebec for a week. Ishbel admired the ease with which Johnny coped with speaking in French at his swearing-in, but complained that although the housekeeper had made the rooms in the fortress "quite cosy," there was barely room for them and their retinue. She enjoyed "watching the light & shades playing about the hills & waters & the constant panorama going on below"; hailed the new Château Frontenac hotel nearby, with its extravagant castellations, as "a triumph for its architect," and tried to master an important social skill for any Governor General's consort:

Dancing in Canada has its own peculiarities. The waltz is particularly difficult to pick up. It is a mixture of deux temps and trois temps danced v. slowly and they always reverse here. Then there is the 'rush polka', and the 'bonton', a pretty graceful Virginian dance something like a pas de quatre—& then the Saratoga quadrilles are v. popular & a much more lively version of our quadrilles, all the couples dancing at once & the top & bottom dancing with the sides instead of with each other. We had a really good bit of exercise before going to bed.

It was not until just before midnight, nine days after making landfall in Canada, that the train hauling the Governor General's private railcar pulled into a siding at Ottawa. Despite the late hour, Ishbel could not wait to see Rideau Hall, their official residence. With Henry Drummond in tow, she left the others sleeping and managed to do "a good deal of exploring before going to bed."

The house had been built in 1838 near a settlement called Bytown by Thomas MacKay, a Scottish stonemason, who used his profits from building canals and other enterprises, which included sawmills, a cloth factory, and a distillery, to establish himself as a gentleman on a one-hundred-acre estate. Local people nicknamed it "MacKay's Castle," but Rideau Hall was, in fact, an elegant two-storey Regency villa with a distinctive bow front and colonnaded wings on either side of its central block. Inside, there was an elliptical drawing room with a Scottish thistle emblazoned on its coved ceiling and a parlor from which, according to a biographer, "the skirling notes of the bagpipes played by the lord of the manor reportedly sounded through the surrounding woods of a summer's evening." MacKay was said to have designed it "out of his own head," but architectural historians believe he borrowed ideas from *Sketches in Architecture, Containing Plans and Elevations of Cottage and Villas and Other Useful Buildings with Characteristic Scenery*, published in 1793 by the English architect Sir John Soane, although how even this most resourceful of pioneers found a copy in the backwaters of southern Ontario eludes them.

Rideau Hall became the residence of Canada's Governors General by default. After Queen Victoria had chosen Ottawa, which had by then absorbed Bytown, as the capital of Canada in 1857, architectural competitions were held for state buildings. But as the costs of constructing the parliament

Ishbel's father, Dudley Coutts Marjoribanks (1820–94). Despite a lackluster career as M.P. for Berwickshire in the House of Commons, he succeeded in becoming a baronet in 1866 and, fifteen years later, in being elevated, as Baron Tweedmouth of Edington, to the House of Lords, where he joined the group of ennobled brewers known as the "Beerage."
HADDO HOUSE COLLECTION

Ishbel's mother, Isabel (1827–1908). Some thought her grim and austere, but the head stalker on the family estate in Scotland disagreed: "I have seen a big number of Ladies at Guisachan, but Lady Tweedmouth was the bonniest and her holy habits and noble character made her a queen among other ladies."
HADDO HOUSE COLLECTION

Guisachan House near Inverness in northern Scotland, another of Dudley Marjoribanks's French châteaux, incongruously sited in Glen Affric, which Ishbel thought "the most lovely glen in all the world." This not-remotely-modest holiday home boasted everything needed by a man of property in the Highlands, including a ballroom and banqueting hall.

Ishbel aged seventeen. Her love of unusual, even eccentric, headwear stayed with her all her life. When she visited Washington, D.C., at the age of forty, a reporter from the *Chicago Chronicle* marveled at her "Scotch hat" decorated with plaid ribbon and pink heather.

Haddo House Collection

George, 6th Earl of Aberdeen (1841–70), photographed just before he fled from his responsibilities at home and went to America, where he changed his name and became a sailor. His family spent three years trying to find him, but, as an inquiry later discovered, "the unfortunate nobleman . . . terminated his experience as a sailor by a sailor's death" when he fell from the deck of a schooner off Nova Scotia.

Haddo House Collection

Johnny and Ishbel in 1878, soon after their marriage. W. E. Gladstone, who had known both of them from childhood, described them as an "edifying couple," and a fellow statesman, John Bright, thought them "kind, religious and good."

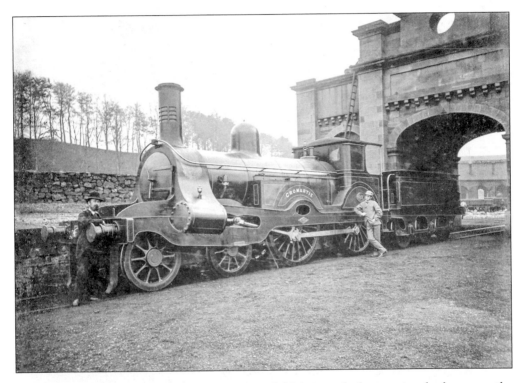

The Earl and the "Duke": Johnny in Inverness with "Cromartie," a locomotive also known as the "Duke," built in 1874 by the Highland Railway Company. But the train Johnny usually drove had the humbler nickname "Meldrum Meg" and plied a branch line of the Great North of Scotland Railway that ran close to the Haddo estate.

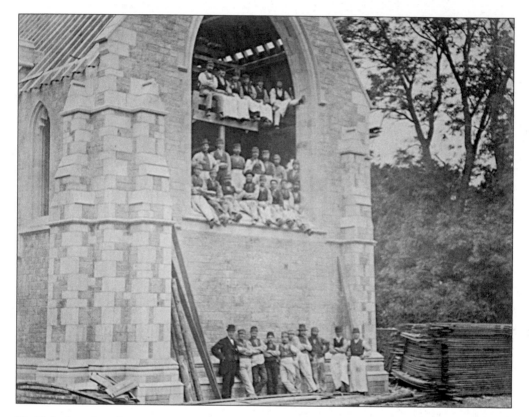

Haddo's chapel under construction c.1880. Ishbel called it a "lovely and sacred meeting place. Baptisms, marriages, funerals, have all taken place within those walls, which hold associations of joy and of sorrow, of hours of difficulty and seasons of great thankfulness."

Ishbel was so proud of creating her magnificent new library at Haddo by combining the billiard room and the prayer room with two corridors that she took this photograph herself. The gentlemen retired there after dinner but were too busy drinking and smoking ever to read any books.

HADDO HOUSE COLLECTION

The household staff at Haddo. Johnny and Ishbel had more than one hundred servants and knew them all by name, rare in an age when supercilious owners of stately homes would address every footman as "James." But their concern for the welfare of their employees sparked rumors, prompting Queen Victoria to ask Lord Rosebery if it was true that the Aberdeens sat down to dinner with their servants.

HADDO HOUSE COLLECTION

Ishbel with George ("Doddie"), Marjorie, and Dudley in 1884. Another daughter, Dorothea, had died in November 1882, aged nine months.

HADDO HOUSE COLLECTION

Guests at the Haddo Open Day in August 1879 gather in front of the huge tent bought by Johnny from King Willem III of the Netherlands. For the next decade, it was the centerpiece of Haddo events—Sunday school picnics, bazaars, and highland games—until bad weather and fraying canvas forced Johnny to replace it with a wooden hall in 1892.

HADDO HOUSE COLLECTION

Littleberries, a hunting lodge in Mill Hill near London, was said to have been the home of King Charles II's mistress, the legendary Nell Gwyn, and the eighteenth-century criminal mastermind Mrs. Margaret Caroline Rudd. But it had long since been restored to respectability by 1880, when Johnny rented it as a weekend retreat and invited Mr. Gladstone to visit.

HADDO HOUSE COLLECTION

Ishbel, an accomplished artist, painted this watercolor of Dollis Hill House, their idyllic five-hundred-acre farm to the west of London, in 1881. The writer Mark Twain called it "paradise," and Mr. Gladstone was so beguiled by its charms that he invited himself to stay every weekend.

HADDO HOUSE COLLECTION

A picnic at Dollis Hill for a charity that deeply interested Ishbel: the Homes for Working Girls. Founded in 1878 to provide "better conditions of living" for some of the 320,000 women employed in the capital, the organization also aimed to provide them with "healthful recreation," something they appear to have found on the tennis court at Dollis Hill.

May 23, 1883. Escorted by cavalrymen of the 3rd Dragoon Guards, Johnny, the Lord High Commissioner of the Church of Scotland, rides with his court through Edinburgh to reopen the newly restored St. Giles' Cathedral. The declaration of a public holiday and exceptionally fine weather brought out huge crowds. Only Ishbel, it seems, missed the pomp and circumstance: she was still in London with Dudley, her newborn son.

Johnny, the Lord High Commissioner, returns to Holyroodhouse after a long day presiding over the General Assembly and visiting local dignitaries. But his duties are not yet done: evenings bring receptions and dinners for more than a hundred guests. "The whole period of residence at Holyrood is of a very busy description," he wrote.

Ishbel and Henry Drummond. Their intense, but probably platonic, relationship fueled prurient gossip in high society. She said, "He was the closest of our friends and comrades." He said, "This lasting friendship was one of the great joys of my life."

HADDO HOUSE COLLECTION

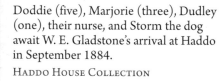

Doddie (five), Marjorie (three), Dudley (one), their nurse, and Storm the dog await W. E. Gladstone's arrival at Haddo in September 1884.

HADDO HOUSE COLLECTION

Gladstone (right); his wife, Catherine (left); and their daughter, Helen (at back), relax with their host and hostess on the terrace at Haddo during their visit—but not for long. The Prime Minister had still to meet a deputation of local Liberals, open a training home for girls, and visit a ruined castle. Doctors had ordered a break from campaigning, but the newspapers reported that he had enjoyed only "comparative rest."
HADDO HOUSE COLLECTION

Ishbel turned herself into a human billboard to promote the work of her Irish Industries Association. According to the *Lady's Pictorial*, her arrival at one of Queen Victoria's drawing rooms in 1888 in this dress "embroidered in gold from Celtic designs copied from old Irish manuscripts" caused the desired sensation.
HADDO HOUSE COLLECTION

A postcard celebrating Johnny and Ishbel's work in Ireland, published when they were suddenly recalled in 1886, attests to their popularity. Ishbel, in her turn, wrote: "Ireland is laid on us to do all in our power for her for ever."

buildings escalated, no one had the nerve, let alone the funds, to embark on a new government house, and the authorities decided to lease Rideau Hall from the MacKay family and enlarge it instead. This work was supervised by Frederick Preston Rubidge, a surveyor and architect from the Department of Public Works. Having dismissed the Hall as "an ordinary house of some eleven rooms," he promptly added forty-nine more. Thus, by the time Ishbel and Drummond made their midnight foray, the building had probably sprouted more extensions than any other viceregal mansion in the empire.

They returned to the house next morning and "ransacked all over the premises & grounds & inspected skating rinks, toboggan slides, curling rinks, etc., etc." Typically, once inside, Ishbel first inspected the servants' bedrooms, which she found "very ample & very comfortably arranged." She thought the ballroom "v. good" and the drawing rooms "roomy," but the rest of the place fell far short of her standards:

> The ordinary dining room is not a good room, is gloomy and smells of kitchen, & after our own staff* and family are disposed of there is v. little accommodation for visitors.

Her predecessor, Lady Derby, had warned her that the house, although "most comfortable," contained little good furniture. The walls, Ishbel discovered, were "absolutely bare," and she was horrified that there were "no lamps in the house at all. No cushions, no table cloths, in fact none of the small things that make a room pretty and comfortable."

But there were more fundamental changes† to be made, which Ishbel

---

* Its members included four aides-de-camp, whose youth and good looks drew all eyes when, arrayed in kilts and military uniforms, they attended Johnny's swearing-in in Quebec. "Never was there such a splendid-looking Staff in the country," said one newspaper story that Ishbel gleefully pasted into her cuttings book.

† One of her predecessors, Princess Louise, the free-spirited sixth child of Queen Victoria, found herself in a similar position on arriving at Rideau Hall in 1878. Although her husband, the Marquess of Lorne, tried to persuade her that the "big and uncomfortable house" was "much superior" to Kensington Palace, their London home, the artistic princess immediately made "everybody work their arms off" to improve the décor and took up her brush to paint sprigs of apple blossom onto the doors of the "Blue Parlour." Louise and Ishbel had much in common: they both supported women's causes and Irish Home Rule and worked hard to ensure the welfare of their servants. But unlike Ishbel, Louise, who longed to be a private individual, was not praised for her good works and was, instead, criticized for being "wayward" and chafing too much against the restrictive conventions of royal life.

listed as she went around. She would ask the Board of Works for "new rooms to be added"; MacKay's old drawing room upstairs would have to be converted into a schoolroom for Marjorie and Archie; and she commissioned a simple wooden chapel for the family's daily prayers, just as she had at the Viceregal Lodge in Dublin.

Ottawa itself she found far less attractive, as she rode in her carriage through "terrible streets . . . so full of pitfalls & ups & downs that it seems wonderful that any springs can stand them." She was not the first to question Queen Victoria's choice of capital. Thirty years earlier, Frances Monck, the sister-in-law of Lord Monck, the first Governor General to live at Rideau Hall, was just as appalled when she visited the town:

> We were much disgusted with the squalid look of Ottawa, though we only saw it by lamplight, which was scarcely any light, such *wretched* gas. The streets were so rough, like dirt roads. . . . It looked as if it was at 't'other end of nowhere'.

Another British visitor dismissed it as a "sub-arctic lumber-village converted by royal mandate into a political cock-pit," when he passed through.

Since they were not due to move into Rideau Hall for several weeks—electric lights, a new heating boiler, and a washing machine were being installed—Johnny and Ishbel continued their "royal" progress, traveling on to Montreal and back to Quebec; meeting politicians and religious leaders; visiting hospitals, universities, and schools; and holding parties for the great and the good, to which, in a radical departure from convention, they even invited the guests' children.

But for Ishbel, the most important stop of the tour was at Toronto, where she had a new cause to promote. In the summer of 1893, just before she and Johnny left for Canada, she had received a cryptic telegram from Rachel Foster Avery, a leading activist in the campaign to win votes for women in the United States. It said:

> You have been elected President of the International Council of Women.

Ishbel was flummoxed, for she "could remember nothing about the International Council of Women," and indeed was not sure that she had ever even heard of it. But when Mrs. Avery's letter arrived, she realized that the organization, which had been founded five years earlier by "a group of splen-did pioneer American women," espoused most of her own ideas about how women's lives could be improved. The council's aims, she would afterwards tell anyone who inquired, were laid out in the preamble to its constitution:

> We, women of all nations, sincerely believing that the best good of hu-manity will be advanced by greater unity of thought, sympathy, and pur-pose, and that an organized movement of women will best conserve the highest good of the family and of the State, do hereby band ourselves in a confederation of workers to further the application of the Golden Rule ("Do unto others as ye would that they should do unto you").

Ishbel took no more convincing, and her first step was to establish a branch of the Council in the Dominion. Hence the gubernatorial caval-cade's stop in Toronto, where an audience of two thousand women was treated to a sight never before seen in Canadian public life: the wife of the Governor General making a speech from the platform, and one, moreover, that was a call to action.

> It is wonderful to feel & see the intense desire & readiness of the women for some such movement as this & it is awe-inspiring to find this work just prepared all ready to my hand—a work to which no one can take exception,

she wrote with relief afterwards. The National Council of Women of Canada, she realized, would help her understand the concerns of ordinary people who would never otherwise gain access to the corridors of power in Ottawa:

> Through them we get our hand on the pulse of the country in a way in which we would never hope to do in the usual course of travelling about, holding formal ceremonies and receptions.

The council would also, she hoped, provide her with cover against the carping of politicians, should any of the reforms she initiated prove

controversial. And she saw enough in the weeks that followed her arrival
to know that these were urgently needed, particularly where medical
services were concerned. On a visit to a hospital in Quebec with Dr.
David Shirres,* the Governor General's surgeon, she was alarmed to find
that, even in the cities, medical services were poor to the point of being
dangerous:

> Did not think much of it as a hospital—v. stuffy & unpleasant & Dr
> Shirres ascertained there was a large percentage of deaths after opera-
> tions from blood poisoning—over 200 patients.

She was even more distressed to hear the story behind the setting up
of the Maternity and Foundling Hospitals in Montreal:

> They were started with a view of coping with the terrible percentage of
> deaths among illegitimate children & children put out at baby farms.
> There is no registration of birth necessary in this province at all—the
> influence of the priests keeps up a very strong feeling about illegiti-
> mate children & the consequence is that it is accepted as a belief that
> the kindest thing is to baptize these children & then facilitate their exit
> from this world as much as possible.

And although she found the hospitals "v. well managed," and was
moved by the valiant efforts of the doctors and nurses to save and improve
the lives of the mothers and babies in their care, she knew that there were
no easy answers:

> In the married women's ward, saw a baby three days old born prema-
> turely at 6 months, in an incubator. Dr Cameron [the consulting physi-
> cian] says lots of delicate babies as well as premature ones are saved in
> this way, but to look at this small morsel of humanity made one wonder
> as to the kindness of making it live to face the world.

---

* Dr. Shirres had begun his career as the general practitioner in Tarves, a village on the Haddo
estate. He stayed in Canada and became the country's first neurologist.

Away from the crowds, in those early days, Ishbel delighted in some less formal outings: to meet a new pony ("he is about 14 hands, bay, and with a star on his forehead and warranted very strong"); to arrange classes with a professor whose "special system" would, she hoped, help her to improve her conversational French; and to a ball, where she and other members of Johnny's household had to dance a Highland reel in splendid isolation, since none of the Canadian guests knew the steps.

But when they finally moved into Rideau Hall, there were still "interminable domestic adjustments" to make. Ishbel had a household of seventy to worry about, almost all imported from home. Its key members included M. Gouffé, their London chef; Miss Wetterman, the Swedish governess; Teresa Wilson,* Ishbel's secretary; and the Reverend James Brebner, their private chaplain. Among the "downstairs" staff were George Germain, the house steward; John Grant, the butler; Mrs. Harriman, Mrs. Grant, and Mrs. Inglis, the housekeepers; Agnes and Alice, the housemaids; Jessie Gunn, Ishbel's own lady's maid; John Keddie, the "leader postilion with the state carriage and four"; Dales, Doddie's valet; Lévy, the "French maid for Marjorie"; Cissy Fletcher, the sewing maid; Willie and Jimmy Black, the stablemen; and Johanna Doherty, a "splendid" dairy maid who had shown off her skills at the Irish village in Chicago and now had to deal with the milk produced by the Governor General's own herd of cows in the grounds of Rideau Hall. They had plenty of work to do, for the house contained 4,810 yards of carpet, 340 of oil cloth, and 272 windows.

One morning, Gouffé, the chef, "appeared with doleful face" and announced that he wanted to leave. "The ways and manners" in Ottawa were "rough and the work heavy," he complained, and he feared he would lose his reputation because "the provisions were not so good." Gouffé was soon "smoothed out," but one problem faced by all the new arrivals could not be swept aside, as Ishbel wrote plaintively to a friend:

Home sickness seems to be an abominable sort of lingering malady; 5 or 6 years away look horribly long.

---

* According to Marjorie, Miss Wilson was "clever, fluent in French and German, a Scot able to hold her own anywhere."

Her own cure for it was to hang pictures of Mr. Gladstone in every room: a defiant touch that horrified Conservative visitors. She also quickly organized the inaugural meeting of a staff association, modeled on the one at Haddo, where John Grant, the butler, "spoke extremely well of the advantages of such a Club." By the end of the evening, a program of activities had been agreed that included classes in singing and carving, "lectures weekly or fortnightly," and a circle to "read up the History of Canada."

Johnny, in the meantime, found himself presiding over what seemed like a permanent political crisis. Immediately after his appointment was announced, Lord Ripon, the Colonial Secretary, had written to him (hoping, no doubt, that Ishbel would also read the letter), explaining that the constitutional status of the Governor General of Canada was very different to that of the Lord Lieutenant of Ireland. While the latter was "essentially a political officer," a member of the government in London, the Governor General of Canada was the "representative of the Queen as a Constitutional Sovereign and Party Politics of any kind are therefore entirely outside his sphere." He added: "Such restrictions are irksome, and you, and I fear Lady Aberdeen also, will feel them so—but I am sure that you will fully appreciate their necessity and will frankly accept them." Johnny replied promising to "adopt & maintain as a fundamental & essential rule, *total abstinence* from all expressions or indications savouring in any way of party politics."

But once on Canadian soil he seems to have realized that his vow would be hard to keep. At his swearing-in in Quebec, he defined the duties of a Governor General in more activist terms:

> His attitude must be that of ceaseless and watchful readiness to take part, by whatever opportunities may be afforded to him, in the fostering of every influence that will sweeten and elevate public life . . . to vindicate, if required, the rights of the people and the ordinances and Constitution, and, lastly, to promote by all means in his power, without reference to class or creed, every movement and every institution calculated to forward the social, moral, and religious welfare of all the inhabitants of the Dominion.

When, thirty years later, Johnny himself looked back on his "reign," he described it as "eventful." He found a country "torn by division and doubt" and politicians struggling to cope with its "definite distinctions of race and religion": confederation, begun a quarter of a century earlier, had not ironed out the deep-rooted cultural, political, economic, and religious differences between the country's French-speaking inhabitants and those for whom English was the mother tongue.

One issue came to symbolize the nation's schisms. In 1890, the legislature of Manitoba had brought in a Public Schools Act, designed to establish nonsectarian schools and deny public funding to those that offered only a Protestant or a Catholic education. Many saw it as a threat to Canada's religious and linguistic cultures, and years of vitriolic debate and political convulsions followed. The act was challenged in Parliament and through the courts, all the way up to the Privy Council in London, leaving Johnny to try to broker peace between the warring parties.

Although "the political atmosphere was heavy, like the lull before a storm," both Johnny and Ishbel got on well with Sir John Thompson, the Conservative Prime Minister, whose party was, by then, deeply divided by the "Manitoba Schools Question," as it had become known. Ishbel, especially, developed a soft spot for this politician "with a playful face." "Many a subdued laugh have we had together in the office," she wrote. "I never met a high official who had less red tape about him, and who never feared compromising his dignity by talking over official & political matters as one human being to another." Thompson and his wife Annie lived modestly, untainted by the allegations of corruption that dogged Canadian politicians at the time, and Ishbel admired the way they had risen to the top, despite difficult starts in life and the snobbish attitudes of Ottawa high society:

> He was educated at the common school & was very poor as a young man. . . . And it is always said that Lady Thompson was employed for a time in some capacity at a shop at Halifax—& for this reason people were not very anxious to call on her at first.

But the Prime Minister did not live long to enjoy their friendship. The Manitoba Schools Question was just one of many political crises that he had had to weather, and Ishbel worried to her diary about the toll these might have taken on his health:

He has been a very hard-worked man, both by day & night & in order
to save time, he gave up coming home for luncheon & practically took
no exercise.

Giving up lunch was too little, too late, and after indulging in Paris's finest cuisine while serving on an international tribunal in France, Thompson's weight had ballooned. Yet at the end of October 1894, ignoring his
doctors' orders and the anguished pleas of his wife, he insisted on traveling
to England to be sworn in as a member of the Imperial Privy Council. The
doctors in London were so reassuring that he perked up, awarded himself
a holiday in Europe, and, for once, took some exercise, climbing the 551
steps to the top of St. Peter's Basilica in Rome. The aftermath was shocking. Ishbel wrote in her diary on December 12:

> A black day indeed for Canada, for Sir John Thompson died suddenly
> at Windsor Castle after being sworn in as Privy Councillor by the
> Queen.... The news could not be believed here.... Unhappily it is all
> too true, & we feel fairly stunned by the double loss to the country &
> to ourselves.

Sir John, it turned out, had stayed on after the ceremony to celebrate
with a group of his fellow Privy Councillors in the Octagon Dining Room
at the Castle. But it was a lunch too far. Soon after sitting down, he fainted
and was taken into another room to recover. There, he came round and
returned to the table, announcing that it seemed "too absurd to faint
like this." But almost immediately, according to a biographer, "without a
sound, he fell backward into the arms of Sir John Watt Reid, the Queen's
doctor, who had been placed beside him."

While the newspapers reported the events that followed—the taking of a plaster death mask so that a statue of Sir John could one day be
erected, the frail old Queen being wheeled out to place a wreath on his
coffin, the embalming of his body and its return to Halifax aboard the
naval cruiser H.M.S. *Blenheim*—Ishbel rushed to Lady Thompson's side.
But the delicacy of her mission did not prevent her from pondering an
urgent question; one that had occurred to editorial writers throughout the
British Empire as soon as Sir John's death was announced:

The party which he led so ably will find it no easy matter to fill his place, and Lord Aberdeen will have an onerous task in the choice of a new Premier.

Ishbel had no intention of allowing Johnny to bear the burden alone, and the entries in her journal for the days that followed Thompson's death justify its editor's assertion that, as her critics always suspected,

> Lady Aberdeen might well be graced with the title Governess-General. Like Victoria's Albert she was a power that could not be overlooked.

From the start, as she socialized with politicians and civil servants or watched debates in the House of Commons, she took it upon herself to act as Johnny's eyes and ears, and in delicate situations where any overt interference from the Governor General would have breached constitutional conventions, she was a useful and enthusiastic emissary. No one was fooled, least of all a young society journalist called Agnes Scott, who followed her progress through the salons of Ottawa with a beady eye. Ishbel, Scott conceded, played the part of decorative consort convincingly, if sometimes to excess, especially at state banquets:

> Her Excellency always has a little page, sometimes two, dressed in the costumes of Louis XIV. They carry her train and run about during dinner carrying notes and messages.

But she also noticed how Ishbel hovered at Johnny's elbow when he was speaking to politicians, "pulling on his sleeve, and offering suggestions." Sometimes she went too far. Sir Joseph Pope, a distinguished civil servant, was no lover of the couple, grumbling in his memoirs that "the Governor-General and Lady Aberdeen apparently belonged to that class of persons whose idea of impartiality consists of being unfair to each side." He therefore seized on a story told to him by John Mortimer Courtney, then the Deputy Minister of Finance, who had been invited to dinner at Rideau Hall:

> Lady Aberdeen backed Mr Courtney into the Governor-General's private office, showed him the Treasury minutes, passed at a recent

meeting of the cabinet and asked him whether he thought they were such as His Excellency could properly be asked to sign. Courtney, rather a choleric gentleman at all times, a radical with a high sense of honour, was furious at being the recipient of this confidence, giving the lady to understand that in the first place, she should never have seen those minutes and secondly, that if Lord Aberdeen had any doubts as to the propriety of the recommendations they contained, his proper course was to consult his Prime Minister, whose name stretched half-way across the page.

On the way to Lady Thompson's, Ishbel considered the possible candidates for Prime Minister. George Foster, the Minister of Finance, was "an able man, a good speaker & a good man, but he has no power over other men"; John Haggart, leader of the Ontario Conservatives, was "the strongest man," but was "a bohemian and also idle." Many thought the job should go to the veteran Sir Charles Tupper, an idea that did not go down well when Ishbel raised it with the grieving widow, who exclaimed: "If *he* were sent for, I should look upon it as an insult to my husband's memory." Ishbel was relieved. She had no time for Tupper either, and nor, she confided, had Johnny:

Never if he could help it should Sir Charles be again in Canadian politics. He is another of those who are able mysteriously to provide for his sons & daughters!

Johnny sent for the man he thought was the safest candidate, Sir Mackenzie Bowell, who had been standing in for Thompson during his trip to England. Ishbel did not disapprove, although she acknowledged that Canada's Roman Catholics might be uncomfortable with so overtly Protestant a Prime Minister. Bowell was "a good and straight man" with "great ideas about the drawing together of the colonies & the Empire."

But he proved to be the wrong man for the job. The Manitoba Schools Question defeated him too. For sixteen months he vacillated, proposing compromises that failed to find favor among the increasingly fractious members of his failing party. Sir Joseph Pope, who thought Johnny should have called on Tupper, was among many who looked on with horror "during days which I never recall without a blush, days of weak and incompetent administration by a man whose sudden and unlooked-for elevation had visibly turned his head, a ministry without unity or cohesion of any kind, a prey to internal dissensions until they became a spectacle to the world, to angels and to men."

Eventually, after a cabinet revolt and more dithering, Bowell resigned, only to be replaced as party leader by Sir Charles Tupper, leaving Ishbel dismayed by the elevation of "that old fox":

> To have to send for a man whose whole life has been devoted to scheming & who will spare no means of any sort which may be of use in securing the return of his party with himself as Premier was a distasteful job.

Tupper did not survive a general election a few months later, but he would not go quietly. He disputed the results, claiming that recounts would show that the Liberals, led by the charismatic French-Canadian Wilfrid Laurier, had not really won. He insisted, too, that he still had the right to make public appointments and drew up a long list of names of senators, judges, and other important officials for Johnny's approval. But Johnny saw through Tupper's plan: most of his nominees were Conservatives, and he feared they would obstruct Laurier's Liberal government for years to come. A furious Sir Charles protested that the Governor General had exceeded his powers, but in the end, Johnny had to step in to prize his hands from the levers of power and insist that "the people had spoken with no uncertain voice as to whom they wished to entrust the duties of government."

He found it all "most uncongenial," but he was relieved that, at last, he had a Prime Minister who might even find the elusive answer to the Manitoba Schools Question.* And Ishbel now felt free to make her feelings clear. She sent her maid Jessie Gunn to the entrance of Rideau Hall

---

* Laurier eventually chiseled out a compromise with the Manitoban Premier, Thomas Greenway, that allowed Catholic education in public schools and the teaching of French in establishments with at least ten pupils. Most people were happy to settle for this classic "fudge," and those Catholics who continued to oppose it failed to win the support of the Pope, Leo XIII, who ruled that it was fair, since very few members of his flock actually lived in Manitoba.

to present Laurier, as he left with the commission to form a government, with a sprig of white heather, "according to the old Highland superstition that if a girl meets a man and gives a piece of white heather as he leaves the house on any quest, that she brings him good luck." Sir Charles Tupper, in the meantime, skulked off into the political shadows to rebuild his party and nurse his resentment.

14

A Fishing Lodge in Quebec and a Hospital in the Klondike

One of Johnny and Ishbel's first houseguests at Rideau Hall was a spirit called Julia. In life, she had been a journalist, the editor of the *Union Signal* of Chicago; in death, she was apparently the ghostly "pen friend" of W. T. Stead, Ishbel's advisor on her *Onward and Upward* magazine, who claimed he could receive letters from her, thanks to his gift for automatic writing. Ishbel was amused:

> He has talked to us a good deal of 'Julia', his double & his various spook friends. . . . But he speaks about it all in such a matter of fact way that one gets to think of them as most commonplace beings & to take it quite as a matter of course that 'Julia' should write her name in our visitor's book.

But Stead, who was nursing a cold and struggling to find backing for a North American paper, had arrived in Ottawa in a low mood, and Ishbel had to work hard to humor him. She had good reason to, for Stead had promised to repay her hospitality by writing an article in his influential *Review of Reviews* about Canada's "present standing & future possibilities."

This, it turned out, was not what Stead had in mind, preferring to publish *Lord and Lady Aberdeen: A Character Sketch*, a long hymn of praise to the couple. Ishbel, Stead wrote, "possesses immense activity and energy, together with a capacity to do things and get them done," while Johnny was tougher than he appeared, for "his ready sympathy, his absolute forgetfulness of self, his natural bonhomie," masked "a strong character."

But there was one odd omission from Stead's long list of the couple's good qualities: their willingness to work tirelessly for the country and their causes. The political dramas that followed the death of Sir John Thompson were probably enough in themselves to make Johnny, as one observer noted, "the most overworked Governor-General in Canadian history," but he and Ishbel, when not organizing the usual round of dinners, dances, and quasi-royal ceremonies, also traveled more widely across the Dominion than their predecessors. They did so, for the most part, in style, in the comfort of their own railway carriage, the "Car Victoria," although, as Ishbel's diaries show, they never shrank from taking to the country's primitive dirt roads in a horse-drawn carriage if, beyond the railhead, there were communities or organizations in need of their help and encouragement. Ishbel-watchers, of whom there were now many in the press and Ottawa society, noted that the Governor General's schedule often happened to take them to places where Ishbel would also have an opportunity to pursue some of her own pet causes.

On August 3, 1895, for example, she awoke in the Car Victoria outside Qu'Appelle in southern Saskatchewan. It was Johnny's birthday:

He is 48 to-day, & I am thankful indeed that this day has been reached. Somehow or other an idea has prevailed & has at times made itself a presence in his own mind, that he must necessarily die at the age of 47, because his father died then & because he is supposed to be so like his father. Gott sei dank that he is now 48.

After she had given him a "little present" of a "White leghorn cock & 3 hens with the intention that they should lay some fresh eggs for use in the train," Ishbel duly held a meeting about establishing a branch of the National Council of Women of Canada in Fort Qu'Appelle, and that evening she and Johnny set off to perform the opening ceremony at a home for young women who had emigrated from Britain.

The twenty-five-mile journey was an endurance test:

The road was v. rough, with innumerable pit-falls, & our driver said he could scarcely see the leaders for the gathering darkness, which was increased by the advent of a thunder-storm. We should have had a good moon, but somehow she managed to hide herself away behind heavy clouds. So our main light was derived from the lightning which after playing about amongst the clouds for a time in picturesque fashion, became extremely busy and unpleasantly forked.

Although they did not arrive until ten o'clock, Ishbel launched into a discussion with the wife of the local bishop about "the folly of sending out to this country for Canadian farm life girls trained in service in gentlemen's houses at home." She did not mince her words: it was "utterly wrong and cruel to encourage such girls to come out." Earlier that day, she explained, a young woman had buttonholed her:

One could not help noticing that she must be a trained servant with her nice neat dress & apron & cap. She lingered in the room for a moment & then asked me if perhaps I could hear of another place for her. She had been head housemaid at Lady Ormonde's and previously at Lady Dartmouth's & had come out because she had heard that wages were higher. Now she was a general servant in a little Canadian village earning $10 a month. She said she expected things to be different from England but not like this.

Ishbel also knew that there were problems in the cities and towns that could not be ignored, and that her investigations would require many more excursions in the Car Victoria:

We had fixed on a plan whereby we were to endeavour not only to entertain at Government House, Ottawa, and at the Citadel, Quebec, where official residences were provided for the Governor General, but we were to find a suitable house in each of the Provincial capitals for a few weeks, during the course of our term of office. By this means, we hoped to get in touch with the people.

An early venture beyond the political hothouse of Ottawa was to Montreal and a temporary home at 919 Rue Sherbrooke which Ishbel found "roomy, comfortable, & decorated in good taste." But Mrs. Grant, the housekeeper from Rideau Hall who had gone ahead to get the house ready, was not so happy, complaining that, though it looked clean, it was "another matter" when she looked under the carpets. Not that Ishbel minded much, since she felt it was essential that Johnny should spend time in Montreal, "for this *is* the metropolis & the place where he can make his influence most felt so as to permeate the country." But meeting the people—the grander ones at least—was not as congenial as Ishbel had imagined. In at least one city, the inhabitants made no effort to hide their feelings. When Johnny and Ishbel arrived at Government House, Toronto, for a six-week stay, they received the frostiest of welcomes from its chatelaine, Lady Kirkpatrick, who, "for some reason* best known to herself appears to have conceived a violent antipathy to us from the outset."

Ishbel was soon aware that Lady Kirkpatrick was not alone:

The Conservatives, of which Toronto is the centre, were against us. . . . The Orangemen were against us for we had too many Roman Catholic friends. . . . The great Army of Temperance was against us—for we had expressed ourselves clearly adverse to prohibition.

Sometimes it was hard to keep smiling, she confided to her diary, as she recovered at home in Ottawa from a tour of small towns:

Here again after another week of 'progress' as it is called through Ontario—that is, being bucketed from one place to another by night & going through the round of being received at the station, addresses presented, a procession round the town, reception at the Fair grounds, an attempt to go round the exhibits in the midst of a huge crowd, a long luncheon with nothing possible to eat, & visits to various schools, hospitals, convents & other institutions. We live our days to the tune

---

* Lady Kirkpatrick was the daughter of a Conservative politician and, just like Ishbel, had fiercely maintained her allegiance to her father's party since childhood. She was also a supporter of Sir Charles Tupper, whom she believed had been badly treated by Johnny.

of God Save the Queen, from the moment the train arrives till it departs, & one sometimes wonders inwardly whether the moment will not arrive when instead of keeping up an inane smile, we will not seize someone & turn them round and shake them or do something desperate to make at least a change.

Often the attacks were personal. In January 1895, their butler John Grant was so incensed by a Sunday newspaper's repetition of the "old chestnut" that his employers fraternized with their servants that he wrote to its editor to protest:

> You tell a story of a 'Vice-Regal reception held at Ottawa' for the truth of which you evidently hold some 'grand military dame' responsible. 'Her Excellency is supposed to be enjoying the company of her servants in the drawing room while the reception is going on.'

The story, he complained, was a "false statement," a distortion of the more creditable truth:

> Their Excellencies know how to treat their servants with dignified kindness, and in turn they receive a loyal, loving, and dutiful service, such as I feel certain is not received elsewhere on this side of the Atlantic.*

But for Ishbel, the pleasures of family life made up for the exhaustion, the tension headaches that still afflicted her, and the occasional attacks of depression: being "down in the dumps," she called it. The children found Canada "an earthly paradise," Marjorie remembered:

> It was a free, full life, with a boundless range of interests and pursuits: we had the New World to explore, and to me it remains El Dorado.

---

* The butler-turned-spin-doctor's protest went unheeded and probably perpetuated the myth. Johnny's successor, the Earl of Minto, a stickler for etiquette, told his brother that he had heard that "the establishment was too awful—punctuality for anything unknown—dinner sometimes not till 10 p.m." Most shocking of all was "the Haddo Club (on terms of equality with the servants every Thursday night) when subjects were brought forward for discussion, in which I hear on one occasion the butler considerably bested H.E.—the servants consequently odious to everyone."

When they could escape from the schoolroom at Rideau Hall, they headed outside with their sports-mad father:

> We tobogganed, snowshoed, skated, played ice-hockey in glittering weather. Our dear Swedish governess, Miss Wetterman, got some pairs of 'ski' from Sweden for us,* and we soon thought this the best sport of all.

Indoors, there were amateur dramatics and *tableaux vivants* in which no one took part with more enthusiasm than the Governor General himself.

For Marjorie, "the treat of the year" was taking the train west to the Coldstream Ranch. At every station along the way, she and Archie, who had been given an air rifle, "sprang out for a run, and especially at the wayside prairie stops where we could explore or shoot at marks." The ranch house at Coldstream was built of wood and had a covered veranda, white-painted windows, and a balcony from which to view Johnny's rolling acres. Ishbel liked its simplicity, but was less keen on its size: "we just fit in," she noted on a plan drawn up by Marjorie. This shows, on the ground floor, a drawing room, a dining room, and small sitting rooms for Johnny and Ishbel, flanking their bedroom. There was a hall for the servants that, for most of them, doubled as sleeping quarters, and a kitchen, scullery, and larder down the corridor. Marjorie and Archie slept upstairs, as did the cook, the valets, the footman, and the ladies' maids.

Marjorie remembered only one cloud in the British Columbian sky:

> On these holidays we had several hours of lessons to do under mother's supervision which we always declared was much stricter than the ordinary schoolroom routine.

However, Dudley, who was then eight, never forgot how their visit in September 1895 was overshadowed by the deaths of Filbert and Atlas, Ishbel's best-loved horses. They had died of carbon monoxide poisoning

---

*Ishbel boasted that Miss Wetterman introduced skiing to Canada, but that honor may more properly belong to the Norwegian émigrés who, in 1891, founded a ski club at Revelstoke in British Columbia, around a hundred miles from the ranch at Coldstream.

when the smoke from the engine got into their open boxcar as the train neared Vernon. And then Archie broke his arm tipping backwards off his pony. But there were better days, like September 28, when the family drove five miles up the valley to a corner of the ranch called the Lower Meadows. Marjorie wrote:

> We took the luncheon basket, and sat down on logs, and had a very good luncheon. Then we looked at the little houses where the men stay when they are feeding the cattle with hay. These meadows are 1040 acres, with a good deal of bush. We saw two stacks of hay of 30 and 25 tons. We fired at a bottle, and then started again. It was delicious after this—the road going through lovely woods, of birch and fir, with a little burn running along. It was just like Scotland. Father compared it to Balmoral.

There were holidays, too, near New Richmond on the Atlantic coast, for on his arrival in Canada, Johnny had bought yet another property, a lodge on the Cascapédia River in Quebec, where, as a perk of the job, the Governor Generals were traditionally granted the fishing rights.

Stanley House, named after Johnny's predecessor Lord Stanley, who had built it, stood nine miles from the river, so that residents could avoid the mosquitoes, blackflies, and sand flies that infested its banks. Like the Coldstream ranch house, the rambling lodge was plain and unadorned: built by the Rideau Hall carpenter of "common pine wood," Ishbel noted, "& the furniture is of the simplest." As usual, she had checked downstairs, where she thought the servants' quarters "good and roomy." Upstairs she found "eighteen bed-rooms, a nice big octagonal drawing-room with a big open fireplace & a brick hearth." Outside there was a "rough stable for 8 horses & a little laundry," as well as the menservants' bedrooms and carpenter's shop. The only improvement needed was a coat of varnish everywhere.

Stanley House appealed to her for another reason. It was "arranged for summer living only," which meant that, in the face of dwindling funds and the cost of life at Rideau Hall, it "reduced expenses for the whole year considerably." Above all, she enjoyed watching the children enjoying themselves:

It is even better than Coldstream, inasmuch as there are no responsibilities involved by our sixty acres, and then, in addition, there is sea
bathing, and both sea and river fishing. The children love their surroundings. Marjorie considers it her ideal for a permanent home, and
Dudley says his greatest idea of bliss is never to change from what he
is, never grow older, and spend all his time between this and Harrow.*

This was the nearest Ishbel and Johnny ever got to the simple life,
although they brought their servants with them, and the usual cares and
duties—catching up with correspondence, looking over their accounts—
were never entirely forgotten.

Ishbel was especially grateful for the peace and quiet of Stanley House
in June 1897, arriving there with "a great breath of relief" after a month of
"perpetual rush and hurry." But she could now begin to relax in the knowledge that a bitterly fought campaign was nearly over, and that she had won.

The year before, the National Council of Women of Canada had debated a motion calling on the national and provincial governments to offer
"inducements" to doctors and nurses to work in the Northern Territories
and "outlying districts," where medical services were virtually nonexistent.
Only the two delegates who proposed it knew that it was a plant by their
president, who was by then wary of provoking criticism from politicians
that she was interfering in matters of state. But as Ishbel listened to the
members' "pathetic stories of cases where young mothers and children
had died, whilst husbands and fathers were travelling many weary miles
for the medical and nursing aid which might have saved them," she became
more determined than ever to get something done.

When, on her own visits to such communities, Ishbel had heard such
tales, she had thought back to the creation in Britain, ten years before, of
Queen Victoria's Jubilee Institute for Nurses, which had sent nurses out
to care for the sick in the poorest parts of the countryside and the disease-
ridden slums of the cities. Now she planned to do the same for Canada, in
honor of the Queen's Diamond Jubilee. The way forward seemed simple:

---

*Dudley remained fond of Harrow School for the rest of his life, often cutting a striking
figure in a suit of Gordon tartan on occasions important enough to warrant his presence as a
Governor.

she spoke to the Prime Minister, who expressed his support, a government grant looked likely, and enthusiastic committees throughout the land were poised to begin a fund-raising drive.

Instead, she met fierce opposition: Toronto's influential Medical Association denounced her plan as "one fraught with danger to the country," while other self-interested practitioners claimed that the nurses would only be "semi-trained" and thus provide poor care. But the nurses were not in favor either. They had struggled, they told her, to achieve professional standing and to command the fees they deserved: her vision of them helping patients with the housework and cooking, as well as providing treatment, would be a loss of status that they would never accept. Ishbel won them over by agreeing to recruit only nursing-school graduates, but persuading politicians and doctors to support her proved far more difficult. Parliament refused to provide funding, thanks to a campaign led by Sir Charles Tupper, who was finally exacting his revenge for the wrongs that he believed Johnny had done him. And Ishbel despaired when the doctors refused to listen even to the revered doyenne of modern nursing, Florence Nightingale, who wrote:

> Heartily do we wish success to the Victorian Nurses and to all Canadian workers in this good cause.

It was not until the end of October 1897 that Ishbel's luck turned. During a trip south to Boston, she recruited a young doctor, Alfred Worcester, who was becoming well known for his innovative methods for training nurses, to work on Canada's most influential medical associations. He soon won round doctors in Ottawa and Montreal, but the resistance of their colleagues in Toronto took longer to crack. However, they, too, fell into line, thanks to the young man's persistence, charm, and the generous supply of drinks, sandwiches, and cigars that Ishbel had laid on for them at a meeting that went on until past midnight. Afterwards at Government House, Ishbel and Worcester celebrated their victory with toast and tea (Johnny rummaged in the pantry for a lemon), but she wasted no more time. She organized a training program, set up four nursing schools, asked Queen Victoria for a royal charter, and launched the Victorian Order of Nurses in the most eye-catching way she think could of.

An appeal from the Reverend Robert Dickey, a Presbyterian missionary from Skagway, Alaska, for nurses to work in the Klondike goldfields
had caught her eye. Ishbel responded with a promise to send him four
"fully trained nurses of great experience." They would, she assured him,
"count the opportunity thus given them of succouring suffering humanity
under very adverse circumstances, a joy and an honour."

And so for Miss Powell, Miss Payson, Miss Hanna, and Miss Scott, the
first members of the Victorian Order of Nurses, an epic adventure began.
The National Council of Women provided them with kit for the trek of
more than two and half thousand miles from Ottawa to Dawson City in
the Yukon, and Ishbel and Johnny threw them a party at Rideau Hall on
the night before their departure. A newspaper reporter who was present
was moved by their ceremonial farewell to the pioneers:

> His excellency conferred upon each of the four young ladies the badge
> of the order, which Lady Aberdeen, with loving fingers, securely fas-
> tened, and one looked with moistened eye at those earnest faces, so
> calm and steady in this trying hour of farewell.

Johnny had already deposited the women's salaries in the bank at Dawson City, along with another $600 for emergencies. To ensure the young
women's safety in the hostile territory that they would have to cross, Ishbel
had prevailed upon a friend, Colonel T. D. B. Evans, the commander of the
Yukon Field Force, to escort them with two hundred of his men. As they
navigated rivers in paddle steamers, rafts, and makeshift boats, crossed
high mountain passes, and slogged their way over the trackless land, she
followed their progress anxiously from Rideau Hall.

Much of the journey, she learned later, was a punishing trek across
"terrible country":

> Boulders and huge fallen trees were the least part of the difficulties,
> for there were horrible swamps, through which they had to wade up
> to their waists. There was nothing to eat but hard biscuits, and rancid,
> strong bacon and black tea, and this in the midst of great heat and
> under perpetual attack from the mosquitoes.

Miss Powell, the chief nurse, put it even more graphically in a newspaper interview:

> From mountain to swamp and bog we went—bogs into whose cold mossy depths we would sink to our knees, and under which the ice still remains; swamps where we trampled down bushes and shrubs to make a footing for ourselves and where the mules stuck many times, often as many as twenty all down at once, sometimes having to be unpacked to be taken out, our baggage dumped in the mud and the mosquitoes held high revelry.

The nurses' clothes and boots, designed to last them three years, were "completely worn out" when they finally arrived at Dawson City and its Good Samaritan Hospital, a log cabin that was still under construction. But there was no time to recover from a journey that even the Yukon Force's commander admitted had been "very bad": an epidemic of typhoid had broken out among the thousands of hopeful prospectors who were living in squalid conditions. Miss Powell told Ishbel:

> I thought I had seen something of typhoid, but nothing like this. Typhoid with pneumonia, with malaria, congestion of the liver, rheumatism, neuralgia, sore throat, discharge from the ears and sore eyes. Such sick men!

As the news filtered south from the nurses' own log house, built with Johnny's emergency money, a wave of pride swept across a country that was still finding its identity and needed heroes. Ishbel confessed: "I would never have dared to initiate it, had I known what was to come," but she was content that after all her battles with physicians and politicians, the Victorian Order of Nurses was at last firmly established.*

But it was, in some ways, a hollow victory, for early in May 1898, while Miss Powell and her colleagues were still gamely struggling through the

---

* The VON is still a vital force in Canada today, with around five thousand professionals and nine thousand volunteers providing healthcare in patients' homes.

swamps, Johnny had suddenly announced that he would be cutting short his term of office and hoped to return home before the end of the year. He wanted to see his "honoured mother," he explained, who was "in very advanced years," and it was "her desire that he should return to the old land before the end of his full term of six years." But there were other, more pressing reasons for his decision: ones that he was reluctant to reveal to the Canadian public and even to Sir Wilfrid Laurier, the Prime Minister.

15

A "Dear House" in Ottawa and a Scottish Retreat

In the weeks that followed Johnny's announcement, Ottawa buzzed with questions and rumors. Was the Governor General really giving up his post simply so that he could see more of his mother? What were the "private and family claims and interests" that he had cited in his letter of resignation, and why were these, as Sir Wilfrid Laurier had acknowledged just as delphically in his reply, "of a nature which must be accepted without questioning"? Tongues wagged even more busily when Sir Charles Tupper accused Johnny of favoring a company chaired by Ishbel's brother Edward in a dispute over a contract for a new transatlantic steamer service. Perhaps, the political gossips whispered, the Governor General had been sacked.

In the press, Johnny fared better. Many newspapers, like the *Ottawa Journal*, paid tribute to "the kindly gentleman and unselfish and earnest public man" who "had endeavoured steadfastly to further our interests and earn our goodwill." From Quebec, *La Patrie* praised Ishbel's contribution too: "Their whole mission," it said, "was one of doing good." But Johnny remained tight-lipped about the reasons for their departure, and Ishbel said nothing in public, confining herself to a single observation in her diary: "People have been wonderfully kind about it."

To her, the "Goodbye days" seemed "an extra heavy time," and she complained of "the turmoil and anxiety with which those months were filled." But she found at least one compensation. It came, as it so often had for Ishbel, in the form of a "dear house" at 578 Somerset Street, Ottawa, a "very charming gift" to her from a rich friend and supporter. Before handing over this "ever so pretty" villa to the Victorian Order of Nurses to use as its headquarters, she delighted in having guests to lunch "in my own house" and made the most of the opportunity to indulge her love of interior design:

> The little Board room is decorated in the two blues of the Jubilee colours & it is furnished with my old Irish furniture from the Irish Village. . . . We have a nice etching of the Queen at one end.

Ishbel had one more important public appearance to make. Two years earlier, sixteen of the country's most talented female artists had been chosen to paint a china dinner service to commemorate the four hundredth anniversary of the explorer John Cabot's landing in Canada. Their brief from the Women's Art Association of Canada was to depict "old forts, battlefields, old gates and other historical scenes, also reproductions of game, fish, shells, ferns and flowers of Canada," on nearly two hundred "blank" plates and coffee cups provided by Sir Henry Doulton, whose London firm produced some of the finest ceramics in the Empire. A dozen Limoges coffee cups completed the set. For the artists, the work was a formidable challenge: each piece had to be painted with a different design, and the president of the association had written to say: "Your best work is expected." But when the service was finally exhibited, the newspapers hailed it as "the most valuable artistic work ever done in Canada, as it will be, practically, an illustrated history of the [country's] scenery and seasons."

The Women's Art Association had hoped that the dinner service would be used at Rideau Hall on state occasions, but the government declined to buy it.* Instead, members of the Senate and the House of Commons

---

* Later governments and cultural organizations regretted this petty act of meanness, and my father-in-law, the 4th Marquess, fielded several inquiries as to whether he could be persuaded to return this spectacular work of art. But the "Elgin Marbles of Canada," as they then became known in the family, have stayed put in their display cabinet, except for one trip to Canada for an exhibition, and they are among Haddo's most precious treasures.

stepped in. They agreed that it would be an ideal farewell gift for Ishbel, because, as one told her, "it is purely Canadian and because it is the result of the efforts of Canadian women, in whom Your Excellency has always shown the deepest interest."

Ishbel's speech of acceptance at the presentation ceremony in Parliament made history, as Lady Edgar, wife of the Speaker of the Commons, noted:

> For the first time a woman's voice thrilled through the august Senate Chamber, as in eloquent and touching words Lady Aberdeen thanked the Members for their gift.

Ishbel spoke simply. The painted service would bring back happy memories of her Canadian houses:

> Again we shall hear the sweet notes of the Canadian robin and blue bird heralding the spring in the woods of Rideau Hall—we shall hear the whirr of the wild geese sweeping over our lovely British Columbia lakes and mountains. . . . How often shall we long for the exhilaration of a toboggan slide on a brilliant Canadian winter's day? How we shall listen for the splash of the paddle as the canoe glides up a stately river amidst sunshine and beauty! And now we shall be speeding over the myriad-hue prairies and anon we shall find ourselves in deep woods amidst the haunts of the wild flowers, whose loveliness we shall see delineated before us!

To Lady Edgar's surprise, many members of Ishbel's audience—even the most hard-bitten of the politicians—were "moved to tears," and perhaps this is why no one seemed to notice that almost all Ishbel's happy memories came from private moments: holidays with the children at Stanley House or the ranches, scenes glimpsed through the windows of the Car Victoria as it trundled across the prairies, or walks in the quiet of the morning before the official business of Government House began for another day. Of her public life she said nothing, perhaps because, as she confessed in her journal, she had often found the stress that it inflicted upon her hard to bear:

It is a comfort that A. can take things lightly, it would be the last straw
if he began to worry. But sometimes I fairly sink under the load—
trying to help him a bit over public business, to be a companion to the
children, with knocks raining on my unoffending door all day, work
for the N.C.W. and V.O. all night, and this gnawing at one's heart over
money. One feels paralysed by the difficulties, so horribly small and
incompetent.

And the couple's five years in Canada had left them exhausted, bruised,
and often bewildered by the animosity shown to them, although Johnny
did not cite these reasons when, in his memoirs some thirty years later,
he finally revealed why they had decided to go home early, despite having
become "much attached" to the country. The explanation he gave was not
one that the gossips had guessed, although it was true that after five years
away without once returning home, he was keen to see his mother, the
eighty-four-year-old Dowager Countess, to whom he was very attached.
Nor, despite the efforts of the vindictive Sir Charles Tupper, does he seem
to have been dismissed from his post, although the Colonial Secretary,
Joseph Chamberlain, was wary of the peace-loving Johnny and would have
welcomed the appointment of his successor, the militaristic Earl of Minto,
who could be relied upon to provide Canadian troops to fight against the
Boers in South Africa.

In fact, Mr. Jamieson, the Edinburgh accountant, had at last prevailed.
They had left, Johnny confessed, because he was running out of money:

The expenses of our regime had been very heavy. Our plan of resid-
ing at the different centres, in addition to Ottawa, and entertaining
at each, whilst being most desirable in itself had added largely to our
burdens. We had had summer sessions every year during our tenure
of office, which prevented us from shutting up Government House
for the summer, and Coldstream's failure to be a source of income,
not to speak of the outlays required there, had placed us at a disadvantage.

Johnny was a casualty of a convention that suited the Colonial Office
and the Treasury in London, but which was beginning to prove unwork-

able as the turn of the century approached. Viceroys and governors general were appointed not so much for their political or diplomatic acumen, but for their ability to subsidize, from their own fortunes, the showy, quasi-royal, lifestyle that they were expected to lead. A few years later, the 7th Earl of Hopetoun, the Governor General of Australia, flounced off home after the Australian Parliament, with an eye to reducing the pomp and circumstance that went with the job, refused to supplement his £10,000 salary with an expenses allowance of £8,000. In Johnny's case, his financial situation was so dire that Joseph Chamberlain felt bound to warn Minto of the problems he might face in succeeding him:

> I think I ought to say that Lord A. informs me that the expenditures
> of the office during his tenure of it had exceeded his salary by about
> £5000* a year.

But Chamberlain was unsympathetic to Johnny's plight, adding that this was "more than is necessary." He had a point. From the beginning, by installing the private chapel at Rideau Hall when there were plenty of churches nearby where they could have worshipped, Johnny and Ishbel's lavish spending had raised eyebrows in spartan Ottawa, and later embellishments to the house, such as adding gilt cornices to the ballroom, were also seen as "more than is necessary."

They entertained constantly: state banquets, parliamentary dinners, "At Homes" with music and dancing once a fortnight, Drawing Rooms and levees. Their guests took full advantage of Ishbel's hospitality, as the journalist Agnes Scott noted, after witnessing "an *omnium gatherum* of men and women who not only sup as if they had not dined that day, but as if that necessary meal had not been enjoyed for weeks." John Grant, the butler, complained that "some would drink four or five glasses of champagne' at ceremonial events, and after one concert Ishbel was put out by the consequences of her liberal hospitality:

> The ladies behaved somewhat boisterously in the cloakroom & quite
> upset our calculations by vaulting over tables arranged for giving out

---

* Around £400,000 ($520,000) in today's money. Johnny's salary was twice that.

the cloaks & insisting on going for their bundles themselves, & as no reasoning or entreaties would make them abstain from this, of course there was dire confusion.

Most extravagant of all, and especially hard on Johnny's fraying purse strings, were the spectacular fancy-dress balls that Ishbel produced with all the brio of P. T. Barnum himself. At one, guests were instructed to dress as characters from Canadian life and history: Marjorie, who came bizarrely arrayed as the "Forests of Canada" with a stuffed chipmunk on her shoulder, easily stole the show. At another, held to celebrate Queen Victoria's Diamond Jubilee and attended by two and a half thousand guests, Ishbel commissioned *tableaux vivants* based on famous pictures and a procession that included brass bands, agricultural machinery, and dancers "representing telephones and motors." Afterwards she wrote, rather nervously:

> We think that the cost will not exceed the 4,000 dollars we intended for it.

Johnny's willingness to provide seed money for Ishbel's projects had also made deep inroads into his dwindling funds, as did his impulsive acts of generosity. When "his" first Prime Minister, Sir John Thompson, died, he immediately offered to pay for his two sons to complete their education, and after Ishbel was rescued from drowning when one of the ponies hauling her carriage lost its footing and tipped her into a river,* he presented the nearby church with a large bell as a token of their gratitude.

With his income from Haddo still faltering and the Cromar estates without a buyer, Johnny had counted on his North American ranches to restore his fortunes. But both the "Honorable Cowboys," as Ishbel's brothers were known, had failed to make a go of their businesses in Dakota Territory and Texas. By the time Johnny became Governor General, Coutts had already abandoned the Horseshoe Ranch and taken up Ishbel's offer of a

---

* The nearest bridge to the scene of the accident at Gatineau, near Ottawa, is now called the Lady Aberdeen Bridge.

job at their Guisachan Ranch in British Columbia. Archie's Rocking Chair Ranch barely outlived the Horseshoe, thanks to John Drew, its manager, who succeeded in stealing most of its cattle before anyone noticed. The syndicate back in London was about to take action against him, when its lawyers pointed out that the unwitting Archie had also signed every false statement of the stock numbers that they had been sent. He was therefore just as much to blame in the eyes of the law as Drew. Both men were sacked immediately, and in the late summer of 1893 Archie traveled north to Ottawa to throw himself on the mercy of his forgiving sister. The land lay unsold for three years before another, more competent, company bought it for less than half the price that Johnny and his fellow investors had paid ten years before.

By now, Johnny and Ishbel were pinning their hopes on the British Columbian ranches, but things scarcely went better there. From the start, Coutts had proved a disaster as a manager, and Mr. Jamieson, whom Johnny had dispatched there in 1892 to report on the prospects, had despaired of his lack of business acumen and common sense. Coutts might well have learned from the cowboys in Dakota, but Guisachan "was in no respect suitable for him: it could never be a cattle ranch." And despite his success at the Vernon Show with the giant pumpkins, cauliflowers, and beets that he grew in his small garden soon after his arrival, "he was not the man," Jamieson concluded, "to sit down to cultivate apples, pears and hops" on an industrial scale. Nor did he have the expertise to set up a fruit farm as large and complex as Coldstream.

Although Jamieson tactfully forbore to mention it, Coutts was wrong for the job for another reason. The "Major," as locals unable to pronounce Marjoribanks had nicknamed him, had begun to conform to the worst stereotype of the hard-drinking remittance man. Charles Mair, the journalist and poet, who encountered Coutts on a visit to the Okanagan, was surprised that Johnny had left the management of his ranches to a "rum stick who goes about dressed as a cowboy, and indulges freely in Scotch whisky." One of his neighbors, the photographer and artist Charles Holliday, described how "he liked to ride at a clattering gallop to pull up short in front of the Kalamalka Hotel where he would dismount for a refresher" and, all too often, some drunken antics. Holliday was amused that Coutts blamed Ishbel for his bad behavior:

In apologising to the ladies for his rough manners he was apt to say, "You know my sister has so much godliness that there wasn't enough left to go round the rest of the family."*

But it was Johnny, not Coutts, who was responsible for the greatest fiasco of those early days. He had advertised for a manager for his pet project, the jam factory that would process the fruit from the new orchards, and in October 1892 the *Victoria Times* announced that the job had gone to a Mr O. W. F. Krauss, who, the paper said, had "learned the confectionary and jam making business at Berlin, and was afterwards manager of a jam factory in California, and is in all respects a suitable man to manage a business."

Krauss turned out to be most unsuitable. He showed his true colors from the start when he suggested buying jam from Scotland, falsely labeling it as being from the "Okanagan Preserving Works," and exhibiting it at the Chicago World's Fair. Johnny appointed him anyway, merely making him sign a contract agreeing "to use none such named tricks of the trade." It was left to Jamieson and Mackay to dismiss Krauss soon afterwards, after he ran up exorbitant bills for furnishing his house and for high living in a hotel. He was also said to have taken $5,000 from another community in exchange for a promise to build the jam factory there and not at Vernon. And there were rumors, too, that Mrs. Krauss had made an "unscheduled visit" to Coutts's home in the hope of blackmailing him.†

Jamieson was worried by what he found during his visit, warning Johnny that the financial situation was "alarming." The return on Gui-

---

*Johnny was less amused by Coutts's contributions to the Okanagan ventures: he later admitted, in a masterly understatement, that they had left him "financially at a disadvantage." I doubt he would have derived much consolation from the news, reported in the *Cowboy Chronicle* a century later, that Coutts had been nominated for induction into a Cowboy Hall of Fame.

† Krauss does not seem to have lain low for long after his dismissal. When, a few months later, newspapers in the United States published a story about a plan for "a jelly factory" at Leavenworth, Kansas, Mr. E. Jameson, the man behind it, received an offer of help "from a Canadian gentleman," who wrote: "If I can be of any assistance to you or your scheme I shall be most pleased to do so. I am well acquainted with British jam and jelly manufacture as well as our usual American canned goods. Hoping you will kindly excuse me, and trusting to hear from you very soon, I am dear sir, Yours Very Truly, O.W.F. Krauss." The would-be jelly makers of Leavenworth do not seem to have availed themselves of Krauss's expertise, however: two years later, with local fruit farmers about to produce one million bushels of apples each season, the *Leavenworth Weekly Times* was still calling for a jelly factory.

sachan had been only $2,393 in the first two years, for an outlay of $34,972, and he feared for the future of "an enterprise that has attracted such wide attention and interest." The problems at Coldstream were even more critical. Jamieson told Johnny that he had paid too much for it, and that he suspected the seller, Colonel Vernon, of bulking out the size of his herd with poor-quality cattle to make the ranch appear more prosperous and saleable than it really was. The large stock of hay mentioned in the prospectus seemed to have vanished with the ranch's former manager, and they would have to buy more feed for the winter. But the Colonel had rebuffed all Jamieson's attempts to renegotiate the contract and had faced down threats to take him to court. Jamieson's conclusion was bleak: Johnny would have to raise $64,785 to keep the ranch going.

As Johnny's losses mounted, he sought advice from Canadian experts, yet due to his characteristic impulsiveness, naïveté in matters of business, or ignorance of the fruit-growing techniques he had never taken the time to learn, he embarked on expensive improvement programs before the experts had reported. And when they did report, he did not heed their warnings that he was paying his workers too much and selling off his best land to settlers at knockdown prices. Ishbel was disappointed when she returned to British Columbia in 1894:

> The fruit at Guisachan is a failure, owing to the alkali & the ground being so near a level with the lake that the water comes in the roots. And so it has been a big loss to plant all those trees down there. We shall probably have to turn it mainly into a pig ranch combined perhaps with dairy. Pigs pay very well . . .

And later, in her memoirs, she put on a brave face as she looked back on the collapse of their hopes for Coldstream:

> How eagerly we repaired thither in the first autumn of our official residence in Canada, how entirely did we feel that the descriptions which we had received of the promise and attractiveness of the property were justified! . . . But the years came and went, and the golden age predicted always receded, and always more capital was called for, so as not to lose what had already been invested.

But although they blamed the failure of the ranches on others—the grasping Vernon, the incompetent Coutts, the slippery Mackay, the duplicitous Krauss—and on the conditions—poor soil, bad weather, unreliable water supplies—the real culprit was Johnny. He only ever visited the Okanagan six times after he bought the ranches; he seemed to think that his worthy speeches condemning absentee landlords in Scotland did not apply to him. He never understood that his plans for fruit farming, however good they might have appeared on paper, would not succeed without the sweat of everyone from the humblest picker to the proprietor himself. One old-timer learned this the hard way:

> No man can sit on his verandah all day and expect his ranch to buy him bread and cheese. Fruit-growing means work—solid, hard work—work from the first glinting of the dawn to the creeping up of midnight. It means an unceasing vigilance. It calls for the constant, daily exercise of a high intelligence. Once again it calls for work, long and strenuous hours.

If it was a relief to leave the problems of the Canadian ranches behind her when she and Johnny finally embarked for home in November 1898, Ishbel did not look forward to dealing with the other "private and family claims and interests" that Johnny had mentioned in his letter of resignation. She had faced some already. Her father, Dudley Tweedmouth, had died in March 1894, which meant that, to her frustration, she was forced to miss the sight of Johnny presiding over the Opening of Parliament, since it took place during the customary six weeks of mourning. Tweedmouth, predictably, bequeathed the bulk of his fortune, which amounted to £650,409 3s 4d (more than £50,000,000 today), to his eldest son, Edward, who also inherited his title. He left £1,000 to Ishbel "to buy some jewel or ornament" to remember him by, and "as a token of esteem," £1,000 in cash to Johnny. This was a substantial sum of money at the time, but nothing like enough to solve Johnny's financial problems.

To Ishbel, the death of Henry Drummond from bone cancer in March 1897, at the age of only forty-five, was the harshest blow, but, as she did so often at a time of loss, she kept her feelings to herself. And even in her diary, she devoted just a few lines to "the dying out of a great light & joy in our lives":

It would be useless to try to write of this—it seems to us that it can have been granted to but few to have known so full & so perfect a friendship with one whose character & nature ever seemed to reveal new richness & new perfection the closer one came to him. . . . It has all been so perfect & there has never been a shade over our relationship since that first evening when he came into the drawing-room at Holyrood in May 1884 & when we seemed to know one another right away.

Her words are a poignant epitaph to a special kindred spirit. He was, she wrote in her memoirs nearly thirty years later, "so intimate a friend that he became virtually a member of our immediate family circle." He was Archie's godfather and her children called him "Uncle Hen." For Johnny in particular, time with the witty, high-spirited, unpredictable, unconventional Drummond was an escape from the stultifying formality and ceremonial that dominated their lives. He was the court jester who enlivened the long, and sometimes distressing, days of visits to factories, hospitals, schools, and the homes of people struggling to make a living, by insisting on "playing rollicking games" in the evenings; the banisher of depression who "seemed to diffuse, like radium, brightness and vivacity"; the traveling companion who could make an adventure even out of inspecting the servants' quarters of Rideau Hall; the replacement brother for Johnny who went on holiday with him while Ishbel was busy at women's conferences; the energetic supporter of their causes (he appointed himself sub-editor of *Wee Willie Winkie*); the "entirely unclerical" cleric whose warmth* and gift for easy intimacy allowed him to become their mentor and father confessor; the charming conversationalist who could be relied upon to bring out the best in even the shyest of house guests.

They dispatched Doddie and George Germain, their house steward, to Drummond's funeral in Stirling, and "had a little service at about the same hour" in the chapel at Rideau Hall. Ishbel was comforted by the way the service was "tenderly conducted," for she was "desolate indeed." Later, they commissioned a bas-relief from one of the leading sculptors of the

---

* Helen Keller, the deaf-blind American writer and political activist, was another of his admirers, thanks to his "strong, warm" handshake, which she wrote, was "like a benediction." "He was the most sympathetic of companions. And it was impossible to feel dull in his presence."

day and installed it in the antechapel at Haddo for everyone to see. Drummond's mother sent Ishbel a lock of his hair: its red-brown sheen was gone and it was "almost white." She hid it at the back of a miniature portrait of her "wonderful friend" and kept it close.

Gladstone was the next to die, in May 1898. Ishbel was not surprised: Johnny's patron and her Grand Old Friend and mentor had long been ailing, but she knew that another landmark in their lives had gone. England, she wrote, would be "a very different place to go back to."

Soon after they returned home, other deaths followed. The first, from pneumonia and "blood poisoning" was Ishbel's sister, in March 1899. While high society extolled Polly's beauty and her skills as a political hostess, Ishbel's response was typically loving and practical. In the face of the "grief and desolation" of Polly's husband, Viscount Ridley, she took him and his children under her wing, always invited them to Haddo for the Christmas holidays, and after Ridley's death in 1904, looked after his young daughters.

Johnny's wish to see his mother, Mary, the Dowager Countess, was granted, but he did not have long with her. After she died in April 1900, aged eighty-five, in a "tribute of loving gratitude" in her *Onward and Upward* magazine Ishbel thanked her for being "ready with sympathy for all, whether in joy or sorrow."

Next came her brother Archie, whom, like Coutts, she had rescued after the failure of his ranch. His long exile in the grasslands of the Texas Panhandle at last over, on his way to Ottawa Archie had stopped at the World's Fair in Chicago, and there, at Ishbel's Irish Village, he had met his future wife, Elizabeth Brown, the daughter of a judge from Tennessee. But when Archie arrived at Rideau Hall in February 1894, everyone could see that he was seriously ill. An agonized Ishbel sent him to a specialist in New York and learned that he was suffering from a degenerative disease.* It was, she wrote, "horrible" to see her brother in its "tightening grip." The consultant's prognosis was stark: he gave him "about 5 years," but warned

---

* Archie was diagnosed with locomotor ataxia, an affliction that affects the connection between the spinal cord and the brain, leaving sufferers unable to control their limbs: symptoms include shaking wildly or staggering when walking. Today the condition is known to have several causes—spinal tumors, congenital defects, and heavy drinking among others—but in the nineteenth century doctors knew of only one: syphilis.

that it could be "much less." She immediately persuaded Johnny to appoint
Archie as an extra aide-de-camp:

> This will give him some sort of occupation & companionship &
> pleasant surroundings, I hope, and I trust we shall be able to make
> him happy & lead him to try to be of use here for the little time left,
> poor boy.

Archie died at Bath in September 1900, after moving back to England
with Elizabeth, who, the newspapers were oddly keen to point out in their
obituaries, was "a charming woman" but "not an heiress." Archie was only
thirty-eight. There were rumors that he had committed suicide. These
may have been true: even before the onset of his cruel last illness, exiled
in his cabin on the Texas Panhandle, his life had been difficult, lonely,
and unfulfilled, and of the cowboy brothers, he was the one who had tried
hardest and suffered most.

There was one more tragedy yet to unfold. Ishbel's brother Edward,
the new Baron Tweedmouth, was the golden boy of the Marjoribanks
family: a noted sportsman, a highly regarded lawyer, and a respected politician, who, on the day after his father's death, had been appointed to the
cabinet by the Prime Minister, Lord Rosebery. But in the eyes of many of
his contemporaries, his most enviable achievement was to have married
Lady Fanny Spencer-Churchill, the beautiful and popular daughter of
the 7th Duke of Marlborough and aunt of Winston Churchill. In 1904,
Fanny died of cancer, her long decline chronicled in the society pages of
the newspapers. Ishbel, who had admired "her joyous zest in all the activities and pleasures of life," was moved by her courage in the face of death,
and by her determination to "live her life out to the very end, meeting
all engagements already made, as ready as ever to enter into the joys and
sorrows of others around her."

Fanny had told Ishbel of her illness at what would otherwise have
been a happy family event: Marjorie's wedding, in July 1904, to Jack
Sinclair, who had been one of Johnny's aides-de-camp in Ireland and
was then the Liberal Member of Parliament for Forfarshire. He was
forty-four and Marjorie was twenty-three, but, despite the large age gap,
they were happy: so much so that he turned down the job of Liberal

Chief Whip a year later because he feared it would take him "altogether from his wife."

Soon Ishbel was plotting another spring-autumn marriage. Worries over Doddie's health and future had been among their main reasons for returning home early from Canada. His childhood and teenaged years had been blighted by epilepsy, and now, in his twenties, he had begun to talk of getting married. But Doddie's condition posed a problem: doctors believed epilepsy was hereditary, and Ishbel and Johnny feared he might pass it on to the next generation. Things came to a head when Doddie announced that he planned to take a flat in London and live there alone, despite the risk of seizures. It was time to find him a wife, Ishbel decided, but one past child-bearing age.

Her eye soon alighted on Florence Cockayne, the widow of one of the owners of a department store from Sheffield, whose son, Edward,* had been one of Doddie's friends at Oxford University. Florence agreed to Ishbel's proposal that she should move into the apartment next door to keep an eye on him. Ishbel waited until she was sure that they got on well, and then suggested to Florence that they should get married. Florence wrote back, aghast:

I love your boy dearly, but had never thought of him in that way, and you know he looks on me as a second mother.

But four months later, *The Times* carried news of their engagement, and the wedding of this most unlikely couple soon followed, in August 1906: she was forty-nine, Doddie twenty-seven. Thirty years later in her memoirs, Ishbel considered it a job well done:

---

*Edward, who, although only eighteen months younger than Doddie, became his stepson, had two distinguished careers: one as a physician specializing in children's medicine and the other as an entomologist. By studying his collection of more than fifty thousand specimens, he made an important contribution to the understanding of the biology and genetics of butterflies and moths. Like Doddie, he became more and more eccentric as the years passed. According to a biographer, "his flat under the rooftops of Westbourne Terrace was furnished with cabinets of dead insects and jars of living caterpillars," and "while he was the foremost diagnostic paediatrician of his age, treatment hardly interested him. One was not expected to telephone him about a patient."

A more happy union it is difficult to conceive. From the first Florence won the hearts of all the family, and of all the people at Haddo, and has been everything both to her husband and to us ever since.

Yet while dealing with all these "private and family claims and interests," Ishbel faced problems of her own. She had returned from Canada exhausted and "down in the dumps," and fleetingly dreamt of retreating from the world into a peaceful garden with a "rosery and grass sloping down to murmuring water, and a whole place full of small birds." There, she wrote hopefully, "the old feverish anxious times will seem long long ago."

Johnny did not buy her a garden: instead, in November 1899, having sold their weekend retreat at Dollis Hill two years earlier, he acquired the lease of another house in London. No. 58 Grosvenor Street was, like its predecessors, in Mayfair, but the three-storey building was in need of refurbishment. Johnny did not hold back, lavishing £10,000* upon it, despite his financial woes. A visiting writer, who called to interview Ishbel for a magazine profile and was given a tour of the redecorated rooms, admired the sweeping staircase, the well-stocked library, Johnny's large office, the airy hall with its Sheraton furniture and grandfather clock, Ishbel's comfortable boudoir, and the dining room that, to her surprise, was hung with fine Old Master paintings, including a Tintoretto and a Titian.

Ishbel, as ever, had supervised the works, although she had had little time to do so. Earlier that year, she had presided over a "great meeting" of the International Council of Women that had culminated in a reception at Windsor and an appearance by a frail and impassive Queen Victoria, who rode slowly past the crowd of delegates in her carriage. Newly galvanized, Ishbel returned to championing Irish Home Rule, a cause that she believed had languished since the brief premiership of her old friend Lord Rosebery a few years before, and she was also fiercely opposed to the idea of war in South Africa.

Fellow Liberals and the members of the International Council of Women were not alone in noticing this new burst of activism. In a letter to Johnny, the local postman remembered how, on a "bitterly cold" winter's night, Ishbel rushed up to him in Grosvenor Street as he was collecting the

---

* Roughly £800,000 ($1,000,000) today.

mail from a postbox at three o'clock in the morning. She asked if he would wait while she put stamps on a pile of letters:

I replied that I could, and seeing that her Ladyship had not waited to throw a wrap round her shoulders, I said that if she would step back into the hall, I would wait till the correspondence was ready. I received her thanks, and was much impressed by the kindness of her words and manner, as similar everyday incidents often pass without a 'Thank you', and are looked upon merely as a duty of a public servant. On the following night I was surprised to find Your Lordship waiting at the pillar-box to thank me for what you were pleased to call my consideration. This gentlemanly treatment to one in my position led me to see that your correspondence secured what is in London an important collection.

Yet Ishbel still felt that her days were humdrum when she compared them to the heady ones spent campaigning in Ireland and Canada, and Johnny made only occasional forays into public life: notably, as a pall-bearer* at the showy funeral of the celebrated actor Sir Henry Irving at Westminster Abbey. Bram Stoker, who managed Irving's Lyceum Theatre when he was not busy writing *Dracula* and other gothic novels, was another.

But at least there was something for both Johnny and Ishbel to look forward to: they had finally decided to start building the house in Tarland that Ishbel had dreamt of on her first visit there more than twenty years before. The design they commissioned from Laurence Aloysius McDonnell, the architect of the Chicago Irish Village, was a grandiose affair. It oozed "Scotchness" with its tower and craggy stonework and detailing that seemed to have been culled straight from the pages of the *Castles of Aberdeenshire, Historical and Descriptive Notices*, published only a few years earlier. McDonnell sent a letter with the plans, to explain that the house would be "long, low and unpretentious, partly manor house, partly cottage" and that a round tower and "the suggestion of a keep at the

---

* The coffin cannot have been much of a burden: Sir Henry was the first person to be cremated before being interred at the abbey.

entrance" would "recall the characteristics of Scottish architecture." Inside, the rooms would be light and airy, many of them opening onto covered verandas with views of the garden. It would have all modern conveniences, including "a bathroom for every three bedrooms," and the servants' quarters would be "large for a house of the size."

But McDonnell did not win the contract, no doubt because his estimate of £15,000* for the building works was more than twice Johnny's budget. The job went instead to Sydney Mitchell,[†] a well-regarded architect from Edinburgh, whose work was influenced both by the "Scottish Renaissance style" and the Arts and Crafts Movement. He clearly enjoyed his collaboration with Ishbel, who, after the long years of dreaming about a house among the hills of Deeside, had plenty of ideas.

How many happy hours have I spent with you over plans and drawings for the House of Cromar,

he wrote.

Mitchell's final design was an oddity, supping at the Scottish baronial style only with a long spoon. Ishbel, who had borrowed from other architectural cultures before—Indian, in the case of the bungalow at the Guisachan Ranch, and Canadian for the community hall at Haddo—may well have been behind this. Architectural historians have suggested that, although its detailing is vernacular, the inspiration for the imposing pink granite hip-roofed pile, with its chunky chimney stacks and plump drum towers, may have come from the Château Frontenac, the Canadian Pacific Railway hotel that she had admired when she arrived in Quebec at the beginning of Johnny's term as Governor-General. Later, on a visit to the Coldstream Ranch in October 1895, their friend Sir William Van Horne, the chairman of the CPR and mastermind of the company's hotels, sketched out a design of a house for them. It, too, had a round tower with

---

* About £1,250,000 ($1,600,000) in today's money.

† It is not clear why McDonnell was not asked to try again, nor why Sydney Mitchell won the commission instead. Ishbel would have known him because he designed the "Old Town" exhibit at the 1886 Edinburgh International Exhibition, where she had her first stand promoting Irish crafts. Another connection may have been through Ernest Auldjo Jamieson, the son of her and Johnny's accountant, who may have been working in Mitchell's office at the time, prior to taking over his father's practice a few years later.

a conical spire. This "lodge" was never built, but Ishbel, who never liked to let a good idea go unused, kept the drawing and could well have shown it to Mitchell.

Such was the scale of the works that the budget of £7,000 began to look optimistic[*] even before the first stone of the new house was laid. Johnny made things worse by commissioning a nine-hole golf course from Tom Morris, the leading designer of the day: a costly indulgence. But in June 1903, the *British Architect* reported that construction was at last about to start:

> The main building will be 102 feet long by 50 feet broad and, in addition to the basement will have two storeys with attics. The drawing room and dining room enter off the central hall and other apartments on this floor are a boudoir and smoking-room and, in a wing, a billiards room. The upper floors are to be used as bedrooms, bathrooms etc. and the basement will contain accommodation for the servants.

A few months later, Johnny and Ishbel held a dinner for the builders in the village hall at Tarland. The stonemasons were congratulated on their craftsmanship; the driver of the traction engine brought in to haul heavy loads was praised for his skillful handling of the cumbersome machine after bad weather had turned the site into a quagmire; Mr. Lawrence, the foreman, thanked Ishbel for providing his squad with a daily "basin of soup" for their lunch; and everyone joined the clerk of works in toasting: "Success to the new house and its inhabitants!"

Many of those present must have wondered how Johnny could afford such expensive new houses. They knew all too well that the Agricultural Depression had cost their landlord dear and that the Cromar estate had failed to sell. They were also aware that in 1897 Haddo had been offered for rent: another plan that had come to nothing. What they had not seen, of course, was the little dining room "gallery" of Renaissance masterpieces in Grosvenor Street, situated conveniently close to a London art world teeming with dealers with commissions from the world's richest collectors.

Ishbel had realized that the easiest—almost the only—way she could

---

[*] It was. The house cost them twice as much.

quickly raise cash was to raid the treasure trove of Old Master paintings collected by Johnny's forebears. She asked Scotland's foremost experts to value them, and when the curiously named P. McOmish Dott and J. Lumgair Dott opined that the Titian she had hung in Grosvenor Street was worth at least £2,000, she discreetly invited offers from dealers. One wrote claiming that the multimillionaire American financier J. P. Morgan was keen to acquire it, but the picture went elsewhere.* Perhaps to save face and avoid trouble from the family, Ishbel kept her sales secret. They remain so today: there is no record of them in the family archives.

Many of the people who had celebrated the start of work on the House of Cromar, as it was now named, met again in the Tarland hall in February 1906. Although the house was finished, the gathering, paradoxically, had been arranged to bid farewell to Johnny and Ishbel. The Liberals were back in power, Johnny had been reappointed as Lord Lieutenant of Ireland, and Ishbel's dream of returning to Dublin Castle was at last about to come true.

---

* The Titian, now known as *An Allegory of Prudence*, had been bought by the 4th Earl from Samuel Woodburn, one of the leading art dealers of the day, in around 1828. One of its previous owners had been Lucien Bonaparte, younger brother of the more famous Napoleon. Ishbel's anonymous buyer may have been another banker, Alfred de Rothschild: it was certainly in his collection when he died in 1918. The woman he left it to, Almina, wife of the 5th Earl of Carnarvon, chatelaine of Highclere Castle and possibly his illegitimate daughter, seems not to have cared for it—or to have had more money than sense—since she sold it almost immediately. Old Master prices had collapsed during the war, and the picture was knocked down for only 28 guineas. One of Ishbel's grandsons tried, and failed, to discover the price paid by de Rothschild, but guessed that it was probably around £600, less than £50,000 in today's money. This reinforced his view—and no doubt his mother Cecile's—that Johnny was "profoundly bad at guarding his resources." After passing through other hands since Almina Carnarvon sold it, the Titian has joined the matchless collection of his works in the National Gallery in London.

16

A Village Hall in Ballsbridge
and a Caravan in Kerry

In December 1905, an Irish priest wrote to a newspaper with the tale of a Good Samaritan. Canon Hugh Gateley from Strokestown in County Roscommon recalled how, during a visit to London a few years earlier, he had gone down to the Houses of Parliament and asked a policeman outside how he could gain admission to hear a debate. At that moment, "a gentleman emerged from the House" and offered to take him inside:

> We ascended the steps to the door, where he said: 'I must give your name here. Please, what is your name?' I said, 'My name is Gateley,' to which he replied: 'My name is Aberdeen.' Somewhat bewildered, I said: 'Can it be you are Lord Aberdeen?' He said, 'Yes.' I replied: 'My lord, I cannot sufficiently express my thanks to you: you are really too kind.' 'Not at all,' he said; 'When I was Lord Lieutenant of Ireland, I received great kindness from the Irish people.'

Thus, Gateley welcomed the return of a Lord Lieutenant who, in his turn, "had always shown a deep and kindly feeling for the Irish people."

But on February 3, 1906, the day on which she and Johnny returned to Ireland, Ishbel knew that not everyone thought that way. For years she had cherished vivid memories of the cheering crowds as they had ridden through the streets of Dublin at the end of Johnny's first term, but twenty years on, the mood in the country felt somber. It did not help that they had landed at Kingstown in a gale "that contained a big suggestion of the cold snap of winter," and that she had not been able to "dress Irish" in one of her elaborately embroidered "Celtic" gowns and, instead, had to wear black because Queen Alexandra's father, Christian IX of Denmark, had died a few days earlier.

Much had changed since 1886: politics especially. Years of parliamentary wrangling in London over Home Rule had led to hardening attitudes in Ireland: the calls for true self-determination were growing louder, and in the north especially, the unionists were becoming increasingly fearful that the bonds that tied them to Britain and its monarchy would be broken. Others saw the Lieutenancy as an anachronism and as a symbol of imperialistic repression. Some went further and agreed with Arthur Griffith, the founder of the republican Sinn Féin Party, that it was "the fount of all that is slimy in our national life," while Richard Barry O'Brien, a writer who made a study of the way Ireland was governed, expressed a widely held view when he called for "a Governor . . . chosen by the Irish people."* Thus, one newspaper editorial published on the eve of Johnny and Ishbel's arrival looked optimistic:

> It has long been one of the most urgent demands of the Irish Nationalists that the Castle, with all that it signifies, shall forthwith be abolished. Now, however, that a Home Rule Government is installed in London, they will probably abate or postpone this article in their programme.

Nonetheless, Ishbel decided that it would be wise "to go very cannily and feel our way."

The crowds in the streets of Dublin, friendly but sparser than before,

---

* O'Brien acknowledged that Johnny's "Home Rule Administration" in 1886 had "possessed the popular confidence more or less." During Johnny's second term O'Brien conceded that the "Administration of Lord Aberdeen . . . enjoys the popular toleration as much as any English administration can or ought to enjoy it," but he also maintained that "peace and contentment will not reign in Ireland while an English Parliament usurps the rights of an Irish National Assembly."

saw a changed Vicereine too. The young mother whose excited young children* had captivated onlookers in 1886 was now almost fifty, and was well aware that, despite having bought "one of those saddles for taking mechanical exercise," her waistline had begun to show the effects of years of official dinners. Yet her enthusiasm and energy were undiminished. "Her Excellency's vitality never ceases to surprise us," wrote one observer, and the writer Katharine Tynan gushed that "no boy and girl could have come with more eager hopefulness and young courage to the task of setting crooked things straight, than the new Viceroy and Lady Aberdeen."

Ishbel was ready for the challenges ahead. "From the moment we landed," she wrote, "there seemed to be always so much more to do than we could possibly accomplish in the twenty-four hours." Before she could begin to address the many social issues that she knew Ireland still faced, there were domestic matters to sort out, even though the Castle and the Viceregal Lodge were not in need of improvement. But after the years of expensive living and travel in Canada, the costs of their retirement home in Tarland, and the failure of the ranches in North America, the same could not be said for their finances. Ishbel knew that it would be hard to keep up appearances, for Dublin society expected, literally, to be royally entertained. Her youngest son, Archie, one of his father's occasional aides-de-camp, described the heavy burden that this placed on his parents in a letter to a friend:

> Imagine giving a dance in London every night of the season to people you didn't know and hadn't asked and having to treat them as tho' they were your nearest and dearest.

While there could be no cutting back of the Drawing Rooms, levees, and other ceremonial events, Ishbel managed to disguise her economies by introducing "novel features" such as "afternoon receptions," to the Castle's program of dinners and dances. She claimed they were "for the benefit

---

* Ishbel thought "it was rather touching to hear one old lady call out, 'but where is Lady Marjorie?' seemingly forgetful that twenty years had passed and that little 'Lady Marjorie,' who had sat with us in the carriage on the occasion of that memorable farewell of 1886, was now herself the busy wife of a Cabinet Minister." Doddie and Dudley did ride in the State Entry procession, but, since they were now in their twenties, as aides-de-camp to their father.

of the non-dancing portion of the community, who liked to drop in, meet their friends, and have a cup of tea."

Many members of the "Ascendancy," as Ireland's Protestant establishment was known, were outraged to discover that they could now dine out less well at Dublin Castle than in the days of Johnny's immediate predecessors: Earl Cadogan, who owned most of the London borough of Chelsea, and the Earl of Dudley, who flaunted his wealth by importing his barber from London whenever he felt in need of a haircut.*

But at least one of Ishbel's guests, her friend Horace Plunkett, who had helped to organize the Irish Village at Chicago, confided to his diary that he found the new arrangements "much simpler (& nicer)." Maurice Headlam, an official of the Irish Treasury, was also understanding:

> It was the fashion to sneer at the Aberdeens' entertaining . . . but Lord Aberdeen confided to me that he never spent less than £6,000 per annum in addition to his annual salary of £20,000—in many years more than £6,000. When I told this to an unsympathetic Dubliner she said that he ought to spend another £20,000—like his predecessors![†]

Johnny's newfound reputation for parsimony was not the only reason why those whom Headlam called the "big Irish peers" boycotted the Castle. They were staunch Unionists and therefore refused invitations from the "Home Rule Aberdeens." Ishbel was hurt and disappointed, because, by their absence, "they greatly diminished the brilliance of our

---

*Lord Dudley's barber was Truefitt's in London. According to the memoirs of Sir Henry Robinson, a senior Irish civil servant, Lord Dudley awoke one day at the Viceregal Lodge in Dublin and decided that he urgently needed a haircut. When, the next morning, his valet told him that a man from Truefitt's had arrived on the overnight mailboat, and was waiting for him, "Dudley said he had an important race at Kingstown and could not stop to have his hair cut, and Truefitt's man would have to wait till next day." But the following morning, Dudley had to go to Meath and then found himself summoned urgently to London. "On arriving in London, he observed, to his surprise, that his hair still wanted cutting, so he had Truefitt summoned by telephone and his hair was cut." When he returned to Dublin the next day, his valet pointed out that Truefitt's man was still waiting. " 'Too late, too late,' said Dudley; 'send him back to London. Why can't these people come when they are wanted?' "

† Not everyone in Dublin thought that Johnny and Ishbel were mean. The playwright Denis Johnston remembered: "When I was a small boy of ten standing at the bottom of Grafton Street with a collecting-box for some primeval flag-day, the Viceregal barouche stopped opposite me, a hand beckoned from the back seat, and I came away with a golden sovereign in my box. A sovereign, somebody said rather jealously, from a half-sovereign."

balls and dinners, and we deeply regretted losing the company of many personal friends." Other socialites, like the aesthete Page Dickinson, were snobbish about mixing with the "middle-class folk" who snapped up the spurned invitations. He found it "rather embarrassing to meet the lady at dinner who had measured you for your shirts the week before." Yet Lady Edith Gordon, who found the Viceregal Lodge "a delightful place to stay in" and was one of only a handful of "Ascendancy" grandees who defended Johnny and Ishbel, dismissed such sneers as "petty and ridiculous stories which did not contain even the proverbial grain of truth."

Twenty years later, when Ishbel wrote her memoirs, the criticism still rankled:

> Apparently . . . the jokes which Aberdonians tell against themselves, and which represent them as extremely thrifty, to say the least of it, got irretrievably connected with our entertainments. . . . We wish our Comptroller could have seen some result of this supposed tendency in our accounts!

Yet everyone agreed that Ishbel did score at least one undoubted social triumph, with the Irish Lace Ball that she held in March 1907. By then, her Irish Industries Association was well established, thanks to the success of the village in Chicago, the popularity of the regular sales organized by her aristocratic friends in their London mansions, and the prosperity of the shops, which now had an annual turnover of £25,000. But although lace had been in fashion since the beginning of the century—Marjorie, like many society brides, had got married in a cloud of it—Ishbel thought that the time was right to promote still further the work of the craftswomen she had recruited in Youghal, Limerick, Blackrock, and Carrickmacross.

Even before the night itself, the *Irish Times* pronounced it a success, for "the mere announcement of the prospective ball brought about renewed industry in all the lace-making centres." Ishbel, who had been suffering from an attack of rheumatism, could only watch the dancing from a wheelchair, but, typically, she made no concessions to her illness as far as her toilette was concerned:

Her Excellency wore a magnificent robe of deep blue chiffon velvet, lavishly trimmed with Irish point lace made at the Youghal Lace Industry; she had a tiara and necklace of diamonds, and kept a handsome stole of white ostrich feathers round her shoulders.

While Johnny does not seem to have entered quite so wholeheartedly into the lacy spirit of the evening in his "Scotch costume, the Gordon tartan, with a scarlet and gold waistcoat, and a profusion of magnificent stars of Orders* glittering on his coat," the *Irish Times* reporter was dazzled by the spectacle:

On every side lovely gowns were to be seen on which Irish lace of every description was lavishly employed; flounces that must have constituted heirlooms met in friendly rivalry the new and up-to-date panels that hailed from distant country villages, where deft fingers plied the needles quickly and skillfully with such charming results.

Encouraged by the ball's success, Ishbel staged another eye-catching event to promote the work of the Irish Industries Association two years later. Again, the *Irish Times* waxed lyrical, hailing the success of "a Pageant which in many respects stands out as the most picturesque ceremonial that Dublin has witnessed for very many years." Picturesque it certainly was, from the men of the 3rd Dragoon Guards in their "bright scarlet uniforms and burnished helmets" to the "prettily gowned maidens and milkmaids, carrying milk, cream and butter." The long procession also included the "tobacco group," who "presented a striking appearance, the ladies' gowns being of browns and greens, showing the big brown leaves of the plant"; the "peat group," carrying "small creels on their backs and baskets of turf in their hands"; and the "soap group," with candelabra and "white hats shaped like inverted candle extinguishers."

Ishbel also seized an opportunity to showcase Irish crafts at an in-

---

*The reporter was exaggerating. Johnny was entitled to wear three stars: that of the Order of St. Michael and St. George, whose Grand Cross he was awarded in 1895 as the holder of a prestigious position in the British Empire, that of Scotland's premier Order of Chivalry, the Order of the Thistle, conferred in 1906, and that of Ireland's Order of St. Patrick, which he wore as its Grand Master.

ternational exhibition, conveniently sited at Ballsbridge, near Dublin, in
1907. Among the exhibits at the Palace of Industries were "facsimiles of
the furnaces of the battleship *Dreadnought*," which also provided heating for the building; and the show at the Palace of Fine Arts included
pictures lent by the King, the Prince of Wales, and Tsar Nicholas II of
Russia. The Canadian pavilion contained "not only displays of minerals, cereals, and industries but a grouping of stuffed specimens of the
fauna of the Dominion"; and every evening the huge dome of the Grand
Central Palace was illuminated by strings of electric lights. There were
spectacular sideshows, including a helter-skelter, a switchback railway,
a stomach-churning water-chute, and the 15,000 visitors each day could
also enjoy an iridescent "Crystal Maze" and the rare chance to look right
inside a huge ants' nest.

Ishbel had annexed plenty of space for her Home Industries, but she
realized that her latest version of an Irish village—a cluster of houses set
around a "village green" that she had persuaded McClinton's, a soap company from Tyrone, to sponsor*—could help her to launch another, different
campaign. One that would be bolder, and potentially more far-reaching,
than any she had attempted before.

Her "crusade," as she quickly came to call it, was inspired by a report
by Ireland's Registrar General. It painted an alarming picture of the way
tuberculosis was cutting a deadly swath through Ireland's population, with
almost twelve thousand deaths from the disease reported in 1905 alone.
Ishbel was particularly shocked to learn from a delegation of doctors,
local government officials, and "various woman workers" who called on
Johnny to take urgent action, that its victims were mainly younger men
and women, between fifteen and thirty-five, "the most important age from
a nation's point of view." They told her, too, that "people were sinking into
a sort of hopeless condition of apathy regarding the disease, believing it to
be a scourge which could not be evaded."

---

* McClinton's were so pleased with the village that they went on to sponsor a bigger and better
one, known as Ballymaclinton ("the place of Maclinton"), at the Franco-British Exposition in
London in 1908. This even boasted a vegetarian restaurant. Its continuing success in selling
"Colleen" soap, to which the charming young women "inhabitants" ascribed their soft com-
plexions, meant that Ballymaclinton was rebuilt for other international exhibitions in the years
that followed.

Ishbel knew otherwise. Just a year earlier, Robert Koch, a German physician, had won a Nobel Prize for his discovery that the disease was not caused, as many believed, by heredity or, as a medical treatise had claimed in 1881, by "depressing emotions," but by an airborne bacillus, which made it highly infectious. This meant that much more could be done, if not to cure tuberculosis, at least to prevent the disease from spreading.

The hotbeds of tuberculosis, the experts told Ishbel, were Ireland's overcrowded towns and cities. And she did not have far to look to see this for herself: just over the wall from the Castle, 20,000 families were enduring the worst housing conditions in the United Kingdom, each crammed into a single fetid and sometimes windowless room of a tenement or of the many collapsing Georgian houses abandoned by the gentry, who had fled to the fresher air of the suburbs. According to census returns, the once-fashionable Henrietta Street epitomized the problem, with 835 people occupying only fifteen houses: of these, 104 all lived at No. 7.

Ishbel set about tackling the problem in her usual manner: she formed an organization, the Women's National Health Association of Ireland, and persuaded religious leaders and some of the world's most eminent experts on tuberculosis to put forward solutions at a conference in March 1907. One of the delegates, Nicholas Donnelly, Auxiliary Bishop of Dublin, suggested that the high death rates could be "to a great extent, reduced by hygienic means and sanitary reforms." But others, including the author of the "Ladies' Letter" in the *Northern Whig*, were skeptical:

Anyone who goes much into the homes of the poor will know that they have a rooted objection to fresh air and personal ablutions, and that, in spite of lectures and teaching at schools, they will not feed infants properly or learn how to do plain cooking.

But such doomsayers merely spurred Ishbel on. She was adamant that education was the answer, and what better place could there be to launch her campaign than her village at the International Exhibition? There she mounted a show that was made all the more striking by the contrast between the prettiness of the rustic buildings from the outside and the grim medical story told within. The village hall was full of statistical charts showing death rates from tuberculosis throughout Britain, pamphlets on methods used by English and Scottish local authorities to try to stop its spread, copies of bylaws such as the one from Manchester that proscribed spitting in public places, models of ideal sanitoria, and photographs showing the impeccably hygienic Royal Sea-Bathing Hospital at Margate in the south of England. A veterinary section went for shock value, featuring the diseased lungs of a raccoon and a leopard among its exhibits, while in one of the quaint cottages, "Various Appliances for Disinfection" were on display for those attending the daily "demonstrations in Sanatorium and Invalid Cooking" given by a specialist chef. When the exhibition closed, Ishbel was encouraged to discover that, in just four weeks, 145,000 people had visited it or heard the accompanying series of lectures. It had been, she wrote proudly in her diary, a "*succès fou.*"

Her next step was to send the exhibition on tour to towns and villages throughout the country. Ishbel often went along, too, and always, to eager audiences, she spoke from her heart, translating the dry statistics of child mortality into an inspiring battle cry:

> If we can once make the mothers—and the fathers too—realise that these deaths need never have been—that it was not God's will that these little ones should perish, and that those who are left can be guarded against such foes if we will take proper precautions—then the victory is ours.

To spread the word beyond the cities, to the smaller settlements across the country, she sent out two horse-drawn "health caravans," which she named "Eire" and "Bluebird." Lecturers who could speak both Irish and English traveled with them, and their program included not only talks on cooking and household management, but also Irish songs and dances to attract the crowds. The strategy was a triumphant success. From Achill Island off the west coast of Ireland, one lecturer reported:

> We met with large appreciative audiences, among them those who after their hard day's work walked eight miles over mountains and through bogs to hear the lectures.

The same story came from Kilfenora in County Clare:

Our audience was so large that we had to lecture in the open air. It was a glorious moonlight night, and the people did not seem to feel any discomfort standing outside for two hours: on the contrary they were loath to go home.

One of the lecturers was a young woman named Constance Fletcher, later known as Constance Spry, who is now better remembered for her subsequent career as a society flower arranger and cook.* Life on the open road was no holiday, as her biographer discovered:

She gave ninety-five lectures in one autumn season, speaking three times a day: to housewives in the morning, schoolchildren in the afternoon and to mixed groups in the evening.

Exhaustion was not the only problem that Ishbel's "crusaders" faced: the caravans often got stuck in the snow or mud in the winter, and one mysteriously caught fire. And, as Sir Henry Robinson, the government official responsible for the administration of health services, remembered, there were myths to dispel:

The caravan was supposed to have had, for demonstration purposes, slides and cultures of various bacilli, and the country people much objected to the importation into their districts for any purpose of these things, dead or alive. They were convinced that it was dangerous as 'some of them microbes might escape' and go joy-riding on the night breezes and 'attacking quiet people when it was too dark to see them and get out of their way'.

---

* Spry arranged the flowers for the weddings of the Duke of Windsor and Princess Elizabeth in the 1930s and '40s and supplied the ones used to decorate Westminster Abbey when Queen Elizabeth II was crowned in 1953. She also started a cookery school and is probably most famous today for having helped to invent the recipe for that staple sandwich-filling "Coronation Chicken." According to Spry's biographer, Ishbel became "a mother substitute" to Connie, who also "picked up many ideas and methods" from her. One was "promoting cheerfulness and taking people out of themselves; others were how to handle people from every kind of background, how to take criticism but ignore snubs, and how to teach using encouragement, praise, and audience participation."

But then the condescending Sir Henry disapproved of Ishbel because "she had too many irons in the fire," and, he claimed, obstructed his officials in their work. Matters came to a head when she applied for a grant from a government fund for combating tuberculosis. Public money, Sir Henry told the Treasury, should not be given to "an association of irresponsible women," but Ishbel, undeterred, went straight to the Chancellor of the Exchequer, David Lloyd George, and extracted £25,000 from him to build a much-needed sanitorium at Peamount in County Dublin. She also promoted a Tuberculosis Prevention Act. This was passed by Parliament, but it lacked teeth because it did not compel tuberculosis sufferers to notify the authorities that they had been infected: a necessity, Ishbel believed, if the "white plague" was ever to be driven out of Ireland.

It was not until the 1920s that she could pause to look back on the campaign. It had come at considerable personal cost to her, although she never allowed the "ups and downs and anxieties attending our efforts" to deflect her. She had long since learned to cope with misogyny and petty officialdom, and if she minded being nicknamed the "Viceregal Microbe" by nationalists, or was hurt when their newspapers alleged that she had invented "the tuberculosis scare," she did not show it. And there were compensations: a prize from TB campaigners in New York, honorary membership of the British Medical Association,* and praise from the *Times* of London for her "good and great and far-reaching work," that would "do more to add to the happiness and prosperity of the Irish race than all the Acts of Parliament that were ever passed."

When their long odyssey was over, her caravan lecturers estimated that more than half a million people had heard their talks or visited their exhibitions. In the end, though, Ishbel wrote, one statistic was the greatest reward of all:

The death-rate from tuberculosis was reduced by one-third between 1907 and 1921.

* Ishbel was the first woman awarded honorary membership of the BMA.

17

A Hospital with a Throne Room

During a visit to Dublin in 1911, Violet Asquith, the daughter of the Prime Minister, H. H. Asquith, and keeper of a lively diary, accompanied Ishbel on a round of "frowstyish functions" to promote her anti-tuberculosis campaign. The twenty-four-year-old had "gladly endured" such meetings before, but this was "a particularly bad one," and "when a woman read a paper on lodging-houses with Zola-esque detail about lice—vice—stench etc.," she noticed that Ishbel not only lacked her usual energy but "dozed in the Chair."

Violet, of all people, should not have been surprised. She knew that Ishbel had good reason to feel exhausted. For four years she had struggled to keep a brave face in public as, in private, family troubles had mounted. And in one instance in which Violet was intimately involved, trouble had turned into tragedy.

The first problem had come in the summer of 1907 with the sensational theft of the Irish Crown Jewels from a safe in the Bedford Tower of Dublin Castle. Ishbel never once referred to the scandal in her voluminous autobiographical writings. She left it to Johnny to tell the tale, and he did so, only briefly and with obvious reluctance, in an account of a visit to Ireland that year by King Edward VII and Queen Alexandra:

When we went to Kingstown to receive their Majesties, as soon as the King had shaken hands, I was conscious that he was scrutinizing the badge of the Order of St Patrick which I was wearing. I was afraid it might have been incorrectly placed, and said, 'Is it not right, sir?' 'Oh yes,' said the King, 'but I was thinking of those jewels.' Alas! Yes, His Majesty was alluding to a very, very sore subject, namely the mysterious, detestable, and disastrous theft of the Crown jewels.

In fact, Johnny was using the term "Crown jewels" loosely, for the stolen gems—a star and a badge encrusted with diamonds, rubies, and emeralds—were, in fact, the regalia of the Order of St. Patrick, Ireland's premier order of chivalry, whose knights were appointed by the King himself.

I cannot recall any individual case to which, during my whole life, I have given so much thought and anxiety as to this,

he later confessed. Two revelations compounded his embarrassment as the police and government officials investigated what some were already calling "the crime of the century": not only had the jewels been stolen from right under his nose, out of a safe in the Bedford Tower of Dublin Castle, but his eldest son, Doddie, was suspected of complicity in the heist.

Such was the importance of the case that a top detective was summoned from Scotland Yard in London. Although, mysteriously, every copy of Inspector John Kane's report has apparently disappeared, the story did unfold at hearings of an inquiry that Johnny set up in January 1908. Appropriately, they were held at the scene of the crime, the library of the Office of Arms, the headquarters of the officials, known as "heralds," who were responsible for organizing the ancient, quasi-royal ceremonies over which the Lord Lieutenant presided. The commission's brief was not so much to try to solve the case, as to investigate how someone could have stolen the jewels from a locked safe in a closely guarded fortress. But the inquiry also had another, barely concealed purpose: to find grounds for dismissing the man responsible for their safekeeping, Sir Arthur Vicars, who rejoiced in the title of Ulster King of Arms.

Six months had passed since the robbery, and the police were floundering: with no solution to the mystery in sight, this was a show trial set up to placate the King, who was demanding a scapegoat. Yet there was only one truly dramatic moment. It came when William Stivey, the office messenger, described Vicars's reaction on opening the door of the safe:

Sir Arthur says, 'I wonder if they are all right,' meaning, I suppose, the Crown jewels. With that, Sir Arthur opened that case and then he opened this, and went down on one knee, and said, 'My God, they are gone,' he said, 'the jewels are gone!'

Otherwise, the commissioners stuck dourly to their brief, which was to decide whether Vicars had "exercised due vigilance and proper care" as the jewels' custodian. It soon emerged that security arrangements in the Office of Arms had not been as stringent as they should have been. Because the safe that Sir Arthur had bought to house the jewels had proved too wide for the door of the strong room, he had decided to leave it outside in the library, in full view of visitors. But the more pertinent question was: How had the thief managed to get into the building and open the safe without leaving any signs of a break-in? That was quickly answered by expert locksmiths who proved that keys had been used: the robbery had been an inside job.

Mrs. Mary Farrell, the office cleaner, told the commissioners of some odd occurrences before the theft was discovered on July 6. On arriving for work three days earlier, she had noticed that the outer door of the building was unlocked; yet when she went inside, the office was deserted. And on the morning the jewels were discovered to be missing, she had found the front door locked, but the door of the strong room inside ajar. Even more curious was a disconcerting encounter at the beginning of the year with a "gentleman" standing at the far end of the library:

I did not like it. I did not know whether he was a gentleman connected with the office or not, and he apparently came down to this end as if to write a note, and he then went out again, and he nodded to me, and I thought he was some gentleman connected with the office, and then I came to see if there was a note on that table, and there was no note.

The implication was clear: Could it be that the keys to the office, the strong room, and the safe, had fallen into the hands of strangers? After hearing five days of evidence that established that an unnecessarily large number of keys had been in circulation and that Sir Arthur had been casual

even with the ones in his possession, the three commissioners surprised
no one with their verdict:

> We cannot acquit Sir Arthur Vicars of want of proper care in the cus-
> tody of the keys of the safe. These keys unlocked the safe which con-
> tained Jewels of enormous value* and importance, for whose safety Sir
> Arthur Vicars was wholly responsible.

Sir Arthur was duly sacked; Kane returned to Scotland Yard; and armchair detectives took up the case with gusto.† They all agreed that the theft
was an inside job, but who, among Vicars's small coterie of heralds, could
have carried off so audacious a crime? One firm suspect soon emerged:
Francis Shackleton, the brother of Sir Ernest, the famous polar explorer.
Francis had had both the motive and the opportunity. He had once been
rich and successful, but now, after the failure of a land deal in Mexico, he
had fallen on hard times. Furthermore, he had shared lodgings with Vicars
on his visits to Dublin, and so would have had countless chances to copy
the keys.

The only flaw in this theory was that Shackleton had not been in
Ireland when the robbery took place. But this was no problem to the armchair sleuths, who promptly identified a likely accomplice: an even more
thoroughgoing rake called Captain Richard Gorges, who was Shackleton's
lover and was in town at the time. Gorges, they reasoned, was known to
need money; he was ruthless and desperate enough to have committed the
crime; and thanks to his friendship with Vicars, he was such a familiar figure at Dublin Castle that his comings and goings would not have aroused
suspicion. By leaving the doors of the office and the strong room open,
he had ensured that the theft was discovered while Shackleton was out of
the country, providing him with an alibi that even Kane of the Yard would
not be able to crack.

But who was the mystery man caught entering the library by Mary

---

* Estimates vary. Johnny's figure was £40,000: around £3,000,000 ($3,900,000) today.

† They included Sir Arthur Conan Doyle, creator of Sherlock Holmes; but, as a distant cousin
of Vicars, his interest lay in backing up Vicars's protestations that he was innocent of any wrong-
doing. Never one to waste a good plot, Doyle also managed to write a short story very loosely
based on the case called "The Adventure of the Bruce-Partington Plans."

Farrell? Had he played a part in the crime? Although she told the inquiry that she had been unable to see him properly because the sun had been in her eyes, the word was that she had identified him to a Dublin detective. He was someone everyone at the castle knew well: Lord Haddo, the Lord Lieutenant's eldest son.

Doddie had, indeed, been in Dublin at the beginning of the year, but it was a confession by one of the heralds that sent the rumor mill into overdrive. Vicars, he alleged, had been in the habit of throwing informal drinks parties in the Bedford Tower, but since he was unable to hold his liquor, he had often collapsed in a stupor. One night, the herald's story went, Doddie, who was a frequent guest, rifled the pockets of his insensible host and took the keys to the safe. He then "borrowed" the Crown Jewels for the night, only confessing to the joke the next morning. And there were whispers, too, that with Vicars out cold, the parties had turned into homosexual orgies orchestrated by Shackleton.

The official hue and cry did not last long. Vicars, who unwisely, many thought, had refused to give evidence to the viceregal commission, continued to protest his innocence; the Office of Arms was "reorganized"; Shackleton was quietly reminded that homosexual activity was illegal in Ireland and warned that he would be unwise to return; no one was charged with the theft; and no trace of the jewels was ever found.

But for years wild theories abounded, much to the amusement of Johnny and Ishbel's enemies in Dublin society. Sir Henry Robinson, the official who had tried to obstruct Ishbel's tuberculosis crusade, especially enjoyed one put forward by a Dublin cabdriver:

> Sure it was the King himself took them! He was afther having great card-playin' with the Duke of Devonshire, and he dropped a power o'money, so he sent round Lord Aberdeen wan night to take them out of the safe and bring them to him and say nothin' at all about it. Sure they were his own, and hadn't he as good a right to take them as he would have to sell his own gould watch and chain?

Perhaps because they discredited the Lieutenancy, the rumors about Doddie's involvement would not go away. He broke his silence only once, when Sir Arthur Vicars sued the *London Mail*, a popular scandal sheet,

in 1913. The paper had concocted a lurid tale that suggested the jewels
had been stolen by a lovelorn woman called "Molly," a former mistress
of Vicars, in revenge for him spurning her in favor of Doddie's wife, Florence. Although the paper's editor admitted before the trial began that
the story was a "myth," Vicars's counsel, James Campbell KC, insisted on
cross-examining witnesses so that everyone smeared by the "atrocious and
abominable libel" could clear their name. Florence, when asked whether
there was "a particle of truth" in the suggestion that she had had an illicit
"friendship" with Sir Arthur, replied:

'None. I scarcely know him.'

Doddie was just as dismissive:

CAMPBELL: Had you anything to do with the removal of the jewels or
    do you know anything about them?
LORD HADDO: Absolutely nothing.

Vicars won damages of £5,000,* but the trial had shed no new light on
Ireland's "crime of the century."

Amidst these goings-on at Dublin Castle, Ishbel had to cope with what,
with some understatement, she called "a sad chapter of family history,"
when her mother, her brother Edward, and her youngest son, Archie, all
died within two years of one another. In March 1908, the Dowager Lady
Tweedmouth, "passed away painlessly and quietly, in perfect peace," but
the opposite was true when it came to the others.

For Edward Marjoribanks, now the second Lord Tweedmouth, the
death of his wife Fanny was, according to his biographer, "a blow from
which he never completely recovered." But by 1904, he was facing other
crises in both his public and private lives, probably brought on by the

---

*This was a considerable sum of money, the equivalent of £400,000 ($520,000) today. One
recent study suggests that the plainly preposterous libel was concocted between Vicars's half
brother Pierce O'Mahony and the London Mail for two reasons: so that the case could be
aired in court and, with the rich O'Mahony guaranteeing the cost of the action, so that the
now ruined Vicars could be provided with funds that he was too proud to accept directly from
his family.

onset of what his friends euphemistically referred to as a "cerebral malady." Despite his huge inheritance, not least of which was more than half the shares in the Meux brewery, Edward had persuaded himself that his fortune was ebbing away. He, like Johnny, had been cajoled by his father into investing in the American ranches, which, thanks to the disastrous management of his brothers, had amassed huge losses. And when the income from the brewery began to dry up—Dudley Tweedmouth and his fellow directors had milked it of funds, leaving it unable to compete with its more modern rivals—Edward panicked. Marjorie remembered how Ishbel, powerless to rescue yet another brother in trouble, had to watch from the sidelines as he "hastily sold Guisachan and Brook House with their treasures*—so carefully built, so fondly collected by his father."

Guisachan was bought by Newton Wallop, 6th Earl of Portsmouth, to add to his portfolio of three other houses and thousands of acres in Devon; while Sir Ernest Cassel, banker and crony of the King, agreed to purchase Brook House, but only on condition that the Grosvenor Estate would allow him to make Tweedmouth's "palace" even larger. Both men paid £60,000 for their properties: knockdown prices† many thought, and finding the right buyer for the Wedgwood masterpieces proved difficult. The Victoria and Albert Museum wanted only a few of them, but the thought of breaking up the world's greatest collection stayed even the desperate Edward's hand. Eventually, the soap tycoon William Lever, later 1st Viscount Leverhulme, came to the rescue with £17,500. The sale of fifty-two of the Brook House pictures at Christie's salesroom in June 1905,

---

* He kept Hutton Hall, his father's constituency bolt-hole in Berwickshire, which he had only recently restored. When his son sold it at auction in 1916, it was bought by a Glasgow solicitor, acting on behalf of a mystery client who was later revealed to be another great collector, the shipping tycoon Sir William Burrell. When Burrell gave his art treasures to Glasgow Corporation in 1944, he stipulated that some rooms from the castle should be reproduced so that they could be properly displayed. Nearly forty years later, his wish was granted and replicas of Hutton's dining room, hall, and drawing room were constructed in the museum in Pollok Country Park, Glasgow, that now houses his collection.

† One newspaper explained the low price of Guisachan thus: "The inaccessibility that was the first Lord Tweedmouth's pride doubtless has something to do with the moderate price realised. A house to be reached only after 25 miles' drive through its Park on alighting from a 578-mile railway journey from London, is not everybody's market." Another said: "Guisachan is purely a residential and sporting domain, the return from the property being practically nil, so that it would be a white elephant except to a very rich man," which Portsmouth certainly was. Edward also sold the furniture to Portsmouth for £12,000. Other items included the servants' bedding for £9, eight ponies for £70, and eleven dogs for "£100 the lot."

however, exceeded expectations. Among what the *Inverness Courier* hailed as "superb, valuable and historical" works were portraits by Sir Henry Raeburn and Sir Joshua Reynolds that fetched record sums. But even the £49,548, 12s realized did not allay Edward's fears that he was heading for bankruptcy.

His political career, hitherto very successful, had begun to founder too. In 1905, he had been appointed First Lord of the Admiralty, a job that he reveled in but soon lost amidst accusations of treason. Edward's "crimes," in the eyes of a British public fearful that Germany was preparing for war, were twofold: he had not only been in touch with the Kaiser, a potential enemy, but he had provided him with confidential details of the Royal Navy's strength and spending plans. In fact, the Kaiser had sent the first letter and Edward's reply had been circumspect. Edward's mistake— another sign perhaps of his mental decline—was to boast about the clandestine correspondence, leaving the Prime Minister with no option but to dismiss him from the Admiralty.*

Ishbel's son Archie, who saw him soon afterwards in April 1908, told Violet Asquith that he found his uncle "quite stricken":

> The poor man is naturally feeling it terribly, not only because he loved his ships and guns, but because in the eyes of the world it is the finishing at a blow of a long career of hard work for the party.

Quite how "terrible" Edward was feeling became apparent soon afterwards. Asquith had allowed him to stay in government as Lord President of the Council, a less influential post, but in July the newspapers announced that he was ill. Most were decorously vague about what was

---

* The letter arrived in the regular post in a green registered envelope postmarked "Potsdam" and addressed to "The First Lord of the Admirality[sic], Lord Tweedmouth, London." The Kaiser, who signed it "William I.R., Admiral of the Fleet" and had sent it without the knowledge of his Chancellor or the naval minister, Admiral von Tirpitz, claimed to be astonished by the controversy that followed. He maintained that he had simply tried to reassure Edward that his warships had been built "against nobody at all," that the German fleet was far smaller than the British, and that he simply wished to modernize it. Some politicians, like the Earl of Balcarres, thought that the Kaiser had deliberately set a trap for Edward, whom he had met on a trip to England not long before. The Kaiser, Balcarres believed, had "taken his measure" of Edward and saw him as a formidable opponent. But he had also spotted his Achilles' heel—a susceptibility to flattery—and had played on this in the hope of forcing him out of his job.

wrong with him, but the Aberdeen *Press & Journal* revealed he had had "a sudden nervous breakdown." The rumors in the smoking rooms of Parliament and the gentlemen's clubs of London went further, and, as the Earl of Balcarres noted in his diary after speaking to Edward's daughter-in-law, they were all too true:

> He seems to be hopelessly insane. For the last few weeks his speeches have contained wandering passages. . . . Now we learn that he is quite off his head.

Ishbel took Edward home with her to Dublin and borrowed a house close to the Viceregal Lodge. And it was here, confined and concealed like a pitiful madman in a nineteenth-century novel, that Edward died in September 1909: probably, as the gossips also averred, by his own hand. He left £204,975, 18s in his will, the equivalent of £16,000,000 today. He had been successful, at least, in staving off bankruptcy, although he had probably never faced it in the first place.

Ishbel's last act of devotion to her brother was to try to restore his reputation by compiling a book of reminiscences from his friends and colleagues. And it was while she was putting the finishing touches to it, one Sunday afternoon in November 1909, that she heard that her youngest son had been involved in a car crash.

Two days earlier, Johnny had watched as Archie, "the very picture of health, strength and buoyancy," drove off from the Ritz Hotel in London in a brand-new Daimler "Silent Knight," at the time one of the most sophisticated cars on the road. On the Sunday afternoon, at a crossroads outside Winchester, a car suddenly shot out of a lane right in front of him. An eyewitness described how Archie's car hit it from behind, throwing its occupants out, before making what an eyewitness described as a "complete somersault." Only when he had been extricated from the wreckage could the true extent of Archie's injuries be seen, and he was taken to the County Infirmary. He later told his mother that during the journey he suffered such "intense anguish . . . that he scarcely expected to reach the hospital alive."

Archie was another "golden boy," a much-doted-upon youngest son and brother. Marjorie, who remembered how, in Canada, they had shared "the whole of life, lessons and holidays, scoldings and treats," was especially close to him:

> His eager step, his happy face were exhilarating: he was always pleased to see you and knew you would be pleased to see him. A sanguine temperament, a clear conscience and freedom of care gave him a childlike power of enjoying life which was attractive to everyone.

At the time of the accident, Archie was twenty-five and something of a dilettante. After Oxford, he had gone abroad, working unpaid at banks in Berlin and Paris. Since his duties were only to "attend to the English speaking visitors," he spent much of his time on the golf course, winning the German Amateur Golf Championship in 1908. He then joined a merchant bank run by the Canadian financier James Dunn* in the City of London, but was soon spending his evenings in the House of Commons, watching debates and flirting with the idea of entering politics like so many of his forebears.

Ishbel was more concerned about Archie's private life than his career. In 1904 he fell under the spell of Ettie, wife of Lord Desborough[†] and mother of Julian Grenfell, later a celebrated poet of the Great War. Ettie was only ten years younger than Ishbel, and although intense relationships with older women were seen as a rite of passage for young men in Edwardian high society, Ishbel soon had her eyes on Violet Asquith as a more suitable consort for her eligible son.

---

* Presumably this "job" was arranged by Johnny and Ishbel, who shared many mutual friends with Dunn: not least the Canadian Pacific Railway entrepreneur Sir William Van Horne, who raised the finance for a venture in Cuba through Dunn. In 1909, thanks to the U.S. stock market crash two years earlier, Dunn's finances were shaky, but he eventually survived fraud committed by employees at his brokerage in Montreal, the disappearance of a partner who saddled him with huge debts, and the drowning of a key client when the RMS *Lusitania* was sunk by a German U-boat in 1915, to become a multimillionaire.

† William Grenfell, Baron Desborough, was an only moderately successful Liberal politician, but he was perhaps the greatest sporting all-rounder of his generation. He represented Oxford in athletics and fencing and twice rowed in the Boat Race against Cambridge, climbed the Matterhorn three times by different routes, twice swam across the pool below Niagara Falls, and explored the Rocky Mountains, where he got lost. He was also president of the Marylebone Cricket Club, the Lawn Tennis Association, and the 1908 London Olympics. Ettie loved him, but perhaps because he sat on no fewer than 115 public committees between expeditions to Africa and India to hunt big game and to Florida to fish for tarpon, she had time to indulge in affairs with young admirers that may, or may not, have been platonic.

Vol. VI. No. 4.

March, 1896.

WEE WILLIE WINKIE

EDITED BY LADY MARJORIE GORDON AND HER MOTHER

Obedient "Dash"

London: PARTRIDGE & CO. | Edinburgh: GEORGE DUNCAN & SON.

The title page of *Wee Willie Winkie*. Articles on the Haddo pets were popular features of what is thought to be the world's first magazine for children. One edition even ran a letter "written" by a Collie dog aggrieved at being forced to live in a "smoky town."

This photograph of the "editorial board" of *Wee Willie Winkie* deliberating in her boudoir at Haddo helped Ishbel to perpetuate the myth that Marjorie, then in her teens and dubbed "the world's youngest editor," was in charge of the magazine. In fact, its driving force was the seasoned editor of the *Review of Reviews*, W. T. Stead.

Coutts Marjoribanks (1860–1924). Exiled to Dakota Territory by his father for unspecified social misdemeanors, Ishbel's brother enjoyed a calamitous career as a cowboy before moving to Johnny's ranches in Canada, where his attempts to reinvent himself as a fruit farmer proved just as disastrous.

Haddo House Collection

Ishbel's youngest brother, Archie (1861–1900), was also sent to America, but the cowboy life on a ranch on the Texas Panhandle was neither to his nor his backers' liking. His one success was in helping, with his dog "Lady," to introduce Golden Retrievers to North America.

Haddo House Collection

Ishbel sketched Archie's Rocking Chair Ranch in North Elm Creek, Texas, when she and Johnny visited in 1887. She was pleased that the place was "perfectly tidy," but Johnny, who had invested in the business, realized that cattle breeding was riskier than he had supposed.

Exterior of 27 Grosvenor Square, the luxurious Mayfair mansion Johnny built in the late 1880s but sold soon after completion, when a mining tycoon made him an offer he could not refuse.

The music room at 27 Grosvenor Square, set up for an "exotic bazaar," one of many charitable events the cavernous space was designed to accommodate. On other occasions, ninety people could comfortably sit down to dinner there.

Ishbel took this photograph of Highfield, a "picturesque Gothic" villa at Hamilton, Ontario, during their visit to Canada in 1890. She enjoyed her family holiday there, remembering it as a place of "sunshine and butterflies." Her only disappointment was the size of the garden: a mere thirteen acres.

HADDO HOUSE COLLECTION

Many of these servants, whom Johnny and Ishbel brought with them from Britain to staff Highfield, stayed on and settled in Canada. "Thanks to the heartiness of Canadians towards newcomers," Ishbel wrote, they found "happy homes."

At Killarney, Manitoba, a community established by emigrants from Britain, Johnny investigates the living conditions of settlers with Mr. and Mrs. O'Brien. Johnny liked the place so much that he wanted to move there, but Ishbel thought, "May Heaven preserve us from ever being fated to banishment to the far-famed wheatlands of Manitoba!"

Ishbel's Irish Village, complete with replica of Blarney Castle and its famous stone, dominated one of the main avenues of the 1893 World's Columbian Exposition in Chicago. Uniquely for one of Ishbel's enterprises, it made a large profit.
ART INSTITUTE OF CHICAGO

Modeled on a bungalow that Ishbel had admired in India, the Guisachan Ranch, the couple's first farm in Canada, was an exotic addition to the landscape of Kelowna, British Columbia. Ishbel thought it "just perfect and delightful."
HADDO HOUSE COLLECTION

Ishbel and Johnny return to the Guisachan Ranch in the farm wagon after church during a holiday in the fall of 1891. Ishbel was relieved that her brother Coutts (back right) and his farm manager, Eustace Smith (back left), had resisted the temptations of the local bar, which she thought "a symbol of mischief in the neighbourhood," and agreed to worship with them.

The Governor General's procession about to leave his official residence, Rideau Hall, Ottawa, for the opening of the Canadian Parliament. Here, as at Holyrood and Dublin Castle, Johnny and Ishbel assumed the full—and sometimes irksome—trappings of royalty: "We live our lives to the tune of God Save the Queen," Ishbel complained.

In 1897, ironically just as their own finances were at a critically low ebb, Johnny and Ishbel found themselves portrayed on a new Canadian one-dollar bill. Two million four hundred thousand were printed.

On the hockey rink at Rideau Hall, Christmas 1895. "What winter sports holidays were those!" wrote Marjorie. "In the grounds we had three high toboggan-slides, two open-air ice rinks for skating and ice hockey, another indoor rink for curling matches; and all around, the Rideau and Rockcliffe woods for snow-shoeing and skiing."
HADDO HOUSE COLLECTION

The barn at the Coldstream ranch in 1896, a year of success with the first crop of fruit and a record yield of hops, of failure when a sharp frost decimated the orchard, of disaster when the ranch office was destroyed in a fire, and of growing anxiety for Johnny and Ishbel as their financial losses mounted.
HADDO HOUSE COLLECTION

Ishbel visiting one of the playgrounds built by the Women's National Health Association of Ireland to improve the health of children from Dublin's slums. "I have witnessed many enthusiastic gatherings," wrote one observer in 1912, "but never such cheering, never such gratitude expressed in a multitude of faces."

Firemen spent twenty-eight hours fighting the fire at Haddo in April 1930. They saved the main part of the house, but could not prevent the destruction of a wing containing Johnny and Ishbel's apartment, a gun room, a kitchen, and twenty-one bedrooms. An oak tree planted nearby by the 1st Earl in 1682 had to be chopped down by a retainer using an ax presented to Ishbel by Mr. Gladstone.

The House of Cromar, the home Ishbel and Johnny built for their retirement. Some experts believe the design of this curious building, so out of keeping with its setting, was inspired by that of the Canadian Pacific Railway hotels Ishbel admired in Canada.

Ishbel and Johnny at the House of Cromar in the 1920s, replying to some of the five thousand Christmas cards they received each year. Their daily postbag usually contained between three hundred and four hundred letters.

Queen Mary and other members of the Royal Family regularly drove over to visit Ishbel and Johnny from their summer residence at Balmoral Castle, twenty miles away. They planted so many trees to mark their visits that the garden of the House of Cromar boasted a "Royal Avenue."

A life come full circle. In this photograph taken at Gordon House just before her death in 1939, Ishbel, now in her eighties, sits beside a fireplace rescued from Guisachan, the beloved home of her childhood.

Ishbel and Violet had not got off to a good start. After a visit to Haddo for the New Year festivities in 1905, the eighteen-year-old Violet told a friend that she was "rather frightened" of her.

> To her Life offers two vocations: suffering and ministering thereto. I fall between both these stools—I am neither maimed nor hurt nor do I do anything to help anyone who is. . . . If I had been lopsided or an orphan—or ever so little forlorn she would have loved me.

But Ishbel thawed when Violet wore her best dress to a dance. It came from the House of Worth in Paris, couturiers to the crowned heads of Europe and Edwardian society:

> I remember feeling a little nervous before going down lest Ly A. should be shocked, as I rather feel with her frumpiness would be accounted to one as virtue. However she was not shocked—on the contrary pleased—she called Archie out of the room and poured unwary dew-drops into his ears.

Over the next three years, despite Ettie Desborough's continuing predations and the gaggle of young men in ardent pursuit of Violet, the tendresse that Ishbel had glimpsed and encouraged between the couple developed into something more. By 1907, Archie, who had signed his letters two years before with a cool "Yr Archie," had turned up the heat, now calling Violet his "dear one." And earlier that summer, she had confided to her diary:

> I had only realized properly in the last two months what an exceptional being he is. . . . What I love about him is this great cleanness and sound-ness of his whole being—the strength and simplicity of his emotions & the courage with which he feels—never holding back for fear of ultimate pain. I think his singleness of heart very rare—& it gives him untold power. He also has undefeated hopefulness & the greatest ca-pacity for joy I have ever seen.

When Violet heard that Archie was lying injured in hospital, she rushed to his bedside. By the time she was allowed to see him, at four o'clock in the morning, the doctors had told Ishbel that Archie was overwhelmed with infection and that they could do no more for him. Violet's account of his last hours is suffused with the passion for Wagner's operas that she and Archie shared.

The room was dimly lit and heavy with the smell of eau de cologne. She found Archie "propped up in bed . . . his arms held out to me." He said:

'Dearest—you've come—how good of you. Now I know what Tristan felt!'

Violet had something to say:

Then I told him in the words Heaven sent me for such a moment that I loved him—that everything I had to give was his. It would be sacrilege to write of what followed—an ecstasy too holy for expression either then or now . . .

She called to the doctor.

'Archie wishes me to tell you we're going to be married,' she said.
    Archie spoke too: 'Yes tho' perhaps at first sight I don't look it Dr. I am at this moment in the most enviable position of any man alive'.

When her father arrived to join Johnny and Ishbel, Archie's brothers, and some friends, Ettie among them, at the dying man's bedside, Violet told him her news.

He said 'I've always wished it Archie—I've always wished it' with tears in his eyes and voice; A. looked a little puzzled—but then suddenly seemed to understand his emotion: 'I know you're giving me the most precious thing you've got Mr. Asquith' 'It's my best—the best thing I've got to give'—A. 'I will try to make her happy'. They talked on about it a little & then A. said in his 'City' voice 'So now we've put all this on a thoroughly business footing Mr Asquith—it's settled up. Then 'Will you kiss me?'—& when father had done so 'Will you bless me?'

Outside in the corridor, some nurses sang "Abide with Me," and Ishbel came back to Archie's bedside and whispered:

'My Benjamin, who never brought anything but joy to his mother.'

Violet sat with him as his condition worsened:

Another lapse of consciousness & then he drew me towards him & whispered 'May we be married in bed darling—now—at once.' 'In bed beloved—why? We can easily wait'—'I don't know why—but I want to be married now—I feel such a strange impatience.' This was the last thing he said to me before he finally became unconscious.

At Archie's burial a few days later in the snow-covered cemetery at Haddo, after the local schoolchildren had sung the twenty-third Psalm and the coffin had been lowered into a grave lined with ivy, which is the emblem of the Gordons,* Violet stepped forward and dropped a wreath of violets onto the coffin and a card that read, "To My Beloved."

For the next few years, Violet became a sort of phantom widow: she wrote her diary as a series of letters to Archie. One, about the opening of a club for poor boys that she had founded in his memory in the East End of London,† began:

My Darling—The Club's first evening is just over—& I feel happier than I have done since you left me.

And it ended: "Wish me luck, Beloved."

Ishbel, too, sought distraction in good works, throwing herself into

---

* After King George II's "Dress Act" banned the wearing of tartan in the wake of the 1745 Jacobite Rising, members of Scottish clans are said to have found an ingenious way to circumvent this law and show their allegiances: they picked a sprig from a plant growing on their family lands—in the Gordons' case, ivy—and pinned it to their bonnet. Whatever the origin of this custom—and it is much disputed—clans today still wear their own distinctive emblems or "plant badges."

† A journalist who visited the club in Hoxton was impressed by Violet's commitment to it: "Miss Asquith visits the club weekly whenever she is in town, and joins the boys in parlour games, story-telling, and painting and drawing. Furthermore, she gives them a fortnight's holiday every summer in camp, and fits them up in clothes and boots before they go away."

them again with an energy that, as far as her friend Lady Edith Gordon could see, never seemed to flag:

> Lady Aberdeen herself is capable not only of existing without food but without sleep, being frequently found by a housemaid, at sunrise, seated in her evening dress at her writing table.

She treated Violet as a daughter-in-law, and enlisted her to help her causes. Violet had long since become an admirer:

> Lady Aberdeen's life really *stupefies* one with wonder and admiration— one thankless (but infinitely fruitful task) undertaken after another out of sheer love of humanity.

When, in 1913, Ishbel took her to America (a clever move since the arrival of the Prime Minister's daughter attracted far more attention than hers), Violet watched her at work, extracting funds from Irish-American businessmen for the sanitorium at Peamount:

> She spoke for almost an hour & the most marvellous response followed—everyone rising & offering everything they could give with the most extraordinary directness spontaneousness & lavishness.

In Dublin, Ishbel had taken a lease on Ely House, a Georgian building that she used as the headquarters for her Irish organizations. She had also annexed a "modest" apartment there, against the day when Johnny's term as Lord Lieutenant was over. Not that there was anything modest about Ely House: even in a city noted for its fine Georgian architecture, the four-storey red brick mansion, with its ionic columns, high windows, and intricately wrought cast-iron balconies, stood out. Inside, a cantilevered staircase of Portland stone swept down from the upper floors into a hall decorated with fine plasterwork. The grand rooms, with their neoclassical ornamentation, had provided a suitable setting for the great art and furniture collection of its previous inhabitant, Sir Thornley Stoker, a distinguished surgeon and elder brother of the more famous Bram. While Sir Thornley was a throwback to a previous era—the writer Oliver St. John Gogarty joked that he lived "in Ely Place, and in the Eighteenth Century"—Ishbel had the house altered to serve her more utilitarian purposes in 1912.

It was from Ely House that Ishbel oversaw her campaigns, notably one to improve housing conditions, which, in the cities and towns especially, she saw as a "blot and a menace." But that campaign faltered in the summer of 1914 as war approached and she turned instead to finding ways to help on the home front. She founded a branch of the Red Cross and leased another elegant Georgian townhouse, 29 Lower Fitzwilliam Street, where the society organized classes in first aid, nursing, and ambulance work, seamstresses sewed shirts for the troops, and Christmas gifts were gathered for soldiers and sailors repatriated to the city. But when she asked the military authorities what else she could do, "the unhesitating reply was made that more hospital accommodation would be required, as it was proposed to bring transports of wounded soldiers to Dublin."

Ishbel did not have far to look. Dublin Castle had plenty of space, but when she proposed converting it into a hospital, she ran, as so often before, into opposition. Some said that the ancient building was unsanitary; others that it would never come up to War Office standards and that she would never raise the £5,000 she would need. But Ishbel outflanked the naysayers by arranging an inspection by the president of the Royal College of Surgeons and his counterpart at the Royal College of Physicians. They opined that the sanitary arrangements were "perfect," and that the building was "in every way suited as an emergency hospital." And when, in December 1914, Ishbel announced that the King had given permission to use the Castle, along with a donation of £100 to the hospital fund, the objectors were silenced.

But it was a hollow victory, for she already knew that Johnny's days as Lord Lieutenant were numbered. In October, he had received a letter from H. H. Asquith. It said:

I propose that when you have completed its ninth year your term of office should come to an end.

The decision had come from out of the blue: not least because the Prime Minister had just been staying with them, and had given no hint that he wanted to make a change. In fact, Asquith had been dithering about whether to replace them for some time. In 1911, when there were rumors that Johnny was going to be offered a new post in South Africa, Violet had "told" Archie in her diary that she had "written a long letter to Father about the removal of yr. F. & M. from Ireland. How I pray it can be stopped. Anyhow I have stretched every sinew."

In fact, Johnny and Ishbel later acknowledged that they should not have been surprised, for there had been a "tacit understanding" that they would retire when the Home Rule finally had passed into law: it had done so a few weeks earlier. But although all parties had agreed that Home Rule should not begin until the war with Germany was over, key difficulties remained: not least the Unionists' demand that Ulster should remain in the United Kingdom. Asquith confided to his close friend Venetia Stanley* that the Chief Secretary for Ireland, Augustine Birrell, thought that Johnny, the Unionists' bête noire, would be more of a hindrance than a help in solving the problem. In fact, Birrell had put it more bluntly: he wanted him "booted out at the first opportunity." Asquith demurred, but soon afterwards told Stanley that he had changed his mind about the denizens of Dublin Castle. "A weaker & more incompetent crew," he wrote "were never in charge of a weaker ship in stormy weather."

Johnny wrote Asquith a seven-page letter begging to be allowed to stay, and Ishbel, distraught, protested to Violet, asking, "How can your Father wreak such havoc on Archie's parents?" But Asquith gloatingly described how he had rebuffed a direct appeal from Ishbel, during a "nerve-harrowing interview":

> I had of course no difficulty in disposing of her arguments about the terrible ruin that would be wrought to Ireland if her 'great work' (sanitoria &c &c) were now to be interrupted. I told her brutally that if her

---

* Asquith became infatuated with Venetia Stanley, the daughter of the 4th Baron Sheffield. He was in his late fifties, married, and Prime Minister of the United Kingdom; she was in her early twenties, unmarried, and a friend and contemporary of Asquith's daughter Violet. From 1910, during the course of one of the strangest and potentially most scandalous relationships in twentieth-century politics, he wrote her more than five hundred affectionate and indiscreet letters, often covering sensitive matters of state. He sometimes even put pen to paper during cabinet meetings. How far the affair went is unknown, and it is not clear what she felt about his attentions, since Asquith destroyed the letters Venetia wrote in reply. After five years, the weird correspondence was abruptly ended by Venetia in 1915 when she became engaged to be married. Asquith, only briefly heartbroken, began writing to her older sister, Sylvia, soon afterwards.

efforts & organisation were of any real value, they would go on after her disappearance from the scene.

But he did soften a little, he told Venetia Stanley:

She wept copiously, poor thing, and you know what a coward I am *au fond*: so in the end I gave them till the beginning of Feb, and he is to write a beautiful letter announcing his wish to retire now that his life-work in Ireland is done, and I am to ask the Sovereign to give him some mark of appreciation.

But even deciding on a suitable "mark of appreciation" caused controversy, both public and private. Asquith was astonished to receive an "extraordinary letter" from Ishbel:

It is almost incredible. She wants them to stay on till *April*, & then that he shd. be made an *Irish* Duke! with a seat perhaps in the Senate of the Home Rule Parliament.

Instead, Johnny was promoted from earl to marquess, but his plan to add an Irish element to his title and style himself "Marquess of Aberdeen and Tara" excited fierce passions. Many people thought it sacrilegious that a Scotsman should associate himself so closely with the Hill of Tara, the traditional seat of the High Kings of Ireland, and even Edward VII was worried. It would be "a matter of regret," his Private Secretary, Lord Stamfordham, explained to Johnny, if taking the title were "to wound the national susceptibilities of that warm-hearted people who are now testifying to their gratitude and affection & their regret at your departure." Eventually, to Ishbel's relief, the matter was solved by a linguistic sleight of hand: they would use "Temair," the Irish form of Tara. It had no royal connotations and was used, she claimed, for places in both Scotland* and Ireland.

---

* Some people found the double title confusing. H. H. Asquith told another inamorata that he had made the King "roar with laughter" with an anecdote that went the rounds soon after he gave Johnny his "step up" the aristocratic ladder: "Lady A. sent to a friend a photograph of herself with a Scotch terrier on her knee signed with the new style. The friend replied with effusive thanks, adding, 'it was so nice, too, to see your little dog Temair.'"

There was just enough time before they left to make sure that the Dublin Castle Auxiliary Hospital was ready. Reporters who were taken on a tour were amused that St. Patrick's Hall had been converted into a games room, surprised to find twenty-seven beds installed beneath the master-pieces in the Picture Gallery, and did their best to convey the exoticism of a ward in a Throne Room, where thirteen wounded officers would be "nursed to convalescence in an atmosphere of dazzling brilliance." And they were enchanted to discover that the golden canopy that hung above the throne in peacetime now sheltered one of the beds.

The King sent Johnny a handwritten letter thanking him for his "con-scientiousness & high sense of duty." He praised Ishbel too: her good works would be "ever gratefully remembered by the Irish people." It eased the pain of leaving, as did the cheers from the crowds that gathered in the streets as they rode out of the city: Johnny on horseback, Ishbel in the state barouche, holding her Kodak high in the air to capture the unfolding scene. Although this was, as Ishbel pointed out, the "last ceremonial de-parture of any Viceroy from the shores of Ireland," it was also the most in-formal. Along the route, the organizations she had founded had mounted tableaux: near the Castle, nurses from the new hospital stood beneath a Red Cross banner; in Grafton Street, a pristine "fairy fortress" celebrated the Women's National Health Association's campaign for hygienic hous-ing; in South Frederick Street the weaving, spinning, dancing colleens from the Irish Industries Association evoked the spirits of the "villages" that had drawn the crowds in Chicago, London, and Dublin itself. And in Nassau Street, a lone voice broke through the hubbub of the people and the band to puncture the pomp and circumstance:

'There they go',

an old woman shouted,

'There they go, with their microbes and crown jules an' all.'

18

A House to Retire To

Johnny had celebrated his sixty-seventh birthday on the day before war was declared, but neither he nor Ishbel, who was fifty-seven, headed home to Scotland in February 1915 with any intention of retiring.

Within weeks, Ishbel had converted the Lodge, their original home in Tarland, into an auxiliary hospital, but it was a far more makeshift affair than the one at Dublin Castle. She put the village physician in charge of treating the wounded soldiers; sent her own housekeeper and cook from the House of Cromar to cater and clean; and arranged for patients to be driven to church in Johnny's car. Convalescents were invited to build up their strength on the croquet and tennis courts at the "Big House," and on the golf course, if they felt up to it. She persuaded local farmers to provide food and organized concerts and a door-to-door collection to raise funds. The money went towards buying postage stamps so that the soldiers could write to their families, and each of them was given the bus fare home when they were discharged.

Yet even though they had spent little time at the House of Cromar since its completion in 1906, Ishbel and Johnny were soon off on their travels again: first to Edinburgh, where Johnny briefly enjoyed one last taste of the trappings of royalty as Lord High Commissioner of the Church of Scotland, and then to the United States on a fund-raising tour for Ishbel's Women's National Health Association.

Their children were horrified because they knew that their parents could not afford to travel abroad in the grand style to which they had become accustomed. Indeed, they could not afford to travel at all, since, as Marjorie bluntly put it, they were "on the verge of bankruptcy." And they could not expect the WNHA to pay their expenses either: it was struggling too. Dudley's wife, Cecile, was particularly incensed, asking Doddie just before Johnny and Ishbel's departure in September 1915:

> Can they really afford it or is it being paid for by Dudley's & Marjorie's allowances? Oh my dear Doddie forgive me if I say that financially your mother is a *menace* to the family. They can go to America & enjoy themselves on the fat of the land & yet dock the children of *their* due.*

Ishbel and Johnny's problems had been compounded by the expense of building the House of Cromar and by giving their tenants a six-month rent holiday to alleviate the hardships of the war, a gesture that had cost him £20,000. They had sold their London house, 58 Grosvenor Street, but they were burdened with borrowings against life insurances and guarantees from rich friends† whose patience they feared was not inexhaustible, and at least one bank had instructed its lawyers to call in a substantial overdraft. Most of their attempts to raise money—selling the Cromar estate and the Old Masters, renting out Haddo—had been unsuccessful or had made little difference. Even the Old Masters Ishbel had quietly extracted from Haddo seem to have gone for a song. As Ishbel had pointed out in her tearful interview with H. H. Asquith the year before, their dismissal from Ireland had been more than a blow to their pride: it had deprived them of their only reliable source of income. They had hoped, she told him, to "make large savings" from Johnny's £20,000 salary, since the social season that they had always had to sponsor had been canceled because of the war.

Yet she was determined to continue her work for Ireland. To put the WNHA and its Peamount Sanatorium "on a firm footing" they had to raise

---

* In fact, Cecile had a pleasant surprise when, after Ishbel's death, at a time when they themselves were short of money, a letter arrived with the proceeds from a life insurance policy that Ishbel had left to Dudley.

† When Johnny wrote to a neighbor, Lord Cowdray, to ask if he would guarantee an overdraft of £3,000, he received a surprising answer. "Certainly not," said the obliging oil tycoon, "£5,000 or nothing."

£20,000 and they would only find it in the United States. Marjorie, like the rest of the family, was worried:

> She might have the will to carry on, but how could she find the cash? First of all, by the sale—on St. Patrick's Day—of her precious jewels,[*] and by other expedients she appeased the banks where A.'s private accounts showed overdrafts; then she insured her life and set off with A. to America.

But the trip proved as dismal as it was mistimed. The days of private railcars, addresses of welcome, luxury hotels, and retinues of servants, aides-de-camp, and secretaries were now distant memories. Ishbel economized as best she could by learning to type, staying in cheap rooms, and traveling by bus. But as they crisscrossed small-town America, speaking in public halls, schools, and churches to any group that would give them a hearing, she was distressed to find "more impediments in our way than we anticipated." When William Mackenzie King, a friend from their days in Ottawa, bumped into them in San Francisco in 1915, he found them depressed and careworn. Johnny in particular, looked "much older and rather delicate," and Ishbel grumbled "that she would like if the people, instead of giving them dinners or entertainments, would give them just what these social events would cost and allow the money to be used for the health work." Yet, Marjorie wrote, they "continued their diligent search for any coin however small," even if that meant standing behind stalls for hours "selling lace and tweed, blackthorns and lucky leprechauns."

Rival Irish causes, not always ones with such peaceful intent, were also seeking funds, forcing them to extend again and again a trip that they had thought would take six months. At least once, their plans went awry with embarrassing consequences. A posse from the New York County District Attorney's office had burst into a meeting that Johnny had called to discuss a concert at Carnegie Hall. They explained they had been tipped off that

---

[*] By then Ishbel's collection was not what it was: she had found friendly jewelers in Dublin and Aberdeen who, whenever she needed some cash, bought the diamonds in a family tiara one by one and replaced them with paste imitations. The jewelers were so discreet and the fake diamonds so convincing that Ishbel's cunning plan went undetected, until, years later, one of her heirs needed an insurance valuation.

a "suspicious promoter" had put on a show there and that the advertised entertainers, who included the film star Charlie Chaplin, had failed to turn up. Johnny was ordered to explain himself to the DA in person and was only exonerated after a two-hour inquisition. The Aberdeens, Judge Swann concluded, were "inexperienced" in the ways of American show business and had been "exploited by interested parties."

At home in Aberdeenshire, Johnny faced trouble too. As Lord Lieutenant, he was nominally responsible for military recruitment and the defense of the county, and his deputies were unhappy about his long absence in a time of war. David Lloyd George, the Prime Minister, was also asking awkward questions and threatening to demand his resignation if he failed to return immediately. Johnny, clearly guilt-stricken, pleaded that he was "communicating with the Secretary for Scotland" and promoting goodwill between Britain and America.

The family's news, at least, was more cheering. Their children had all volunteered to help the war effort, but Doddie's attempts to sign up were rejected four times by medical boards: a blow he made sure to include in Who's Who to stave off accusations of cowardice. He found plenty to do instead on the home front, working for the Red Cross and the Young Men's Christian Association to such effect that he was awarded the Order of the British Empire in the Civilian War Honors. In Madras, where her husband was Governor, Marjorie was emulating her mother, raising money to equip an innovative hospital ship that brought wounded soldiers from Africa and Mesopotamia back to India for treatment. She, too, was honored for her war work and became one of the first Dame Commanders of the British Empire.

Dudley had joined the Gordon Highlanders, and at the Somme in 1916, the "magnificent courage" of the quiet thirty-three-year-old engineer inspired his men to write to their commanding officer suggesting he deserved a medal. The top brass made him wait a few more months, but Dudley won the Distinguished Service Order for another act of gallantry: the citation spoke of his "fearlessness and disregard of danger" under heavy fire.

Johnny and Ishbel returned to Scotland in May 1918. They had reached their £20,000 target, but it had taken them two and a half years to do so, and in their absence, their financial crisis had intensified. In his letter to Lloyd George, Johnny had complained that, because of the war, he had received no income from his estates, and that he had made a substantial loss after tax. That it was time to face facts was immediately brought home to them: they could not afford the expense of opening up the House of Cromar or Haddo and had to stay in a hotel in Aberdeen instead. It was now Dudley's turn to complain to Doddie that their parents were living beyond their means:

> I can't help feeling that it would be so much better if they could per-
> suade themselves to retire absolutely and live quietly at Haddo or
> Cromar instead of racing about to London & Dublin.

Johnny was not the only landowner in financial difficulties at the end of the hostilities. The point he had made to Lloyd George was justified. In the 1870s, he had paid £800 a year in tax on his estates, but fifty years on, his annual bill, levied by a government that urgently needed to pay for the war and provide jobs for its demobilized troops, had increased to £19,000. These taxes, combined with punitive death duties, the after-effects of the Agricultural Depression and declining revenue from their farms, drove so many landowners to sell their estates that it is said that one-fifth of Scotland changed hands between 1918 and 1921.* And Johnny, who had sacrificed most of his income to help his tenants, borne the expenses of fifteen years of viceregal entertaining, provided seed money for Ishbel's many charities, and who was still losing money on his fruit growing enterprise in British Columbia, was in a worse position than most to weather the harsh realities of the peace.

His first step was to transfer Haddo House and the thirteen thousand

---

* The English aristocracy was selling up too. A rather florid article in the London *Times*, lugubriously headed "Changing Hands, A Note of Resignation," began by lamenting the "sacrifices" being made by the "privileged classes" who found themselves forced to see their patrimony laid out in "in the beautiful illustrated book(s) to be had on application to the land agents." "What will not be found there," it added, "are the intangible things; the loving care the estate has received from each successive owner; how each in turn grew to know every nook and corner of his vast possession, from his earliest days when as a nursery child he played with the acorns under the trees, or later made adventurous expeditions on lake or river, or in adolescence shot over every corner, knowing the haunts of the wildfowl and the hare, or from the old-world stables . . . rode forth to the meet, his duty to the place ever before his mind." But the article ended on a more cheerful note of welcome for the new owners: "Let the next generation blend the new ideals and aspirations with the old experience and traditions—then, though England will have changed hands, the old spirit will remain."

acres immediately surrounding it to Doddie, thus doing his duty to his eldest son and ensuring the continuation of the family's 450-year-old presence in Aberdeenshire. Then, on March 3, 1919, the Aberdeen *Press & Journal* announced that Johnny had sold fifty thousand acres, most of them to a London businessman who immediately put what his agents boasted was Britain's "largest purely Agricultural Estate that has ever been offered" back on the market.[*]

Next, Johnny had to extricate himself from the disastrous fruit farming operation in British Columbia. He had sold the Guisachan Ranch at the turn of the century, but had kept the Coldstream. He had offset some of his liabilities by taking on outside shareholders, but the fruit farm remained disastrously unprofitable, thanks to the prodigious expense of irrigating the land, labor costs that his advisors deemed unnecessarily high, poor harvests, and his staff's ignorance of even the basic techniques of tending orchards. Eventually, one of the shareholders, Sir James Buchanan, a fellow Scot who had made a fortune as a whisky blender, took over. This far cannier businessman was soon turning the profits that Johnny and Ishbel had so fondly dreamt of thirty years before.

But even then, Johnny's problems were far from over. The sale of the Haddo lands had yielded £445,000, but after he had paid off all his debts and mortgages, he was left with only £4,918. Not only was this not enough to sustain him and Ishbel even in modest style at the House of Cromar, there were outstanding debts on that estate too. In the end, a friend and neighbor from Tarland came to the rescue. Sir Alexander MacRobert, a self-made millionaire who had made his fortune from woollen mills in India, undertook to pay off the debts of the Cromar estate, which amounted to £44,850. He also agreed to meet its spiraling annual deficit: in 1919 this was £1,900, but it had increased to £2,670 three years later.[†] Sir Alexander who was, in effect, providing them with their entire income, exacted a high price for his munificence: when they died, Johnny and Ishbel would have to surrender the house and estate to him.

They now had the best of all possible worlds: or so they thought. With

---

[*] Much of the land was sold to Johnny's tenants, as he had hoped. At an auction in June 1919, more than a hundred of them bought the properties that they had previously rented.

[†] In today's money, the debt amounted to about £1,500,000 ($2,000,000) the 1919 deficit to £55,000 ($72,000), and the 1922 deficit to £77,000 ($100,000).

the threat of bankruptcy no longer hanging over them, they could enjoy what one member of the family called "their version of retirement," and because the agreement with Sir Alexander had been made in secret, they could carry on as though nothing had changed. The reinvigorated laird and his lady immersed themselves happily in their duties: there were rural skills to celebrate at the local agricultural show and at plowing matches in the fields surrounding the house, parties and cinema shows for local schoolchildren, and widows to be rescued from penury with discreet and generous handouts. In the grounds of their elegant new mansion, Johnny tended his flock of turkeys and Ishbel supervised a "rabbitry" stocked with Chinchillas, Havanas, Blue Beverens, and Black Alaskas. They played host to what one member of the family described as "a continuous house party of a changing sequence of guests from rapacious old harridans to greedy grandchildren."

The American activist Helen Keller and the Archbishop of Canterbury were among those who called by to enjoy their still unstinting hospitality. Members of the Royal Family regularly popped in from their summer residence at nearby Balmoral Castle and soon had planted enough commemorative trees to form a "royal avenue." While the Irish writer Katharine Tynan, ensconced in her "suite of three delicious rooms," exulted in "the song of the fountain" in the "beautiful Italian garden" that was Ishbel's pride and joy. The "greedy grandchildren," one of them remembered, enjoyed their visits for less elevated reasons:

> We guests came down to the dining-room, never sooner than nine o'clock, often later, to consume porridge and cream, eaten standing up, then to fall on a row of those silver entrée dishes containing fillet of sole bathed in cream, or perhaps kedgeree, then kidneys, scrambled, fried or boiled eggs, bacon, sausages, fried bread.

Another visitor, unaware that Johnny and Ishbel could only afford a minimal staff, was pleasantly surprised by the informality of the place:

> We sat around the fire in a cosy lounge in chairs that were easy to sit in. And we just talked. For them the simple life is the happy one. They have no domestic staff of haughty retainers.

With the war over, Ishbel could return to her crusades, but for her, as for everyone else, the world had changed. She was still president of the International Council of Women, and although women around the world were winning the battle for the vote,* there were other causes to fight for. At the Council's Congress in 1899, she had seen, Marjorie remembered, "a glimpse of a new universe at work where women of the future, educated, freed, enlightened, would everywhere move forward together," to secure a lasting peace.

While she lobbied the newly formed League of Nations, she was also crisscrossing the Irish Sea to Dublin, where amidst the birth pangs of the Free State, she found running her charities from Ely House more difficult—and dangerous—than before:

> I must admit to feeling rather eerie . . . when I was left alone in my boudoir preparing for next day's work. The house had two staircases and two doors into the street, and when I heard shots not very far off and steps in the street, I used to try to make up my mind whether it would be best to remain and face the invaders, whom I nightly expected, or if I should slink down the other stairs and take my chance of getting away somewhere outside.

But in Scotland, their money worries soon returned. Sir Alexander MacRobert died in 1922, and his second wife Rachel proved to be far less tolerant of what she saw as unreasonable demands,† balking especially

---

*While Ishbel certainly believed that women should be allowed the vote, her position on how suffrage could be won was cautious. She angered activists by condemning violence as a means of winning the argument and insisted, to the annoyance of the leading activist Millicent Fawcett, that arguments against, as well as for, the idea should be heard at the International Congress of Women in 1899. Fawcett refused to take part, but held a separate campaign meeting at the same time. Ishbel and Johnny were much criticized by militant suffragettes for not standing alongside them.

† Rachel MacRobert, born in Massachusetts in 1884, was the daughter of William and Fanny Workman, who both came from rich families. After the death in infancy of their son Siegfried, the couple left Rachel in the care of tutors and nannies and set off on their bicycles from their home in Germany to explore the world. One cycle trip took them to Egypt. Fanny also became a famously competitive mountaineer, setting altitude records for female climbers in the Himalayas and other ranges. When a rival claimed that she had climbed Mount Huascarán in Peru and reached a higher point than any woman in history, Fanny sent surveyors to check the height of the mountain. They found that it was one thousand feet lower than Pinnacle Peak in the Himalayas, which Fanny had conquered earlier.

at a bill for expenses Johnny had run up while performing his duties as Lord Lieutenant of the county. In desperation and without telling Johnny, Ishbel agreed, in exchange for more funding, that she would move out of the House of Cromar within six months if he died first.

In the meantime, they did their best to earn some money. In 1925, they published their joint autobiography, *We Twa*,* to praise from the critics. Reading it, the *Dundee Courier* said, was like overhearing "a chat between old friends," while the *Scotsman* liked the way it was "full of the milk of human kindness." The Aberdeens, everyone agreed, had found a winning formula, and the first printing of *We Twa* sold out in only three days.

Soon afterwards, Johnny published a slim and very different volume of his own. *Jokes Cracked by Lord Aberdeen*† was the result of a series of storytelling competitions‡ between Johnny and Sir James Taggart, a former Lord Provost of Aberdeen,§ who told, it was said, at least a thousand jokes a year. Johnny poked gentle fun at skinflint Aberdonians with tales told in the local dialect:

'Jock, will you dine with me tomorrow night?'
   'Aye, Sandy, I will.'
   'Guid! Eight o'clock at your hoose.'

Both Johnny and Sir James were in their late seventies when they reached the zenith of their joke-telling careers at a "Grand Story-Telling Symposium" that topped the bill of a Burns's Night Concert in Aberdeen's Music Hall in 1926. But offstage Johnny had little to laugh about. He was now laird only in name, and as relations with Lady MacRobert soured, he found it harder to keep up appearances. Decisions about the estate had to

---

* The title comes from two verses of probably the most famous poem in the Scots language, Robert Burns's "Auld Lang Syne": *We twa hae run about the braes / And pu'd the gowans fine; / But we've wander'd mony a weary fit / Sin auld lang syne* and *We twa hae paidl'd i' the burn, / Frae mornin' sun till dine; / But seas between us braid hae roar'd / Sin auld lang syne.*

† The book was reprinted in 2013. The marketing campaign billed it, unkindly, as "the world's worst joke book." Others think that title was more deserved by Johnny's rival, whose *Stories Told by Sir James Taggart* was sadly not thought worthy of reissue.

‡ One competition, held to raise funds for local hospitals, lasted three hours. Johnny and Sir James each had to tell forty jokes. Johnny won, scoring 1,788 points to his rival's 1,722.

§ The equivalent of mayor in some of the larger Scottish cities.

be referred hugger-mugger to her trustees, and the worry made him ill. He had grown deaf as he reached his eighties and was exhausted from trying to keep up with Ishbel, who still regularly worked through the night on her voluminous correspondence. The frailty that their Canadian friend William Mackenzie King had glimpsed in 1915 was, by 1930, plain for all to see.

The day of reckoning came on March 7, 1934, when, late in the evening, after a longer-than-usual letter-writing session—"six weeks work in one night"—Johnny suffered a stroke. He was eighty-six. Ishbel wrote in her diary:

> I arrived just in time to take him into my arms like a tired child going to sleep, before he woke to find himself free of all human frailties, in the enjoyment of that new life about which we so often had spoken. I thank God for taking him thus and for the daily close companionship of recent years: and that he was not the one to be left alone. He could not have borne the silence.

A few days later, the *Scotsman* described how Johnny's tenants and friends were invited to the House of Cromar to walk round his coffin in tribute "to one so greatly beloved as a laird and so thoughtful and kindly as a neighbour." And after "an impressive service" in the church below the house, the whole village turned out to bid him farewell.

The Aberdeen *Press & Journal* published a photograph of the hearse leaving Tarland, taken at the pass above the village. This was the place where, on that sunny afternoon more than fifty years before, the newly married Johnny and Ishbel had been welcomed to the valley and the cheers of its people had rung out across the hills. Now the scene was bleak: patches of snow lay on the roadside and the high moors were darkening beneath a lowering sky.

Five hundred people had gathered at Haddo, among them a representative of the King. A reporter from a local magazine watched as the funeral procession wound its way through woods "bright with the first promise of spring" to the little family cemetery half a mile from the house:

> It was a scene not lightly to be forgotten. There were in the throng men in Highland dress; men and women in uniform of many kinds—the

Army, the Salvation Army, the Red Cross, the Boys' Brigade; farmers with tile* hats and grave, whiskered faces; women with children by their skirts; the Magistrates of Aberdeen in crimson gowns; peer, merchant, and ploughman, all come on the same errand.

Violet Asquith, long since married, had sent blue violets "to Archie's father," while the card on Ishbel's wreath of red carnations said:

From his wife, blessed above women in her close comradeship for 56½ years. Until the day dawns and the shadows flee away.

At the graveside, a piper played "Lochaber No More," and Ishbel dropped a sprig of ivy into the grave. Then, said the reporter:

We left him there, remembering him as he had been in life—a little over middle height, with a generous breadth of brow, deep eyes, features shaped to laughter rather than solemnity but showing the strong and even temper of the man and his authority. The beard, not neatly trimmed but handsome, did not so much conceal as emphasise the qualities of that face, and his upright frame which carried uniform bravely was well suited to the kilt. This was indeed a Scottish laird and a link with a day that is, to most of us, dead beyond imagining.

---

* The Scottish slang term for a silk top hat.

19

Ishbel's Lost Houses

To spare Ishbel embarrassment, Robert Hunter, the family solicitor, used a loophole in the law to avoid publishing Johnny's will. For sixty years after coming into his extraordinarily rich inheritance, Johnny had died with only £204* to his name. But Lady MacRobert's lawyers were not so well disposed. With what the family considered to be indecent haste, they invoked not only the agreement that Johnny had made with Sir Alexander but also the secret deal made by Ishbel with his wife. The time had come for her to hand over the estate, they said, as well as the house and all its contents. When, they asked, would Lady Aberdeen be leaving?

Ishbel played for time. She had nowhere to go, she replied, since the suite of rooms she could have occupied at Haddo had been destroyed when the family wing burnt down in 1930. But the lawyers had their instructions and pushed ahead. The negotiations were bruising: at one point, Doddie, the new marquess, complained that his mother was being bullied by the obdurate solicitors. Lady MacRobert hid behind them, and although she lived less than a mile from the House of Cromar, she repeatedly rebuffed Ishbel's pleas for a face-to-face meeting.

An inventory was drawn up: it included even the smallest household objects, an old toaster among them. As the weeks passed, relations between the grandes dames deteriorated even further. Lady MacRobert,

---

*Barely £10,000 ($13,000) today.

stung by suggestions in the press that she was callously turning a grieving old lady out of her home, insisted that Ishbel should reveal the reasons for the handover in a humiliating announcement in the *Scotsman*. Ishbel, on her part, made no secret of her unhappiness about having to leave so many family treasures behind, especially the portraits of her children and mother let into a wall of the dining room. But the MacRobert lawyers were insistent, although they did agree to make one concession: for £40, Ishbel was allowed to buy back the dinner table at which Mr. Gladstone had so often sat, and one other piece of furniture was unexpectedly rescued.

Queen Mary came to tea at the House of Cromar and saw Ishbel's distress, particularly at the prospect of handing over an eighteenth-century satinwood secretaire that Johnny had given her as a souvenir of their time in Ireland. Later that day Ishbel was surprised to hear from Lady Victoria Weld-Forester, who had accompanied the Queen:

> To-night Lady Victoria telephoned that the Queen wished to purchase my bookcase by valuation and give it me—wonderful! Lady MacRobert has consented to sell; valuation Monday.

A price of £30 was agreed and the next day a carrier arrived from Balmoral. The secretaire was loaded aboard; but instead of going west to the Queen's Castle, the van took it north to Haddo. It is still there in the morning room today.

Ishbel, finally reconciled, sent each of her neighbors and tenants a handwritten letter to say goodbye. In church on the Sunday before she left in September 1934, the minister, the Reverend W. Marshall Low, spoke feelingly of the many ways in which she and Johnny had been "helpful and kind" to the people of the neighborhood:

> We recall the privilege so often accorded of their beautiful estate, of their interest in the school, of their sympathy in the joys and sorrows of young and old, of their consideration for the sick, and, above all, of their love for God's house and His worship. Lady Aberdeen's philanthropic labours will not cease on leaving Cromar. Like Wesley, the whole world is her parish.

Ever the Viceroy's wife, Ishbel gave a farewell garden party before leaving Tarland. Without the MacRobert payments, she now had virtually no income and would have to rely on Doddie to provide her with living expenses and somewhere to live. Although he himself had struggled—he narrowly avoided having to sell Haddo in 1927 by selling yet more pictures from the family collection—he found her an extraordinary, and to many eyes, ugly, home in Aberdeen: built in 1881 by a granite merchant, the rambling gothic building, which Doddie renamed Gordon House, has been described by an architectural historian as "spooky" and like "something out of Transylvania." Ishbel's next problem was to find furniture, since Lady MacRobert had claimed all that she owned at the House of Cromar. Her lawyer, who had acquired many of the finest fittings from Guisachan, lent her some, including a satinwood writing table, the drawing room curtains, and even one of her father's treasured fire surrounds.

Amidst these reminders of her childhood, much to Marjorie's relief, Ishbel felt content in the city, far though she was from her beloved hills:

> Here was a garden in front of the open window where she could sit and write as at Cromar. She could see her beehives standing in the sun, her Cairn terriers scampering on the lawn, a crowd of birds around the bird-table, the flowers from the seeds she had ordered growing into a blaze of colour, the blue and the white Saltire Cross of St Andrew flying from her flagstaff.

In Aberdeen, Ishbel made new friends and greeted old ones. Among them was William Mackenzie King, then in his third term as Prime Minister of Canada, who called at Gordon House in June 1937 on his way to Germany. They had forged a strange and secret bond: both had been converted to spiritualism by another friend of Ishbel's, W. T. Stead.[*] Ishbel

---

[*] It is not clear when Stead convinced Ishbel that it was possible to communicate with the dead. It could have been during his visit to Rideau Hall in Ottawa with the ghostly "Julia" in 1893, or perhaps it was after her son Archie's death in 1909. Stead also lost a son that year and was consoled when he apparently got in touch. He believed that this contact confirmed "the reality of the unseen world around us." Stead had gone down on the *Titanic* a quarter of a century before King's visit, but history does not relate whether Ishbel and King tried to contact him.

had wasted no time in trying to contact Johnny. In the lonely hours after his death she wrote in her diary:

> We promised one another we would try everything and to-night the little OUIJA table pointer spelled out, 'I am happy do not grieve try writing!'

When King died, his diaries revealed, sensationally, that he had regularly consulted the dead* while in government, and that he had used all kinds of signs, portents, magic numbers, and even shapes in his shaving foam, to guide him in making decisions. Such supernatural "advice" had inspired his quixotic mission to lobby Hitler to try to avert the Nazis' growing threat to peace.†

On the first evening of King's visit, the two friends sat down after dinner. King described a séance that Ishbel had arranged for him in London with Mrs. Leonard, one of the mediums she consulted; and she shared "revelations" from the former Prime Minister Henry Campbell Bannerman and his wife Charlotte, who were among her regular "correspondents" from beyond the grave.

That Ishbel was often preoccupied with death was not surprising. She had not only outlived Johnny and two of her children, but almost all the Marjoribanks dynasty too. After their father's death in 1894, her brother Coutts had given up the struggle to grow fruit in Canada and had returned to Scotland. But the call of the Okanagan was strong and the old cowboy went back there in 1910. There he married a widow and built himself a large and solid house of a kind he can only have dreamt of in his shack at the Horseshoe Ranch in his salad days. Coutts died in 1924, fondly remembered by a nephew as "a big man with a voice like the roar of an old bull . . . but under that big voice was a nice old man."

---

* King, who never married (though he did confess that Marjorie was his ideal woman), was very attached to his mother and "communicated" with her and three other members of his family who died between 1915 and 1922.

† The spirits do not seem to have had a baneful influence on King's governance of Canada, although his visit to Hitler was a hubristic blunder. The peace-loving Ishbel had supported his mission and telegraphed him when he reached Berlin with words of encouragement from Psalm 91: "For he shall give his angels charge over thee, to keep thee in all thy ways." But King was gulled by the German dictator, gushing: "Hitler said to me, my support comes from the people—the people don't want war.—This impressed me very much and a real note of humility."

Ishbel shrugged off her eightieth birthday in 1937, exclaiming in her diary:

It seems ridiculous, but one goes on feeling just the same.

She had at last been honored for her work and was now a Dame Grand Cross of the British Empire, but she refused to rest on such laurels and was as busy as ever: reluctantly drawing upon the resources of her organizations to travel across Europe to meetings of the International Council of Women, to Dublin to continue her crusade for health, to Glasgow to organize the construction of a "Peace Pavilion" at the Empire Exhibition,* and to England to try to revive the fortunes of the Liberals. A delegate marveled at her appearance at the party's assembly that year:

The venerable lady stood there, in the dignity and beauty of old age, and in a clear voice that carried all over the great hall, she told us about her last conversation with Mr Gladstone at Hawarden; how he had said that the task of his time had been to remove barriers . . . and then had added, his eyes gleaming with their old fire: 'Above all, never be afraid.'

But in her diary entry for Easter Day 1939, Ishbel acknowledged, uncharacteristically, that she was ailing:

Dr Fraser forbade my going to church to-day, owing to a recurrence of those annoying lack-of-breath spells, due he says to a toxin of that slight inflammation affecting the heart a bit, so there is nothing for it but to keep quiet for a few days.

Ishbel died from a heart attack nine days later, on April 18. Despite her frailty and her age—she was eighty-two—she had worked until the end. It came as no surprise to Marjorie, who had been with her, that the last entry in the long series of diaries that her mother had begun in child-

---

*Ishbel had a garden laid out around the pavilion with a cairn as a centerpiece. King George VI and Queen Elizabeth, who opened the exhibition in 1938, brought a stone from Balmoral and others came from governments and organizations throughout the world. The Peace Cairn still stands in Bellahouston Park, Glasgow.

hood concerned Peamount, the pioneering TB sanatorium that she had founded in Ireland.

There were so many mourners at her funeral a few days later that two services had to be held at Haddo: one in the private chapel, another in the hall. In his address, Professor Archibald Main, the Moderator of the General Assembly of the Church of Scotland, said of Ishbel:

Every cause of human healing and social welfare, of relief of distress and defence of liberty, of women's opportunities and responsibilities, of world-wide peace and spiritual culture; every good and noble cause found in her not only a loyal friend but a stalwart champion.

But, he added:

The picture of memory would not be complete if we were to forget that she who was Her Excellency in Government House or Viceregal Lodge was as perfectly and graciously at home in the cottage as in the castle. Her friendships broke through all restraints of class or convention.

His praise was echoed in obituaries throughout the world.

Otherwise, Ishbel's funeral followed a now familiar pattern: a piper leading the procession to the little cemetery that she had commissioned after the death of Dorothea in 1882;* the coffin, made of a beech tree from the Haddo woods, draped with a pall of Irish poplin embroidered with a golden cross; farmers, estate workers, peers, and politicians, black-suited, bareheaded, silent together in the chill Aberdeenshire wind; women from the charities she had founded, proud in their uniforms; roses and tulips and daffodils and her favorite red carnations tied with ribbons of Gordon tartan; wreaths entwined with ivy leaves; the voices of children singing "The Lord's My Shepherd" and the strains of "Lochaber No More" hanging in the air. Now she was reunited with the baby she had lost, with Archie, the cherished son who had died too young, and with Johnny, the other half of "We Twa," the husband who had always called her his "priceless blessing."

---

* The cemetery was designed by the doyen of Victorian Gothic architects, Alfred Waterhouse, who was also responsible for the Natural History Museum in London.

Many of the six hundred mourners at Haddo that day would have known that just before her death, Ishbel had fought her last and most poignant campaign. Twenty years earlier, in 1919, the Earl of Portsmouth had offered her childhood home in the Highlands for sale. But at auction Guisachan did not attract a single bid. When it reappeared on the market sixteen years later, Ishbel, who was in no position to buy it back herself, persuaded her lawyer Robert Hunter to acquire the estate. He soon resold the land, but no one wanted the house, even at the knockdown price of £3,500. Ishbel was determined to save it, but unwittingly sealed its fate by suggesting that it would be the ideal venue for a summer school sponsored by the government's National Fitness Campaign. But the keep-fit enthusiasts who frolicked naked in the lake beside the farmhouse nearby outraged its occupant, Lady Islington, the widow of a former Governor of New Zealand. She persuaded Hunter to sell her the mansion for £1,500 and immediately ordered its demolition. Ishbel was horrified: "It seems unbelievable and has upset me terribly," she wrote in her diary. She asked the County Council to step in, but its members regretted that they had no authority to intervene. Her local Member of Parliament and the Secretary of State for Scotland gave her the same reply. Two weeks after Ishbel's death the demolition squad moved in, took the roof off Dudley Marjoribanks's fine house, and stripped it of its fixtures and fittings. These, to the last block of parquet flooring and the smallest window fittings, were sold the following month. Guisachan is now a picturesque ruin, visited mainly by Golden Retriever owners who revere it as the birthplace of the breed.

After buying Brook House from Edward Marjoribanks, Sir Ernest Cassel, Edward VII's banker, made it even more palatial and ostentatious: it had twenty-four bedrooms, a ballroom, and a dining room that could accommodate a hundred people. And, with eight hundred tons of Italian marble that took a year to extract from a quarry in Italy, he created an entrance hall in which even Dudley Marjoribanks can never have dreamt of dwelling. Predictably, it became known around town as the "Giant's Lavatory." Cassel's granddaughter Edwina, who inherited it after his death, made yet more changes after she married Lord Louis Mountbatten in 1922, reflecting her husband's love of the Royal Navy in the décor of their bedroom which, with its portholes and brass fittings, was "designed to represent the cabin of a battleship."* The building was partly demolished in 1933, and the Mountbattens lived in the luxurious penthouse of the flats that replaced it.

Dollis Hill was pulled down in 2012 after a long campaign to save it: a "theatre space" now stands where Gladstone read Homer on Sunday afternoons. Nos. 27 and 37 Grosvenor Square were also demolished, to make way for the neo-futurist charms of Eero Saarinen's Embassy of the United States, now itself redundant. The cabins from which Coutts and Archie sallied forth with packs of hounds and, more reluctantly, to inspect their cattle, vanished long ago into the grasslands of Texas and North Dakota, and the log-cabin hospital in the Klondike goldfield was closed in 1918 and replaced by a more modern medical complex.

Other houses are still standing, though greatly altered. Littleberries, home of the notorious Mrs. Rudd, ironically, became a convent, which in its turn has been converted into luxury flats. The contents of Gordon House—everything from Ishbel's picnic basket to her umbrella—were auctioned over two days in August 1940, but the wartime buyers kept their hands in their pockets. The top lot, a magnificent George III mahogany bookcase that had covered a whole wall of the hallway, fetched only £51,† and the Guisachan dining room curtains went "for a song." Since then, the house has gone through many transformations: student lodgings, a hotel, and, more recently, the offices of an engineering company. In British Columbia, the bungalow at the Guisachan Ranch is now a restaurant, but the Coldstream still flourishes in the valley where Coutts so singularly failed to produce enough fruit for Johnny's jam factory. Ely House is now the headquarters of the Order of Knights of Saint Columbanus, an organization that promotes Catholic values and principles. Haddo has proved both a victim and a beneficiary of the couple's fluctuating fortunes. The estate now flourishes, but the expense of maintaining the house defeated my father-in-law, who bequeathed it to the National Trust for Scotland. Ishbel's improvements remain its scintillating glories.

---

*The room's most eccentric wonder was its light switch, according to the Mountbattens' daughter, Lady Pamela Hicks. Her father, she wrote, had designed it, "so that when turned down it emitted a low hum, like that of a ship's engine, and this helped him get to sleep."

† About £2,000 ($2,600) today. What may be the same bookcase has appeared in salesrooms in the last thirty years with at least a couple of noughts added to its value.

The House of Cromar, the home that Johnny and Ishbel dreamt of through their years of exile in Ireland and Canada and finally built, still stands in the village where I live. It has proved an unlucky house and its story is a sad one. After Ishbel handed it over in settlement of her debts, Lady MacRobert gave it to her sons. By the end of 1941, however, all three were dead: one killed in a prewar air crash, the other two with the RAF in combat. Their mother's response was robust: she sent a check for £25,000* to the Air Ministry to pay for a Stirling bomber, known as "MacRobert's Reply." The house, renamed Alastrean House, became a holiday hotel for officers from the armed services and their families. Later, it was turned into a care home. Little now remains from Johnny and Ishbel's time: in 1952, a fire gutted the building and the family portraits and much of the furniture that Ishbel was forced to leave there were lost. But one tradition they established persists. The gate on the drive was never closed, and today, like all those royal visitors, celebrities, and delegates from their charities, local people can enjoy the woods that surround the house.

I walked there often as I tried to work out why Johnny and Ishbel lost so great a fortune. At first sight, Ishbel was following the example of her acquisitive father, who spent lavishly on his houses and on the pictures, porcelain, and fine furniture with which he decorated them. But for her, houses were not just for living in, they were places from which to launch social projects and where she could further charitable causes: on the lawns of Haddo there was space to entertain the farmhands and servant girls who might otherwise have yielded to the less sedate temptations of Aberdeen; in Grosvenor Square her Indian music room could accommodate bazaars, religious meetings, and sales of Irish crafts; an invitation to dine at Rideau Hall or the Viceregal Lodge or Dublin Castle helped to raise funds; the Coldstream Ranch would bring a new industry to British Columbia and provide land where émigrés could settle and make their fortunes.

And though she was given most of the credit for their good works, "We Twa," the name they chose for themselves, told the real story. Ishbel and Johnny were a team: like-minded, earnest, prodigiously hardworking, forward-thinking, and kind. Like Johnny's father, the 5th Earl, with his coach piled high with furniture for the poor and his anonymous funding

* About £1,000,000 ($1,300,000) today.

of churches, children's homes, and ragged schools, they believed that their privileged position and old money should provide churches, hospitals, housing, and even railways, for the communities through which they passed. In an age when politicians, aristocrats, and even social reformers spoke of "the masses," Johnny and Ishbel saw individual people with problems and worries and afflictions of their own. It never mattered to them who anyone was or where they had come from: those who espoused their campaigns and crusades had their ear and those in need of help would be given it.

But, as their hand-wringing bankers and despairing daughter knew only too well, they were singularly ill-equipped to pursue so generous a program of philanthropy. Marjorie could barely contain her exasperation at her mother's financial naïveté:

> She would never learn to balance her own resources, either in cash or in health, against the common interest. To get things done she habitually overspent both and thereby gave herself and those around her endless anxiety.

And Johnny, usually far from Aberdeenshire, seems to have paid little attention to the accounts of estates whose workings he never fully understood, and until it was too late, to have turned a deaf ear to his lawyers' warnings. They were not, as one friend and admirer said, "of this world."

But, to the last, Ishbel was unrepentant. "I suppose we made many mistakes," she confided to one of her grandsons not long before she died, "but I like to think we did more good than harm."

ACKNOWLEDGMENTS

I first became interested in Ishbel's life story when, as a teenager, bored and desperate to escape from a fractious house party at Haddo in the dreary days between Christmas and New Year, I decided to explore the old "downstairs" staff quarters. Many of the rooms were still in occasional use, among them a cavernous kitchen with an enormous range and a *batterie de cuisine* that would not have disgraced an Edwardian grand hotel. Next door was a butler's pantry lined with pine cupboards crammed with hundreds of crested plates, tureens, and dishes, and where, on the wooden draining board stretching for yards on either side of the huge sink, stood a curious Victorian knife-cleaning machine.

But there was one room whose purpose, at first glance, was hard to make out. Towers of filing boxes and ribbon-tied papers covered every surface: a long table, the mantelpiece, the splintery floor. As the afternoon wore on, I lost myself in an extraordinary treasure trove: the Gordon family archives. A bundle of press cuttings told of a libel case and a famous Edwardian crime; photograph albums chronicled a lost world of Victorian high society posing in the drawing rooms of ornate London mansions or disporting themselves on the balconies and terraces of country houses; the files revealed letters from the great and the good, the diaries of small children, and correspondence from lawyers and bank managers (rather a lot of them); tin boxes spilled over with rent books, crop records, and financial ledgers recording the business of generations of a landowning family.

Such was the state of the family archives half a century ago, and their rescue and preservation in a fine muniment room are just two of the many ways in which Alexander Gordon, the 7th Marquess of Aberdeen and Temair, modernized the estate and generously made its resources accessible. I could not have written this book without his help, so freely given. Research can be a drudgery, but he made it fun, for no one knew the family's history better or loved it more, and he was as interested in the foibles and eccentricities of his ancestors as he was in their achievements at home in Scotland and in the wider world. It is a great sadness to me that Alexander did not live to see the publication of this book.

I am also immensely grateful to his wife, Joanna, for her kindness, support, and hospitality. There are many others in Aberdeenshire to whom thanks are due, not least the archivist Nicola Mills, for her expert and thoughtful cataloguing of all those files, albums, press cuttings, and tin boxes. I also thank Mark Andrew, Moira Minty, and Marge Pocknell from the Haddo Estate; Innes Catto, James Burnett of Leys, David Fasken, William Gordon, Professor Marjory Harper, Moira Minty and Alexander Milne of John Milne Fine Art Auctioneers, the Reverend Frank Ribbons, and the Trustees of the David & June Gordon Memorial Trust. In Tarland, the Cromar History Group has kindly allowed me to clarify my ideas through inviting me to give talks and contribute to its annual publication, *Echoes from Cromar's Past*, and thanks are due to Rita Barnes, Peter Craig, David and Lesley Ellis, Nigel and Janet Healey, Patrick Heron, Ann Miles, Marion Miller, Anne Robson, Veronica and Irvine Ross, and Morna Stewart. Alison Donaldson, Simon Power, and Stephen McCallum of the MacRobert Trust have also provided me with useful information and help, as have Anke Addy, Sandy Cooper, David Currie, and David Vardy.

I also acknowledge, with gratitude, the help of many friends and experts from further afield: Alastair Bruce of Crionaich, Christopher Coles, Tace Fox of Harrow School, Pete Hammar, John Hill, Peter Hunter, Jeremy Lemmon, Huon Mallalieu, Mary Miers, Mary Montefiore, David Morgan, Ian Parkinson, George Pirie, Charles Sebag-Montefiore, Catriona Stewart, Professor Veronica Strong-Boag, Professor David M. Walker, David W. Walker, and Adam and Humphrey Welfare. Professor Carolyn MacHardy and Peter Costello have been particularly generous in sharing their knowledge of the Aberdeens' sojourns in British Columbia and Ireland respectively. At Atria Books, I thank Fiora Elberts-Tibbitts and at 42 Management & Production, Emily MacDonald. My account of Archie Gordon's death draws heavily upon Violet Asquith's vivid and touching diary for December 14, 1909–May 29, 1910 (© the Trustees of the Asquith and Bonham Carter Papers) lodged in the Bodleian Library, Oxford (MS. Bonham Carter 8), and I thank the Bonham Carter family for kindly allowing me to do this.

The history of Haddo lies at the heart of this book. The house is now owned by the National Trust for Scotland, Scotland's leading conservation organization. Independent of government and supported by its worldwide membership, the Trust has maintained Haddo for more than forty years and welcomes thousands of visitors to enjoy its treasures. Ishbel and Johnny, pioneers of opening houses to the public, would surely have approved, and I am grateful to the Trust's staff, past and present, particularly Ian Gow, Christopher Hartley, and Jennifer Melville, for the benefits of their wisdom and for the unstinting help that they have given me. The Trust has also kindly provided many of the pictures in this book.

I offer especial thanks to my literary agent Eugenie Furniss who has patiently nurtured this project over many years, to Trish Todd, my editor at Atria, and to my friend John Fairley who has read the drafts of this book, for their encouragement, advice, and enthusiasm, and to my wife Mary who has so graciously tolerated my obsession with another woman.

SIMON WELFARE

SELECT BIBLIOGRAPHY

To say that Johnny's and Ishbel's lives are well documented is an understatement. In the second half of the nineteenth century, the comings and goings of the British aristocracy were chronicled in exhaustive detail in the society columns of the newspapers. Readers could follow dukes and duchesses from stately home to stately home, welcome the arrival of heirs and "spares," wring their hands at the declining health of a venerable dowager, wonder why a countess was selling part of her estate, marvel at the high price that a landowner had obtained from selling a prize bull, or learn that a former Prime Minister was "engaged most of each day in his study." And since Johnny and Ishbel were public figures, too, it is perhaps not surprising that, according to the British Newspaper Archive, there were more than twenty thousand mentions of Ishbel in the British press alone between the date of her wedding in 1878 and the turn of the century. Thus, I have drawn extensively and with gratitude upon online newspaper databases from around the world in the course of my research.

Johnny's and Ishbel's own highly readable writings and those of their descendants have, naturally, proved an invaluable resource, and I recommend them and the other books that I list below. This is by no means a comprehensive bibliography, but these sources do provide more information (and invariably the proverbial "good read") for anyone who wishes to know more about this fascinating couple and their world. And since Johnny and Ishbel covered much ground, both literally and figuratively, and embraced many causes in their long and busy lives, I have listed the books according to the themes or episodes that they cast light on.

Books by Johnny and Ishbel:
Aberdeen and Temair, John Campbell Gordon, Marquess of, and Ishbel Gordon, Marchioness of Aberdeen and Temair. *More Cracks with "We Twa."* London: Methuen, 1929.
————. *We Twa.* London: W. Collins Sons & Co., 1925.

Books by Johnny:
Aberdeen and Temair, John Campbell Gordon, Marquess of. *Jokes Cracked by Lord Aberdeen.* Dundee: Valentine & Sons, 1929.
————. *Tell Me Another.* Edward Arnold & Co: London, 1925.

Books by or Edited by Ishbel:
Aberdeen and Temair, Ishbel Gordon, Marchioness of. *Edward Marjoribanks, Lord Tweedmouth, K.T., 1849–1909.* London: Constable, 1909.
————. *The Musings of a Scottish Granny.* London: Heath Cranton, 1936.
————. *Onward and Upward.* 2 vols. London: Partridge & Co., 1891 & 1892.
————. *Through Canada with a Kodak.* Edinburgh: W. H. White & Co., 1893.
Drummond, James, ed. *Onward and Upward: Extracts (1891–96) from the Magazine of the Onward and Upward Association Founded by Lady Aberdeen for the Material, Mental and Moral Elevation of Women.* Aberdeen: Aberdeen University Press, 1983.

Books About Ishbel and Johnny
Pentland, Marjorie. *A Bonnie Fechter: The Life of Ishbel Marjoribanks, Marchioness of Aberdeen & Temair, 1857–1939.* London: B. T. Batsford, 1952.
Shackleton, Doris French. *Ishbel and the Empire.* Toronto: Dundurn Press, 1988.
Strong-Boag, Veronica. *Liberal Hearts and Coronets: The Lives and Times of Ishbel Marjoribanks Gordon and John Campbell Gordon, the Aberdeens.* Toronto: University of Toronto Press, 2015.

Archie Gordon
An Album of Recollections of Archie Gordon. Privately Published, 1910.
Bonham Carter, Mark and Mark Pottle, eds. *Lantern Slides: The Diaries and Letters of Violet Bonham Carter, 1904–1914.* London: Weidenfeld & Nicolson, 1996.

Coutts, Archie, and the U.S. Ranches
Brisbin, James S. *The Beef Bonanza, or, How to Get Rich on the Plains.* Philadelphia: J. B. Lippincott, 1881.
Clay, John. *My Life on the Range.* Norman, OK: University of Oklahoma Press, 1962.
Macdonald, James. *Food from the Far West.* London: W.P. Nimmo, 1878.
McFarlane, Larry A. "British Remittance Men as Ranchers: The Case of Coutts Marjoribanks and Edmund Thursby, 1884–95." *Great Plains Quarterly* 11, no. 1 (Winter 1991): 53–69.
Pagnamenta, Peter. *Prairie Fever: British Aristocrats in the American West 1830–1890.* London: Duckworth Overlook, 2012.
Tinkler, Estelle. *Archibald John Writes the Rocking Chair Ranche Letters.* Burnet, TX: Eakin Press, 1979.

————. "Nobility's Ranche: A History of the Rocking Chair Ranche." *Panhandle-Plains Historical Review* 15 (1942).

Zuehlke, Mark. *Scoundrels, Dreamers & Second Sons: British Remittance Men in the Canadian West*. Vancouver, BC: Whitecap Books, 1994.

Family and Friends

Chamberlain, Muriel E. *Lord Aberdeen: A Political Biography*. New York: Longman, 1983.

Chapman, J. K. *The Career of Arthur Hamilton Gordon: First Lord Stanmore 1829–1912*. Toronto: University of Toronto Press, 1964.

Chenevix Trench, Charles. *Charley Gordon: An Eminent Victorian Reassessed*. London: Allen Lane, 1978.

Corts, Thomas E., ed. *Henry Drummond: A Perpetual Benediction*. Edinburgh: T. & T. Clark, 1999.

Drummond, Henry. *The Greatest Thing in the World*. Birmingham: Samford University Press, 1997.

Elliott, Edward Bishop, ed. *Memoir of Lord Haddo, in His Latter Years Fifth Earl of Aberdeen*. London: Seeley, Jackson & Halliday, 1873.

Gordon, Archie. *A Wild Flight of Gordons*. London: Weidenfeld and Nicolson 1985.

Jenkins, Roy. *Gladstone*. London: Macmillan, 1995.

Simpson, James. *Henry Drummond*. London: Oliphant, Anderson & Ferrier, 1901.

Taggart, James. *Stories Told by Sir James Taggart*. London: Valentine and Sons, 1926.

Guisachan

Emmerson, Robin. *Wedgwood at the Lady Lever Art Gallery*. Liverpool: Bluecoat Press, 1995.

Gow, Ian. *Scotland's Lost Houses*. London: Aurum/National Trust for Scotland, 2006.

Harris, Eileen. "Adams in the Family: Wright and Mansfield at Haddo, Guisachan, Brook House and Grosvenor Square." *Furniture History* 32 (1996): 141–58.

Miers, Mary. *Highland Retreats*. New York: Rizzoli, 2017.

Wood, Lucy. *The Lady Lever Art Gallery*. Liverpool: Bluecoat Press, 1999.

Haddo House

Fasken, David. *The Earl of Aberdeen's Railway: The Great North Branch That Never Was*. Aberdeen: Great North of Scotland Railway Association, 2018.

Guidebook to Haddo House. Edinburgh: National Trust for Scotland, 2013.

Linklater, Eric. *The Music of the North*. Aberdeenshire, UK: Haddo House Choral & Operatic Society, 1970.

Welfare, Mary. *Growing Up at Haddo: A Scottish Childhood*. London: Weidenfeld and Nicolson, 1989.

Ishbel and Johnny in Canada

Gwyn, Sandra. *Private Capital: Ambition and Love in the Age of Macdonald and Laurier*. Toronto: McClelland and Stewart, 1984.

Harper, Marjory. "A Gullible Pioneer? Lord Aberdeen and the Development of Fruit Farming in the Okanagan Valley, 1890–1921." *British Journal of Canadian Studies* 1, no. 2 (December 1986): 256–81.

Holliday, Charles W. *The Valley of Youth*. Caldwell, ID: Caxton Printers, 1948.

Hubbard, Robert Hamilton. *Ample Mansions: The Viceregal Residences of the Canadian Provinces*. Ottawa: University of Ottawa Press, 1989.

———. *Rideau Hall: An Illustrated History of Government House, Ottawa, from Victorian Times to Present Day*. Montreal: McGill-Queen's University Press, 1977.

MacHardy, Carolyn. " 'Kodaking and Being Kodaked': The Guisachan Album of Ishbel, Lady Aberdeen." *Journal of Canadian Art History/Annales d'histoire de l'art Canadien* 34, no. 2 (2013): 179–209.

MacRae, Marion, and Anthony Adamson. *The Ancestral Roof: Domestic Architecture of Upper Canada*. Toronto: Clarke, Irwin & Co., 1963.

Middleton, R. M., ed. *The Journal of Lady Aberdeen: The Okanagan Valley in the Nineties*. Victoria, BC: Morriss Publishing, 1986.

Saywell, John, ed. *The Canadian Journal of Lady Aberdeen: 1893-1898*. Toronto: The Champlain Society, 1960.

Wuest, Donna. *Coldstream: The Ranch Where It All Began*. Pender Harbour, BC: Harbour Publishing, 2005.

Ishbel and Johnny in Ireland

Brooke, Raymond F. *The Brimming River*. Dublin: Allen Figgis & Co., 1961.

Carruthers, Dr. Frances and Martin Duffy. *The Viceregal Microbe: Politics and the Battle Against Tuberculosis in Ireland*. Leicester, UK: Matador, 2018.

Costello, Peter. *Dublin Castle in the Life of the Irish Nation*. Dublin: Wolfhound Press, 1999.

Craik, Dinah Maria Mulock. *An Unknown Country*. New York: Harper & Brothers, 1887.

Headlam, Maurice. *Irish Reminiscences*. London: Robert Hale Ltd, 1947.

Helland, Janice. *British and Irish Home Arts and Industries 1880–1914: Marketing Craft, Making Fashion*. Dublin and Portland, OR: Irish Academic Press, 2007.

Johnston, Denis. *Orders and Desecrations: The Life of the Playwright Denis Johnson*. Dublin: Lilliput Press, 1992.

Keane, Maureen. *Ishbel: Lady Aberdeen in Ireland*. Newtownards, UK: Colourpoint Books, 1999.

Shepherd, Sue. *The Surprising Life of Constance Spry*. New York: Macmillan, 2010.

Tynan, Katharine. *The Years of the Shadow*. London: Constable & Co., 1919.

Ishbel and Johnny's London Houses

Sheppard F. H. W., ed. *The Survey of London: Volume 40, the Grosvenor Estate in Mayfair, Part 2 (The Buildings)*. London: Athlone Press for the Greater London Council, 1980.

Tarland and the Cromar Estate

Miller, Marion. *Cawnpore to Cromar: The MacRoberts of Douneside*. Moray, UK: Librario, 2014.

Sharples, Joseph, David Walker, and Matthew Woodworth. *The Buildings of Scotland: Aberdeenshire: South and Aberdeen*. London: Yale University Press, 2015.

Welfare, Simon. *Home Front: Aboyne & Tarland 1914–18*. Tarland, UK: Cromar History Group, 2014.

The Theft of the Irish Crown Jewels

Appendix to the Report of the Vice-Regal Commission Appointed to Investigate the Circumstances of the Loss of the Regalia of the Order of Saint Patrick. Dublin: HMSO, 1908.

Duncan, Myles. *The Stealing of the Irish Crown Jewels: An Unsolved Crime.* Dublin: Town House, 2003.

The World's Columbian Exposition, Chicago, 1893

Guide to the Irish Industrial Village and Blarney Castle. Chicago: Irish Village Book Store, 1893.

General

Cannadine, David. *The Decline and Fall of the British Aristocracy.* New Haven, CT: Yale University Press, 1990.

Horn, Pamela. *Country House Society: The Private Lives of England's Upper Class After the First World War.* Stroud, UK: Amberley, 2013.

Sutherland, Douglas. *The Landowners.* London: Anthony Blond, 1968.

Tinniswood, Adrian. *The Long Weekend: Life in the English Country House Between the Wars.* London: Jonathan Cape 2016.

PHOTO CREDITS

————

Before she and Johnny left on their trip to Canada in 1890, Ishbel summoned a salesman from the Eastman Dry Plate and Film Company to her house in London and bought two of the revolutionary Kodak cameras that George Eastman had invented only two years before. Designed for amateur photographers, they were portable and easy to use. Eastman's beguiling marketing slogan, "You point the button, we do the rest," meant just that. The camera came loaded with a roll of film, and when the photographer had taken a hundred "snapshots," they simply sent the whole camera off to Kodak's factory, where it was reloaded once the images had been developed.

Ishbel took her cameras everywhere, recording her travels, her family life, and the great and the good of the Victorian and Edwardian ages at play, and she also collected the images produced by many of the photographers who "kodaked" her. Today, the legacy of all that button-pushing can be found in the bulky albums that line the shelves of the Haddo Estate archive, and it is from these that I have chosen most of the photographs in this book. I am grateful to the Marquess of Aberdeen and Temair for generously allowing me to explore and make use of this extraordinary treasure trove and to Ian Thorn who copied the pictures with his customary skill and patience.

Most of the color plates were supplied by Susanna Hillhouse of the National Trust for Scotland, and I thank her, too, for her help in difficult circumstances. *Dinner at Haddo House 1884* was provided by the National Portrait Gallery, London; the painting of Brook House by akg-images; and the photograph of Ishbel's Irish Village by the Ryerson and Burnham Archives of the Art Institute of Chicago.

Lord and Lady Aberdeen (Stead), 223–24
Lorne, Marquess of, 211n
Louise, Princess, 211n
Lyttleton, 4th Baron, 101n

Macassar Oil, 146
MacDonald, George, 173–74
Macdonald, James, 156, 157, 165
Mackay, G. G. "Gee Gee," 18, 183–84,
    189, 190, 192–93, 197, 242
MacKay, Thomas, 210
Mackenzie, Sir Kenneth, 128
MacLagan, Thomas, 173, 179
MacLennan, Duncan (Guisachan's head
    stalker), 14–15
Maclise, Daniel, 149
MacRobert, Lady (Rachel), 290–91,
    294–96, 302
MacRobert, Sir Alexander, 288–89
Mair, Charles, 241
Manchester Ship Canal, 103
Manitoba Schools Question, 217,
    220–22
Mansfield, George, 22, 27, 66–69, 74
Mar, Earl of (Fergus), 77n
Margaret, Princess, 127n
Maria Alexandrovna (Duchess of
    Edinburgh), 128
Marjoribanks, Annie (Ishbel's sister), 7
Marjoribanks, Archie (Ishbel's brother)
    childhood of, 7
    death of, 246–47
    photo, P3–3
    Rocking Chair Ranch (Texas) and,
        156, 158–63, 165–66, 241
Marjoribanks, Coutts (Ishbel's brother),
    7, 27n
    Canada meeting with sister, 180,
        183–84
    Coldstream Ranch, 198, 228–29, 238,
        241–44
    Cowboy Hall of Fame induction of,
        242n
    death of, 297
    father's disapproval of, 156
    Guisachan Ranch and, 191, 192, P3–10

Horseshoe Ranch and, 27n, 163–66,
    180, 183, 240–41, 297
Mouse River Live Stock Protective
    Association, 163–64
photo, P3–3
Marjoribanks, Dudley Coutts (Ishbel's
    father). *See also* Guisachan;
    Marjoribanks's homes
    art collection of, 2, 22–24, 26–28, 67,
        100n, 271–72, 284
    as Baron Tweedmouth of Edington, 156
    business and wealth of, 1–5
    death of, 244
    Gladstone's friendship with, 98–99
    Golden Retriever breed and, 17–18, 300
    Horseshoe Ranch purchased by,
        163–66
    hunting by, 15, 19–20
    influence of, 13
    on Ireland, 150–51, 154
    on Ishbel and Johnny's finances, 185
    Ishbel's childhood and, 1–3, 8–9,
        11–12, 97
    on Ishbel's education, 29
    marriage and family of, 6–12
    as Member of Parliament for Berwick-
        upon-Tweed, 17, 46, 271n
    photo, P2–1
    Rocking Chair Ranch purchased by,
        158–63, 165–66
    as Scottish laird, 18–20
    Tarland Lodge advice of, 79
    temper of, 8–12, 79n
Marjoribanks, Edward (Ishbel's brother)
    as 2nd Baron Tweedmouth of
        Edington, 247
    childhood of, 6, 17–18
    death of, 273
    as First Lord of the Admiralty, 272
    investment in American ranches by,
        159, 271
    on Ireland, 150–51
    as Member of Parliament, 156
    scandal involving, 272
    sister's wedding and, 47
    wife of, 30, 86, 143, 247–48

ABOUT THE AUTHOR

Simon Welfare has had a long career as a television producer. At Yorkshire Television, part of ITV, one of Britain's major television networks, he produced scientific and medical programs for a general audience, including the internationally popular *Mysterious World* series with the science writer Arthur C. Clarke, and coauthored the bestselling books based on them. Among the subjects of other programs were Nobel Prize–winner Linus Pauling, physicist Richard Feynman, and neurologist Oliver Sacks. His own company, Granite Productions, also specialized in history and adventure. Notable productions included Stanford historian Robert Conquest's account of Soviet Russia, *Red Empire*; the equally revelatory *China Rising*, and *Nicholas & Alexandra*, presented by H.R.H. Prince Michael of Kent; and quests for a lost city in Guatemala, the truth about Zombies in Haiti, a gigantic meteorite in Mauretania, and the bones of Peking Man in China. Simon Welfare lives in Scotland, just a mile across the fields from the house that the subjects of *Fortune's Many Houses*, the 1st Marquess and Marchioness of Aberdeen, built for their retirement. Welfare's wife Mary is their great-granddaughter, and she spent her childhood at another of their houses, the magnificent eighteenth-century stately home of Haddo House near Aberdeen.